Approaches to Teaching
Vergil's *Aeneid*

Approaches to Teaching
World Literature
Joseph Gibaldi, series editor

For a complete listing of titles,
see the last pages of this book.

Approaches to Teaching Vergil's *Aeneid*

Edited by

William S. Anderson

and

Lorina N. Quartarone

The Modern Language Association of America
New York   2002

For information about obtaining permission to reprint material from
MLA book publications, send your request by mail (see address below),
e-mail (permissions@mla.org), or fax (646 458-0030).

Library of Congress Cataloging-in-Publication Data

Approaches to teaching Vergil's Aeneid / edited by William S. Anderson
and Lorina N. Quartarone.
  p. cm. — (Approaches to teaching world literature, ISSN 1059-1133 ; 74)
Includes bibliographical references and index.
ISBN 0-87352-771-2 — ISBN 0-87352-772-0 (pbk.)
1. Virgil. Aeneis. 2. Epic poetry, Latin—History and criticism.
3. Aeneas (Legendary character) in literature.
4. Epic poetry, Latin—Study and teaching. 5. Virgil—Study and teaching.
I. Anderson, William Scovil, 1927– II. Quartarone, Lorina N., 1959– III. Series.
PA6825 .A75 2002
    873'.01—dc21   2002022917

Cover illustration for the paperback edition: *Tu Marcellus eris:
Virgile lisant le sixième livre de l'*Eneide *à Auguste*. By Jean-Auguste-Dominique Ingres.
Toulouse, Musée des Augustins. Photographer: STC

Printed on recycled paper

Published by The Modern Language Association of America
26 Broadway, New York, New York 10004-1789
www.mla.org

CONTENTS

Appendixes

PREFACE TO THE SERIES

In *The Art of Teaching* Gilbert Highet wrote, "Bad teaching wastes a great deal of effort, and spoils many lives which might have been full of energy and happiness." All too many teachers have failed in their work, Highet argued, simply "because they have not thought about it." We hope that the Approaches to Teaching World Literature series, sponsored by the Modern Language Association's Publications Committee, will not only improve the craft—as well as the art—of teaching but also encourage serious and continuing discussion of the aims and methods of teaching literature.

The principal objective of the series is to collect within each volume different points of view on teaching a specific literary work, a literary tradition, or a writer widely taught at the undergraduate level. The preparation of each volume begins with a wide-ranging survey of instructors, thus enabling us to include in the volume the philosophies and approaches, thoughts and methods of scores of experienced teachers. The result is a sourcebook of material, information, and ideas on teaching the subject of the volume to undergraduates.

The series is intended to serve nonspecialists as well as specialists, inexperienced as well as experienced teachers, graduate students who wish to learn effective ways of teaching as well as senior professors who wish to compare their own approaches with the approaches of colleagues in other schools. Of course, no volume in the series can ever substitute for erudition, intelligence, creativity, and sensitivity in teaching. We hope merely that each book will point readers in useful directions; at most each will offer only a first step in the long journey to successful teaching.

Joseph Gibaldi
Series Editor

PREFACE TO THE VOLUME

It does not seem overstated to suggest that Vergil's *Aeneid* has been the most continually read and discussed work by a Roman author in the history of Western literature. His poetic contemporaries refer to him, his successors allude to him, and ancient grammarians have left behind copious commentaries on his works. His poetry is a direct ancestor to such later eminent poets as Dante, Chaucer, Spenser, Shakespeare, Milton, and Pope. His works were translated by Thomas Phaer, William Webbe, Richard Stanyhurst, John Dryden, John Ogilby, Richard Lauderdale, Christopher Pitt, Percy Shelley, William Wordsworth, John Keats, William Morris, C. H. Sisson, Rolfe Humphries, Henry Surrey, and C. Day Lewis, among others. Despite the criticism Vergil received from many eighteenth- and nineteenth-century poets (including Samuel Johnson, George Crabbe, Samuel Taylor Coleridge, and Lord Byron), who found fault with what they perceived to be his political agenda and indebtedness to Homer, he was still imitated by many of these writers as well as by Wordsworth, Walter Savage Landor, and Samuel Rogers. Alfred Tennyson greatly revered him, as did Robert Fitzgerald; T. S. Eliot obliquely referred to him (mostly through Dante), and W. H. Auden responded to his work.

All this attention, both positive and negative, should not be surprising. In Vergil we have a poet of consummate talent; one who observed tradition but was no thrall to it; one whose work is an intricate nexus of poetic allusion, historical allegory, traditional adaptation, innovation, and artistic subtlety. All these facets have contributed to a continual interest in his poetry, all reveal a poet so nuanced and complex as to encourage lively debate still today, and all make the *Aeneid* a challenging poem to teach. That Latin was dropped as a standard requirement for college students in the late 1960s and early 1970s only exacerbates difficulties for teachers of this text. Furthermore, since the *Aeneid* has more recently become a familiar feature of courses such as Epic in Translation, Survey of Classical Literature, and other great-books and humanities courses, the text is reaching perhaps more students than ever and being taught by more instructors who are not formally trained in classics. While it is primarily toward the less-experienced and nonclassically trained teachers that we have oriented this volume, we hope that its essays will open avenues of approach to the poem for both the novice and the seasoned instructor of the *Aeneid*.

Part 1 of this volume, "Materials," is based on the results of our survey of teachers of the *Aeneid*. We received completed questionnaires from numerous instructors who furnished information on over a hundred courses utilizing the text in all levels of Latin instruction and varied courses in translation. For their assiduous responses we owe a great deal of gratitude. We have assembled their collective experience and advice as efficiently as we could and culled from them a compendium of resources devised to guide teachers to the most useful materials as quickly as possible. Our initial section on translation is designed to introduce readers and teachers to some of the difficulties of rendering Vergil's verse in English, so that those with less command of Latin may feel better equipped in selecting the appropriate translation for their classes. In our listing of reference and critical materials, we have often supplied short descriptions but have by no means attempted to assess fully the potential worth for the prospective user; such worth is determined by a number of factors we could not possibly presume to know. We do not claim to have presented an exhaustive bibliography; rather, we have attempted to offer starting places for continuing research. Assuming a primarily English-speaking audience, we have focused on the scholarship available in English, even though much influential criticism on Vergil has appeared in German, French, and Italian. For any oversights that these modi operandi have caused, we beg pardon; the array of criticism on a scholar of Vergil's status is enormous, and limitations imposed by both space and purpose necessitated that we make choices with which not all readers would agree. Our aim throughout has been to guide those who seek assistance without dictating their direction.

In part 2, "Approaches," we have assembled a collection of essays that offers something on many areas of interest, with a balance between newer and more traditional approaches to the text. Our roster of essayists includes those whose teaching experiences are in high schools and private academies, workshops and community colleges, small liberal arts colleges and large universities. Many have been involved in designing courses and setting curricula, and the sheer number of publications this group has produced, in addition to the variety of issues it addresses, is impressive. Most important, these contributors are incontrovertibly dedicated to the craft of teaching. The essays reflect this dedication as well as the varied interests and experiences of the writers, whose formal training ranges from classics to comparative literature, from medieval to modern literature, and from history to archaeology.

We are indebted to many for their assistance on this volume. *Nihil soli facimus* ("we do nothing alone"), and the truth of this phrase rang clearer each day that we worked on this project. In addition to thanking both the survey respondents and the essayists, without whom this volume would not exist, we must also thank many more whose contributions have been invaluable in one way or another. To our series editor, Joseph Gibaldi, whose patience and wisdom are boundless, our humblest thanks. To our copyeditor, Michael Kandel, our deepest appreciation for tireless labor on our behalf. To two anonymous readers, sincere gratitude for many influential comments and suggestions. To numerous family and friends, who have provided both emotional and professional support, apologies for not having expressed our appreciation often and loudly enough. Our indebtedness is ineffable to our students past and present, and above all to our numerous teachers. In fact, there are so many mentors to thank, so many scholars whose works have been influential, so many students from whom we ourselves have learned how to teach, that it would be impossible to credit them all here, and so it is to these many lovers of literature that we offer our gratitude; they are the ones who have truly given this volume its shape and substance.

> [. . .] semper honos nomenque tuum laudesque manebunt,
> quae me cumque vocant terrae.   (*Aen.* 1.609–10)

> [. . .] your honors and title and praises will last forever,
> wherever I may go.   (trans. ours)

WSA and LNQ

Part One

MATERIALS

Texts

Latin Editions and Commentaries

The standard edition of the complete works of Vergil is the Oxford Classical Text (OCT), edited by R. A. B. Mynors, *P. Vergili Maronis opera* (1969, reprinted with corrections in 1972). This volume, which includes an introduction on the manuscript tradition (composed in Latin) and an apparatus criticus (a listing of variant manuscript readings), is the most popular choice for use in both graduate-level courses and upper-division undergraduate Latin courses. The standard dual-language edition is from the Loeb Classical Library, which is issued by Harvard; the translation, first published in 1916 by H. Rushton Fairclough, is serviceable for its line adherence and facing-page correspondence but lacks the elegant language of less dated or strictly literal translations. Its appendix offers notes of interest to Latinists and refers frequently to the contemporary J. W. Mackail commentary on and translation of the *Aeneid* (1930). Fairclough's two-volume set contains the *Eclogues*, *Georgics*, and the first half of the *Aeneid* in the first volume; the second contains the second half of the *Aeneid*, the *Appendix Vergiliana*, and a compendium of proper nouns, including an index and definitions. An online text of the *Aeneid* is accessible at several Internet sites (e.g., ftp://sailor.gutenberg.org/pub/gutenberg/etext95/anidl10.txt; http://patriot.net/~lillard/cp/verg.html).

To supplement the text in higher-level courses, two excellent series of ancillary works are available, both of which produce single-volume commentaries on the individual books of the epic. One series, published by Cambridge, includes volumes compiled by foremost scholars such as K. W. Gransden (books 8 and 11), Philip R. Hardie (book 9), and Richard Tarrant (book 12). The other series, which is produced by Oxford, offers similarly stellar editions by R. G. Austin (books 1, 2, 4, and 6), R. D. Williams (books 3 and 5), C. J. Fordyce (books 7 and 8), and S. J. Harrison (book 10). All the single-volume commentaries give the text of the appropriate book of the *Aeneid*, which is usually based on the Mynors OCT; introductory comments on both the book and the epic as a whole; a scholarly commentary; and pertinent bibliography. The introductions normally contain information about Vergil and his poetic techniques. Harrison's commentary on book 10 is a dual-language version. The three-volume commentary on Vergil's works by John Conington and Henry Nettleship, first published in the late nineteenth century, remains a reliable resource despite its age. Any of these commentaries may be helpful to the non-Latinist who seeks detailed information on specific passages, phrases, and words but are written for those who possess some command of Latin.

For lower-division Latin readers, many instructors find the Williams (*Aeneid*) and the earlier T. E. Page work on the *Aeneid* quite useful, as each contains a full commentary (volume 1 treating books 1 through 6, volume 2 treating books 7 through 12). Both Williams and Page provide more basic assistance with Latin translation than do the Oxford and Cambridge commentaries. Some instructors find Page archaic, and although many consider his notes superior to Williams's, more by far actually employ the work by Williams. They consistently consider it more useful and rate it higher than any other commentary, while recognizing that it can be difficult and at times not as helpful as Page for those students who require more rudimentary assistance. By far the most frequently employed text, with notes for the lower-division college and the advanced high school level of Latin is *Vergil's* Aeneid by Clyde Pharr, which contains only books 1 through 6, has notes and vocabulary on the page accompanying the text, and a pull-out glossary; although until recently difficult to acquire, it has been revised and is currently available from Bolchazy-Carducci. On the one hand, the Pharr work may coddle too much; on the other, it allows students to read substantially more of the poem by offering grammatical assistance and diminishing the time spent looking up vocabulary. Similar to Pharr but not as well-known is a volume entitled *Latin Poetry* edited by Wilbert L. Carr and Harry E. Wedeck; it has the *Aeneid* books 1 through 6 and selections from several other Latin authors. Its format, with text, brief grammatical notes, and vocabulary all on one page, also helps students focus on the Latin and read more in less time. The Jane Harriman Hall and Alexander G. McKay edition of selections from the *Aeneid* books 1, 4, and 6, which is part of the Longman series, likewise contains a glossary and helpful notes.

English Translations

The selection of the appropriate poetic or prose translation often depends on the level of the course and the ability of the students to tackle a rendition of some sophistication. In our survey, many instructors voiced concern about students reading the *Aeneid* simply as a narrative and not as a poem. Although recognizing that the density of the language sometimes challenges students so much as to discourage them, professors remain convinced of the virtues of using verse translations. Of the currently available translations of the *Aeneid*, most are in verse. On the whole, professors find these versions adequate but not outstanding, and many acknowledge that this problem may be irremediable. As one respondent observes, "It is not that we lack competent translators; English just will not do the things Latin can do." Part of the challenge lies in the difficulty of combining an accurate, literal translation with the power and beauty of Vergil's verse. We might add that many poets, let alone translators, are simply not Vergil. But those who have applied their talents to this daunting task deserve our respect. William S. Anderson offers a brief but detailed discussion of the challenge of translating the *Aeneid*, in which he analyzes the stylistic elements and difficulties of translating the last several lines of book 12 (*Art* 101–09). His more recent "Five Hundred Years of Rendering the *Aeneid* in English" discusses the principal translations from William Caxton (1490) and

Gavin Douglas (1512) to Allen Mandelbaum (1971) and Robert Fitzgerald (1983) in terms of their formal (e.g., metrical) organization and their cultural adaptations of the hero Aeneas and his imperial mission. For a different perspective on various translators' interpretations of the *Aeneid*, we recommend Colin Burrow's "Virgil in English Translation." Burrow focuses on several British poets' renditions of the epic and their relation to contemporary political concerns and climate.

To demonstrate briefly a few aspects of translating the *Aeneid*, here is an excerpt from the poem accompanied by my literal prose translation.

> Musa, mihi causas memora, quo numine laeso
> quidve dolens regina deum tot volvere casus
> insignem pietate virum, tot adire labores
> impulerit. Tantaene animis caelestibus irae? (*Aen.*1.8–11)

> Muse, recount for me the reasons why, on account of what injured divine power or grieving at what did the queen of the gods compel a man, distinguished for devotion, to undergo so many misfortunes and to encounter so many toils. Is there such great wrath in divine spirits?

The initial juxtaposition of *musa* ("muse") and the pronoun *mihi* ("for me"), which refers to the poet-narrator, emphasizes the solidarity or near unity of the poet and his inspiration. The alliteration of *m* connects these two words with the first verb, *memora* ("relate" or "mention"). This device combines three important elements: the muse and inspiration, the poet, and the past: this story is a legend, not contemporary but of great significance to the Romans and their history. (Memory itself is a worthwhile element to pursue throughout the poem, as it serves as a catalyst for the actions of several characters, particularly Aeneas and Juno.) Each line concludes with a powerful and negative word (*laeso* ["injured"], *casus* ["misfortunes"], *labores* ["toils"], and *irae* ["wrath"]), and since final words stand in a position of emphasis in Latin verse, this feature produces a heavy impact and a sense of foreboding. The two central lines contain a parallel structure in their final three words: *tot*, an adjective meaning "so many," is followed by the infinitives *volvere* ("to undergo") and *adire* ("to encounter"), and the infinitives are followed by their respective direct objects, *casus* ("misfortunes") and *labores* ("toils"). These two phrases frame the three words defining the protagonist, *insignem pietate virum* ("a man distinguished for devotion"). *Pietas* is a term that deserves attention and is untranslatable with a single English word; it means "a sense of duty or devotion to one's family, country, and gods" (see app.). Capturing the Latin word order is perhaps impossible in English, but the order is significant, for the sequence clearly indicates that the hero is hemmed in by troubles (the two parallel phrases described above) on either side. It is also arguable that the "injury" (*laeso*) and "grief" (*dolens*) attributed to Juno reflect Vergil's sympathy for her as well as for Aeneas. The enjambment of the verb *impulerit* ("compelled" or "forced") stresses Juno's direct action and significant role in the poem. In the last line, the framing of "tantae [. . .] irae" ("such great wrath") around the heavenly spirits is impossible to represent sensibly in English but indicates that divine beings remain a central force and are themselves captured by their emotions. This type of close analysis is, of course, impossible to maintain in a reading of the poem where time is limited and the students know no Latin; we offer it here, however, so that readers may observe these elements at work and be better able to evaluate the extent to which each of the following three translations represents these nuances. Another important matter is how clearly each translator renders the essential import of the passage.

A little over half the instructors polled prefer the Mandelbaum translation. Despite the major complaint that the line numbers do not correspond to the Latin text (which also applies to most other translations), Mandelbaum's translation receives kudos for everything from having nobility without pomposity to being cheap and readable, elegant and trustworthy, and the easiest for students to follow. This praise is not insignificant, since the poem can be confusing, particularly for first-time readers and those lacking appropriate background in Roman history, mythology, and literature. Mandelbaum's nearly uniform lines of ten and eleven syllables, intended to approximate iambic pentameter, can be read aloud to students in order to simulate, in some guise, the Latin meter of the poem, dactylic hexameter. The volume also contains a useful glossary of proper nouns, complete with a pronunciation and transliteration guide, as well as a brief bibliography. That Mandelbaum has also translated both Homer and Dante is of particular interest to those who read these poets in courses that survey Western literature. Mandelbaum's view of Vergil's text as reflecting "a sense of the lost as truly irretrievable" (viii) and his impression that "no man ever felt more deeply the part of the defeated and the lost" (xi) comes through in his translation.

> Tell me the reason, Muse: what was the wound
> to her divinity, so hurting her
> that she, the queen of gods, compelled a man
> remarkable for goodness to endure
> so many crises, meet so many trials?
> Can such resentment hold the minds of gods?   (1.13–18)

Mandelbaum's rendition is fairly literal. He captures the essence of the passage well and maintains the parallel phrases "to endure / so many crises, meet so many trials?" with asyndeton (lack of a connective), although he cannot make them surround the "man" as they do in Latin. While his translation is clear, his rendering of the important phrase *insignem pietate virum* as "a man remarkable for goodness" is inadequate; "goodness" simply does not express the essence of *pietas*. In general, Mandelbaum's translations of *pietas* (e.g., "goodness," "righteousness," "honors," and "loyalty") are weak. His phrasing of the final question "Can such resentment hold the minds of gods?" is powerful and well devised. Its emphasis on the near disbelief of the narrator through the modal "can" underscores the unusual nature of Juno's wrath. The insertion of "hold" as a verb, which does not occur in Latin (Latinists would understand an appropriate form of the verb "to be"), offers an appropriate depiction of the tenacious anger that will pursue Aeneas throughout the poem. Mandelbaum's question thus fittingly leads us to the next passage, in which the poet describes the reasons for Juno's resentment toward the Trojans and Aeneas.

The next most popular translation is Fitzgerald's. According to our survey respondents, the Fitzgerald translation is praiseworthy for being accessible, good old-fashioned poetry and neither too sentimental nor simplistic. It is criticized, however, for needing a better introduction and notes, being too politically oriented, and being readable often at the expense of accuracy. Those instructors who prefer Fitzgerald rank his rendition lower in terms of overall satisfaction than those who favor Mandelbaum. His lines, like Mandelbaum's, display an attempt to approximate iambic pentameter but are less consistent in the number of syllables, which ranges from six to twelve. In addition to a brief glossary of proper nouns, Fitzgerald includes an informative postscript that supplies pertinent historical, literary, and biographical context.

> Tell me the causes now, O Muse, how galled
> In her divine pride, and how sore at heart
> From her old wound, the queen of gods compelled him—
> A man apart, devoted to his mission —
> To undergo so many perilous days
> And enter on so many trials. Can anger
> Black as this prey on the minds of heaven?   (1.13–19)

"Galled" and "sore" may seem less than poetic word choices, but they convey the vehemence of Juno's wrath more powerfully than Mandelbaum's "wound" and "hurt." Yet Fitzgerald is less true to the Latin; for instance, his references to "pride" and "heart" do not render actual Latin words. Thus, although he emphasizes the personal nature of Juno's injury, which is important in understanding her role at the poem's start, he does not translate the text as clearly as Mandelbaum. Fitzgerald's choice to employ the pronoun "him" and separate the appositive "A man apart, devoted to his mission" by dashes is laudable, for it heightens the distinctive character of Aeneas, but at the same time it does not convey that character with enough thrust: the vague "a man apart" does not forcefully relate Aeneas's distinction to reverence, respect, and duty, nor does "devoted to his mission" completely capture the sense of *pietas*. The loss of asyndeton in the parallel infinitive phrases diminishes their impact. Fitzgerald's phrasing of the final question is powerful but again less true to the Latin, and it contains an adjective, "black," that is the sort of word students are likely to seize on and invest with a meaning such as evil or wicked, which the original does not connote. In short, Fitzgerald's translation is more interpretive than Mandelbaum's, which is a plus only if one agrees with Fitzgerald's interpretations. His various expressions for *pietas* include "loyalty," "piety," and "devotion." Devotion is perhaps the best one-word equivalent in English.

The most popular prose translation is that by David West. Respondents laud this translation for its modern and concise prose and for being complete and affordable. Complete it is, containing an appendix on the underworld procession that provides a sequential list of the proper names in that episode and an appendix on the shield that explicates the historical scenes in it. The West translation also includes maps and genealogical trees of the Julian line and the house of Atreus. For the instructor who desires ready assistance with such matters, this volume may be the best available; its primary drawback, however, is that the poem is rendered in prose (with the corresponding line numbers in the margins).

> Tell me, Muse, the causes of her anger. How did he violate the will of the Queen of the Gods? What was his offence? Why did she drive a man famous for his piety to such endless hardship and such suffering? Can there be so much anger in the hearts of the heavenly gods?   (p. 3)

West's attribution of responsibility to Aeneas with "How did he violate [. . .]?" and "What was his offence?" is objectionable because it alters the sense of the original and casts Aeneas as guilty of insulting Juno. It is important that he does not offend her—rather, it is her anger against Troy in general (which begins with Paris) and the prophecy that the Trojans will one day destroy Carthage, as the poet explains in the next passage, that cause Juno to harass Aeneas in an attempt to keep him from both Carthage and Rome. Thus, this translation can be misleading regarding Aeneas's role. Furthermore, casting him as guilty undermines the ensuing description of Aeneas, "a man famous for piety," which is the best rendition of the Latin phrase in the three translations. West's removal of the sense of grief (*dolens*) from Juno is puzzling and inaccurate, but the accessibility of his prose is laudable. Instructors who employ this or another prose translation should continually remind students that the *Aeneid* is a poem, not a novel. A poetic translation inevitably suggests to students that word choice is significant. West's translations of *pietas*, however, are reliable and include "goodness," "piety," and most frequently "devotion."

To round out the comparison of these translations, let us consider a few key phrases in the poem whose impact is crucial. The first occurs in book 1, where Aeneas examines the images on the Temple of Juno at Carthage. The Latin reads "atque animum pictura pascit inani" (1.464), literally "and he nourishes his soul on a lifeless picture." The word *animus* means "mind," "soul," or even "memory" and is related to the word for breath or life, *anima*. The subtle verbal echo with *inanis* ("lifeless," "insubstantial," or "empty") is difficult at best to capture in English, and a good translation should attempt to render the paradox of feeding something integral to life with something that is insubstantial. Mandelbaum seems to render it best: "he feeds / his soul on what is nothing but a picture" (1.658–59). Fitzgerald's "to feast his eyes and mind on a mere image" (1.633), while fairly literal (excepting the inclusion of "eyes"), is less powerful; West's "he was feeding his spirit with the empty images" (p. 18) is close to the Latin but lacking in power, although it comes near to conveying the irony of the phrase.

In book 6, Aeneas receives instruction from Anchises in the Underworld:

> tu regere imperio populos, Romane, memento
> (hae tibi erunt artes), pacisque imponere morem,
> parcere subiectis et debellare superbos.   (6.851–53)

> Remember, Roman, to rule nations with supremacy—these will be your skills—to introduce the way of peace, to spare the defeated, and to subdue the haughty.   (trans. mine)

Several words demand a translator's decision. *Imperium* is "(right of) command" or "authority," "mastery," even "supremacy"; overtones of military power, and the fact that the term eventually fosters the English word *empire*, cannot be divorced from it. *Artes* generally means "skills" or "crafts" but in a wider sense may mean "ability," "means," or even "character." There is a sense that what is *ars* is something fashioned, worked at, not natural but the product of discipline and effort. *Imponere* yields the English "impose"; less forcefully it means "establish," more so, "dictate." *Mos* (*morem*) has meanings ranging from "custom" and "usage" to "law" and "habit"; the phrase *mores maiorum*, the "customs of our ancestors," evokes tradition as well as morality, as does the use of *mos* in this context. The verb *debellare* is not commonly used and ranges in meaning from "fight it out with" and "wear down" to "subdue." The adjective *superbus* also may ring either positively ("proud," "magnificent," and the English cognate "superb") or negatively ("arrogant," "tyrannical," "disdainful"). There is in warfare, it seems, a sense of tension about defeated peoples: if they succumb to defeat, they deserve to be subjects; but the victors can feel still more superior if the conquered are a people of some stature and are worthy opponents. *Superbus* carries both senses in Latin, a difficult dichotomy to reproduce with a single English word.

Mandelbaum's translation "remember, Roman, these will be your arts: / to teach the ways of peace to those you conquer, / to spare defeated peoples, tame the proud" (6.1135–37) is quite close to the Latin, and his rendering of *imponere* as "to teach" rather than as the more forceful "to impose" conveys a positive feeling about the mission of the empire. Fitzgerald's rendition betrays his interpretation: "Roman, remember by your strength to rule / Earth's peoples—for your arts are to be these: / To pacify, to impose the rule of law, / To spare the conquered, battle down the proud" (6.1151–54). He brings out a more violent sense of the passage through choices such as "by your strength" for *imperio* and "battle down" for *debellare* and again deviates from the Latin original in the extension of two infinitive phrases, "to pacify, to impose the rule of law" out of the single *pacisque imponere mos*. West's translation falls somewhere between Mandelbaum and Fitzgerald in its sense of force or violence: "Your task, Roman, and do not forget it, will be to govern the peoples of the world in your empire. These will be your arts—and to impose a settled pattern upon peace, to pardon the defeated and war down the proud" (p. 159). West captures the goal of the Romans more diplomatically through choices such as "govern," "a settled pattern of peace," and "pardon"; furthermore, his option of the more forceful "war down" elicits the tension between ruling by strength and ruling with mercy.

One final phrase for consideration is Aeneas's confrontation of Lausus in book 10: "quo moriture ruis maioraque viribus audes? / fallit te incautum pietas tua" (10.811–12). "Why are you, about to die, rushing (into it)? Why do you dare things greater than your strength? Your devotion is deceiving you, (making you) heedless" (trans. mine). That Mandelbaum renders the vocative future participle, which is awkward in English, more smoothly as a prepositional phrase helps convey the sense of imminent death suggested by the participle: "Why are you rushing to sure death? Why dare / things that are past your strength? Your loyalty / has tricked you into recklessness" (10.1113–15). Fitzgerald similarly alters the participle but renders the phrase less potent by removing the second-person verb and falls into a colloquialism that is almost silly: "Why this rush deathward, daring beyond your power? / Filial piety makes you lose your head" (10.1136–37). West is less terse than either the original or these other translators but manages to capture the essence in a moving manner: "Why are you in such a haste to die? Why do you take on tasks beyond your strength? You are too rash. Your love for your father is deceiving you" (p. 268). West emphasizes the adjective *incautum*, which stands in apposition to *te* ("you"), by rendering it in a sentence all its own, "You are too rash." Neither of the other translations achieves such a focus on this important adjective.

To sum up, Mandelbaum's translation remains, in most cases, the truest to the Latin while maintaining clarity and still offering a poetic rendition. Fitzgerald is poetic but at times slips into colloquialism; he is also more prone than the others to impose his interpretation. West offers a fine translation, save for its prose form. All are serviceable; the choice depends on the desires and needs of the instructor.

History of the Text

The *Aeneid* boasts the best manuscript evidence of any ancient Latin poem that we study. For the most part, all twelve books of the epic can be read against the strong witness of three beautiful manuscripts dated in the late fourth or early fifth century and written in the block-letter style known as rustic capitals, once called Vergilian letters because of their particular use in transmitting Vergil's text. One of those three manuscripts (named the Romanus) also preserves nineteen illustrations. Four other manuscripts of the fifth century have come to us in a fragmentary condition, supplementing the authority of the first three. One of the four, a collection of pages in the Vatican Library (Vergil MSS Vat. lat. 3225), has preserved fifty very important illustrations (plus traces of several others). At the time of the Carolingian Renaissance in the ninth century, there was a rush to copy the entire text of Vergil, above all of the *Aeneid*, and we possess many of these manuscripts. Mynors listed thirteen of these in his Oxford text, but he found few occasions on which he considered it necessary and useful to cite their readings. The earliest three remain our best and most legible witness to the text of Vergil.

Since Vergil's poems became a standard fixture in education almost immediately (Suetonius mentions lectures occurring in Rome on Vergil and other poets during the 20s BCE, even before Vergil's death [*De gramm.* 16]), there is also a lengthy tradition of discussion and commentary on the text. Four principal and influential commentators all date from the fourth and fifth centuries. The Servian commentary has enjoyed the most fame; it exists in a shorter version, considered to be the work of Servius himself, a fourth-century grammarian, and in a longer portion now generally thought to be an addition produced during the seventh or eighth century and derived from the now lost fourth-century work of Aelius Donatus. The Servian commentary preserves readings not in agreement with the fourth-century rustic-capital manuscripts as well as interpretations of other, earlier scholars, not always named. Don Fowler's brief article "The Virgil Commentary of Servius" provides a thoughtful description of what one may expect to find there, including examples and an assessment of utility.

Of the other three earliest commentaries, the *Scholia Veronensia* contains notes of a consistently high caliber, but the work is fragmentary; it also appears to have been composed either slightly before that of Servius or simply without knowledge of it. In his *Saturnalia*, Macrobius comments on and praises Vergil's poetry. *Saturnalia* is important for us principally because it includes early poetic models for Vergil, some of which are no longer extant. It is not a commentary in the traditional sense but was composed by Macrobius to educate his son. Similarly, Tiberius Claudius Donatus wrote his *Intepretationes Vergilianae*, chiefly a prose paraphrase of the *Aeneid*, which contains discussions of difficult verses and allusions and shows a special concern with moral issues. All these commentaries are valuable in that they are the work of native Latin speakers; at the same time, although they are closer in time to Vergil than we, they remain four centuries distant from him. They can be helpful and instructional but are not above question.

For an overview of the history of the text, we suggest three resources of varying length and breadth. S. J. Harrison, in his commentary on book 10 (Aeneid *10*), presents a concise description of the early history of the text and the roles of the major ancient commentators. Stuart Gillespie's *The Poets on the Classics* offers a chapter chronicling the influence of Vergil's poetry on English literature into the twentieth century. The most expansive treatment is the volume edited by Charles Martindale, *Virgil and His Influence*, which devotes separate chapters to tracing the reception and influence of Vergil's poetry since Dante.

The Instructor's Library

Reference Works

There are several trustworthy general reference works that offer background on Vergil's poetry and the historical developments and political climate of the first century BCE. *The Cambridge Ancient History*'s comprehensive essays on the Late Republic and Early Principate (Bowman) are an excellent starting place. *The Oxford History of the Classical World* (Boardman, Griffin, and Murray) offers the chapters "The Founding of the Empire," "Augustan Poetry and Society," and "Virgil." The first two provide a straightforward summary of the social and political atmosphere in which Vergil wrote; the third is devoted to the poet's works, with a section on the *Aeneid*, composed by Jasper Griffin, focusing on Vergil's relationship with Augustus and how Vergil tackled writing the epic. The *Oxford Classical Dictionary* and the *Oxford Companion to Classical Literature*, both organized in encyclopedic form, also make valuable reference tools. The former is broader in scope and includes literary, historical, and cultural information; a brief bibliography follows most entries, and there are many general topics, such as "Travel" and "Arms and Armour," that offer detailed and informative discussions. The latter volume is narrower in focus and offers brief but thorough entries on literary authors, titles, characters, and place-names. This handy reference, available in paperback, makes a good supplement for undergraduates in classical literature courses.

Bibliographic resources on Vergil are numerous and easy to obtain. The annual journal *Vergilius*, available at most college libraries, features yearly bibliographies by Alexander G. McKay on books and articles on Vergil. The bibliographic reference work *L'année philologique* is produced annually (although it has recently been running a couple of years behind) and is the quintessential resource for finding all published works on the ancient West. It is a standard feature of college and university libraries, and it always includes several pages listing the most recent publications, in English and several other languages, under the heading "Vergilius." A comprehensive bibliography on Vergil, covering the period of 1875–1975, was compiled by Werner Suerbaum for a volume of *Aufstieg und Niedergang der römischen Welt*. For a few worthwhile online bibliographic resources, see "Internet Resources" below.

Background Studies

Most instructors agree that exposure to the Homeric poems is the single most important resource for enhancing an appreciation for the *Aeneid*. Since Vergil's use of allusion and intertextual reference is extensive, a familiarity with Homer's works is invaluable. (We provide a chart of Homeric parallels in appendix A to make comparison easier.) Vergil also alludes to many other ancient texts, including the *Homeric Hymns*, Plato's *Republic*, Apollonius's *Argonautica*, Polybius's *History*, Ennius's *Annales*, Lucretius's *De rerum natura*, and Catullus's *Carmina*; a familiarity with these sources enriches understanding of Vergil's accomplishment in the *Aeneid*.

For overall background on the *Aeneid*, we recommend R. D. Williams's article on the poem, found in *The Cambridge History of Classical Literature: The Age of Augustus* ("*Aeneid*"). It briefly treats matters such as culture, history, literary background, meter, and style and is perhaps the most comprehensive assessment available.

Since the *Aeneid* is frequently taught in epic-in-translation or humanities courses in which students receive historical and cultural background in lecture, many instructors do not require specific reading on the history of the period. But for upper-division and graduate-level Latin courses, scholars consider familiarity with ancient historical sources imperative. Livy's book 1 (*Ab urbe condita*) gives an account of the founding of Rome that attempts to reconcile the different traditions about Aeneas and Romulus. In Augustus's *Res gestae*, the emperor himself provides a record of his achievements. Tacitus's *Annales* (book 1) begins with a summary estimate of the principate of Augustus. Suetonius, Tacitus's younger contemporary, composed biographies of both Vergil and Augustus. His work *De poetis* ("On the Poets") gave a life of Vergil that was later expanded by the fourth-century grammarian Donatus; Suetonius's *Divi Augusti vita* ("Life of the Divine Augustus") is a valuable resource on Rome's first emperor. While Tacitus's works contain a discernible antidynastic sentiment, his writing is often compelling; Suetonius is perhaps less obviously biased, and his texts are the efforts of a chronicler who rarely offers interpretive or analytic perspectives on his subjects. Still, his writings are worthwhile for their presentation of facts, anecdotes, and his clear debt to primary sources.

On the century of civil discord that preceded Vergil's writing of the *Aeneid*, two works have become standards for classical scholars and students. H. H. Scullard's *From the Gracchi to Nero* offers a complete account of the civil war (beginning 133 BCE) and its ramifications through to the end of the reign of the Julio-Claudian line (Nero, 68 CE). Chapter 8, "The Second Triumvirate," traces the rise of Octavian; chapter 10, "Art, Literature and Thought in the Late Republic," is centered on the influence of Greece on Rome; and chapter 11, "The Augustan Principate," is perhaps the most comprehensive short account of Augustus and includes a brief section on Vergil and other Augustan writers. Ronald Syme's *Roman Revolution* is a gripping and in-depth record that focuses on the events preceding the rise of Augustus and his en-suing principate.

More recently, Karl Galinsky's *Augustan Culture: An Interpretive Introduc-tion* discusses *auctoritas* ("power," "influence," "authority," or "leadership") as the crux of the Augustan regime. R. O. A. M. Lyne, in the eloquent and insight-ful "Vergil and the Politics of War," discusses the Roman tendency to idealize war as a means of securing peace and in this light examines Aeneas's actions in the second half of the poem. In "The Evolution of Augustus' Principate," Ed-ward T. Salmon discusses the gradual establishment of Augustus's power through successive measures and observes his adaptability to circumstances. Robert Gurval, in *Actium and Augustus: The Politics and Emotions of Civil War*, repudiates the notion that the Augustan poets' treatment of the Battle of Actium indicates their collusion with or apostasy from Augustan politics. David Quint's *Epic and Empire: Politics and Generic Form from Virgil to Milton* also explores the connections between Vergil's epic and imperial ideology.

Williams's "The Purpose of the *Aeneid*" opposes the traditional purposes as-signed to the poem, such as the glorification of Rome and the adaptation of Homer. Williams focuses on how Vergil explores the implications of the ideal of Rome that are at odds with the circumstances of various characters, Homer, heroism, and myth. Richard Tarrant's article "Poetry and Power: Virgil's Poetry in Contemporary Context" is perhaps the best short discussion of Vergil and his times; it marries seamlessly the issues of what we know of Vergil's life experi-ences and relationship to Augustus with his multivocal expression in the *Aeneid*. Paul Zanker's *The Power of Images in the Age of Augustus*, translated into En-glish by Alan Shapiro, examines Augustan art with the premise that civic art and architecture reflect the values of a society; Zanker views the art of the Augustan regime as both a catalyst and outgrowth of Augustan ideology.

Critical Studies

Books

Of the vast number of books on the *Aeneid*, many are more suitable for the classicist than for the general reader. Described below are those books sug-gested by survey respondents as important for beginning instructors of Vergil's poem. We have clustered them with respect to their primary goals and focuses (even though many works defy such simplistic categorization) in an effort to present them in an accessible manner. These resources are all reliable and offer substantial assistance in interpreting the poem as a whole.

For a superior general introduction to the text, Anderson's *The Art of the Aeneid* is the most frequently cited and, in the estimation of many, the best available treatment of literary aspects of the poem. Anderson discusses the epic in pairs of books and devotes attention to the poet's debt to Homer, his use of imagery and symbolism, the structure of the epic, and Aeneas as an allegory for

Augustus. Similar to Anderson's work is William A. Camps's *Introduction to Virgil's* Aeneid, which is praised for its attention to detail and conciseness. Viktor Pöschl's *The Art of Vergil* has also had lasting influence. Pöschl examines imagery in the *Aeneid* and elucidates how the poem is symbolic of both Roman history and human life. His focus on Aeneas, Dido, and Turnus is a worthwhile analysis for teachers of the text. His work was translated from German into English in 1962. In his brief book *Virgil*, Jasper Griffin offers a chapter on the *Aeneid* that is accessible to teachers and undergraduates alike. He discusses both the historical and literary aspects of the poem's complexity. For Latinless readers, David R. Slavitt's *Virgil* may be one of the best critical introductions available. Half the book concentrates on the *Aeneid*, the rest on Vergil's previous poems. Slavitt's work receives praise for its readability but also criticism for his less than adequate consideration of the historical aspects of the poem. It is certainly an excellent concentration on the human aspects of Vergil's poetry, with many useful analogies to modern literature and art. For college professors, graduate students, and those who are seasoned in Vergilian scholarship, Nicholas Horsfall's *A Companion to the Study of Virgil* is an important resource; its lengthy chapter on the *Aeneid* examines specific themes, introduced book by book, with in-depth and focused discussion rather than broad treatment. Christine Perkell's *Reading Vergil's* Aeneid offers an excellent introduction to the epic, providing hefty essays on each of the twelve books of the poem and four other essays on noteworthy issues. The contributors to the volume are all distinguished Vergil scholars and make this collection a valuable resource.

During the second half of the twentieth century, Vergilian criticism has been largely divided into two opposing interpretive camps, simply labeled the optimist and the pessimist. Largely, the optimist readers (also known as the Augustan or panegyric camp) are European scholars who view the epic as proimperial or pro-Augustan in essence and emphasize the poem's positive commentary on the Augustan regime and empire. The Harvard school or pessimist reading focuses on the ambivalence of Vergilian verse while frequently emphasizing its darker or anti-Augustan aspects. Francis Cairns's *Virgil's Augustan Epic*, as is discernible from the title, fosters a pro-Augustan reading of the poem, placing Aeneas in the role of the good king who is met by various opposing characters; Cairns finds the *Odyssey* of more influence than the *Iliad* and is perhaps a bit one-sided. In *Virgil's* Aeneid: *Cosmos and Imperium*, Philip Hardie explores the ramifications of the word *urbs* ("city") in the poem, particularly how Vergil employs it to stand for the world (*orbis*); this use implies that the Roman state is analogous to a natural order. Hardie examines several characters and episodes from this perspective; of special interest for teachers is his analysis of the shield in book 8. W. R. Johnson's *Darkness Visible*, the most frequently cited work associated with the Harvard school, is an excellent introduction to the complex nature of the poem's narrative. Lyne's *Further Voices in Vergil's* Aeneid is something of an extension of an earlier article by Adam Parry, "The Two Voices of Virgil's *Aeneid*" (discussed below). Lyne proposes that an overarching epic voice in the poem supports patriotism and

Augustan imperialism, but that other, smaller voices question or subvert what that epic voice promotes. This book provides an excellent illustration of tension in the poem. Also evocative of the Harvard school but more a product of New Criticism is Michael C. J. Putnam's *The Poetry of the* Aeneid*: Four Studies in Imaginative Unity and Design*, which explores Vergil's use of symbols and key terms to create a specific design in each book. In *Virgil's Epic Designs: Ekphrasis in the* Aeneid, Putnam analyses six of the epic's ecphrases, each in its immediate context, and argues that each embraces the themes of the entire poem. In his provocative article "Which *Aeneid* in Whose Nineties?," Joseph Farrell very reasonably calls for a departure from these either-or positions and suggests that more progressive, modern theories of interpretation may be applied fruitfully to the poem.

In *Vergils epische Technik*, Richard Heinze became the first scholar of the twentieth century to deal in depth with Vergil's use of the Homeric texts. His original German work was translated into English in 1993 (*Virgil's Epic Technique*) and may be somewhat specialized for nonclassicists but is still often cited by scholars. Brooks Otis's *Virgil: A Study in Civilized Poetry* remains a basic assessment of Vergil's use of structure and Homeric models. Otis asserts that it is imperative to view Vergil's works in concert, and his book is an important resource for those who wish to read the *Aeneid* in conjunction with the earlier poems. Otis focuses on how Vergil's use of symbolism and form differs from Homer's and explores how Vergil's verse emerges as a new kind of narrative. He deals with all of Vergil's poetry but begins and ends with the *Aeneid*, and his two weighty chapters "The Odyssean *Aeneid*" and "The Iliadic *Aeneid*" should be of particular interest and use to teachers of the epic. K. W. Gransden's *Virgil's* Iliad*: An Essay on Epic Narrative* is the premier text for lovers of the *Iliad* and those who seek edification on the second half of Vergil's poem. His work is especially recommended for its accessibility to first-time readers and nonspecialists. Although there are no footnotes, Gransden is an accomplished classicist, and that fact pervades his sensitive reading of the poem. Georg N. Knauer produced the hefty *Die* Aeneis *und Homer*, which contains an extensive index of Vergil's Homeric allusions that even Anglophones can use.

For consideration of the hero in a slightly larger Western context, Thomas Van Nortwick's *Somewhere I Have Never Travelled* assesses the poem in light of two earlier epic poems, *The Epic of Gilgamesh* and Homer's *Iliad*. Van Nortwick focuses on the spiritual development of the hero and its apparent and concomitant diminishment of the self. His work is another excellent resource for nonclassicists. Concentrating on the hero in the *Aeneid*, C. J. Mackie, in *The Characterisation of Aeneas*, usefully assembles all the appearances and speeches of the protagonist for analysis, focusing on the portrayal of *pietas*. Owen Lee's *Fathers and Sons in Virgil's* Aeneid is dismissed by some scholars because of its Jungian analysis, but this study can be worthwhile. Lee gives special attention to the suffering of sons and the failure of fathers in helping their sons.

Susan F. Wiltshire's *Public and Private in Virgil's* Aeneid is a must-read book on the *Aeneid*. Wiltshire provides a both balanced and ambivalent reading of the poem through her examination of its feminine aspects, such as maternal, gentle, domestic features, focusing on the grief of women, *pietas* and *amor*, and promotes a perspective that diminishes the gap between polarities (e.g., male/female, pessimist/optimist) rather than emphasizes their opposition.

Two scholars choose to focus on the role of prophecy in the poem. Elisabeth Henry's *The Vigour of Prophecy: A Study of Virgil's* Aeneid is highly recommended, offering a solid interpretation of the Stoic aspects of the poem. Henry, an accomplished writer, brings numerous talents to bear on her reading of the poem, which emphasizes matters often overlooked, such as memory and joy. She frequently relates the poem to English poets, both traditional (Shakespeare and Dryden) and modern. James J. O'Hara's *Death and the Optimistic Prophecy in Vergil's* Aeneid focuses on prophecies in the poem and their often none-too-positive realization. He covers some of the same territory as Henry; but Henry's reading is more balanced, O'Hara's more negative.

Collections of Essays

There are several excellent collections of essays on the *Aeneid*, any one of which has much to offer an instructor of the text. Descriptions of the contents are brief here, since many of the articles are described in the following section. It is customary for such compilations to include articles on all of Vergil's works, with an emphasis on the *Aeneid*.

The single most popular collection mentioned in the survey is that edited by Steele Commager, *Virgil: A Collection of Critical Essays*. This slim volume contains several important and helpful articles by illustrious scholars such as R. A. Brooks, Wendell Clausen, Otis, Parry, Pöschl, and Bernard Knox, most of which are discussed below. Despite its publication date of 1966, the selection is superb and many of its articles still influential.

S. J. Harrison's *Oxford Readings in Vergil's* Aeneid is an outstanding collection, featuring reprinted essays by a long list of eminent Vergilian scholars such as R. D. Williams, Harrison, Horsfall, Denis Feeney, West, Anderson, Galinsky, Lyne, and L. P. Wilkinson. The collection is organized in a sequence that follows the text and treats central issues ranging from specific characters to cultural context. Although it is perhaps the best recent collection, many of the reprints date from the 1960s.

Charles Martindale's *The Cambridge Companion to Virgil* is likewise excellent and contains not reprints but newly commissioned articles addressing matters both traditional and timely, such as gender and sexuality (Oliensis), narrative (Fowler, "Virgil Commentary" and "Virgilian Narrative"; Barchiesi, "Virgilian Narrative"), intertextuality (Farrell, "Virgilian Intertext"), and characterization (Laird). This volume, with its newer perspectives, would be well employed in conjunction with either the Commager or Harrison collections, which feature older reprints.

The collection edited by Ian McAuslan and Peter Walcot similarly includes several articles extremely helpful in undergraduate teaching, most notably those by Robert Coleman, Gransden ("Fall"), Kenneth McLeish, J. L. Moles, A. Hudson-Williams, and R. D. Williams and C. J. Carter. This set of reprints includes articles from the 1970s and 1980s and sticks to mainstream issues.

Virgil's Aeneid: *Interpretation and Influence* reprints articles by Putnam, offering a survey of a single scholar's work over two decades. For those who favor New Criticism as well as the Harvard school it is a particularly worthwhile collection. Putnam is both a careful and insightful scholar.

Horsfall's collection is not unlike Putnam's. His *A Companion to the Study of Virgil* contains a few articles by other scholars, but his work dominates. The intended audience of the volume is both scholars and students who seek a reliable and rigorous treatment of not only Vergil's works but also his life. Horsfall's amazing mastery of bibliography and the level of his scholarship will be most appreciated by those with a solid background in Vergilian studies.

For those teaching the text in a wider and more forward-reaching context, Martindale's *Virgil and His Influence* is an excellent collection. It is especially geared toward those who seek a proleptic perspective or teach the poem in a later European context. Individual essays address reading the *Aeneid* in conjunction with Dante, Shakespeare, and Milton and give attention to various genres and concerns.

The remaining collections currently available received only occasional reference in our survey. That by Robert Wilhelm and Howard Jones contains three useful articles on women, John Patrick Sullivan's "Dido and the Representation of Women in Vergil's *Aeneid*," Pierre Grimal's "Les amours de Didon ou les limites de la liberté," and Charles Babcock's "*Sola . . . Multis e Matribus*: A Comment on Vergil's Trojan Women." Harold Bloom's two collections—*Modern Critical Interpretations: Virgil's* Aeneid and *Virgil: Modern Critical Views*—which appear to support a rather negative attitude toward Vergil's poems, were mentioned not only rarely but disparagingly as well. Still, Bloom's 1986 volume (*Virgil*) reprints the important Parry article ("Two Voices"), offers a good essay by J. William Hunt ("Ways") that promotes a balanced reading of the poem, and contains a useful article on Aeneas by Douglas J. Stewart. In Bloom's *Modern Critical Interpretations*, Barbara Bono's article on Dido is important, Pöschl's essay "Aeneas" is to be recommended, and Gransden's "War and Peace" focuses on the more-difficult-to-teach second half of the poem and proposes that there are degenerative aspects at work both in the character of the hero and in the poet's own circumstances and artistic expression.

Articles and Chapters

If the attention paid to Vergil's poetry in book form is considerable, the number of articles worthy of distinction in the vast sea of Vergilian criticism is even more so. In fact, the scholars surveyed listed articles more often than books as material that helped them develop their interpretations of the *Aeneid*, that influence their teaching, and that they would recommend to students. Most articles tend to focus on specific books of the epic, episodes, characters, or other limited matters; we group them by book for ease but begin with articles about the protagonist.

On Aeneas there are several meaty essays. In "Aeneas Imperator," R. G. M. Nisbet focuses on Vergil's depiction of the authority and command of Aeneas. His interpretation of the poem's final scene conflicts with that of Hans-Peter Stahl, who in "The Death of Turnus" finds Aeneas's slaughter of Turnus both moral and justified. Stewart's "Aeneas the Politician" offers a balanced view of the poem with respect to the choices the hero must often make. On Aeneas's relationship with women, an excellent beginning is Perkell's "On Creusa, Dido, and the Quality of Victory in Virgil's *Aeneid*." Perkell questions the humanity of Aeneas and argues convincingly that inattention and a lack of responsibility characterize his dealings with women. For an analysis of the poem and its multivocalism, Parry's "The Two Voices of Virgil's *Aeneid*" offers a superb start for any teacher. His concentration on Aeneas as a fusion of several figures—namely, Achilles, Odysseus, Augustus, and Mark Antony—demonstrates how Vergil evokes the presence of many conflicting voices at once. In his article "What Does Aeneas Look Like?," Mark Griffith reviews the words describing Aeneas's appearance and shows that Aeneas is "faceless and indistinct" and that discrepancies and omissions are characteristic of his person (314).

On book 1, Diskin Clay's "The Archaeology of the Temple of Juno in Carthage" finds echoes of both Iliadic and Odyssean scenes in Aeneas's arrival in Carthage and reflections of the first "Iliad" of the poem, the viewing of the temple doors, in books 6 and 12. Williams's "The Pictures on Dido's Temple" discusses Vergil's choices of the depicted scenes and their function in the book and poem as a whole. Putnam's first chapter in *Virgil's Epic Designs* does the same.

On book 2, Bernard Knox provides the most frequently recommended article for teachers as indicated by our survey. In "The Serpent and the Flame" he offers a close analysis of Vergil's use of language and metaphor in book 2, concentrating on the image of the serpent and how Vergil employs both it and allusions to it throughout the book. Knox's New Critical reading, which is straightforward and accessible to students, can eloquently introduce less experienced readers to the sort of work in which many classicists engage. A. M. Bowie's "The Death of Priam" illustrates how familiarity with historical events elucidates Vergil's allegorical technique.

On book 3, Archibald Allen, in "The Dullest Book in the *Aeneid*," sees Polydorus as a symbol for all the dead at Troy and notes that this book marks a break with the past. He remarks on Vergil's creation of a sense of weariness and his use of the adjective *fessus*. Robert Lloyd's article "*Aeneid* 3: A New Approach" examines the structure of book 3, commenting on the relation of individual episodes to one another and the development of Anchises's role as a seer. In his follow-up "*Aeneid* 3 and the Aeneas Legend," he considers book 3 in the light of extant material on the legend and concludes that Vergil did not allow such material to affect either his details or his overall design. In "Aeneas and Andromache," Richard Grimm reads the episode at Buthrotum as pivotal between hopes for the future and wistful remembrance of the past.

On book 4 there are several fine essays that comprise a range of approaches and concerns. Denis C. Feeney's "The Taciturnity of Aeneas" offers an analysis of Dido's and Aeneas's speeches and explores them in the wider context of the elements of speech and its effectiveness throughout the poem. The chapters on Dido in the books by Cairns, Wendell Clausen, Heinze, and Pöschl are all clear and accessible, and Bono's "The Dido Episode" examines Dido in the light of pertinent Roman history and explores both the past- and future-looking stance of the poem. In "Dido in the Light of History," Horsfall considers historical legend and discussions of Carthage in earlier Roman authors and their potential influence on Vergil's portrayal of Dido.

Putnam approaches book 5 in his chapter "Game and Reality" in *The Poetry of the* Aeneid. He examines Vergil's Homeric models for book 5, symbolism and imagery (particularly the image of offerings), and provides a compelling and sensitive reading that focuses on many important details in this book.

On book 6, Putnam analyzes the doors, fashioned by Daedalus, on the temple to Apollo (*Virgil's Epic Designs*, ch. 3). R. A. Brooks's "*Discolor Aura*: Reflections on the Golden Bough" concentrates on interpreting the important symbol of the bough through the text itself. In "History and Revelation in Vergil's Underworld," Feeney examines the influences of Plato's *Republic* and *Phaedo* and Cicero's "Somnium Scipionis" on Anchises's presentation of the afterlife. In "Science and Tradition in *Aeneid* 6," Thomas Habinek argues against inconsistency in the speeches of Anchises and finds in him a combination of philosophical mentor and traditional Roman father figure. Friedrich Solmsen's "The World of the Dead in Book 6 of the *Aeneid*" repudiates a tripartite division of the book and supports its duality, finding it balanced in representations of Tartarus and Elysium. Williams, in "The Sixth Book of the *Aeneid*" discusses the poetic, folkloric, religious, and philosophical heritage of the poet. He asserts that, as patriotic as book 6 is, its main purpose is to refocus attention on the character of Aeneas and his experiences. West's "The Bough and the Gate" is a scholarly but accessible account that poses possible answers to questions regarding the two important symbols of bough and gate in book 6.

For book 7, in "Some Aspects of the Structure of *Aeneid* 7," Edward Fraenkel discusses the pivotal nature of the book and examines some Homeric parallels. Putnam's "*Aeneid* VII and the *Aeneid*" examines metamorphosis and its symbolism, relates many incidents in this book to the rest of the poem, and offers a reading of the epic's close.

For book 8, Galinsky discusses the assimilation of Aeneas to Hercules in "Hercules in the *Aeneid*," tracing the symbolic import of theme and imagery in the episode. Robert Gurval in *Actium and Augustus* devotes the discerning chapter "The Battle of Actium on the Shield of Aeneas" to this scene. West's "*Cernere erat*: The Shield of Aeneas" takes a less than traditional look at

Vergil's illustrative methods, arguing that they depict images that would be "conceivable and effective" on a tangible piece of equipment (297).

For book 9, George E. Duckworth's "The Significance of Nisus and Euryalus for *Aeneid* IX–XII" elucidates the connections between this episode and the final quarter of the poem. Duckworth argues that the errors characters commit and the penalties they pay are a recurring theme in the final books. This observation applies to Nisus and Euryalus and particularly to the portrayal of Turnus. In "Epic Tragedy in Vergil's Nisus and Euryalus Episode," Barbara Pavlock explores the scene's parallels to Euripides's *Rhesus* and elucidates the tension Vergil creates between epic heroism and tragedy.

Herbert Benario examines book 10 in the light of the key figures Pallas, Lausus, and Mezentius. In "The Role of Mezentius in the *Aeneid*," P. F. Burke evaluates Vergil's use of both Homeric parallels and the existing traditions about Mezentius to suit his own poetic purposes. Andreola Rossi's concern in "Reversal of Fortune and Change in Genre in *Aeneid* 10" is the Hellenistic historiographical tradition and its influence on scenes in this book.

For book 11, in "Vergil's Camilla: A Paradoxical Character," W. P Basson sees the inevitable nature of war and the futility of participating in battle in the figure of Camilla. In "Chloreus and Camilla," Grace West focuses on Chloreus as a symbol for Trojan weakness and luxury and finds his destruction by native Italians emblematic of Italian strength.

Galinsky has offered two important and insightful articles on book 12. "The Anger of Aeneas" explores Aeneas's anger in the light of Epicurean philosophy and construes it as unequivocally human. He finds the hero's anger, although evocative of Homeric tradition and contemporary philosophical concerns, realistic. Galinsky's "How to be Philosophical about the End of the *Aeneid*" argues that Aeneas's anger is the product of reflection and justifiable. Perkell's insightful "The Lament of Juturna: Pathos and Interpretation in the *Aeneid*" finds in Vergil's presentation of Juturna an appeal for mercy from the victorious and inspiration for hope to the conquered. In "The Death of Turnus," Stahl argues that the poet's presentation of Aeneas's final act is positive. Stahl acknowledges the influence of historical allegory but explores implications of Aeneas's killing of Turnus in the text itself. These favorable views of Aeneas's final anger attempt to repudiate the interpretations of Putnam, Johnson, and others of the Harvard school.

Periodicals

Vergilius is the foremost periodical on Vergil, publishing articles, reviews, and an annually compiled bibliography of recent works. Other classical periodicals that generally contain a significant percentage of articles on Vergil's works are the *Classical Journal* (CJ), the *American Journal of Philology* (AJP), *Classical Philology* (CP), *Latomus, Euphrosyne, Gymnasium* (mostly in German), and *Classical World*. For reviews of books on Vergil and other pertinent matters (such as religion, history, gender studies, intertextuality) the periodicals *Gnomon*, *Bryn Mawr Classical Review* (BMCR), *Phoenix*, *Greece and Rome*, and *Classical Outlook* are important resources. There are many other periodicals devoted to classical literature and culture, too extensive in number to mention here, that also provide articles and reviews on Vergil; they are listed in the annual bibliography *L'année philologique*.

The following framework of the history of modern scholarship on the text is provided by Daniel M. Hooley.

Twentieth-Century Critical Perspectives

What Vergil offers in this poem that other poets do not is a passionate, grieving, but uncommitted meditation on man's nature and on the possibilities and impossibilities of his fate. It is the free and open dialectic of Vergil's polysematic fictions that makes possible this kind of meditation, and we misread the poem and refuse the wisdom (it is not knowledge) that Vergil makes possible for us [. . .] when we reduce his many allegories to one allegory and pervert his good fictions to bad myths.   (22)

So writes W. R. Johnson in *Darkness Visible*, arguably still the most intelligent general book in English on the *Aeneid*. It is not a polemical study, but polemic lies scarcely latent in the second sentence above. Not surprisingly, for it is a notable fact that the *Aeneid* has been over the course of the twentieth century the most contested of classical poems. There are reasons why a poem so old should matter enough to be thus contested in a nearly Latinless era: it is a big poem, an epic, and epic still, despite its decidedly antique feel, bears something of its old generic respectability. The periodic shifts of fashion and attention that since the very composition of the *Aeneid* have so curiously held Homer and Vergil in a kind of cycling or alternating counterpoise have lately turned to Vergil after the nineteenth century's clear preference for Homeric epic. The twentieth century was a period of cataclysmic shock; of disintegration and fragmentation; of aggressive, destructive nationalisms; of disillusionment; of human slaughter on an epic scale whose presiding reason does not answer to inherited (Homeric) epic paradigms or values. In this light, the world wars; the Holocaust; the nuclear abyss; Vietnam; the ungovernable inhumanities of Cambodia, Africa, and central Europe—all have contributed to a tragic sense of ending along with, for some, the hope that with due diligence we might come to an end of this ending to another beginning. Perhaps not precisely Aeneas amid Troy's flames, but we seem near enough to find something of our own in Vergil's haunting voice.

Yet twentieth-century reception of Vergil was anything but consistent. Readers' and critics' responses to the great poem took on local color, sometimes evolving into larger movements, conflicting positions. For the anglophone reader seeking orientation to the history of this scholarly reception, good surveys exist (Commager 1–13; Johnson, *Darkness* 1–22; Nethercut [for American scholarship] 309–14; Harrison, *Oxford Readings* 1–20; Martindale, *Cambridge Companion* 1–18). Philip Hardie's topic-oriented critical survey (*Virgil*), focusing on recent years, came to me too late to incorporate properly into this essay, but it is a valuable resource, full of good things. The reader looking for a broader history of Vergilian presence in twentieth-century letters and culture will find much in Theodore Ziolkowski's excellent survey. For a yet greater reach, one that embraces ancient and modern critical reception, Richard Thomas's *Virgil and the Augustan Reception* is invaluable.

Since much of the ground covered in these surveys is uncontroversial, I summarize with an eye to the more accessible and available critical works, then move on to more current areas of discussion. A great deal must be omitted. Some prominent Vergilians who work primarily on the nonepic poems cannot be mentioned here; and those, like R. G. Austin and R. D. Williams, whose major work has been confined to commentary do not fit comfortably in descriptions of critical trends, and their importance is thus underrepresented here. Also omitted from discussion are the smaller-scale, general introductions to Vergil and to the *Aeneid* in particular; these are intended for first-time readers of the poem but are usually designed to be independent of larger interpretive movements. Hence, they too receive short shrift. By way of partial restitution, I note William Anderson (*Art*), William Camps, Jasper Griffin, and Richard Jenkyns (*Classical Epic*). All are good for their purposes. On a more ambitious scale, but still introductory (intended "for the nonspecialist faculty and general reader" [3]), Christine Perkell's excellent collection of essays by various hands (*Reading*) should be consulted by readers of this volume. It devotes individual chapters to readings of (aspects of) each of the *Aeneid*'s books, all hospitably written, original essays by major critics (Perkell; Johnson, "*Dis Aliter Visum*"; Hexter, "Imitating"; Spence, "*Varium*"; Farrell, "*Aeneid* 5"; Leach, "Viewing"; Mack, "Birth"; Boyle, "*Aeneid* 8"; Wiltshire, "Man"; Feeney, "Epic Violence"; Anderson, "*Aeneid* 11"; Putnam, "*Aeneid* 12"). The collection provides supplementary pieces on the poem as foundation story (Miles), the women of the *Aeneid* (Nugent), the influence of Apollonius (Beye), and a discussion of the poem in selected English translations (Anderson, "Five Hundred Years").

There is no single story of the *Aeneid* in this past century. Rather, multiple stories carried on at different levels of scholarly engagement and focus. There are, however, discernible broader movements. Within the other stories of more specialized scholarly regard there has been bracing controversy and debate; for orientation one should turn initially to S. J. Harrison (*Oxford Readings* 11–17) and to the bibliographies composed by George Duckworth ("Recent Work"), by Alexander McKay ("Recent Work"), and by McKay annually in *Vergilius* from 1973 onward. German work for the first three-quarters of the century is summarized by Antonie Wlosok. For the hundred years prior to 1975 in German work, consult Werner Suerbaum.

> Thou majestic in thy sadness
> at the doubtful doom of human kind

Tennyson's "To Virgil," written in 1882 as the nineteenth century was beginning to think about its own end, betrays what had become the common tenor of Vergilian appreciation in respect to the *Aeneid*. Always "less" than Homer (especially for the Romantics, and of these, most infamously Coleridge), the Latin epicist's strengths were his warm affinity with nature, accomplished artistry (Tennyson's "stateliest measure"), and haunting melancholy. Heroic characterization, originality, dramatic power, verve, brilliant scenic description, and other traditionally valorized features of epic were Homeric qualities. As Walter Savage Landor put it in the context of *praising* Vergil, "we find him incapable of contriving, and yet more incapable of executing so magnificent a work as the *Iliad*" (qtd. in Gillespie 230). The situation in Germany was virtually identical, with major lights like Barthold Niebuhr and Theodor Mommsen dismissive of Vergilian epic. All that changed dramatically in 1903 with the publication of Richard Heinze's *Vergils epische Technik*. Heinze undertook to examine the relation between Vergil's literary techniques and his larger artistic intentions, not by ignoring the shade of Homer but by investigating exactly what Vergil did with his great predecessor. This examination meant, effectively, a certain kind of source-oriented close reading, and from it emerged an altogether different poem that contrived to foreground human psychology and emotion in ways Homer did (or could) not and that presented a developing central protagonist who grows into a new (non-Homeric but very Roman) Stoic heroism.

Heinze's book had enormous influence, not all of it immediate; most important, it turned scholars' attention to Vergil at a moment when history would conspire to make the *Aeneid* a cultural paradigm. Although the crisis of modernity can be traced in some of its origins to earlier and other elements, the Great War of 1914 shattered Europe and along with it older, optimistic assumptions about progress and providence. In this context of disrupted values and vertiginous passage from one state of civilized life to something darker and less easy of rational construal, Vergil was, surprisingly, handed a big role. Not that he was read in greater numbers than before the war; the *Aeneid* was still an artifact of high culture. But Heinze had opened awareness to the psychological constructions of the new Stoic hero, his uncertainties, confusions, doubts, and this awareness was clearly the right frequency of thought for much of the postwar generation. Other forces, too, were at work. The bimillenary celebration of Vergil's birth took place in 1930–31, and celebratory festivities in Italy especially became occasions for asserting the strains of Roman triumphalism (whereby the poem is seen to celebrate the achievements of the Augustan principate) many have found in the epic. In this context Vergil became, blatantly, the centerpiece for Italian Fascist propaganda. Again, however, this reading was not universal, and its conspicuous antitype was found in the fierce anti-Nazi Theodor Haecker (*Vergil: Vater des Abendlandes*). Haecker's book denied the political parochialism of the Fascists and other nationalists, instead positing Vergil as emblematic of Western spiritual identity. For Haecker that identity was Christian, and he viewed Vergil's depiction of the roles of *pietas*, devotion, persistence, and suffering in a greater cause a proto-Christian masterpiece. It is impossible to summarize in this short space the impact of Haecker's book, but among its most conspicuous legacies were the two celebrated essays by T. S. Eliot, "What Is a Classic?" (1945) and "Virgil and the Christian World" (1951). Ziolkowski has demonstrated how secondary, thin, and distant Eliot's actual acquaintance with Vergil was (119–34), but Eliot by the mid-1940s had acquired the mantle of sage, and his depiction of Vergil as "the classic of all Europe" (130) was mildly electrifying in the world of humane letters. "What Is a Classic?" was the inaugural address of the Virgilian Society, and one might readily catch the whiff of special pleading in a lecture praising Vergil's centrality before an audience of Vergilians. But its themes of cultural maturity, access to tradition, continuity, and moral seriousness—along with its latent burden of imperialist apologia—found resonance for good reasons. World war had again worked its disastrous ways, and the West had once again barely escaped catastrophe. In some respects it had not. Eliot's was a perhaps desperate, certainly derivative, but widely appreciated attempt to rediscover the center (Johnson, *Darkness* 7).

Two Englishmen had anticipated crucial elements of Eliot's thesis in ways that concern us more directly here. C. S. Lewis and Maurice Bowra both raised and discussed the still useful distinction between "primary" (oral) and "secondary" (literary) epic. If primary epic is spontaneous, naive, of "brilliant clarity" and "unhesitating sweep," secondary epic is reflective, complex, the product of a "mature civilization." Lewis's words have the Eliotic ring that represents our mid-century, grown-up Vergil:

> I have read that his Aeneas [. . .] is hardly the shadow of a man beside Homer's Achilles. But a man, an adult, is precisely what he is: Achilles had been little more than a passionate boy. You may, of course, prefer the poetry of spontaneous passion to the poetry of passion at war with vocation, and finally reconciled. Every man to his taste. But we must not blame the second for not being the first. With Virgil European poetry grows up. (66)

There is more in this formulation than sweeping generalization: implicit in both Lewis and Bowra are viable insights for reading Vergil: the Stoicism Heinze had identified, originality of characterization, construction of a public heroism that made sense of sacrifice and loss, full recognition of the force of history in the epic, thematic design not of derivative Homeric mimesis but of its own coherent artistic purpose.

It was another German, Viktor Pöschl (*Art*) who would take this and like interpretive material and develop it into a satisfactory reading through close consideration of Vergil's imagery and symbolism. Pöschl's analysis, though to a degree schematic, is not crude; his symbolic readings often have a powerful ambivalence. Yet certain symbols adumbrate "basic themes" (13–33) in the poem: Jupiter and Juno stand as counterpoised forces, one representing peace, suppression of disruptive energies, the triumph of order, the other war, *furor impius* ("unholy madness"), unreason, violence. Other figures line up in analogous polarity: Aeneas, Anchises, Evander, Pallas, other allies (all male) against the likes of Allecto, Dido, Turnus, Amata, Mezentius, though not always unambiguously or, in the case of the latter group, not without accruing sympathy even when on the wrong side. The underlying thematic course of the epic is the long struggle to subdue the demonic—hence Pöschl places a greater stress on the second, martial half of the poem than was traditional—and to establish an order ultimately reflected in the abiding political dispensation of emergent Rome: *imperium sine fine* ("imperium without end"). This optimistic perspective on Rome and order triumphant despite enormous personal cost responded to postwar anxieties and came to be held widely among European scholars (e.g., Büchner; Klingner), thus its tag, "European optimism" (but see also the American Otis, *Virgil*).

A major response to the Europeans grew up quickly. Originating in America, its proponents came to be called the American pessimists or the Harvard school by those, beginning with Johnson, who traced it to the Harvard-based work of Adam Parry, R. A. Brooks, Wendell Clausen ("Interpretation"), and Michael Putnam (*Poetry*); *ambivalent* and *bivocal* are other terms that have been used to describe the general critical tendency. Parry's article ("The Two Voices of Vergil's *Aeneid*") struck the distinguishing note:

> The nostalgia for the heroic and Latin past, the pervasive sadness, the regretful sense of the limitations of human action in a world where you've got in the end to end up on the right side or perish [. . .] the continual opposition of a personal voice which comes to us as if it were Vergil's own to the public voice of Roman success: all this is felt by every attentive reader of the poem. (111)

Yet for many, Parry contended, this all amounts to rich background noise, secondary to the Roman triumph that is the larger message of the poem. He revalorizes:

> Aeneas' tragedy is that he cannot be a hero, being in the service of an impersonal power. What saves him as a man is that all the glory of the solid

achievement which he is serving, all the satisfaction of "having arrived" in Italy, means less to him than his own sense of personal loss.   (123)

Vergil's "personal voice" (111), which intimates the dark side of the epic, has been explored by a number of critics on a small and large scale, and their work has been influential among anglophone readers into (and in some cases beyond) the 1980s. These often powerful ambivalent readings of the poem locate points of stress between its celebrated moments of redeeming promise (e.g., the prophecies of Jupiter, the incandescent tableaux of foredestined glory in books 6 and 8, the triumphant ecphrasis of Aeneas's shield) and the actualities of the human struggle to realize these things. Rather than see the grinding labor of Aeneas (and so many others his story brings him into contact with) as a painfully necessary prelude to something better, these critics have found an irresolvable gap between the two orders. The ascendancy of Rome and achieved peace under Augustus may or may not be good in themselves, but the poem's most compelling moments are those of scruple and resistance, when, like the talismanic golden bough, it manifests its reluctance to share in the great Augustan project. Hence its focus on the tragedy of those lives, great and little, caught up in the motions of dehumanizing historical process, and on the sacrifices and compromises of self and principle. Aeneas, Dido, Turnus, Mezentius, Amata, and the rest, rather than be simply either proto-Roman heroes or anti-Roman impediments of an earlier construction, are found to share virtues and weaknesses. All, in some respect, are not quite up to the huge pressures they have been subjected to—though in this failure luminously human.

Of particular note are the works of Putnam (*Poetry*, *Vergil's* Aeneid, and *Virgil's Epic Designs*) and Johnson (*Darkness*). Putnam's reading—especially of the poem's problematic ending when Aeneas, in killing Turnus, may be said to accede to or be overcome by the very forces of vengeance, anger, and passion he is meant to oppose—is based on analysis of repeated language and images. Putnam's work with patterns of artistic structure in the poem underscores the affinity between literary formalism and criticism of an "ambivalent" orientation. Bernard Knox's seminal article "The Serpent and the Flame," for instance, in laying its methodological groundwork invokes Cleanth Brooks's *Well Wrought Urn*, and Kenneth Quinn's *Virgil's* Aeneid is an extended analysis strongly colored by the New Criticism. In general, these scholars' focus on symbolism, imagery, and significant language has considerably enriched the poem for the modern reader while, inevitably, revealing some of the limits of formalist literary analysis. Charles Martindale's "Descent" is perceptive about these limits while perhaps overstating the programmatic influence of the New Criticism. (See, *contra*, the wide-ranging work of A. J. Boyle in *Chaonian Dove* and "Canonic Text.") Johnson's book comes near the end of the great pessimistic movement in Vergil studies and is in many ways an endgame itself. While offering a relentlessly dark reading,

Johnson shows signs of dissatisfaction with prevailing critical tendencies. Consequently, he stresses the openness of the text, its blurred images, its deeply resident uncertainties, and the play of restive fictions that resist secure thematic diagnosis.

Further work deriving from Parry's vision of the thematic plurality or multivocality of the poem continued to be written in America and Europe (e.g., G. Williams; Lyne, *Further Voices* and *Words*; Toohey; Farron, *Vergil's Aeneid*). Other, not unrelated, tendencies emerged: for instance, following William Anderson's important article "Vergil's Second *Iliad*," K. W. Gransden (*Virgil's* Iliad) and others began to focus attention on the neglected second half of the *Aeneid*, a tendency that has produced some important new commentaries on those books. In wider terms, the mid-1980s marked a new turn in work originating chiefly in Britain, whose scholarly establishment never fully embraced the bleaker views promulgated widely in America. Hardie (*Virgil's* Aeneid) looks back to Pöschl in readdressing the panegyrical themes of the poem but breaks new ground by exploring Vergil's use of cosmological myth in the positive formulation of an Augustan imperial program. Francis Cairns offers a treatment of Aeneas as the virtuous king portrayed in contemporary philosophical theorizing, in contrast to Dido and Turnus—as well as a discussion of the generic influences of elegy, lyric, and Homeric epic: a rich, composite analysis. Nicholas Horsfall, perhaps the most prolific and learned of modern Vergilians, has provided an almost steady commentary over the past years in reviews and smaller-scale pieces of local and scholarly focus, generally in the spirit of a positive Augustanism. Two of his books (*Virgilio* and *Companion*) offer some integration of his views, in which there is often the edge of brusque common sense and impatience with Vergilian ambivalence—an attitude evident in Galinsky's strong-minded Augustanism as well ("Anger," "How to Be Philosophical," and "Damned"). Horsfall and Galinsky shake free from what is often seen as the pessimistic humanism of the post-Vietnam climate, a charge that Thomas opposes (*Virgil*). Equally triumphalist though broader in scope, covering the entire Vergilian corpus and related poetry as well, is Jenkyns's multidimensional exploration of nature in Vergil (*Virgil's Experience*).

To judge from these works, it might be fair to say that the new Augustanism is currently the dominant voice in Vergilian scholarship, but in one sense that would be misleading. For while some recent studies clearly represent the reassertion of certain aspects of an earlier (European) tradition, expressed with yet more scholarship and verve, much newer work is neither merely an instauration of the Heinze-Pöschl approach nor simply a retreat to a rough-and-ready pragmatism. Among Vergilians of the current generation, there is flexibility, ingenuity, and a degree of theoretical sophistication. Where their work turns away from the individualistic humanism of the 1960s, 1970s, and 1980s (not all of it does; see, e.g., Thomas, "Isolation"), it tracks current critical tendencies and concerns. The work of Gian Biagio Conte, for instance, founded in semiotic assumptions about the marked nature of the literary text, considers the related problems of literary intertextuality and the functionality of generic systems. In respect to the *Aeneid*, Conte focuses on the distinction between epic "code" and "norm": code entails the stock of generically determined possibilities, the things epic can do; norm, the historically and ideologically dictated features of this epic. While the epic norm bears Augustan and Roman themes without compromise, the code, by virtue of its representing a number of generic possibilities, opens the norm to revision and second thought. Conte has lately reconsidered some of the more formalist elements of his work, but his scholarship has been undeniably influential. Work in allusion and intertextuality has long been carried forward across the Vergilian corpus by Thomas (in collected form, *Reading Virgil*); see too, for methodological orientation, Farrell, *Vergil's* Georgics.

In another direction, David Quint's *Epic and Empire*, a study comprehending many more works than the *Aeneid*, might seem another exercise in the new Augustanism. Quint does reject traditional ambivalence, averring that it depoliticizes an inherently political art form, but he breaks new ground. Epic for Quint is teleological narrative that comes to, enables, resolution; the *Aeneid* is a narrative that "plots out empowerment [. . .], the struggle not of the individual psyche but of a collective political nation" (51). He describes how "drawing on the two narrative models offered to it by the *Iliad* and the *Odyssey*, Virgil's poem attached political meaning to narrative form itself. To the victors belongs epic, with its linear teleology; to the losers belongs romance, with its random or circular wanderings" (8–9). The *Aeneid's* totality explores both; after the romance of the first six Odyssean books, the epic, Iliadic half permits the Trojans-Romans to repeat their disastrous past but as winners rather than losers. There are paradoxes and conflicts in Vergil's "winners' story" (52), but Quint maintains that they are part of an overtly political literary medium. This analysis does considerably more than make observations about Vergil's pro- or anti-Augustanism; it establishes a central narrative paradigm that influences major elements of subsequent European literature.

Quint's reading of the *Aeneid* has been fairly criticized as too schematic, but it has been valuable in opening the poem to a wider sense of political implication. Hardie's second book (*Epic Successors*), published, like Quint's, in 1993, shares many of its theoretical and methodological assumptions: it builds on the idea of epic as repetition, either to reenact or alter the past. Vergilian epic is seen as an overtly totalizing form, again a deeply politicized narrative, but like all such narratives it is locked in a contextual temporality (note Mack, *Patterns*) that disallows closure. Hence it exposes itself to readings after the fact: "the instability of the Virgilian world is an open-ended invitation for succeeding epic poets to revise and redefine" (3). Hardie conducts, then, a reading of these subsequent readings as well as of the *Aeneid* itself through the epic eyes of Ovid, Lucan, Valerius, Silius, and others. Martindale speaks in similar terms of the Vergilian "shuttle between the aspect of time and the aspect of the timeless"

(*Cambridge Companion* 4), with its attendant political complications, and finds it one of the underpinning thematic continuities in the very useful collection of essays he has edited. These essays range over a variety of topics and are hardly uniform in approach, but together they point to fertile areas of critical interest: Vergilian reception; the politics of literary genre and the ways, in general, in which literature may become an active vehicle for fostering the interests of one group over those of another (see Wofford; and on political context in general, Stahl, *Vergil's* Aeneid); religious and philosophical ideas; the passions (see Fowler, "Epicurean Anger"; Wright; Gill; Braund and Gill; Hershkowitz [on madness in the *Aeneid* and elsewhere]); intertextuality; aspects of Vergilian narrative (see Ahl; Fowler, "Virgilian Narrative"; Johnson, *"Dis Aliter Visum"*); readerly complicity (see Feeney, "Epic Violence"); sexuality and gender. In this last category, there has always been critical attention focused on the prominent female characters of the poem: Dido, Juno, Amata, and others. Criticism has begun to approach the poem with the more specialized theoretical tools of gender and feminist studies, though much good work remains to do (see Fowler, "Vergil on Killing"; Suzuki; Mitchell; Sullivan; Hexter, "Sidonian Dido"; Putnam, "Possessiveness"; Oliensis; Fantham; Spence, *Varium*; Mack, "Birth"; Nugent, "Women" and "Vergil's 'Voice'"; Keith).

I close this brief survey with a few notable miscellaneous items. The general area of the metaphysics of epic—the nature, literary character, and functionality of its gods—has been thoroughly explored by Denis Feeney (*Gods*), on which general subject see Susanna Braund. On Augustan religious politics, see both G. Gottlieb and David West ("End"). The connection of divine ordinance and the problematic nature of prophecy in the epic has been the subject of a useful study by James O'Hara (*Death*; see also his *True Names* on "etymological wordplay" in the poem). Don Fowler has been the most persuasive exponent of a specifically narratological consideration of point of view in the *Aeneid* ("Virgilian Narrative"), opening another approach to the poem's multiplicity of theme and perspective. His "Deviant Focalisation in Virgil's *Aeneid*" links contemporary narratology to the tradition of Vergilian subjectivity from Heinze through Brooks Otis's important *Virgil: A Study in Civilized Poetry*, particularly in respect to Otis's influence on the narratological work in Italy over the past few decades culminating in Conte and Mariza Bonfanti. In "Narrate and Describe," Fowler also addresses narrative and ecphrasis (descriptions of images or works of art wherein the larger epic narrative pauses and yields to an enclosed narrative). Others to consult in this area are Thomas ("Virgil's Ecphrastic Centerpieces"); A. J. Boyle (*Roman Epic*); Alessandro Barchiesi ("Rappresentazioni"); Michael Putnam (*Virgil's Epic Designs*); and Eleanor Winsor Leach ("Viewing"). As Barchiesi puts it, ecphrasis interests because it presents issues of narrative dynamics, self-reflexivity (texts within texts, texts reading texts), and "various approaches to realism and representation" ("Virgilian Narrative" 272). It further entails, as

Putnam points out, issues of perspective, gender, and larger contextuality. An ecphrastic passage is not only contained in the narrative but also opens the narrative up to the real, visualized world outside the poem, the world in which the poem itself is just another expressive element. That complexity of perspective and, particularly, the role of the reader in ecphrasis, Leach adds importantly, open to question the issue of where interpretive authority is located. In this respect and others, ecphrasis is part of a larger preoccupation with "the power of images" in Augustan culture (see Zanker; Galinsky, *Augustan Culture*). That power is largely seen in political terms, reflecting the assertion of (changing) values in the rising Augustan principate, as both Fowler ("Opening") and Hardie ("Fame") seek to show in their investigations of Vergil's treatment of the political symbols and rhetoric of his day.

In these and too many other critical inquiries to account for adequately in this brief account, the *Aeneid*'s explicit and latent politics spill out of pessimistic and optimistic categories into a messy interpretive space where the critical vocabulary opens up again. In making its own claims, current criticism sees the epic as not merely the great literary monument of its sometime reputation but also as part of a wider tapestry of contested values. The twentieth century's most important legacy may be this awareness of the *Aeneid* as art that matters in more than literary terms, as poetry that is, consequently, ground of intense dispute in larger and evolving frames of debate and understanding. Which leaves us at another century's beginning with the responsibilities and pleasures of sorting through the unsettled and unsettling qualities that have ever been—along with the dark sublimity of Vergil's poetry—at the heart of his epic's abiding appeal.

Internet Resources

Several sites offer downloadable versions of the Latin text of the *Aeneid* as well as English translations. Some are the Internet Classics Archives at MIT (http:// classics.mit.edu/Virgil/aeneid.mb.txt), the Perseus Project (http://www.perseus .tufts.edu/cgi-bin/ptext?doc=Perseus%3A1999.02.0055), and Project Gutenberg (in Latin ftp://ibiblio.org/pub/docs/books/gutenberg/etext95/anidl110.txt and in English ftp://ibiblio.org/pub/docs/books/gutenberg/etext95/anide10.txt). Joseph Farrell's *The Vergil Project: Resources for Students, Teachers, and Readers of Vergil*, also offers everything from downloadable texts to lists of resources and is well worth spending some time investigating (http://vergil.classics .upenn.edu).

For bibliographic resources on the Internet, that of David Wilson-Okamura at http://virgil.org is quite useful; its subheadings, such as "bibliography" and "Augustus," include a link to Amazon.com for books currently in print. The "Augustus" subfile has an excellent compendium of resources-background, primary sources, and modern essays. Shirley Werner's bibliography (www. vroma.org/~bmcmanus/werner_vergil.html) is an excellent place to begin searching for anything related to the *Aeneid* and includes snippets from reviews on the more recent publications. For those particularly interested in gender studies, *Diotima* at http://www.stoa.org/diotima offers general bibliographies on women in the ancient world and a specialized bibliography on women in Vergil (www.stoa.org/dio-bin/diobib?vergil).

Audiovisual Materials

The most popular ancillary medium employed by instructors is the presentation of slides. Representations of the poem's mythological background such as the Trojan War or the judgment of Paris and characters such as the gods, Aeneas, or Laocoön inspire today's visually oriented students. Scenes of Rome and her monuments, particularly the Ara Pacis, help provide a sense of history and tangibility. Furthermore, since such scenes are depicted in both ancient art (e.g., vase and wall paintings, sculpture) and in later European art (particularly in painting from the Renaissance onward), there are many interesting visual interpretations available. Books containing good plates for the production of such slides include those by Thomas H. Carpenter (*Art and Myth in Ancient Greece*); Karl Galinsky (*Augustan Culture*); Susan Woodford (*The Trojan War in Ancient Art*); Paul Zanker (*The Power of Images in the Age of Augustus*); and two books on the Ara Pacis, one by David Castriota and one by Diane A. Conlin. Zanker is particularly good on imperial coinage and sculpture. Nigel Llewellyn's article "Virgil and the Visual Arts" is a good initial source on later European art.

The influence of the poem on other art forms is also easy to demonstrate. Many instructors enjoy presenting to their students selections from Henry Purcell's opera *Dido and Aeneas* and Hector Berlioz's opera *Les troyens* (Berlioz was a great lover of the *Aeneid*). Gustav Holst's suite *The Planets* offers entertaining aural portraits of Mercury and Venus. Ottorino Respighi's *Pines of Rome* and *Fountains of Rome* as well as his other works (part of his *Three Botticelli Pictures* was inspired by Botticelli's famous *Birth of Venus*) all make good accompaniments to slide presentations.

Less directly related are a few films. Survey respondents favor a number of films for their different relations to the text: Joseph Mankiewicz's *Cleopatra* (1963, with Elizabeth Taylor and Richard Burton) offers some historical underpinnings, portions of which include good clips of battle scenes; Roman Polanski's *Chinatown* (1974, with Faye Dunaway and Jack Nicholson), like the *Aeneid*, presents a mythological foundation of a city, deliberately confuses the audience with respect to its genre, includes the unnecessary and dramatic death of the heroine, and makes frightening suggestions concerning the political milieu of its author and times; Francis Ford Coppola's *The Godfather* (1972, with Marlon Brando and Al Pacino), because of the clear distinctions between personal and business matters, provides an interesting modern parallel to

Aeneas's public and private senses of duty. Finally, the original *Star Wars* (1977, now released under the full title *Star Wars Episode IV: A New Hope*, dir. George Lucas, starring Alec Guiness, Harrison Ford, Mark Hamill, and Carrie Fisher) offers a number of episodes that parallel the action of the *Aeneid*, particularly the leaving of home in quest of self- and personal fulfillment, the loss of the father-mentor, and the final duel between the hero and his opponent.

For those who teach the *Aeneid* in a course on the history of the epic or on classical civilization, a number of more classically oriented films are available. A longtime favorite is the old Italian version of *Ulysses* (1955, starring Kirk Douglas and Anthony Quinn, dir. Mario Camerini) as a quick (104 minutes) recap of the adventures of Odysseus; although it is now out of print, it is still available at some of the smaller, independent video rental shops. The more recent *The Clash of the Titans* (1981, starring Burgess Meredith, Harry Hamlin, Maggie Smith, and Laurence Olivier, dir. Desmond Davis), a visual fantasy based on a book by the classical scholar Beverly Cross, relates the story of Perseus. *Jason and the Argonauts* (1963, dir. Don Chaffey) contains numerous special effects that depict the power of magic in antiquity. A film version of the *Aeneid* was produced in Italy, entitled *La leggenda di Enea* (also known as *The Avenger* or *The Last Glory of Troy*, 1962, starring Steve Reeves as Aeneas, dir. Albert Band and Giorgio Rivalta); it is available from Sinister Cinema in Oregon. *La guerra di Troia* (*The Trojan Horse* or *The Trojan War*, 1962, dir. Giorgio Ferroni) features John Drew Barrymore as Ulysses. Stanley Kubrick's *Spartacus* (1960; fully restored version 1991, starring Kirk Douglas, Peter Ustinov, and Laurence Olivier), offers an account of the slave revolt in Italy (73 BCE, shortly before Vergil's birth) and an interesting depiction of the working of the Roman senate. A recent favorite among students is Ridley Scott's *Gladiator* (2000, starring Russell Crowe, Richard Harris, Derek Jacobi, and Joaquim Phoenix). Although the events portrayed occur during the reign of Marcus Aurelius (late second century BCE), there is pertinence to the political climate of Vergil's time. The jealousy that the accomplished general Maximus incurs conveys the power that military leaders could attain as well as the dangers they faced in creating enemies (consider Marius, Sulla, Pompey, and Caesar).

A number of hour-long programs related to Vergil's world are available for purchase from the History Channel, Discovery Channel, or A&E. These include *Byzantium, the Lost Empire*; *Deadly Duels*; *Ancient Rome*; *Roman Emperors*; *Hail Caesar*; *The Odyssey of Troy*; and *Augustus, the First Emperor*.

NOTE

Throughout this volume, wherever text and translation line numbers are given together, even if a quoted English word or words precede the Latin, the first number indicates the Latin, the second the English. To give an example of such citing, "Italian excellence" ("Italia [. . .] virtute") (12.827; 1099): in book 12, line 827 is from Vergil's text, line 1099 is from the Mandelbaum translation. When this order is not followed, a phrase (e.g., "in Latin") will be used to make that clear.

Part Two

APPROACHES

Introduction

The factors and challenges associated with teaching the *Aeneid* are numerous and multifaceted. As with any work that has been translated from another language, teachers depend on the accuracy and interpretation of the translator, which they may not be able to assess. Familiarity with cultural and historical background is important, and knowledge of genre and literary tradition indispensable. The subtleties involved in interpreting Vergil's poetry further complicate matters. Making a text that has come to us from another culture and time meaningful and appealing to students demands understanding, sensitivity, and plain hard work from the instructor. Thus, before we speak about the essays in this collection, we offer a few practical ideas for teaching the *Aeneid*, many of which emerged from our survey. The trained classicist already knows much of this information. But since many who teach the epic today do so in humanities or Western-survey courses and are experts in disciplines other than classics, the following suggestions may make their less familiar path a little easier. Just as the Romans were accustomed to adopt and assimilate ideas or practices that struck them as worthwhile, so we hope that our readers will not hesitate to employ whatever in the following pages strikes them as an interesting or exciting approach to teaching the *Aeneid*.

If an instructor has any Latin—or knows someone who does—we recommend even a brief recitation of some of the original Latin lines when Vergil is introduced in a class or lecture. This practice gives students at least an impression of the sound of the original. If one possesses enough knowledge to recite the dactylic hexameter with confidence, so much the better. It is also instructive to ask students to repeat the Latin after they hear it. This exercise is beneficial in that it emphasizes two important matters students are apt to forget: that the *Aeneid* is a poem, not a novel or book (as they are generally accustomed to calling it), and that they are dealing with a translation. Too often students approach a classic without much awareness that what they are reading is remote in a very real manner: it was written centuries ago and in the context of another place, culture, and language. While this remoteness may dissuade some from developing any bona fide relationship to this work, it may encourage others to put extra effort into learning more about the pertinent language and culture. To this end, a brief analysis of the poem's opening words *arma virumque cano* can help students see how close Latin and English are: when prompted, they can easily observe that *arma* and *arms* are cognate, that *vir-* is the stem that gives us *virile*, and that *cano* is reflected in *incantation*. Such a demonstration of the linkages between Latin and English may help them discover that Latin is not as remote as they thought and that it has had a very tangible impact on English.

Moving from the Latin influence on our language to the Roman influence on our culture, an instructor might ask students to take from their pockets a dollar bill, on the reverse of which they will find the Latin words *annuit coeptis* and *novus ordo seclorum*. Students are normally surprised to learn that these are the words of Vergil. The first phrase echoes *Aeneid* 9.625, where Iulus shoots his arrow and asks Jupiter to "be kind to my / audacious try" (Mandelbaum 9.834–35). (The word *annuit*, derived from *ad* + *nuo*, literally means "nod to" or "give assent to," while *coeptis*, from the verb meaning "to begin," may be translated as "undertaking" or "attempts.") The second phrase on the dollar bill alludes to another of Vergil's poems, the fourth *Eclogue*, in which he predicts the birth of a child whose presence will usher in a new age, when "the great order of the centuries arises from the beginning" ("magnus ab integro saeclorum nascitur ordo"). Hence, the motto on the dollar bill is translated as "A new order of the ages has nodded to our undertakings." The fourth *Eclogue* (line 5 is quoted) is one of the reasons that Christians revered Vergil and made special efforts to preserve his manuscripts—they considered him, although he was a pagan, a prophet who anticipated the birth of Christ; the poem also inspired Dante to select Vergil as his guide through the Underworld and place him in Limbo (in the *Inferno*). A belief in Vergil's prophetic powers seems to have emerged during the Late Roman Empire and was particularly prominent during the Middle Ages, when people employed Vergil's opera, calling them the "Sortes Virgilianae" ("Vergilian oracle"), as a tool to assist them in making decisions: they would ask a question or consider a problem, close their eyes, open the text, and place a finger on a page. The line on which one's finger landed was supposed to offer some guidance or response to the questioner. This tradition is the source of the alternate spelling of Vergil's name, "Virgil," since the Latin word for a divining rod or magic wand is *virga*; thus, the *e* in Publius Vergilius Maro was altered to an *i*, and the popular spelling of his name became "Virgilius" as a result of this association with clairvoyance. Today many scholars, particularly in the United States, prefer to spell his name with the original *e* (e.g., the Vergilian Society), but "Virgil" has become traditional, especially among the British (e.g., Virgil Society). Although *virga* originally evokes a sense of fertility and growth (and thus is cognate with the English word *virgin*), Vergil himself employs the term at 7.190 to refer to Circe's magic wand (rendered as "gold rod" by Mandelbaum [7.251]).

Students may also have heard the tradition that the poem is unfinished, and indeed it is, but not in the sense that they believe. The poem ends just where Vergil intended. From his biographers we learn that he first wrote the story of Aeneas in prose; he then altered that prose into poetic form, not always producing complete hexameter lines. Once the whole was converted into poetry, he embarked on the task of polishing the poem and completing those lines that were not full hexameters. He did not set about this refinement in chronological sequence, however; the number of incomplete lines in book 2 far exceeds that of any other, while several books yield no incomplete lines at all. When his death was imminent, Vergil requested that the poem, still unfinished, be destroyed. It is an incalculable benefit to Western literature that it was not, for had the *Aeneid* not existed, the works of Ovid, Lucan, Statius, Dante, and Milton, to name but a few, would have lacked an important model.

This brief list of names should not imply that Vergil's epic influenced only works that have become a central part of our canon. Over the centuries the *Aeneid* has exerted tremendous influence on works of various genres, and it has directly contributed to the development of the national epics of several countries. With the tenth-century poem *Waltharius*, the form of epic begins to fuse with Christian concerns but still focuses on heroic exploits, national identity, warfare, romantic interests, and issues of obligation and loyalty; *Waltharius*'s form and details are frequently a direct response to or inversion of *Aeneid* books 2 and 4. In the *Chanson de Roland*, stories about an actual eighth-century battle of Charlemagne eventually take the form of a tenth-century poem that bears the flavor of heroic poetry and only barely preserves the details of its origin—the relation of poem to stories echoes that of the *Aeneid* to tales of the legendary foundation of Rome. In some ways, the closeness of Roland and Olivier recalls that of Aeneas and Pallas; but Roland and Olivier together also express two sides of Aeneas, one daring and the other prudent. Alda, the betrothed of Roland, is as nondescript as Lavinia yet similar to her in physical portrayal: her paleness is a distinguishing feature, and her responses to circumstances are swift and effusive. In the twelfth century, the French *Roman d'Enéas* retells the *Aeneid*, emphasizing Aeneas's relationships with Dido and Lavinia and bringing the epic closer in style to romances of courtly love. The *Roman* directly spawned the German epic *Eneit* by Heinrich von Veldeke (or Hendrix or Henric van Veldeke). At the same time, the *Roman de Troie* by Benoît de Sainte-Maure, based on *Aeneid* 2, became a popular romance chronicling the fall of Troy.

In the fourteenth century Petrarch carried epic and the influence of the *Aeneid* into the Renaissance with his unfinished Latin epic *Africa*, which places Italy's illustrious past, concentrated in the achievements of Scipio Africanus, and the issue of national identity at its center. *Aeneid* 1 through 3, 6, and 8 are *Africa*'s most significant models, but the work also echoes the *Aeneid* as a whole in that it too finds important predecessors in Homer, Ennius, and Cicero (Petrarch also makes much use of Livy, Lucan, and Saint Augustine). In addition to the complexities both poems share, Petrarch's apparent ambivalence about progress and glory, whether literary or historical, marks his sensibilities with a Vergilian tinge.

In 1428, Maffeo Vegio composed a thirteenth book of the *Aeneid*, which extols the morality of Aeneas and depicts his apotheosis; for the better part of the next two centuries, this added ending became a standard fixture in printed editions of the text. Girolamo Vida exhibits the *Aeneid*'s influence in both his *Christiad* (1535), with Christ as the central heroic figure, and *De Arte Poetica* (1527), a work on the mechanics of writing epic poetry that praises the *Aeneid* and ends with a hymn to Vergil. In the *Christiad*, Christ's labors differ from those of Aeneas, but the goal of the Pax Christiana parallels the eventual achievement of the Pax Romana through the deeds of Aeneas and his descendant Augustus.

At about this time (the sixteenth century), many authors move epic into the vernacular. In Italian, Ludovico Ariosto's epic treatment of the Roland story in *Orlando Furioso* seeks to extol the Este family in a manner that parallels Vergil's elevation of the Julian gens. In Portuguese, Luíz Vaz de Camões's *Lusiads* models Vasco da Gama's voyage on Vergil and Ariosto, and in French Pierre de Ronsard attempts to produce the great national epic with *La Franciade*. Torquato Tasso's epic *Gerusalemne liberata* depicts the exploits of Godfrey of Boulogne during the First Crusade and, like the medieval epics, develops the threads of love and adventure within the epic structure. Edmund Spenser's *Faerie Queen* may draw less visibly on the *Aeneid*, but Spenser consciously patterned his literary career after Vergil's and traces of Vergil's influence are clear. Spenser's presentation of moral issues through allegory reflects the continuing interest in interpreting the *Aeneid* allegorically (e.g., understanding Aeneas as Augustus or, in Christian readings, Saint Peter or Christ). Voltaire later threw his hat into the epic ring with his portrayal of Henry IV in *Henriade*.

Not all works influenced by the *Aeneid* have maintained a heroic aura, however. In 1673 John Phillips published his *Maronides; or, Virgil Travesty*, an English burlesque treatment of *Aeneid* 6. Charles Cotton followed suit with *Scarronnides; or, Virgil Travestie* (1807), a mock epic rendition of *Aeneid* 1 and 4. The Ukrainian poet Ivan Kotlyarevsky (Petrovych) composed his parody *Eneida* in 1842.

During the twentieth century, many writers evoked Vergil to support their own political causes; the most striking examples are André Bellessort's *Virgile, son œuvre et son temps* (1920) and Robert Brasillach's *Présence de Virgile* (1931), both of which focus on fascist concerns. Theodor Haecker's *Vergil: Vater des Abendlandes* (1933) (translated as *Virgil: Father of the West*, by A. W. Wheen in 1934) attempts to evoke the Christian spirit of Vergil's work. In 1937 the anecdotal tale of Vergil's instructions to burn the unfinished *Aeneid* inspired Hermann Broch's fictional, psychological account of the poet's dying thoughts, *Der Tod des Vergil* (translated into English in the 1940s by J. S. Untermeyer). At the center of this work lie modern concerns about the function of prophecy, the loss of creative control, and the nature of art and its ability to convey the human experience. Highly germane to modern literary theoretical issues ranging from stream of consciousness to the death of the author (Barthes), Broch's novel is also integral to Gabriel Josipovici's play *Vergil Dying*, first performed on radio in 1979, which revolves around the ideas of exile, the continual movement involved in the human condition, and the necessary acceptance of that movement.

Such far-reaching influence shows how easy and interesting it would be to incorporate a reading of the *Aeneid* into a wide array of humanities, literature, comparative literature, history, and modern language courses. It also further supports the maintaining (or reestablishing) of the *Aeneid* as a standard fixture in the liberal arts institution's core curriculum, since a reading of the poem will familiarize students with one of the most widely influential works of the Western canon.

Before we can engage students in intertextual readings of the *Aeneid* and later works, however, we must help them understand the text itself. The road to that understanding is long, and students require guidance and encouragement to help them traverse it. For a cultivated appreciation, they need to be exposed to a substantial array of earlier Greek and Latin literature, and certainly the *Iliad* and the *Odyssey* are the places to begin. They must also become familiar with Greek and Roman history, mythology, and philosophy. Since a significant factor in determining students' success with and enjoyment of the poem is their finding it pertinent and meaningful, the instructor must adopt approaches to the text that make it accessible and relevant. Even though the practice of reading the text in selections is perhaps the single greatest hindrance to developing student appreciation for the poem, many instructors opt for an abridged reading, sometimes as a result of time constraints. Below, we discuss, using information obtained from our survey, ways of making such selections in Latin and translation courses.

While reading only portions of the poem is unavoidable in lower- and even upper-division Latin courses, many instructors begin their course with a reading of the entire poem in English, a practice we highly recommend. Lower-division Latin courses most frequently require portions of books 1, 2, 4, and 6 and at times supplement this with brief portions from books 7, 8, 10, and 12, but the focus seems to remain on Dido, Aeneas, and the fall of Troy. Some professors, even at this level, assign a single book in its entirety, most frequently book 1, 2, or 4, with the rationale that students must learn to work with the consecutive narrative and not be coddled by having to read only the more exciting episodes. In upper-division Latin courses, this single-book assignment sometimes expands into two books, but the purple-passage method of selection tends to prevail. A fair number of upper-division courses focus on the second half of the epic so as not to repeat predictable lower-division readings; they concentrate most often on selections from books 7 and 8. On making the transition from high school to college-level Latin easier for students, see *Articulating the Curriculum from School to College*.

In translation courses where the entire poem is not assigned, there are clear patterns of making selections. Almost uniformly omitted are books 3 and 5, and in the second half most often 9 and 11, with 8 and 10 following closely. For some, the guiding principle is a thematic pursuit, such as the character of Aeneas or the presentation of Roman history; others choose the more dramatic segments. Many try to provide some semblance of the whole by including episodes that appear to maintain a consecutive narrative. While it may be possible to construct a fairly complete condensation (e.g., a focus on Aeneas and his exploits would include books 1, 2, 4, 6, 7, possibly 10, then 12), this manner of presentation encourages students to view certain portions of the text as dismissible or unimportant. The primary disadvantage of such condensation is that students lose the sense of Vergil's sympathy for certain characters (such as Pallas, Evander, Nisus, Euryalus, Lausus, Mezentius, and Camilla). They also miss some of the more interesting episodes (the false starts and "little Troy," the Iliadic funeral games for Anchises, the meeting with Evander, the shield, Hercules and Cacus, the phantom Aeneas). Most professors in our survey do not recommend abridgement of the text, feeling that it does not allow students to savor the complexities of the work. While we are aware that time constraints often dictate such matters, we believe that the responsibility of teaching the text should entail a dedication to teaching the whole text. The survey responses overwhelmingly agree with us.

Instructors generally concur that this exciting and challenging poem presents difficulties that are peculiar to it. The *Aeneid* is a work that combines tradition and innovation; history, legend, and contemporary politics; apparent contradictions or ambivalence; and a hero who is complex and himself a composite of tensions. An overwhelming majority of instructors report that books 2 and 4 are by far the most exciting and engaging to teach. Students respond positively to these riveting narratives, which are not as dependent on a knowledge of background as other segments of the poem. The breach between Aeneas and Dido is a particular favorite, but there must be some effort not to allow the discussion in class to become too pat. Students might be given two opposing clichéd interpretations to help them flesh out complexities and see the absurdity of simplistic conclusions. Two such interpretations of book 4 might be "Dido is a modern, independent woman who expects equal commitment from her mate—and doesn't get it" and "Dido is a collection of misogynist clichés about women and their supposed susceptibility to passion." Focusing on the conflict in Aeneas between his love for Dido and his devotion to destiny may elicit a discussion of such primary thematic concerns as the role of destiny, the cost of empire, the meaning of *pietas*, and the nature and character of the hero.

Many instructors find a direct comparison with the Homeric poems the single most fruitful exercise, whether considering specific episodes or the character of Aeneas. (For assistance with such comparisons, Lorina Quartarone has compiled a chart of Homeric parallels in appendix A.) This exercise is an expedient way of discussing the text at large, since most instructors agree that analyzing certain key scenes is crucial because there is usually not time to read and discuss the entire work. The focus on Aeneas, particularly for first-time readers, is of central importance, since the character of Aeneas qua hero is difficult for students to comprehend; they seldom find him sympathetic. It is thus helpful to examine those passages in which Aeneas clearly recalls Achilles and Odysseus, then explore how he differs from them and how he evolves into a hero of another sort. A discussion of Augustan politics and culture may emerge from this consideration of Aeneas, helping students forge connections between literary and historical contexts. A useful exercise on the poem's conclusion is to have students briefly record their initial response to the scene, then ask them to rewrite the scene. While they rewrite, the initial responses are collected, then presented to the group and discussed. Finally they are returned with the questions "Do you still want to revise the ending? If so, why?" The trick is not to give in to the notion that the *Aeneid* is culturally remote. If, for example, students respond to emotion rather than to responsibility or duty, our task is to help them view duty as something both positive and central to Roman culture. To address such challenges, instructors must limit themselves to the elements they feel are most important. A common lament among survey respondents is that there simply isn't time to discuss the poem fully.

In this volume's essays we present an assortment of approaches to the text that we hope will enable instructors to make the most of their time as they explore the *Aeneid*. The essays are arranged in seven sections, but the alert reader will find that essays from each section cross the boundaries of others.

In the first section, "Preliminary Considerations," two essays, each in a different way, introduce the *Aeneid*. Sarah Spence shows how the relation of the poem's opening words, "I sing of arms and the man," to *furor* and *pietas* provides a meaningful discussion for those interested in rhetoric. She argues that Vergil's work, unlike Homer's, displays the presence of an active poet rather than one who subordinates the poetic process to the poem. William S. Anderson develops a thought-provoking analysis of the various epithets for the Trojans, carefully studying the meanings behind names that one could dismiss as variants used for the sake of polyphony or even metrical convenience. His examination involves both historical legend and mythological background to the epic.

In the second section, "Aeneas and Heroism," three essays consider the character of Aeneas and his status as a hero. Shirley Werner concentrates on character portrayal, bringing to light the differences between ancient and modern methods of characterization. She discusses Vergil's narrative technique, how Vergil establishes point of view, and how he employs patterns of conversation and speech. She presents an interesting assessment of the exchanges between Dido and Aeneas and finds that through the complexity of character portrayal Vergil forces us to be active readers and to make interpretive decisions. John Breuker, Jr., combines a number of traditional approaches to understanding the heroism of Aeneas by looking at his actions and the careful wording with which Vergil describes them. He gives a condensed account of traditional scholarly concerns that include *pietas* and heroic behavior, public and private voices and responsibilities, and optimist and pessimist readings of the poem. Barbara Weiden Boyd addresses the challenges of teaching the final scene of the poem, approaching the text from issues of point of view or focalization in character development to Vergil's narrative technique. Comparing the *Aeneid* with the *Iliad*, she moves from the duality of polar opposites to a triangular, less simplified reading that encourages an appreciation for the complexities of the text.

The two essays in "Homeric Intertextuality" ably demonstrate how Vergil's text engages with the poems of Homer. James J. Clauss assesses Aeneas's heroism through the models of Achilles, Odysseus, and Jason (Jason in Apollonius's

Argonautica). He traces the evolution of the hero through the workings of *pietas* and argues that Aeneas's subjugation of personal desires to public responsibility leads to his depersonalization. Randall Colaizzi concentrates on the second half of the epic, offering much-needed assistance to those who find it more difficult to teach than the first half. He elucidates the text through both a discussion of Iliadic parallels and an analysis of Vergil's convolutions of *pietas* and studies how Vergil sets up unequally matched battles among the principal warriors.

Under "History and Material Culture," three essays link the *Aeneid* with either Vergil's contemporary cultural climate or the material remains of his culture. Michael C. J. Putnam, providing important historical background to the epic, deals with the Italian civil war that pervades the century before the poem's composition and traces how Vergil re-creates the aura of that war in the second half of the poem. He also brings to light Vergil's allusions to the questionability of some of Augustus's actions. Patricia A. Johnston seeks to provide a correspondence between the anger of Juno in the poem and historical legend on the foundation of Rome. She analyzes material remains of the cult of Juno in Sicily and Italy and compares them with the information gleaned from the poem as well as supplied by Livy's *History*. Mary Jaeger discusses memory and landscape. Concentrating primarily on book 8, she unravels the multiple layers of historical underpinnings in the Roman locales mentioned in the text and suggests that we read places and landscapes as historically layered entities.

In the first of the three essays in "Gender Issues," Sharon L. James presents an overview of women in the poem. She demonstrates, by comparing them with the women of the *Iliad*, their diminishing social roles, specifically their loss of activity and individuality, during the course of the founding of Rome. Lorina N. Quartarone marries a modern theoretical approach, ecofeminism, to the traditionally examined themes of *pietas* and *furor*. She argues that in the poem's first half, Vergil presents women and nature as similarly oppressed by patriarchal society; but in the second, his development of *pietas* and the ramifications of *furor* cross gender boundaries and suggest society's oppression of both sexes. Judith P. Hallett theorizes that Vergil employed the letter of a famous Roman matron, Cornelia, as a template for the speeches of several of his noble women. Hallett suggests that in this way, instead of modeling their speeches on conventional literary predecessors, Vergil sought to portray real character.

In "Classroom Techniques and Strategies," two essays offer specific avenues of approach to the poem to utilize in the classroom. Scott Ward and Gary S. Meltzer lead us through selected passages, illustrating how to inspire in students an appreciation of Vergil's poetry. They examine his simile, personification, and imagery, presenting a how-to model for teaching them. Nancy Ciccone addresses the practical difficulties many professors face when they try to coax active participation out of a modern, diverse, and often overworked group of students. She provides an illustration of a carefully constructed in-class writing assignment and follow-up discussion. Using book 7 as a starting point, she guides the students as they examine issues of plot, narrative, and focalization.

Our final section, "Integrating the *Aeneid* into Larger Academic Contexts," links the *Aeneid* with other texts in the Western canon. Ann Engar describes her experience teaching the poem in a Western literature survey course and speaks of understanding the text as a piece of tragic literature. She uses both ancient and modern definitions of tragedy as templates in examining the text. Rachel Jacoff's essay takes up key issues in reading the *Aeneid* and *The Divine Comedy* in tandem. Patrick J. Cook's appraisal of the interplay between Vergil and Milton concentrates on the interpretation of allusions in a reciprocal fashion and serves as a guide to teaching the *Aeneid* as a pre-text to *Paradise Lost*.

Although this volume presents a wide variety of approaches, we recognize that no collection can be exhaustive; witness the several collections of essays on the *Aeneid* currently in print. Our essays, informed as they are by our experiences in teaching Vergil, should nevertheless provide some inspiration and guidance to other teachers of the poem. This volume's contributors and we have benefited not only from teachers who inspired us, who gave us guidance, and who unselfishly offered us their example but also from scholars whose works have assisted us in understanding the poem and in developing our own interpretations. To these many influential people we extend our gratitude and an acknowledgment that this volume is but a small part of a long and valuable tradition.

> [. . .] omnemque suorum
> forte recensebat numerum, carosque nepotes
> fataque fortunasque virum moresque manusque.   (*Aen*. 6.681–83)

> [. . .] as it happened, he was retelling the whole account
> of his people, and his beloved descendants, and their
> fates and fortunes and characters and deeds.   (our trans.)

Pietas and *Furor*:
Motivational Forces in the *Aeneid*

Sarah Spence

Everybody has memorized the opening words *arma virumque cano* ("I sing of arms and the man"). Second only perhaps to *amo, amas, amat* as Latin everyone knows, these words are learned now as they have been since ancient times. Every visitor to Pompeii is shown the graffito: "fullones ululamque cano, non arma virumque" ("I sing of fullers [cleaners of wool] and an owl, not arms and the man") (*Carmina latina epigraphica* 1936), and Propertius (*Elegiae* 2.34.63–64), Ovid (*Tristia* 2.533–34 and *Metamorphoses* 14.476–79), and Seneca (*Epistulae* 113.25 [*Select Letters*]) among others make reference to Vergil through these precise words (Austin, *Primus* 25–26). Yet it is surprising how little attention is really paid to this phrase in the classroom and how much will be yielded if more attention is paid. This essay shows how the opening half line can serve as an introduction to the main themes of the poem.

There is no question that these words point first and foremost to Vergil's primary influence: Homer. Many, from Servius on, have argued that the arms and struggle of the Trojans inform the second six books of the *Aeneid*, which recount the struggle of the Trojans against the Italians after Aeneas has landed on the Italian peninsula, while the "man" or hero that is the focus of the odyssey of Ulysses offers inspiration for the first half, the wanderings of Aeneas from Troy to Sicily and Carthage and finally to Italy and Rome (Anderson, *Art* 5-9; Knauer, "Vergil's *Aeneid*"). As clear as the debt is, Vergil's swerve from his predecessor is equally evident (see Heinze, *Technique* 201–05; Hardie, *Virgil's Aeneid* 302–03). I note two significant differences: first, Vergil inserts his authorial presence through the first-person, lyric verb *cano* (a verb he also uses in the *Eclogues* [esp. 4.1, 3 and 6.3] to emphasize the singer and his task). This act is important as it distinguishes him precisely from the position taken in the opening lines of the *Iliad* and the *Odyssey*, where the Muse is invoked and the poet presents himself as merely a conduit: here the poet is clearly the active shaper of words and events in the poem (Anderson, *Art* 9–10). Second, while *arma virumque* does in fact follow the order of Homer's epics, with the war preceding the journey, it does not describe the plot of the *Aeneid*, where the journey precedes the war. One result of this difference in order is to increase the reader's awareness of the poet's control. "I sing of arms and the man," the poem starts, "and"—it suggests—"I do it differently from the way it was done in Homer." The bibliography on Vergil's adaptation of Homer is immense (the locus classicus is Knauer, *Die* Aeneis; for more recent commentary, see Conte; Barchiesi, *Traccia*, ch. 4; Hinds).

Yet of these four words, the most important for unlocking the poem for students is, I would argue, the enclitic *-que* ("and"). It is the *and* in "arms and the man" I wish to focus on. The opening half line makes it clear that, unlike Homer, Vergil will craft a poem about not one but two things and that these two things are of equal importance. The dual focus is key to understanding the structure of the poem, precisely because the poem is about creating or establishing a tension. What the poet announces in these first few words can and should be taken literally. This single poem is about the interaction of two subjects; it is about both arms and the man. The wording does not suggest that it is about one then the other, or one or the other, or one over the other.

Gesturing toward the Homeric past, toward the *Iliad* and the *Odyssey*, the opening words at the same time set up the problem of the present work: the creation of a poem (emphasized by *cano*) that is about the interaction or tension between arms and the man. What Homer dealt with sequentially this poet will deal with simultaneously; what Homer channeled from the Muse this poet will construct in poetic, often ironic, fictions. The simultaneity of *arma* and *virum* works together with *cano* to suggest that the tension that will be created is a poetic tension, the essence of metaphor, of poetry. The poem will always be considering more than one thing; moreover, the poet will be deliberately casting two things in relation to each other, the arms to the man, the man to the arms. The first line states that the poem serves a historic and a poetic purpose.

To what do *arma* and *virum* refer? We have mentioned the preexisting Homeric context, which suggests one interpretation: they are the battles from books 7–12 and the wandering hero Aeneas. Vergil encourages this reading in lines 1–10 as he first identifies the man as Aeneas and then, repeating *virum*, marks him in the second line as the object of the goddess Juno's wrath, despite the fact that he is *insignem pietate virum* ("a man marked by piety"). This phrase establishes an identification between man and *pietas* that continues throughout the book, particularly but not exclusively in relation to Aeneas. Aeneas is the hero of the book not only because he is the man mentioned at the start but also because he is marked, at least at the start, by *pietas*. As a result, any act or indication of *pietas* falls into the category of heroism (see Putnam,

Vergil's Aeneid, esp. 201–15). Again I point to the opening line: the man and his *pietas* are only part of the story. There is in fact no story without the *arma*, the struggle, labeled first as the wanderings of Aeneas (*fato profugus* ["exiled by fate"]) and then identified more closely with the goddess Juno ("saevae memorem Iunonis ob iram" ["on account of the mindful wrath of harsh Juno"]). *Arma*, perhaps first echoed in the superlative *asperrima*, reappears in line 16 in relation to Juno's weapons, which she keeps stored in her beloved Carthage. The word thus becomes affiliated with war, love, and memory, all presided over by Juno.

Arma and *virum* appear together twice more in the opening 156 lines of book 1. The first occurrence is in line 119 ("apparent rari nantes in gurgite vasto, / arma virum tabulaeque et Troia gaza per undas") ("A few men swimming surfaced in the welter. / So did shields, planks, precious things of Troy" [Fitzgerald 164–65]), the second in lines 150–51 as part of the first simile of the poem:

> ac veluti magno in populo cum saepe coorta est
> seditio saevitque animis ignobile vulgus;
> iamque faces et saxa volant, furor *arma* ministrat;
> tum pietate gravem ac meritis si forte *virum* quem
> conspexere, silent arrectisque auribus astant;
> ille regit dictis animos et pectora mulcet;
> sic cunctus pelagi cecidit fragor [. . .].   (148–54; emphasis mine)

> When rioting breaks out in a great city,
> And the rampaging rabble goes so far
> That stones fly, and incendiary brands—
> For anger can supply that kind of weapon—
> If it so happens they look round and see
> Some dedicated public man, a veteran
> Whose record gives him weight, they quiet down,
> Willing to stop and listen.
> Then he prevails in speech over their fury
> By his authority, and placates them.   (Fitzgerald 201–10)

These two appearances of *arma* with *virum* work together. While the first is clearly less developed than the second (and is not a true echo, as *virum* is in this case a syncopal version of *virorum* [of men]), they both speak to a necessary interdependence between the two forces: in the first, it is the arms of the men that are tossed about in the storm Juno causes, neither more powerful than the other; in the second, an ordering hierarchy is established, yet that hierarchy alludes to a necessary interdependence between the two forces.

The pairing of the terms that occurs in the first simile of the poem fully glosses the poem's first half line. We find *virum* once again associated with *pietas* ("tum pietate gravem ac meritis si forte virum quem / conspexere"), but now, in a balancing move, *arma* is linked with *furor* ("furor arma ministrat"). That these terms are linked in a simile, the first grand poetic gesture of the poem, calls up an echo of *cano* even as it establishes a significant connection for the rest of the poem between arms and the man.

The simile must be read against two backdrops: the immediate context of the opening scene of the poem, in which Juno convinces Aeolus to create a storm off Sicily, and the historic context of the Augustan world of the poem and, in particular, the poem's image of and attitude toward orators. I touch on each briefly.

The simile alludes to a vast network of associations. The image of a riot takes the reader back not only to the *pietas* of Aeneas and the weapons of Juno but also, and perhaps more strongly, to the storm winds that in lines 50–63 are likened to horses kept in check only because the king of winds, Aeolus, who is put in charge by Jupiter, knows how and when to rein them in ("et premere et laxas sciret dare iussus habenas"). So, too, *arrectis auribus* ("pricked-up ears") likens the raging crowd to horses. Through this connection between the winds and the crowd Vergil suggests a connection among those controlling the *igno-bile vulgus* ("undistinguished crowd") in each case—Aeolus, Jupiter, Neptune, the orator. The text establishes a clear dichotomy between the raging forces of the winds, the storm, and the mob of the simile and the ordering powers of the authority figures who control the rage. Strikingly, the winds in the earlier passage are linked with the feminine through the suggestion that their residence is actually a womb ("loca feta furentibus Austris" [51; "place pregnant with the raging south wind"]), while the figure of order in each instance is referred to as being explicitly male (*pater omnipotens* ["almighty father"], *regem* ["king"], *virum* ["man"]).

Through the allusions present in the first simile the opening words of the poem are contrasted (even opposed) on many levels: Juno and Aeneas, *furor* and *pietas*, beast and man, female and male. The question then becomes, How are these terms defined in relation to each other? Is *pietas* necessarily superior to *furor*; does *pietas* exist or thrive in the absence of *furor*? When I am teaching this section, I find it useful to bring in a brief discussion of certain tenets of feminist theory, in particular the notion that difference need not constitute opposition (Mulvey). In its efforts to uncover binary oppositions and disassociate them from hierarchical ordering, a feminist reading of this passage would query whether *pietas* is a utopian state that would thrive best if *furor* were completely exiled or whether the terms are not related in a more complex and intertwined fashion. For example: if *pietas* is a quality that is best defined in the absence of *furor*, then why introduce both *arma* and *virum* as topics of the poem? Why have the voice of *furor*, Juno, speak first and with such passion and sympathy? Why even suggest that King Aeolus's livelihood is dependent on the raging winds imprisoned in his mountain, a mountain described as *feta* ("preg-nant") and thus, at least on some level, associated with the feminine? Perhaps the most striking question is, Why echo the opening lines of the poem first in the chaos of the storm, the disorder of Juno's wrath? *Furor* and *pietas* are on the same level there as *arma* float next to *virum*.

To turn to the political register, the first simile certainly points to Augustus's efforts to establish political order out of the chaos of the civil wars (Anderson, *Art* 25). Moreover, it harks back to the power attributed to the orator in republican culture. In the *De inventione* Cicero describes the origins of oratory:

> For there was a time when men wandered at large in the fields like animals and lived on wild fare; they did nothing by the guidance of reason, but relied chiefly on physical strength; there was as yet no ordered system of religious worship nor of social duties; no one had seen legitimate marriage nor had anyone looked upon children whom he knew to be his own; nor had they learned the advantages of an equitable code of law. And so through their ignorance and error blind and unreasoning passion satisfied itself by misuse of bodily strength, which is a very dangerous servant. [. . .] At this juncture a man—great and wise I am sure—became aware of the power latent in man and the wide field offered by his mind for great achievements if one could develop this power and improve it by instruction. Men were scattered in the fields and hidden in sylvan retreats when he assembled and gathered them in accordance with a plan [. . .]. When through reason and eloquence they had listened with greater attention, he transformed them from wild savages into a kind and gentle folk. [. . .] Certainly only a speech at the same time powerful and entrancing could have induced one who had great physical strength to submit to justice without violence [. . .].   (4–7)

Cicero asserts that rhetoric is a civilizing force. In particular, oratory is shown to be the tool used by a "great and wise" man to control and even silence desires by transforming the "wild savages" into a "kind and gentle" people (Spence, *Rhetorics* ch. 1; see also Cicero 166–69).

Read in isolation, the first simile of the *Aeneid* would appear to articulate similar values, values Augustus might wish to espouse and restore. Yet the *Aeneid* is not a rhetorical tract, it is a work of literature. In particular, Vergil's similes often juxtapose, undermine, or ironize the surrounding text. For example, when the Trojans are likened to ants in 4.401–07, the simile works not only through the strict comparison of men to small trudging insects but also through opposition to the comparison made earlier in the epic in which the Carthaginians are likened to productive bees (1.430–36; the comparison is in turn rooted in the long and largely positive discussion of bees in the fourth *Georgic*). The storm-as-mob simile is arguably also ironic. For one thing the power of rhetoric *per se* rarely, if ever, wields the civilizing powers Cicero ascribes to it. For another, as the text progresses, the struggle between the forces symbolized by the orator and the crowd takes center stage; the relation between Juno and

Jupiter, between Dido and Aeneas, between Aeneas's private will and his public duty are each versions of this conflict. In each case, the scenario proposed
by the simile—that *furor* and its representatives should be silenced, quieted,
exiled—is undermined by the sympathetic context granted *furor*. When the
raging Dido is abandoned by *pius Aeneas* ("dutiful Aeneas") (so described at 5.
26) at the end of book 4, she is described as *accensa furore* ("burning with
rage") (4.697); while Aeneas himself is described as *furiis accensus* ("burning
with avenging rage") as he contemplates killing Turnus at the close of the epic
(12. 946). In each instance the text problematizes a simple reading that would
label *pietas* as all good and *furor* as all bad and that would insist on the necessary separation of the two. I often discuss the fact that after Juno and Jupiter
reach a compromise at the end of book 12, Jupiter reaches down beneath his
throne and draws out one of the two Dirae or Furies who live there. That he
has used the powers of *furor* to attain his goal remains hidden until this point;
that Vergil reveals the interdependence of chaos and order at the end is significant (Feeney, "Reconciliations"; Johnson, *Darkness*). At this point it is useful,
if possible, to bring in discussion of Hesiod and Aeschylus: even as chaos pre-
dates order in the cosmogonies of the *Theogony* and is incorporated into the
city structure of Athens in the *Oresteia*, so in the *Aeneid* Vergil suggests that
pietas is perhaps rooted in or dependent on *furor*.

   In short, the epic is about the interaction and necessary interdependence of
pietas and *furor*, of arms and the man. The opening line suggests a connection
between the forces; the ultimate scene confirms that they are often insepa-
rable. What Aeneas does in killing Turnus is arguably both an act of *pietas* and
an act of *furor* at the same time. While the epic's first simile would seem to
suggest that *pietas*, and the man marked by *pietas*, is a desirable force of order
and antithetical to chaotic *furor*, the sympathy the author establishes for Juno,
Dido, even Turnus, to name just a few, undermines a simple reading of the
pair. The forces of *furor*, after all, are not usually animals but rather other
beings, mortal or divine, of the same order as those of *pietas*. The calming of
chaos by reason and order can also be seen as its silencing, precisely the impo-
tence that Juno rails against in her opening monologue (1.37–49).

   It is useful, finally, to compare the first simile of the epic with the last, in
which Turnus tries futilely to escape from Aeneas.

> ac velut in somnis, oculos ubi languida pressit
> nocte quies, nequiquam avidos extendere cursus
> velle videmur et in mediis conatibus aegri
> succidimus—non lingua valet, non corpore notae
> sufficiunt vires nec vox aut verba sequuntur:
> sic Turno [. . .].   (12.908–13)

> Just as in dreams when the night-swoon of sleep
> Weighs on our eyes, it seems we try in vain

> To keep on running, try with all our might,
> But in the midst of effort faint and fail;
> Our tongue is powerless, familiar strength
> Will not hold up our body, not a sound
> Or word will come; just so with Turnus now.
> (Fitzgerald 12.1232–38)

We are explicitly drawn in (*videmur* ["we seem"], *succidimus* ["we give way"]) and made to identify with the wordless, powerless Turnus. Not only is our sympathy with *furor* encouraged but also our role in the text is made more complicated as we literally enter into the work on the side of the victim and against the dutiful hero. If we stood with Neptune (and, implicitly, with Aeneas) during the opening simile, we stand with Turnus (and, this time explicitly, against Aeneas) at the end. The braiding of the two forces of *pietas* and *furor*, the insistence on their interdependence, is made not only thematically in the text but also experientially in its reading. We become increasingly involved as active players in the work, until, finally, we identify with the character of Turnus, the speechless character so similar in many ways to the unruly mob of the first simile.

The *Aeneid* is a poem about many forces but most notably those of *pietas* and *furor*. The opening line, together with the poem's first simile, especially if set against the action of the entire text, suggests how the interaction of these two forces comes to be explored and refined through the course of the work, until, by the end, the compromise between Juno and Jupiter acknowledges the necessary interdependence of arms and the man.

Trojan, Dardanian, Roman:
The Power of Epithets in the *Aeneid*

William S. Anderson

In these days of nationalistic hostilities and of fierce American politics, we are all familiar with the power of epithets and their varying connotations in the mouths and writings of people. Vergil's world knew similar use and abuse of epithets, and Vergil thematized that phenomenon in his epic poem. From the perspective of the poet and his Roman audience, as the opening indicates, the poem narrates the arduous journey of the defeated Trojans under Aeneas to their promised land and a future as Romans. But this anachronistic perspective is not shared by the Trojans, who cannot imagine being anything but Trojans, or by their various enemies, who use *Trojan* and its various synonyms as opprobrious epithets. It takes half the poem for Aeneas to stop thinking and feeling as a Trojan half-heartedly seeking a new home; it takes the entire poem for him to earn the right and gain the power to be an Italian and proto-Roman. This essay follows, in the epithets, that trajectory, both geographic and moral, which links Troy and Italy, Trojans and future Romans, Aeneas and Augustus.

Vergil uses a series of nouns and adjectives for *Trojan*. In part, of course, he is consulting his own and our desire for variety; in part, he is yielding to the demands of the hexameter. For instance, some words for *Trojan* provide him two initial long syllables, some a complete dactyl, one a single long syllable (*Tros*), and one two short syllables (to fill out a dactyl: the noun *Phryges*, the adjective *Phrygius*). Statistically, far the most common word used by Vergil to refer to the Trojans is *Teucrians* (*Teucri*). It occurs in 130 instances, almost three times as many as the next most common word, *Troianus*. Although *Teucri* is immensely useful in the meter because of its two long syllables, I believe that the poet made a distinct virtue of metrical necessity in order to explore, with Aeneas and us, the meaning of being a Trojan and the value in leaving behind the various negative aspects of the Trojan past. He looks to a Trojan future that will slowly work itself out in one particular variant for *Trojan*.

The poetic narrator chooses as his first word for *Trojan* an easy noun, *Troas* (1.30; Mandelbaum 46).[1] But when he gives Juno an angry speech against the sailors happily heading for Italy, he lets her call them "Teucrians" (1.38; Mandelbaum [57] makes it easy for the modern reader with "Trojan"). Although we know that Latin audiences had heard this word before, at least once in the learned poetry of Catullus (64.345), though not in Homer, it is not clear how familiar the full Teucrian myth used by Vergil was to his contemporaries. For the modern reader, some commentary is necessary. Vergil offers us two later notes that are of some help; first, at 1.619–26 (in English 868–77), Dido reports that a Greek named Teucer visited her city, praised the Teucrians, though enemies of the Greeks, and proudly declared himself related by birth to them. The Greek's praise obviously is a way to get special testimony for the noble qualities of the Trojans. Second, at 3.104 (136–53) Aeneas's father, Anchises, attempts to interpret an oracle from Apollo directing them to seek out their "ancient mother." He thinks of Crete as their mother because of Teucer (3.108–09; 142–44), who long ago left Crete and sailed to the shores where later Troy would be founded through his descendants. Following Anchises's interpretation, which proves erroneous, the Trojans sail to Crete and try to create a settlement where they may go on with their lives. They call it after Troy's alternate name of Pergamum, but a disastrous plague and blight on their crops force these survivors to head to sea again. The word *Teucrian* is a false link to their future, though an important connection to their past (still known at least to the older generation of Trojans). Troy does not simply signify a place on the coast of Asia Minor that was demolished by the victorious Greeks; it has prehistoric links with parts of the western Mediterranean.

Later in book 1, Vergil starts using another word for *Trojan*, which seems unappreciated by the characters at the time and might baffle modern audiences. In Carthage, as he studies from concealment the paintings on the Temple of Juno, then sees Dido approaching, Aeneas is suddenly called "Dardanian" (494; "Dardan," more conveniently for Mandelbaum at 698). Still unseen, he watches his Trojan friends appeal to Dido for help, at the end of which they are "sons of Dardanus" (*Dardanidae* [560]) in both Mandelbaum (789) and Fitzgerald (759), in an unfinished Latin line that consists of that single word. Finally, Aeneas uses the adjective in 602 (846) when he emerges from his protecting cloud and identifies himself to Dido, who then uses it herself at 617 (865). (Vergil's Romans had met the word frequently in Homer and in a few earlier Latin poets, such as Catullus [34.367], Propertius [1.19.14], and Horace [ode 1.15.10].) Who is Dardanus, we may well ask, and why does Vergil at this stage make a point of the Dardanian aspect of his Trojans?

The ancient commentator Servius briefly explained the connections between Teucer and Dardanus at the first appearance of "Teucrian" at 1.38. Dardanus was already on the future site of Troy when Teucer and his people arrived from Crete. He welcomed Teucer, in due course married Teucer's daughter, and honored his father-in-law by calling the united races Teucrians. (Alternatively, in his note on Teucer in *Aeneid* 3.108, Servius says that some sources claim Teucer married Dardanus's daughter.) However, the important point is that Dardanus lived on the site of Troy (in Dardania) before the arrival of Teucer, and his eponymous influence takes priority over that of his Cretan relative. The matter is settled, until we learn more in book 3, where Anchises's error about returning to Teucer's Crete is corrected.

Aeneas is recounting to Dido at this point his painful experiences and failed settlements en route from fallen Troy to Carthage, so this correction, that Teucer is less important to the Trojans than Dardanus, while new to us, has already been absorbed by the leader and his men, at least to some extent. When they first consulted Apollo on the island of Delos, the oracle addressed them alliteratively as "durable Dardanians" (*Dardanidae durae* [3.94; trans.

mine]), the significance of which totally escaped every one of them. But those words were in fact a clue, if they had only realized it, to the identity of the "ancient mother" whom they should seek out. Later, the night before sailing away from their accursed settlement in Crete, a dream to Aeneas himself established what Anchises had missed: that their Dardanian heritage was their key to the future (154–71; 197–227).

This time the Penates, the gods of Troy whom Aeneas is taking to their eventual home, direct him. They say they have been sent by Apollo. They have attended Aeneas since Dardania burned and will continue with him across the sea and ultimately exalt his descendants (obviously the Romans) to world empire and glory. Crete was the wrong destination (161–62; 215); the correct goal is a place farther west (the meaning of *Hesperia* [163]), which can be called a settlement that belongs to them (167; 222). How is that possible? Because in Italy, in the town of Corythus (later Cortona), Dardanus was born, and from there he made his way eastward eventually to Asia Minor and the site of Troy. In fact, Aeneas obscurely refers to this origin when he meets his mother, Venus, in 1.380: "I seek out Italy, / my country, my ancestors born of Jove" (1.538–39). To steer for Italy, then, and settle there would indeed be to seek and find the original mother of the Trojans. Our handbooks spell out this complicated genealogy of Troy and the Trojans as follows. Dardanus was the son of Jupiter and the nymph Electra. He moved from Italy to the Hellespont and settled, where, as we have heard, he was joined by the Cretan Teucer, whose daughter he married. They had a son Erichthonius, whose son Tros in turn was the founder and namer of Troy (see chart and *Iliad* 20.215–40).

For Aeneas and Vergil, however, the descendants of Dardanus are less important, now that Troy has fallen, than his links back to Italy. The homeless Trojans, defeated and harshly punished by the Greeks, need to find a new home that is free of their tainted past and acceptable to the gods above and to the household gods, the Penates, which they are carrying with them. After talking over his dream with his father, who vaguely recalls that mad, hence unreliable, Cassandra had prophesied a future home in the west, in Italy (3.185; 243–44)—but said nothing about Dardanus—Aeneas does sail westward, to the foot of Italy and then, to avoid the dangers of the straits of Rhegium, around Sicily, from which his men are hopefully and happily sailing for their Italian home at 1.34. Vergil's audience should be able to infer from this Dardanian connection his theme that the Trojans are, as proto-Italians, destined to resume their Italian identity and nationality, to leave behind their connection with a badly flawed Troy, and symbolically to cease being Trojans. It is not so easy for Aeneas and his men to accept that change, since their entire existence has been bound up with the Troy they sadly left behind; and it is not easy, indeed almost impossible, for most Italians to accept these newcomers, who seem Trojan invaders, as returning Dardan sons of their native Italy.

Aeneas looks back longingly to Troy for most of the first six books of the poem. In the storm of Aeolus, he famously wishes he had died at Troy rather

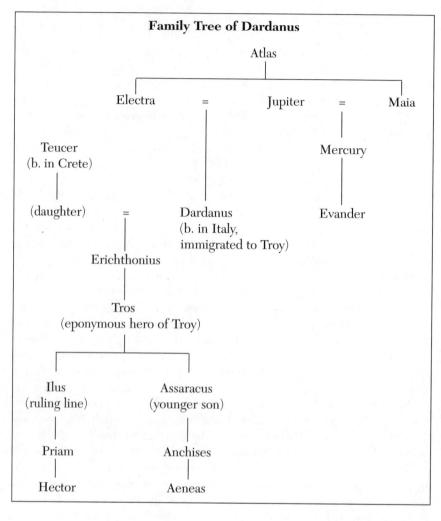

Family Tree of Dardanus

Atlas

Electra   =   Jupiter   =   Maia

Teucer
(b. in Crete)

Mercury

(daughter)   =   Dardanus
              (b. in Italy,
              immigrated to Troy)

Evander

Erichthonius

Tros
(eponymous hero of Troy)

Ilus   Assaracus
(ruling line)   (younger son)

Priam   Anchises

Hector   Aeneas

than risk being drowned off Africa (1.94–101; 133–43): those are the first words we hear from him. When he defends himself from Dido's accusations of perfidy (4.340–44; 460–67), he asserts that he would prefer above all to go back to Troy, that he heads for Italy much against his will (4.361; 491–92). He wastes more time in Sicily in book 5, commemorating his dead father rather than pressing on to Italy. (He does, however, address his men as *Dardanidae* as soon as he lands [5.45; 61], and Vergil plants five other references to the Dardanian connection throughout the book.) The descent to the Underworld in book 6 functions in large part to convince Aeneas (and us) that his Trojan past is dead and, to a great extent, damned. In the Fields of the Blessed, however, he glimpses the noblest representatives of Troy, including Dardanus (6.650; 861). Soon, Anchises reveals to him and us the hopeful succession of Dardanian descendants (*Dardaniam prolem* [6.756; 1000]) who mark the future. He links their appearance directly with Rome when pointing out Romulus to Aeneas (777–87; 1026–43), whose people he calls his son's Romans (*Romanos tuos* [789]; 1045). This development climaxes in Anchises's famous apostrophe to Aeneas as "Roman" (*Romane* [851]; 1135), the first and only time he is so addressed in the epic. But that glorious Roman future dims for Aeneas after he leaves by the Ivory Gate. He must start again with Dardanus as his immediate link with the future.

Dardanus forms a major element of Trojan negotiations with King Latinus after the Trojans land near the Tiber River. Aeneas sends Ilioneus as his legate and rich gifts with him. Latinus immediately hails the Trojans as *Dardanidae* (7.195; 257) and links that epithet properly with the Italian origins of Dardanus, of which he has heard long ago from his elders (205–11; 272–79). In response to this welcome, Ilioneus starts and ends with emphatic allusions to Dardanus. He reminds Latinus that Dardanus was Jupiter's son (219–20; 288); later he asserts that, since Dardanus had his origins here in Italy, the Trojans are coming back at the urging of Apollo (240–42; 315–18). Latinus happily accepts this idea and proposes a dynastic marriage between his daughter Lavinia and Aeneas (268–72; 351–57). This arrangement, which will eventually come to pass, angers Juno, who foments a war between the native Italians and the newcomers, to postpone the inevitable.

It is the sight of Aeneas happy again, as at the start of the poem in 1.35, and of his Dardanian fleet (7.288–89; 382–83) that arouses Juno's fury. She exploits the hellish Fury Allecto as her instrument of disturbance, to create hostility in the influential Italians Amata and Turnus and then among the Italians in general. Amata responds to the Fury's poisonous effects by passionately denouncing the Trojans (7.359–72; 474–95), talking of them not as a changed people with Dardanian links to Italy but as the corrupt race of "Teucrian exiles" who sponsored the "Phrygian shepherd" Paris (7.363; 481) on his adulterous liaison with Helen of Sparta. In Amata's rhetoric, Aeneas is another Paris, a "perfidious pirate" (362). Allecto goes on to whet the fury of Turnus, whom she tries to arouse by first asking him indignantly whether he will tamely allow all the power that he won by warlike deeds to be meekly transferred to "Dardanian colonists" (7.422; 562). Her epithet "Dardanian" obviously means "outsider." That ploy does not work on the more controlled Turnus, but the Fury soon has her way: before long, we hear Turnus ranting publicly against the Teucrians and Phrygian race (7.578–79; 760–61) and demanding war. War there is.

Turnus, as commander of the Italians, attempts to gain allies against the intruder Aeneas, whom he now calls the "Dardanian man" (8.13–14; 17); *Dardanian* means Trojan without redeeming Italian aspects. Aeneas also seeks reinforcements for his gravely outnumbered people. In this atmosphere of hatred, focalizing Italian bias, Vergil aptly calls him "Laomedon's heir" (8.18), evoking one of the worst kings of Troy. (Mandelbaum omits all reference to Laomedon here and earlier, at 7.105). Aeneas goes up the Tiber River to the future site of Rome, now called Pallanteum, to talk to King Evander and his son, Pallas. He announces himself and companions as "chosen leaders of Dardania" (8.119–20; 155–56). Then, in a longer speech to Evander, he spells out a useful version of his Italian origins that allows him to link his people with Evander's and thus justify an alliance. Dardanus, "the first father and founder of Troy," was son of Electra, Atlas's daughter (8.134–42; 175–86). We have not heard this before, only that Jupiter was Dardanus's father. Through Electra Aeneas can claim a blood relationship with Evander, for Evander is son of Mercury, who in turn is son of Maia, the sister of Electra (see chart). Therefore, Aeneas concludes, their two families split from a common bloodline (8.142; 186); relying on that connection, he has come to plead for support. Evander is happy to give him the little he has in his tiny kingdom, which principally is Pallas; but he also alerts Aeneas to the opportunity of enlisting major assistance from the Etruscans.

Significantly, this dialogue is the end of references to the Italian-Trojan ancestor Dardanus and to the region of Dardania that he founded in Asia Minor before Troy. But the Dardanian epithets continue to play a part in the definition of the Trojans until the end of the poem. Aeneas is often called "descendant of Dardanus" (*Dardanides*) and his men Dardanidae. The adjective "Dardanian" functions in every book. We can see the clash of associations in books 10 and 12. Juno harangues the gods about Paris, "the Dardanian adulterer" (10.92; 131); but Aeneas, as he rages over the death of his relative and friend Pallas, is Dardanian in the more positive sense (10.546, 603; 752, 828). At the opening of book 12, when he can no longer postpone the duel with Aeneas, Turnus labels his enemy with contemptuous alliteration "the Dardanian deserter of Asia" (12.14–15; trans. mine; cf. Mandelbaum 18). In the late stages of the duel, after each has thrown his spear without success and Turnus's sword has shattered on the armor of Aeneas, Aeneas needs another spear, Turnus a new sword. The last epithet Vergil uses in the epic for his hero, as Aeneas tries to pry loose his spear from a tree, is *Dardanides* (12.775; 1026). Eventually, by divine intervention, each warrior does get his weapon and they stand there, ready to renew the breathless combat (12.789–90; 1045–48).

Choosing to show the easy way in which the gods can settle their frictions while human beings must die to produce even an unsatisfactory close, Vergil stages a reconciliation between Jupiter and Juno over the Trojan-Italian conflict. Jupiter tells Juno that she can go no further in her destructive opposition (12.806; 1066). She puts on a submissive expression but argues that there is leeway in the fatal decrees to permit the survival of the Latins and the disappearance of the name "Trojan" (12.819–28; 1088–100). "Don't," she begs, "force the native Latins to change their ancient name / and become Trojans and be called Teucrians, / to change their language and their dress. / Let Latium exist; [. . .] / let there be a Roman stock powerful in its Italian manhood. / Troy has perished: let it be dead along with its very name." Jupiter assents: "Mixed only in body, / the Teucrians will sink (into oblivion)" (12.835–36; cf. Mandelbaum 1109–10).

Neither mentions the Dardanian connection, because, as we have seen, that is Italian as well as Trojan. But in the future the sense that Aeneas and his descendants are even partially outsiders will vanish as they build a Latin and Roman people that effaces the powers of Greece and Asia alike.

The major theme of finding a new national greatness in Italy thus gains acceptance among the gods, and Juno retires happy at last (12.841–42; 1118–19), having won what she considers a victory in this compromise with Jupiter. Back on Italian soil, human reality does not permit such easy solutions. The duel between Aeneas and Turnus must somehow be settled. Jupiter intervenes against Turnus, weakens him, and robs him of the assistance of his sister Juturna. Alone, face to face, unequally armed—Aeneas has the advantage with both spear and sword—the two men face each other, unable to stop without bloodshed. When Turnus tries to use a huge stone in place of a spear (12.896–927; 1192–236) and lacks the strength, in this nightmarish moment, to launch it effectively, he is vulnerable to Aeneas's spear, which strikes his leg and puts him on the ground helpless. Throughout this sequence, Vergil refers to the duelers only by their proper names, Turnus and Aeneas: they no longer specifically represent opposing nationalities, different races, Italian and Trojan (or even Dardanian). Human beings, they cannot work out a human compromise; Aeneas cannot fully respond, though he is initially moved, to a reminder of his father's love. Thus, the great theme of Trojans, viewed as returning Dardanians, finding a new and powerful nationality in Italy becomes pointedly queried or even flawed as Vergil depicts the fiery denial by Aeneas of Turnus's appeal. Is not Rome here starting off with a ruthless murder that is as impious as Priam's murder at the fall of Troy and anticipates the future murder of Remus by Romulus? Can brothers and kinsmen, let alone alien races, ever finally unite in friendship? It seems a tragic possibility that there will be many more Troys and Trojans.

NOTE

[1] In this essay, the English translation used, unless otherwise indicated, is Mandelbaum's.

"Frigid Indifference" or "Soaked Through and Through with Feeling"? Portrayal of Character in the *Aeneid*

Shirley Werner

A major obstacle to appreciation for many readers of the *Aeneid* is the character of its hero. "He is always either insipid or odious." No, he is "worse than insipid: —he disgusts by his fears, his shiverings." He "alternately excites our contempt and disgust. His piety has the air [. . .] of bragging ostentation and hypocrisy." "Aeneas exhibits few traits which either conciliate our affection or command our respect: and after all the efforts which have been made to interest us in his favour, we dismiss him at last from our recollection with frigid indifference." Is Aeneas, even in the least, praiseworthy or admirable? The statements quoted above (gathered by R. Williams, "Changing Attitudes" 132–33) happen to have been expressed by Romantic readers rather than by readers of the twenty-first century, but such criticisms of Aeneas are still voiced today. Many contemporary readers are indignant—furious—at Aeneas's abandonment of Dido. For these readers the words "frigid indifference" well describe Aeneas's perceived lack of emotion. A potential consequence is the resentful reader's own frigid indifference to Aeneas.

Yet this view is astonishingly different from two statements made at the beginning of the twentieth century by the German scholar Richard Heinze. First: "The most characteristic thing about Virgil's narrative is that it is soaked through and through with feeling." Second: "Virgil generally presents his characters in the grip of some emotion" (*Technique* 362, 285). One of my aims in teaching the *Aeneid* is to help my students understand that Heinze's statements might be true. The characters of the epic, including Aeneas, are often shown in the grip of some emotion that reveals inner character. An important focus is therefore how Vergil constructs character in his narrative.

Without attempting to absolve Aeneas from blame—if he deserves it—I want to make my students sensitive to the fact that Vergil's epic narrative constructs character quite differently from a modern novel. Although a contemporary reader can usefully apply back to the *Aeneid* some of the theoretical understanding of narrative and point of view that has been gained from studies of the novel, epic character and point of view are conveyed in ways that are remarkably diverse and at times unfamiliar to the modern reader.

The ancient practice of portraying character by type rather than through the piling up of idiosyncratic and incidental details is one of the most important differences between Vergil's technique and that of the novel. Old men act the way they do because they are old men: they are restrained and sober in their judgment, they speak calmly, they enjoy giving advice to younger people, they like to talk about the past, they may be long-winded, and many of them have special insight into the will of the gods. Young men are impetuous, impulsive, energetic; they are inexperienced and sometimes incautious; they long to do heroic things; they have lots of emotion. All those qualities are typical characteristics that apply, more or less, to every man who is old or young.

Sometimes Vergil's emphasis on type even leads to logical contradictions. Consider the portrayal of Aeneas's son, Ascanius. When Troy falls, Ascanius is barely more than a baby who has to trot alongside Aeneas with little steps not equal to his father's big heroic steps. About seven years later, in Carthage, Ascanius is still enough of a baby to be climbing around on Dido's lap—that is, Cupid is climbing around pretending to be Ascanius, but no one can tell the difference. But when the wars begin in Italy, only a very short time afterward, Ascanius is old enough to take his place on the battlefield and to fight with youthful fervor against heroes. He "grows before our very eyes from childhood to young adulthood" (Heinze 220).

In all the episodes in which the young Ascanius plays a role, he is portrayed as a type, in a way that the ancient reader would expect a boy to act. Logical inconsistencies in the portrayal are, from that reader's point of view, undisturbing—although they contradict the expectations of the modern reader, who is accustomed to learning bits of information about characters in the casual, detail-cluttered style that we have learned to think of as realistic. But from the ancient perspective, it could be argued that portraying characters by type, even when there are inconsistencies in the portrayal, enriches the characterization rather than diminishes it. The youthful Ascanius is more deeply understood if the reader imagines him reacting like a boy in various circumstances, at various youthful ages, and not just at one or two moments in time. The ancient reader did not care whether Ascanius was seven years old or fourteen at a given moment; instead the reader wanted to know how Ascanius reacted as a boy when he found himself in a particular situation. Through the unfolding of the story the reader discovers who Ascanius is.

One other point needs to be made about the ancient practice of portraying character by type. Despite the ancient belief that character may be conveyed through the sketching of only a few conspicuous, typical features, it does not follow that typical characters have no personality, or that a modern reader cannot respond feelingly to a character's perceptions, emotions, and situation.

How then does Vergil convey a sense of individual character? Let us start with an aspect that engaged the attention of the ancient scholars who wrote about Vergil's epic: the not so obvious but quite fascinating technique by which Vergil reveals point of view—what characters know, what emotions they feel, how they judge a particular situation (see Fowler, "Deviant Focalisation"; O'Hara, "Dido").

We are familiar with the concept of point of view from our reading of modern novels. Sometimes the narrator of a novel is also a character in that novel, and the first-person narration acquaints us with that character's point of view throughout. Just as familiar is the novelistic device whereby a narrator who is not a character in the story takes the reader into the thoughts of a character and reveals them to us, removing the barrier between reader and character and enabling the reader to spy on a character's inmost thoughts. Novelists have various sophisticated techniques of achieving this effect.

What Vergil does is both more and less. He reports both direct speech and unspoken thoughts but less frequently than a novelist does. Perhaps the most distinctively unusual technique Vergil created—and it was his own invention—is the curious establishment of patterns of conversation (Highet; Feeney, "Taciturnity"). Characters in the *Aeneid* speak to and answer each other but never in a casual and naturalistic way. Rarely do we find conversations that go on at length between two people. Most of the time, one character speaks to another, and the other character does not answer. Often one person speaks, and another person answers. Less frequently, one person speaks, the other person answers, and the first person speaks one more time. Those are the typical patterns of conversation in the *Aeneid*. More prolonged conversations are surprisingly rare. We should not conclude from this restricted use of speech that all the speakers in the *Aeneid* are unnaturally inhibited and incapable of having normal human relationships. Very often there is a real desire to continue the conversation, but it is frustrated by circumstance. Sometimes the conversation does continue, but the narrator simply does not tell us what else was said. The most poignant example of an unfinished conversation is Aeneas's attempt to speak to Dido's ghost in the Underworld (6.456–66; Fitzgerald 613–28): he pleads with her to understand him, but she turns away. An example of an utterance that was never expected to have an answer is the tyrant Mezentius's address to his horse, Rhaebus (10.861–66; 1206–14)—though readers of Homer will know that an epic horse sometimes does answer when you speak to it (*Il.* [Fagles] 19.483–94; in Greek 408–17). An utterance to which the reader never hears the answer is Queen Amata's tearful plea to King Latinus when she tries to dissuade him from doing what he has already done, that is, from betrothing their daughter Lavinia to Aeneas (7.359–72; 495–514). Vergil does not report Latinus's reply, because the reader knows already what it inevitably had to be. The formal structures of conversations in Vergil's epic are consequently laden with a significance not to be found in the novel, where conversations do not tend to have fixed structures. Still, from the modern reader's point of view, the epic's limiting of conversation conveys less of a character's thought than we would get in a novel. The beginnings and endings of many epic conversations are untold and implicit, where a novel would give us a more naturalistic rendering, a more ordinary give and take.

In other ways, too, Vergil gives us both less and more than a novel does. Speech in the *Aeneid* can simultaneously reveal and conceal what a character thinks. When Aeneas is shipwrecked on the shores of Africa—it is almost the first thing that happens to him in the epic—he comforts his friends with an affecting speech. "Perhaps some day it will be pleasant to remember even these adversities," he says (1.203; trans. mine, here and throughout). The narrative continues, "These words he says aloud, and though sick with enormous cares / he feigns hope on his face; the pain he buries deep in his heart" (1.208–09). Here Vergil's narrative reveals to the reader what Aeneas conceals. And in showing so clearly that Aeneas conceals, Vergil is also giving the reader a clue about how to interpret speech. When characters speak, the reader must bear in mind the possibility that they are not revealing their whole thought (Laird 285).

Aside from Vergil's use of direct speech and his indirect narration of thoughts, the reader discovers other, less familiar techniques by which a character's inner self is revealed. Sometimes a word or phrase in the narrative represents not the impersonal point of view that we would assume belongs to the narrator but instead the subjective attitude of one of the characters (Fowler, "Deviant Focalisation"). At other times the narrative reveals to the reader, and to other characters, facts that were previously unknown (see Ahl 21). This backward-looking device may cause the reader to reinterpret character. A dramatic revelation is made in that painful conversation in the fourth book when Dido, in her panic and despair, wildly pleads with Aeneas. Aeneas, after a pause, answers her at last (4.331–61; 459–99). He says that he is grateful for what she has done, that he was never married to her, and he says many other things that infuriate her. A disturbing revelation that Dido has no patience to hear is that Aeneas has been dreaming of Anchises every night. We learn about these dreams for the first time here. Our realization colors what we think about Aeneas's past actions and his hidden emotions. Even while he was engaged in the joyful activity of building Carthage, even while he was absorbed in his passion for Dido, he was having recurring nightmares about his father's ghost. To put it in anachronistic psychological terms, he has been having guilty dreams at night and has been suppressing his unhappy guilt during the day. To put the same thought in ancient terms, Aeneas has been ignoring the dutiful love he owes his father.

Dido, of course, would passionately disagree with that point of view. Her perspective cannot possibly be reconciled with that of Aeneas. Indeed one of the most striking qualities in Vergil's narrative is its incorporation of various points of view, various perspectives. Absolutely the most striking instance of this technique is the narration of the tragedy of Dido in book 4. We see Dido's tragedy through her eyes, not through the eyes of Aeneas. Vergil reveals almost nothing of Aeneas's perspective. Aeneas and Dido have only one conversation after she knows that he is leaving; she later sends messages by Anna, but we do not know whether Aeneas replies, and as it turns out Aeneas and Dido never again speak face to face. In their first and last quarrel, we learn only what Aeneas says to Dido; we have only his bare words, not knowing whether he spoke them tenderly, coldly, angrily, or with indifference. In fact, the narrative plainly indicates that it will not give a full account of Aeneas's thoughts and that even those thoughts that are known to the reader will never be known to Dido. When Dido abruptly tears herself away from Aeneas, she leaves him "in his fear hesitating to say many things, and preparing / [to do so. . . .] / Though he longs to soothe her, in her agony, / by comforting her, and to turn aside her pains with his words," he does not (4.390–91, 393–94). That description temporarily parts the curtain and exposes Aeneas's hidden thoughts to the reader. But elsewhere the narrative of this book is extremely reticent about Aeneas's feelings, revealing them only through hints to which the careful reader must learn to be attentive.

In the other books as well the reader must work to understand who Aeneas is. I think that this narrative mysteriousness is a deliberate technique. If Vergil had given us a flat, cartoon hero whose actions and decisions were unambiguous, then we would not be that interested in Aeneas. There would be nothing to decide. Instead Vergil withholds easy answers. He plays a game with the reader, and the effect is to force the reader to interpret, to be an active reader, instead of passively trying to discover the narrator's point of view and accepting that point of view as the true or right one.

But narrative open-endedness does not mean that Aeneas is a mere shadow, a hollow figure devoid of identity. Let us consider a memorable passage in book 1, when Aeneas, desolate on the shores of Africa, discovers the pictures of the Trojan War that are displayed on Juno's temple in Carthage (441–97; 600–77). In subtle ways, this passage defines the character of Aeneas—his judgment, his way of looking at the world, the depth of his emotions, his sense of humanity, and the limits of his understanding—all the contradictory traits that show who he uniquely is.

Hardly has Aeneas entered the unknown city of Carthage than he finds himself in an ominous grove (a grove full of omen) where a temple to Juno is being built. There he is astounded to discover an artistic representation of his own people's sufferings in the Trojan War. The discovery of these pictures and Aeneas's reaction to them are told almost in the same breath: "There he saw the entire story of the Trojan War, battle by battle, / the war that was famous throughout the world, / and he saw the sons of Atreus, and Priam, and Achilles, who was furious against both of them. / He stood still, and, weeping, said to Achates [. . .]" (1.456–59). Aeneas weeps, but tears in the *Aeneid* do not always mean the same thing, and the tears shed by him in the temple in Carthage are complex tears. Contradictory emotions mingle: profound sorrow, a sudden release from fear, and a feeling of wonder.

The temple episode is not the only passage in the *Aeneid* in which Aeneas's emotions are revealed when Aeneas remembers his sufferings at Troy. The second passage comes at the beginning of book 2, at Dido's royal banquet, just before Aeneas begins his unforgettable narrative of Troy's destruction. It is worth considering for a moment what his emotions are at this banquet, because they are different from what he feels when he first discovers the story painted in the temple.

Dido has been asking Aeneas question after question about the Trojan War. Finally, she begs him to tell her the whole tale of the destruction of Troy from the beginning. He answers, "Although my mind shudders to remember and shrinks back in grief, / I will begin" (2.12–13). His response to the memory of the war earlier, when he saw the representation of it in the temple, was not entirely different, yet it was not quite the same. At the banquet, while he says that he feels grief, he refrains from openly demonstrating it, and he avoids tears. After all, he must tell his painful story for the pleasure of the banqueters there. Before, when he stands unobserved in the temple with his trusted companion Achates, he wails and groans. Yet instead of recoiling from the memory of suffering, he feasts his soul on it. The Latin reads, "He lets his heart graze on the empty picture" (1.464), using the verb *pascit*, which one would use of a herdsman tending his goats or sheep and letting them graze. At the end of the temple description of the war, with its many events and episodes, the narrative reminds the reader once again that Aeneas is still entirely absorbed in the memory: "While he stands dumbfounded, and clings, fastened with one unbroken gaze [. . .]" (1.495).

Thus in different situations Aeneas shows different possible responses of the mind to sorrow: shrinking back from the memory of it or feasting on its representation.

What does he crave when he feasts his soul on these sorrowful pictures? Why does he not draw back from the pain of remembering? First, he recognizes that the danger threatening him in Africa seems to be over. He clings to, and feasts his soul on, the representation of the past with what is almost a kind of joy. Yet the war is not shown in any way that can comfort him or lighten his cares (see Johnson, *Darkness* 103). The mercilessness of the pictures is especially jarring to the reader. If anything, the destruction of Troy is painted in even bleaker terms in the temple than the sufferers themselves would have used to describe what they experienced. The ransoming of Hector's body, for example, is represented as a heartless financial transaction. Achilles is shown "selling his lifeless corpse for gold" (1.484). The cold inhumanity of that depiction contradicts what the reader knows from the *Iliad*. No reader of Homer can forget the heartrending episode in which Achilles and Priam, deadly enemies though they are, mourn together in Achilles's tent over their separate losses. The ghastly picture in Carthage contradicts not only that Homeric scene but also Aeneas's own memory in the *Aeneid*. When Aeneas tells Dido about the fall of Troy, he recounts what Priam said to Achilles's son, Pyrrhus, about Achilles before Pyrrhus murdered Priam at the altar. These are Priam's last extraordinary words: "Achilles did not / treat Priam, his enemy, so; but he had shame before the rights and trust / of a suppliant. He returned the lifeless corpse of Hector for burial, / and sent me back to my kingdom" (2.540–43). The Latin word for the phrase "he had shame" is *erubuit*. It means "he blushed." The blush is a sign that Achilles had scruples and was abashed before Priam, and that his character was not monstrous but human.

What touches Aeneas so deeply in these pictures that are harsher even than the reality he remembers? Let us look more closely at his words: "Achates, what place, / what land on the earth does not contain our sorrow? / There is Priam! Here, too, what is praiseworthy has its reward, / there are tears for one's plight, and things mortal touch the mind" (1.459–62). These few lines contain various perceptions, emotions, and judgments, and the sequence of these enables the reader to follow Aeneas's thought as it unfolds.

His first emotion is wonder. He thought he was wandering in the wastelands of Libya, a land inhabited by wild animals. Instead he finds a city with a flourishing culture and to his astonishment discovers that the story of his own sorrows has become the subject of a magnificent work of art. Is there a place on earth that is not touched by the tale of Trojan suffering? Next Aeneas defines, to Achates and for the benefit of the reader, the meaning that he finds in the pictures. To Aeneas, the intention of the pictures is praise for those represented, and the motivation behind that praise is a noble sense of humanity, a generous sympathy for the sorrows of others, even for those whose lives are distant and whose troubles are not one's own (see Clay 197). Aeneas's interpretation of the pictures leads him to a final judgment. "Release your fears," he says to Achates. "This fame will bring you some deliverance."

What Aeneas feasts his soul on, then, is the noble and generous humanity that from his perspective inspired these pictures. And the person in whom that noble humanity resides is Dido. Without knowing it, Aeneas is now prepared for the emotions of profound gratitude and ardent admiration that he will experience on meeting her. The wonder he feels, as he stares in rapture at the pictures in the temple, is a prelude to his love for her.

Aeneas's perceptions, emotions, and unique understanding of Dido's generous humanity are unusual. Another observer might not discover in Dido or her people the intentions and motivations that Aeneas describes to Achates. The uniqueness of his perspective is brought into focus by the sharply contrasting situation and perceptions of another character, the Trojan Ilioneus, who of course does not fall in love with Dido.

Ilioneus was on one of the ships that were separated from Aeneas in the storm. He comes into the plot just after the temple episode. While Aeneas and Achates are contemplating the pictures, Dido enters and takes her place on a throne. Ilioneus and a shouting crowd of Trojans burst into the place. As soon as the turbulence of their entrance has quieted, Ilioneus speaks.

He has a different story to relate from that of Aeneas. After his part of the fleet drifted to the shore of Africa, they met with a belligerent reception from the inhabitants. They were not even granted the right to touch land. In Ilioneus's words, "we are denied the protection of the beach; / [. . .] they will not let us set foot upon the border of their land" (by "border" he means the shoreline); indeed, the inhabitants "are making preparations to fight us" (1.540–41). The fleet is so severely damaged, it cannot sail; thus its being beached can hardly be seen as an aggressive act. Yet the Africans, without taking the trouble to find out why the ships have come to shore, regard the fleet's presence as hostile and are threatening to set fire to it.

Although Ilioneus shows deference for Dido's queenly dignity, his speech contains a strongly worded protest against her people's threatening to burn the Trojan ships. The reader learns about this danger for the first time here. "What kind of people is this?" Ilioneus says. "What kind of nation is so barbarous as to allow this treatment? [. . .] / If you have no respect for humankind and the weapons of mortal men, / at least know that the gods are mindful of what is right, and what goes against divine laws" (1.539–40, 542–43). Ilioneus's mention of Trojan weapons is a threat of his own, and he counters with indignation the hostility shown him by the Carthaginians. But even as he protests strongly, he speaks with words calculated to defuse tension. He is a diplomat.

The contrast between Ilioneus's perspective and Aeneas's could not be stronger. Aeneas said to Achates, "Here, too, what is praiseworthy has its reward, / there are tears for one's plight [. . .]." Those words would have amazed Ilioneus if he had heard them. He might have wondered whether Aeneas had gone mad. Ilioneus has seen no sign of human recognition, no tears of sympathy. The brutish people preparing to burn the fleet do not have the least idea who the strangers are. They want simply to destroy them.

Whose impression of Dido's people is closer to the truth, that of Ilioneus or that of Aeneas? Interestingly, both are true. What gives rise to such contradiction is the gulf that separates the experiences of the two men. But that gulf also depends on the character of the men, on who they essentially are. Aeneas has a deeper understanding of Dido's history because he is the son of Venus, and Venus has told him Dido's story (earlier, at 1.338–68; 460–503). Only through Venus's words does Aeneas, and the reader, know how Dido's brother murdered her husband in secret, how she dreamed of her husband's ghost, and how she plotted to escape. Ilioneus is just an ordinary man with an ordinary human understanding. He, as the reader learns, has also somewhere heard a version of Dido's history. We know that he is not uninformed, because his first words to her are, "O Queen, whom Jupiter has granted to found a new city, / and to curb arrogant peoples by justice [. . .]" (1.522–23). Ilioneus does not document the source of his information, and we do not know what else he knows. But we can guess what he doesn't know. The secret motivations, Dido's private anguish, the plans that were never revealed, would be impossible for anyone but a god to know. The reader can easily see that whatever Ilioneus has heard, presumably from other people, is not enough to create in him the sympathy for Dido that Aeneas and the reader have.

What about the reader? Let us enter the text as characters for a moment. We too bring to the reading of the temple episode a perspective that is different from that of Aeneas. As readers of Vergil's narrative, we have a privileged understanding of the depth of Juno's hatred and of its mythological and historical causes. Juno hates the Trojans with a hatred more profound, because it is divine, than any hatred known to humans. Yet Aeneas has no misgivings when he discovers the ruthless pictures of Trojan humiliation displayed in Juno's temple. Instead, strangely, he begins to hope (see O'Hara, *Death* 36, 183). His lack of awareness reveals to us how slight must be his human knowledge of Juno's centuries-long and historically motivated hatred. We shudder, because Aeneas does not.

Readers must work to understand the character of Aeneas. The kind of work depends, of course, on the kind of reader. For a modern reader, some of the work is the necessity of coming to terms with ancient narrative techniques that are different from those of the novel. Aeneas is often reticent, a quality that leads at times to ambiguity in the narrative and doubt in the reader. But ambiguity of character is not the same as absence of character. Nor should the reader's uncertainty about what Aeneas is thinking lead to a persuasion of his "frigid indifference." Persons in the *Aeneid* are often shown in the grip of an emotion that discloses character. The complex tears wept by Aeneas in the temple of Juno in Carthage reveal his way of looking at the world, his sense of humanity, and the limits of his understanding. The discrepancies between what he sees in the pictures, the meaning he finds and defines, and what the reader knows are instructive. Aeneas's perception of the Carthaginians' humanity also differs sharply from the indignant stance taken by Ilioneus. Thus the interpretations, emotions, and judgments of Aeneas are shown to be distinctive. His tears, together with the "tears for one's plight" that he believes he has found in Carthage, give a splash of emotional color to the narrative and lift the curtain for a moment from his elusive character, affording the thoughtful reader a glimpse of who Aeneas uniquely is.

The Public and Private Aeneas:
Observations on Complex Responsibility

John Breuker, Jr.

Considerable discussion about the *Aeneid* in the past four decades has centered on the issues of optimism versus pessimism, the European school versus the Harvard school, ambiguity, the two voices (public and private), and so on. (Helpful summaries of these debates may be found, inter alia, in Johnson, *Darkness* 1–22; Harrison, *Oxford Readings* 1–20; Stahl, "Aeneas" and *Vergil's* Aeneid xiii–xxxiii; and Galinsky, *Classical and Modern Interactions* 74–76.) It has been, however, generally agreed that Vergil, while writing in the tradition of Homer when he undertook his epic task, had no intention of writing another Homeric epic. Vergil's complicated Roman society emphasized not the brilliant individual heroism of an Achilles or an Odysseus (the events of the past century had made individualism's costs all too clear) but social qualities—those responsibilities and obligations that required the individual to submit personal desires to the good of the community: family, country, gods, and friends and dependents (Galinsky offers especially perceptive observations on this point [77–85]). In a word, Vergil's *heros* had to have *pietas*. An examination of the poet's use of *heros* to refer to Aeneas provides insights into Vergil's modified concept of what constituted heroism.

It is noteworthy that the word *heros* does not appear in books 2 and 3 during Aeneas's lengthy retelling to Dido of the events of Troy's fall and his trip through the Mediterranean in search of a new home. It is in *Aeneid* 1 that the word first appears, but not until after Aeneas has been introduced expressing the conventional heroic ethos as he faces imminent shipwreck in Juno's storm. Once Neptune calms the storm, the Trojans head for the nearest shore. Unsuccessful in spotting any other ships, Aeneas slays deer as food and distributes the meat to the hungry survivors.

> Vina bonus quae deinde cadis onerarat Acestes
> litore Trinacrio dederatque abeuntibus *heros*
> dividit, et dictis maerentia pectora mulcet.
> > (1.195–97; emphasis mine)

> Then the hero divides the wine which good Acestes had loaded in jars on the Trinacrian shore and had given to them as they departed, and with words he soothes their grieving hearts. (trans. mine, here and throughout; parallel passages in Fitzgerald are cited for the reader's convenience: cf. 264–67)

Though *heros* is commonly read in apposition to *bonus Acestes* ("good Acestes") (as both Austin [*Primus*] and R. Williams [Aeneid] ad loc. strongly urge), its effect is at least felt by *dividit* ("divides"), whose subject is Aeneas, and this essay demonstrates that in eight of the other ten occurrences when *heros* is similarly located at line's end, it must be taken with the verb or verbs in the following line(s), as I propose here (cf. Mackail, ad loc.). In this proposed reading, the action Vergil describes as heroic is Aeneas's providing food and drink for his men and attempting to soothe their grieving hearts with words of encouragement. Then "curisque ingentibus aeger / spem vultu simulat, premit altum corde dolorem" ("weary with vast anxieties, he feigns hope on his countenance, but [adversative asyndeton] checks his grief deep in his heart") (1.208–09; cf. 284–86). After they have refreshed themselves with the venison and wine, Aeneas joins with his men in discussing the fate of their lost companions.

> Praecipue pius Aeneas nunc acris Oronti,
> nunc Amyci casum gemit et crudelia secum
> fata Lyci fortemque Gyan fortemque Cloanthum.   (1.220–22)

> Especially loyal Aeneas laments with himself the misfortune now of spirited Orontes, now of Amycus, and the cruel fates of Lycus and both brave Gyas and brave Cloanthus.   (cf. 300–03)

Pius ("loyal") Aeneas privately (*secum*) laments their misfortune and cruel fates. The context of the initial appearance of heroism in the poem, therefore, stresses the internal value of responsible concern for others (Heinze, *Technik* 281; Heinze, *Technique* 228; Galinsky, *Classical and Modern Interactions* 89) and highlights three concepts: Aeneas as a hero, Aeneas as loyal, and Aeneas as sensitive to the difference between his personal private feelings and his public corporate action.

The next appearance of *heros* is in *Aeneid* 4. After Mercury's visit to Aeneas and the subsequent confrontations between Dido and Aeneas, the queen flees into her palace. The point of view shifts to *pius* Aeneas:

> At pius Aeneas, quamquam lenire dolentem
> solando cupit et dictis avertere curas,
> multa gemens magnoque animum labefactus amore
> iussa tamen divum exsequitur classemque revisit.   (4.393–96)

> But loyal Aeneas, although he desires to soothe the grieving one by consoling her and to turn aside her cares with words, lamenting many things and staggered in spirit by his great love, nevertheless carries out the orders of the gods and revisits his fleet.   (cf. 545–51)

Then, in the moving apostrophe at 408–12 ("Quis tibi tum, Dido [. . .]"), the point of view shifts briefly to Vergil himself. Dido next begs Anna to plead on her behalf that Aeneas change his mind and remain in Carthage. As this episode ends, Aeneas is likened in a famous simile to an oak tree pounded by Alpine blasts:

> haud secus adsiduis hinc atque hinc vocibus *heros*
> tunditur, et magno persentit pectore curas,
> mens immota manet, lacrimae volvuntur inanes.
> (4.447–49; emphasis mine)

> not at all otherwise is the hero pounded from this side and that by the incessant words, and he feels deeply the cares in his great heart: but [adversative asyndeton] his mind remains unmoved, the tears roll down without effect. (cf. 617–21)

The episode, starting with *pius Aeneas* (393) and concluding with the *heros* (447), does not have its focus on physical action by the *heros*. The passive voice of "pounded," the "tears [. . .] without effect," and the "mind [. . .] unmoved" stress Aeneas's feelings and inner resolve, while "feels [. . .] the cares" and the appearance of "tears" indicate the depth of his emotional empathy and inner struggle.

At the conclusion of the boat race in *Aeneid* 5, prizes are awarded; finally Sergestus brings his damaged ship and its crew safely to shore. Then

> Sergestum Aeneas promisso munere donat
> servatam ob navem laetus sociosque reductos. (5.282–83)

> Aeneas presents Sergestus with the promised reward, joyful because of the saved ship and restored comrades. (cf. 365–66)

Vergil bases Aeneas's joy on the safe return of the ship and crew ("servatam ob navem [. . .] sociosque reductos"); this joy in the safety of others, an aspect of *pietas* (see Mackie 100–01), prepares the way for *pius* Aeneas to lead the throng to a grassy plain where he organizes the foot race.

> Hoc pius Aeneas misso certamine tendit
> gramineum in campum, quem collibus undique curvis
> cingebat silvae, mediaque in valle theatri
> circus erat; quo se multis cum milibus *heros*
> consessu medium tulit exstructoque resedit.
> (5.286–90; emphasis mine)

> When this contest was finished, loyal Aeneas hastens onto a grassy field which woods on winding hills encircled all around, and in the middle of a valley was the circle of a theater [i.e., a natural running course]; the

> hero came to the midst of this assembly with many thousands and sat
> down on a raised platform.   (cf. 369–74)

This episode again focuses on Aeneas's inner feeling (*laetus*), his *pietas*, and his effective leadership. It is this kind of Aeneas that Vergil chooses to call a *heros*.

Vergil describes Aeneas as *heros* three times in *Aeneid* 6. The book begins with *pius Aeneas* (6.9) after he has lamented for his lost helmsman Palinurus, going to visit the sibyl as Helenus and Anchises had instructed (see 3.441–62 and 5.724–39; Fitzgerald 3.591–616 and 5.940–62). After Deiphobe offers her fearfully mysterious prophecy of more war, another Achilles, et cetera (6.83–97; Fitzgerald 128–47), *heros* Aeneas responds with equanimity.

> incipit Aeneas *heros*: "Non ulla laborum,
> o virgo, nova mi facies inopinave surgit;
> omnia praecepi atque animo mecum ante peregi."
>   (6.103–05; emphasis mine)

> Not any new or unexpected aspect of toils arises for me, maiden; I have
> anticipated them all and been over them already in mind by myself.
>   (cf. 155–58)

He has privately (*mecum*) anticipated and pondered everything. Vergil clusters three concepts: Aeneas as *pius*, Aeneas as *heros*, and Aeneas privately engaged in mental activity ("omnia praecepi atque animo mecum ante peregi"). He emphasizes Aeneas's acumen and mental preparation rather than deeds of prowess. Aeneas then requests that the sibyl instruct him how to find his father (6.106–09; Fitzgerald 158–63), and she announces the three mysterious conditions he must fulfill in order to effect this meeting (6.124–55; cf. 185–225): he must obtain the golden bough, properly bury a comrade of whose death he is ignorant, and offer appropriate sacrifices as his *prima piacula* ("first expiatory sacrifices") (6.153). Aeneas leaves, pondering her words ("caecosque volutat / eventus animo secum" ["and he privately considers the dark events"] [6.157–58]), and is joined by Achates. The two shortly come upon the corpse of Misenus, word quickly spreads, and the collective mourning begins. "Ergo omnes magno circum clamore fremebant, / praecipue pius Aeneas" ("Therefore all lament with loud shouting, especially loyal Aeneas") (6.175–76; cf. 252–54). Concluding the preparations for Misenus's funeral rites, Aeneas works alongside his men, encouraging them ("hortatur socios" [6.184]), privately pondering all these recent events ("haec ipse suo tristi cum corde volutat" ["he considers these things with his own sad heart"] [6.185]), and finally uttering a prayer that the bough show itself. In immediate response, twin doves appear. "Tum maximus heros / maternas agnovit avis laetusque precatur: / este duces [. . .]" ("Then the greatest hero recognized his mother's birds and hap-

pily prays: 'Be my guides [. . .]'") (6.192–94; cf. 275–78). Again the familiar
cluster of three concepts is present: *pius* Aeneas, the *heros* Aeneas engaged in
mental activity ("volutat [. . .] animo," "agnovit [. . .] precatur"), and doing so
privately (*secum, suo tristi cum corde*).

Having secured the bough, Aeneas returns to the sibyl's shrine; then *pius*
Aeneas (231) joins the other Trojans in the actual rites for Misenus and obeys
the sibyl's command to sacrifice to the Stygian deities. On their *facilis descen-
sus Averno* ("easy descent to Avernus") (6.126), Aeneas and the sibyl pass Tartarus, soon seeing Charon at the Styx. When he resists their initial attempts
to board his ferry, Deiphobe informs him of her companion's identity and
mission, highlighting his paternal *pietas* before showing Charon the golden
bough.

> 'Troius Aeneas, pietate insignis et armis,
> ad genitorem imas Erebi descendit ad umbras.
> Si te nulla movet tantae pietatis imago,
> at ramum hunc' (aperit ramum qui veste latebat)
> 'agnoscas.'   (6.403–07)

> Trojan Aeneas, distinguished in loyalty and arms, goes down to his father
> in the deepest shadows of Erebus. But if no likeness of such great loyalty
> moves you, still you should recognize this bough (she reveals the bough
> which was lying hidden in her robe).   (cf. 542–50)

Once across the river, past Cerberus and in the Mourning Fields, they find in
a great forest, among others, those who died for love. In their midst recently
deceased Dido is wandering.

>   quam Troius *heros*
> ut primum iuxta stetit agnovitque per umbras
> obscuram [. . .]
> [. . . . .]
> demisit lacrimas dulcique adfatus amore est [. . .].
>   (6.451–53, 455; emphasis mine)

> as soon as the Trojan hero stood close to her and recognized her dimly
> through the gloom [. . .] he let his tears fall and addressed her with sweet
> love.   (cf. 606–12)

Vergil almost immediately underscores Aeneas's inner world of feelings, words,
and tears:

> Talibus Aeneas ardentem et torva tuentem
> lenibat dictis animum lacrimasque ciebat. (6.467–68)

Aeneas kept trying to soothe her with such words, as she was burning in spirit and gazing grimly at him, and kept arousing tears.   (cf. 628–30)

Dido finally flees to Sychaeus's loving embrace, with Aeneas in pursuit.

Nec minus Aeneas casu percussus iniquo
prosequitur lacrimis longe et miseratur euntem.   (6.475–76)

Nor does Aeneas, shaken by her inequitable misfortune, any less follow her a long way in tears and he pities her as she goes.   (cf. 638–39)

The verbs that define the actions of the *heros* Aeneas, the "likeness of such great loyalty," during this emotional meeting with Dido—"[he] stood close [. . .] and recognized," "he let his tears fall and addressed her with sweet love," he "kept trying to soothe her with [. . .] words," "he kept arousing tears," "shaken by her inequitable misfortune, he follows her a long way in tears," and "he pities her as she goes"—describe the inner world of feelings and emotions. The reader recalls the earlier comparison of Aeneas to a stout oak tree, shaken (*concusso stipite* [4.444]) by the storm of Anna's pleas but standing firmly rooted in Tartarus (*radice in Tartara tendit* [4.446]), and notes that he is shaken again (*casu percussus iniquo* [6.475]) here in the Underworld, still dropping leaf-large tears.

The next appearances of *heros* are in book 8. Early on, Turnus and the other Latin leaders make preparations to deal with the Trojan invaders and send Venulus as an emissary to seek help from Diomedes.

Quae Laomedontius *heros*
cuncta videns magno curarum fluctuat aestu,
atque animum nunc huc celerem nunc dividit illuc
in partisque rapit varias perque omnia versat.
        (8.18–21; emphasis mine)

The hero, offspring of Laomedon, seeing all these things, rides on a great tide of cares, and divides his quick mind now to this place, now to that, and sends it in every direction and turns it through everything.
        (cf. 26–30)

Five verbs of the inner world define the actions of this *heros*: *cuncta videns, fluctuat, animum* [. . .] *dividit, [animum] rapit,* and *versat.* Later, Evander entrusts Pallas to Aeneas's care, and the surrounding group witnesses the heavenly appearance of clashing weapons, a sign from Aeneas's mother, Venus. Vergil highlights the different reactions.

Obstipuere animis alii, sed Troius *heros*
agnovit sonitum et divae promissa parentis.
        (8.530–31; emphasis mine)

Others were astonished in their spirits, but the Trojan hero recognized
the sound and promises of his divine parent.   (cf. 719–22)

Though the others are amazed, Aeneas understands, and for his insight Vergil
calls him *heros*.

The final three appearances of *heros* show a more traditional type of hero.
As the battle rages after Turnus slays Pallas, Lucagus and Liger tauntingly challenge Aeneas, who replies with his spear rather than with words.

> Sed non et Troius *heros*
> dicta parat contra, iaculum nam torquet in hostis.
> (10.584–85; emphasis mine)

But the Trojan hero does not also ready words in response, for he twirls
his spear at the foe.   (cf. 818–20)

Still, it is a *pius* Aeneas (10.591) who, having wounded Lucagus, addresses him
with bitter words (*dictis amaris*) as Lucagus lies dying, and then Aeneas slays his
brother, Liger, as well. Later, when Mezentius and Aeneas are dueling, Mezentius circles him and throws spears until Aeneas's shield resembles a forest.

> Ter circum astantem laevos equitavit in orbis
> tela manu iaciens, ter secum Troius *heros*
> immanem aerato circumfert tegmine silvam.
> (10.885–87; emphasis mine)

Three times he rode around him, as he stood there, in circles going to his
left, throwing spears with his hand, three times the Trojan hero brings
around with him a huge forest [of spears] in his bronzed shield.
                    (cf. 1240–43)

These two instances display Aeneas as a stalwart warrior, engaged in physical
action and able to withstand a foe's fierce attack. In the poem's final invocation
too, Vergil refers to the horrendous slaughters accomplished by both Turnus
and Aeneas.

> Quis mihi nunc tot acerba deus, quis carmine caedes
> diversas obitumque ducum, quos aequore toto
> inque vicem nunc Turnus agit, nunc Troius *heros*
> expediat? Tanton placuit concurrere motu,
> Iuppiter, aeterna gentis in pace futuras?   (12.500–04; emphasis mine)

What god is to disclose to me now by song so many bitter sufferings, the
differing slaughters and destruction of the leaders whom now Turnus,

now the Trojan hero drives across the whole plain and one after the other? Did it please you, Jupiter, that peoples who were to be in eternal peace should meet in such great conflict?   (cf. 680–86)

These last three occurrences of *heros*, all in decidedly martial contests, describe feats more traditionally ascribed to a Homeric hero. There is but one association with *pietas*, and there is no focus on the inner world of the spirit.

Several observations arise from this examination of the contexts in which Vergil employs *heros* to refer to Aeneas (space precludes a discussion of contexts in which *heros* refers to others, e.g., Helenus, Entellus, Misenus, Musaeus, Evander, or to a group). First, *heros* at line's end has its verb(s) in the following line(s) in eight of the ten occurrences, supporting the proposed interpretation of the eleventh occurrence of *heros* at 1.196, that it refers to Aeneas rather than to Acestes (which would make it nine of eleven occurrences). Second, each instance of Aeneas as *heros* in books 1–6 occurs in a context of Aeneas's *pietas*, as does one in book 10. Third, three of these instances in books 1–6 emphasize the contrast between Aeneas's private feelings and his public persona. Fourth, every instance in books 1–8 shows a *heros* engaged in mental actions rather than physical deeds, or as one concerned for the well-being of others for whom he has some responsibility. It is only in the battle scenes of books 10 and 12 that the *heros* is assigned verbs such as *torquet* ("twirls"), *circumfert* ("brings around"), and *agit* ("drives").

The combination of a different sort of heroism, *pietas*, and a sensitivity to private versus public roles observed above may help the reader find a common ground and a perspective from which to interpret the character of Aeneas and, perhaps, the ending of the *Aeneid*. For we have discovered a figure characterized by thought before action, by a focus on inner rather than outer values, by an awareness of the need to subjugate his private feelings to the greater public good, and by a willingness to subordinate his individual personality to the requirements of his social duty. This was Vergil's concept of heroism: *pius heros*.

Throughout the poem, Aeneas struggles to understand what such heroic *pietas* entails. As a result, there is an ambivalence about the poet's characterization of Aeneas (private individual, public leader) that Adam Parry described as Vergil's "two voices," the public and the private. Others (e.g., Pöschl, *Art* 34–60, 122–38; Hunt, *Forms* 67–81; and R. Williams, "Purpose" 25–35) refer to two aspects of the character called Aeneas—Aeneas the man and Aeneas the symbol. Aeneas the private man is usually unhappy; he often weeps and is in despair. He sometimes seems a bit slow to learn, especially in the first half of the poem. In book 2, for example, it requires Hector, Panthus, Venus, and Creusa to get him to leave Troy and to lead both his family and a group of refugees to found a new home. At the same time, Aeneas is also a displaced person, pursuing a future home and city of which he himself is not really to be a part. He loses every human bond (wife, home, city-state, father, friends, nurse—all from the past) except for his son (the future). He is, consequently, complicated, moody, and hesitant on his quest to define his identity and to discover the relations embraced by this *pietas*. Sometimes he fails to subjugate his immediate wishes and passions to the claims of that *pietas* (as at Troy in book 2 and the new Troys of book 3, with Dido in book 4, or after the burning of his ships in book 5), but his understanding of *pietas* and his perspective on it are enlarged from book 2 to 4 to 6.

Aeneas the public symbol represents the civilized man: responsible, willing to give in and to sacrifice himself in order to establish or retain order in society. In this representative role too, he is not heroic in the Homeric sense. He is too unsure, too cautious, too reflective. He generally senses his responsibilities to his dependents—unlike Achilles, for example, for much of the *Iliad*. Aeneas also seems elected to carry the cross of fate, a theme introduced in the poem's opening lines: *fato profugus* (Fredricksmeyer). This representative Aeneas is not all that happy about his lot in life, but he does his best. When he kills Turnus, the Latin Achilles (see 6.89–90; Fitzgerald 134–36), Vergil does not specifically comment on the rightness or wrongness of this act of vengeance, as he commented on the "marriage" to Dido (4.169–72; cf. 233–38) and on Turnus's killing of Pallas (10.501–06; cf. 701–07). But many readers sense that he does end the poem on a note of disquiet over Aeneas's action and of sympathy for Turnus (see R. Williams, Aeneid at 12.887–952; R. Williams, "Purpose" 35). Since there are these two aspects to Vergil's Aeneas, as private man and public symbol, Parry's reference to the poet's two voices is sensible.

The poet's public voice deals with Aeneas as the symbol of the patriotic Roman and gives the poet's public statement, which is optimistic in outlook and focused on the state. The Romans were, in Vergil's view, the chosen of heaven. Jupiter's prophecy in book 1, Anchises's ringing statement of the Roman arts in book 6, and the scenes portrayed on Aeneas's divinely wrought shield in book 8 proclaim the poet's view, which is never lost sight of. In the real world, as Vergil knew and experienced it, the Romans did in fact serve as civilizing agents who brought peace and order. For him, this was historical reality: all roads did, after all, lead to and from Rome. For many in the Mediterranean world of the first century, it seemed Augustus really had initiated a golden age as it occurred in Stoic thought (and was vividly predicted at the end of Jupiter's prophecy [1.291–96; cf. 391–98], when the *impius furor* of civil war is chained and imprisoned under Augustus as the introduction of such an age). Aeneas himself does not gain full understanding until book 6's parade of future historical Roman heroes when Anchises excitedly says to him, "Hic vir, hic est [. . .] / Augustus Caesar, divi genus, aurea condet / saecula qui rursus [. . .]" ("this is the man, this is the one [. . .] Augustus Caesar, son of the deified, who will found again golden ages [. . .]") (6.791–93; cf. 1062–66). Here the reader hears the poet's public, patriotic, and optimistic voice.

The poet's private voice deals with Aeneas as a man and gives the poet's personal sentiment, which is more pessimistic in outlook, Epicurean in background, and focused on the individual. The Roman (Augustan) accomplishment, though glorious, was in Vergil's view and experience attained at considerable personal cost. Consequently, the poet has compassion for the suffering in the lives of both the victors and the vanquished, and those who must be eliminated for Rome to be born are painted in realistic and often in sympathetic colors. Few readers are not attracted to Rome's sacrificial victims: to Dido; to Camilla, "the apotheosis of Italian heroism, the incarnation of Italian *virtus*" (Gransden, Aeneid *Book XI* 21); to the youthful Lausus and Pallas; even to Turnus, the antagonist. The *Aeneid*, therefore, implicitly raises the problem of evil in the world: are the gods and the universe really benevolent since they allow such suffering (Fredricksmeyer 14-15)? The poet's first question is "Tantaene animis caelestibus irae?" ("Do celestial spirits have such great anger?") (1.11; cf. 18–19), and his last is "Tanton placuit concurrere motu, / Iuppiter, aeterna gentis in pace futuras?" ("Did it please you, Jupiter, that peoples who were to be in eternal peace should meet in such great conflict?") (12.503–04; cf. 684– 86). These two questions frame the entire poem and provide a context in which readers recall that Vergil qualifies Anchises's panorama of future Roman greatness in book 6 with the tragic and premature death of Marcellus, the chosen heir of Augustus; in which, for some readers, Aeneas's triumph over Turnus in the final line is filled with plangent questioning of the need for Turnus's death, as much as for Camilla's. Vergil does not claim to understand evil's presence but does assert that divine will works through evil; life and history are like this, he says. Here the reader hears the poet's private, personal, and pessimistic voice.

There are, then, different perspectives from which to view the poem's concluding scene (Burnell reviews several): optimistically as Aeneas's triumph and pessimistically as his failure. The pessimistic view (as argued, e.g., in Putnam, *Poetry* and *Vergil's* Aeneid; Johnson, *Darkness*) stresses that the sacrifice of enemies and of individuality, even that of the hero, is necessary for Rome to result. This necessity, it is argued, was historical reality for Vergil. The pessimistic view notes that Vergil does not give the typical Judeo-Christian answer to the question of evil, or even a pat answer, and asserts that this absence of an answer may be one of the most civilized aspects of the poem, since it recognizes and admits the tensions and ambiguities of civilized society and life.

The optimistic view (as argued in Gransden, Aeneid *Book XI*; Stahl, "Aeneas," "Death," and *Vergil's* Aeneid; and Galinsky, *Classical and Modern Interactions* and *Augustan Culture*) allows that in the final duel Aeneas is filled with wrath but sees that wrath not as personal failure but as the direct outcome of the war and treaty breaking by the Latins, so the wrath is in direct response to those two impious events. The optimistic view stresses Aeneas's responsibility to Evander and the dead Pallas: this responsibility too is part of *pietas*. In addition, the optimistic view notes that Vergil shows Aeneas as a *pius* suppliant (12.311; cf. 427) who urges that the broken treaty be renewed even as he tries to halt the outbreak of new fighting and notes that it is at this very point that he is wounded. The wounding of the *pius* suppliant Aeneas, then, is a critical element in the final scene, for it transfers to the Latins the guilt of *impietas* in breaking the treaty. When Aeneas as representative head of his people kills Turnus as representative head of the Latins, he avenges that *impietas* (Petter). This avenging is his public responsibility.

In a sense, then, the optimistic view argues that the *Aeneid* has two endings, one on the divine level, the other on the human level. On the divine level, Juno's reconciliation (12.791–842; cf. Fitzgerald 1069–143) completes the motif of her opposition, a major unifying device in the poem. The reconciliation recalls the early Jupiter-Venus scene (1.254–96; cf. 347–98), and so in a way the poem's end was already found in the poem's beginning. On the human level, the death of Turnus completes the narrative. Aeneas, however, reenacts the Iliadic vendetta not just to avenge the personal loss (Pallas-as-Patroclus motif) but also to secure the future that was earlier predicted by Jupiter. He is therefore both a private individual who, being moved, hesitates (a moment Clausen refers to as "an extraordinary moment; for the epic warrior never hesitates" [*Virgil's* Aeneid 99]), and the public head of state who, aware of the obligations of *pietas*, acts. Note that the public head of state cannot fulfill his city-founding purpose (*dum conderet urbem* ["until he might found a city"] [1.5; cf. 10]) unless the private man *ferrum condit / fervidus* ("buries his sword hotly") (12.950–51; cf. 1295). The hotly buried sword is the foundation on which the destined city and empire will be built. "Tantae molis erat Romanam condere gentem" ("Of so great a burden was it to found the Roman race") (1.33; cf. 48–49).

"Tum Pectore Sensus Vertuntur Varii": Reading and Teaching the End of the *Aeneid*

Barbara Weiden Boyd

> The best key to a poet's partiality is found in those
> passages where he tries to influence the subconscious
> self of his reader.
> —Stahl, "The Death of Turnus"

No single scene in Latin literature has proved to be as great an ideological battleground as the end of the *Aeneid* (12.887–952; Mandelbaum 1178–271). For decades, a war of words has been waged among Vergilians over the best, or only, way to describe and make sense of the killing of Turnus by Aeneas and the final confrontation leading up to it. It would be presumptuous—if not impossible—for me to attempt even a survey of the views expressed in no uncertain terms about this scene; instead, for an up-to-date evaluation of the debate and its central terms, I refer my readers to Hans-Peter Stahl ("Death") and to Richard F. Thomas ("Isolation"), and to the bibliography collected therein. Meanwhile, I have set for myself a slightly different, and more modest, task: to consider the scene from the point of view of a teacher whose job it is to introduce this scene to a group of first- or second-time *Aeneid* readers. I am thinking in particular of undergraduates and high school Latin students, who come to Vergil's conclusion from a focus on the first half of the *Aeneid* and whose tendency to see ethical and moral issues in black and white is almost inevitable, particularly if they can maintain their detachment from the experience of a literary fiction. A delicate challenge for even the finest of teachers awaits in this episode: How to make the characters other than cartoon superheroes or villains? how to understand their humanity or lack thereof? how to know what is in fact right and what Vergil meant and to be confident that these two things are essentially the same? Such questions acquire an especially urgent tone when we note that this scene has now been admitted to the canonical syllabus for a first course in Vergil promulgated by the Educational Testing Service as a means to prepare for the Advanced Placement examination on the *Aeneid*. My primary aim, therefore, is to provoke in these students, as well as in other readers, a personal involvement in finding answers for the questions this scene asks. A central component of our task as teachers, after all, is to make what we teach matter to our students by engaging them in the questions a text raises. The answers themselves are another matter entirely; their discussion would require among other things that we look beyond this scene to numerous episodes leading up to it. For now, it is enough to attempt a first survey of shifting perceptions of self and other in the final moments of the *Aeneid*.

In twenty-five years of reading and rereading and thinking about this epic, I have learned much from other readers, from Servius to the moderns, from

Richard Heinze and Viktor Pöschl to Alessandro Barchiesi and Richard Thomas, and what I have read has naturally shaped and given nuance to my view of Vergil. I nonetheless approach this scene from a vantage point slightly different from that taken by most critics, whose focus especially in recent years has been on character—the characters of the two men weighed in the balance, as it were, with individual emphases tipping the scales one way or another. The typical reading of this episode is in terms of a series of binary oppositions: Aeneas versus Turnus, Augustan versus anti-Augustan, Greek versus Trojan, Trojan versus Rutulian, past versus future. Even the terms most commonly used to describe the conclusion, *ambiguous* and *ambivalent*, reflect the duality posited at the heart of the scene: there is one ending with two characters, a victim and a victor; one death, two destinies; one loss and one triumph. I want to move away from this strict duality over which an omniscient narrator seems to preside and instead triangulate, and so complicate, our relation with the text by focusing on our experience as readers and on the means by which Vergil invites our involvement in this scene. One powerful device Vergil uses in particular is to locate us in the scene, at least as onlookers; the paradoxical effect of this device is to enhance our sense of the inaccessibility of the epic past.

On this premise, I look at four moments in the concluding scene of the poem to consider how the representation through language of one series of events or narrative moments in turn evokes our participation through recollection of other moments, other events, other conclusions, other poems (Barchiesi, *Traccia* 91–122). In particular, I focus on features of syntax, diction, and word order that are most likely to catch the attention of new readers and demand clarification. In each of these moments, the superficially binary character of the scene gives way to the blurred vision we experience as we see the events in our mind's eye from the perspectives of both Aeneas and Turnus as well as from our own.

1.

> sed neque currentem se nec cognoscit euntem
> tollentemve manu saxumve immane moventem;
> genua labant, gelidus concrevit frigore sanguis.   (12.903–05)

> But he recognizes himself neither as he runs, nor as he goes, nor as he lifts and moves with his hand the huge rock; his knees give way, and his blood, icy from cold, has congealed.   (trans. mine, here and throughout)

Facing Aeneas on the battlefield for their final confrontation, Turnus lifts a massive stone and prepares to hurl it at him. But something interferes; Turnus suddenly loses all strength, his knees give way, and he becomes a stranger to himself. How can this be? How can Turnus not know who he is? Vergil's language enhances the effect: the four present participles (*currentem, euntem, tollentem, moventem*) create a sort of verbal slow motion, freezing the physical form of Turnus yet making him unrecognizable to himself as viewer ("neque [. . .] se [. . .] cognoscit"). The psychological or intellectual self of Turnus is trapped in a foreign body, it seems; the placement of the reflexive *se* at the very center of 903 replicates visually, through the words on the page, the trapping of Turnus inside himself in a sort of schizophrenic nightmare. At the same time, his uncontrollable physical response, knees failing and blood chilling involuntarily (905), is described with detachment: visible from without, unsensed from within. This description could be focalized by Turnus as he watches himself from some point outside (Fowler, "Deviant Focalisation"); by Aeneas, whose inaction as he observes Turnus is implicit; or by us, the readers, who recognize the sense of disembodiment Turnus experiences in his slow-motion last effort as something we too have experienced in moments of great fear. The engagement of the reader is subtle but effective: the physical transformation of Turnus has been depersonalized and universalized. The failing knees and cold blood that Vergil describes could be Aeneas's or our own.

The conflict between physical and psychological responses to fear captured in this passage eerily fulfills the taunting command uttered by Aeneas a few lines before:

> Verte omnis tete in facies et contrahe quidquid
> sive animis sive arte vales; opta ardua pennis
> astra sequi clausumve cava te condere terra.   (891–93)

> Transform yourself into all shapes and bring together whatever [i.e., resources] you can, whether through courage or through skill. Choose to chase the steep stars on wings or to hide yourself shut up in the hollow earth.

Aeneas's general suggestion that Turnus try to escape by becoming something other than himself ironically recalls the description of Proteus given by Cyrene in the fourth *Georgic*—"ille [. . .] formas se vertet in omnis" ("that one [. . .] will transform himself into all shapes") (411). The options Aeneas proceeds to suggest—for Turnus to fly up to the heavens on wings or bury himself in the earth—are neither of them real; no Proteus, Turnus cannot in fact alter his physical form. Instead, he must face his opponent with the few resources he has left, even as his physical strength disintegrates. We, meanwhile, present as onlookers, are still unsure which side to choose.

The binary structure of the confrontation is compromised by Turnus's loss of self. Aeneas's ironic allusion to Proteus suggests an imprecise but useful metaphor for the scene as a whole: one character is constantly standing in for, or in the shadow of, another, struggling to escape his very individual destiny. R. O. A. M. Lyne has demonstrated that, for the use of a stone as a weapon against Aeneas, a scene from the *Iliad* (5.302–10) is the primary model for Turnus: in Homer, Diomedes successfully heaves a stone at Aeneas and brings him to his knees (*Voices* 132–35). But Vergil's Turnus is not Homer's Diomedes, and his cast fails to stop Aeneas; presently, Aeneas will tower over Turnus instead. This reversal echoes the turnabout of *Iliad* 20.285–87, when Homer's Aeneas picks up a stone to hurl at Achilles (Putnam, "Turnus" 62–64): the intended victim in *Iliad* 5, Aeneas becomes in the later scene a new Diomedes, if only momentarily. The intervention of Poseidon to save Aeneas from Achilles in *Iliad* 20, however, limits the aptness of Vergil's reference to the Diomedes-Aeneas scene in *Iliad* 5 even as it reinforces our awareness that Aeneas's destiny and identity are not yet fixed by Homer. Neither victor nor vanquished, Aeneas departs from the *Iliad* essentially unproven; the deus ex machina who acts to move Aeneas's destiny outside the framework of the Homeric narrative refrains from intruding on the Vergilian confrontation of Aeneas and Turnus. Thus, the destiny averted in Homer remains fixed in the Vergilian scene. While both Aeneas and Turnus have a whole series of Homeric analogues, neither can escape from the identity or the destiny shaped for him in the *Aeneid*.

Vergil's play with focalization enhances the effect: we see Turnus as he sees himself, yet we can recognize him even when he cannot; our eyes are like those of Aeneas, watching him up close and comprehending his inner split. Do we view this scene with fear, in anticipation, or from a clinically objective distance? Or is our assumption of objectivity and control, like Turnus's own, an illusion? Vergil offers a clue to our position as he describes the stone Turnus lifts as so great that even twelve men nowadays would have difficulty lifting it ("vix illud lecti bis sex cervice subirent, / qualia nunc hominum producit corpora tellus" [899–900]). We are those modern mortals or could be; but the gulf that separates us from Turnus is almost unbridgeable. Even Turnus, called "hero" for the last time (*heros* [902]) just as he prepares to hurl this stone, could not complete his assault on his foe; we are capable of far less. Vergil invites our sympathy for Turnus even as he denies its efficacy.

2.

> ac velut in somnis, oculos ubi languida pressit
> nocte quies, nequiquam avidos extendere cursus
> velle videmur et in mediis conatibus aegri
> succidimus—non lingua valet, non corpore notae
> sufficiunt vires nec vox aut verba sequuntur: [. . .]. (12.908–12)

And just as in sleep, when sluggish quiet has pressed our eyes with night, we seem to want in vain to extend our eager running, and in the middle of our attempts, we fall, unwell; the tongue has no strength, and the familiar resources in the body are not sufficient, and neither word nor speech follows; [. . .].

Turnus's physical failure continues, and with it his mental agility disappears; he is like a dreamer trapped in a body over which he has no control. Vergil's vivid simile depicts verbally the interior landscape of a dreamworld, a world we can only imagine; yet as we do so, we enter the poem through first-person verbs ("velle videmur [. . .] / succidimus"), and Turnus's dream is ours. Here again, Vergil plays with focalization, shifting constantly from Turnus to Aeneas to us, so quickly that the different perspectives are hard to separate (Thomas, "Isolation" 290–91). The frame provided by the simile sends us back to Homer again, as we read the confrontation in the shadows behind and before this one, that of Achilles and Hector (*Il.* 22.199–201). Yet our inclusion in the simile radically alters the past; Homer placed both his heroes in the simile, as two men in a dream, but left his audience outside. In Vergil we stand with Aeneas and so share the double vision of Turnus and of Aeneas watching him. It is true, as Thomas notes (291), that we share here the point of view of the victim; equally suggestive, however, is the implication that this point of view is shared by the victor, too.

3.

> [. . .] miseri te si qua parentis
> tangere cura potest, oro (fuit et tibi talis
> Anchises genitor) Dauni miserere senectae
> et me, seu corpus spoliatum lumine mavis,
> redde meis.   (12.932–36)

> [. . .] If any concern for a wretched parent can touch you, I beg you (for such was your father Anchises to you), pity Daunus's old age and return me, or if you prefer, return my body deprived of the light of life to my people.

Turnus appeals to Aeneas as one son to another, summoning to Aeneas's mind the memory of his father, Anchises. The appeal suggests a close identification between the two men: they are more alike than they are dissimilar, motivated by the same basic emotions and understanding the same basic laws of civilized human nature. But Turnus's frame of reference immediately moves outside the poem and beyond these two men; the words "miseri [. . .] parentis / [. . .] cura" ("concern for a wretched parent") evoke first and foremost the plight of Priam, who in *Iliad* 24 seeks from Achilles the return of Hector's body for burial. Yet this echo is imprecise; Homer had given us a supplication to one man's son by another's father, while here it is to one son by another. Even in noting this contrast, however, we must correct ourselves: Aeneas, once a son, is a son no more but father to Ascanius and surrogate father to Pallas; and Turnus has no son on whose behalf to plead. Thus, Turnus is like both Hector and Priam, and again, like neither; and Aeneas is like both Achilles and Priam, and again, like neither. The shadows cast by the Homeric heroes ultimately do not fit the features of

Vergil's men; yet it is to this ostensible similarity that Turnus appeals and on which his life depends.

The impression of inexactness is underlined, at least temporarily, by Turnus's phrase "miseri te si qua parentis / tangere cura potest." Is the genitive *miseri parentis* to be interpreted objectively or subjectively? Is it the concern of Anchises for Aeneas that Turnus asks Aeneas to recall, or is it Aeneas's own love for his father that Turnus invokes? A third possibility presents itself—the care Aeneas might feel as surrogate father for Pallas. Vergil thus blurs our view of Aeneas again, suggesting that no one clear model can inform this hero's epic stature. Our evaluation of Turnus's plea and of Aeneas's response pulls us toward the *Iliad*, urges us to read its ending into this one; at the same time, the failure of the comparison becomes obvious under scrutiny. Turnus is not Hector, not Priam; Aeneas is not Achilles. The identities they determine for themselves as they are isolated from family and friends move outside the framework provided by the clear vision of Homer.

4.

Tune hinc spoliis indute meorum
eripiare mihi? Pallas te hoc vulnere, Pallas
immolat et poenam scelerato ex sanguine sumit.   (12.947–49)

Are you now to be taken from me here, clothed in the spoils of my people? Pallas offers you up with this wound, Pallas, and exacts the penalty from your defiled blood.

Aeneas's last words ring in Turnus's ears and in ours. The language of sacrifice Aeneas uses draws attention to the religious framework against which the Roman reader would have read this speech. But another, equally remarkable, phenomenon of language creates a blurred vision here: after his use of hyperbaton in the first sentence to establish an emphatic opposition between *tu* ("you") and *mihi* ("me"), we hardly expect Aeneas to replace himself as actor with the memory of the dead Pallas. Yet this is exactly what he does: Aeneas becomes Pallas, losing himself in his rage and wrath (*furiis et ira* [946]) as he asserts that it is Pallas who now acts; his repetition of Pallas's name (948) is an assertion of the transformation, a transformation that can transcend logic through language. This transformation again casts shadows, as for one last time we measure Pallas against Patroclus and Aeneas against Achilles. And these shadows give way to others in turn, when Turnus dies in the same terms used earlier in the poem to describe the despair of Aeneas (12.951 is similar to 1.92) and the death of Camilla (12.952 is the same as 11.831; see Putnam, *Poetry* 200–01; Anderson, *Art* 106). If we follow a recent suggestion made by Sarah Spence ("Polyvalence" 157), these shadows may have at least the hint of a divine cast as well: the Pallas in whose name Aeneas claims vengeance here also recalls by name Pallas Minerva, who at the very opening of the *Aeneid* (1.39–45) was mentioned by Juno as the wreaker of successful revenge on Oilean Ajax. In a nice instance of ring composition, then, the last act of revenge in the poem echoes the first described in it, through the emphatic repetition of the name Pallas. Yet this act of textual memory brings in its wake a sort of cognitive dissonance for us: however like the divine avenger Aeneas may unconsciously style himself, we see him overpowered here by an awareness not of divine insult but of human loss.

The bonds that unite Aeneas and Turnus transcend the usual limits of identity and even the difference between victory and loss: in asserting himself as Pallas's alter ego, Aeneas utters a self-fulfilling prophecy, and becomes, for the endless moment in which the poem ends, both victor and victim. Yet this understanding, it must be clear, belongs to us as readers, not to Aeneas; the backwards look that opens up this ending for us is closed to him in his isolation. Finally, as Turnus's soul departs to the Underworld, we move out of the frame of the poem into which we have been pulled by Vergil; ultimately we leave Aeneas standing alone.

This brief discussion shows some of the ways in which the epic identities of both men who confront each other at the end of the *Aeneid* are compromised. The concept of blurred vision describes the strange but inescapable sensation we have as we read this scene of seeing shadows cast over Aeneas and Turnus by other poems and other heroes. It also captures the odd sensation created by this scene that we are there, both trapped in Turnus's panic and observing it from Aeneas's point of view. The effect of all this blurring is profoundly destabilizing, emphasizing at once our emotional and intellectual experience of the scene as participants (*videmur*) and our physical experience as outsiders. Yet by the end of the book, a final radical transformation in the characters and in our relationship to them has occurred: drawn by his memory of Pallas's death (*saevi monimenta doloris / exuviasque* [945–46]), Aeneas is now pulled—as are we—into the emotional space left empty by the death of Turnus. As Turnus moves beyond the constraints of history, Aeneas assumes its burden and invites us to determine on whom next to bestow the baldric of Pallas. It has already sealed the fates of two great heroes; are we to imagine Aeneas himself wearing it and transmitting its legacy to his Roman descendants? For both Vergil and his readers, the century with which Roman republican history comes to its tormented conclusion might well be thought to bear the baldric's impression.

As a poet, Vergil has the power to engage us in and through his creative imagination; as readers, we have the power to respond. And as teachers, we have the opportunity to instill in our students a respect and love for both these processes, by beginning—but only beginning—a questioning in these students of what, and how, and why they read. I have illustrated here a few of the moments during Vergil's concluding scene in which such questioning is particularly fruitful; but like the end of the *Aeneid* itself, this questioning is only a beginning.

Vergil's Aeneas: The Best of the Romans

James J. Clauss

In the book *The Best of the Achaeans*, Gregory Nagy has drawn out the implications of an intriguing passage in the *Odyssey*, and the results of his discussion have been extremely important for our understanding of the hero in the ancient epic tradition. The passage in question is in book 8, lines 72–82. There, Homer reports the topic that the bard Demodocus sang at a banquet honoring Odysseus on the island of Phaeacia as follows:

> But when they had put from them the desire of food and drink, the Muse moved the minstrel to sing of the glorious deeds of warriors, from that lay the fame whereof had then reached broad heaven, even the quarrel of Odysseus and Achilles, son of Peleus, how once they strove with furious words at a rich feast of the gods, and Agamemnon, king of men, was glad at heart that the *best of the Achaeans* were quarrelling; for thus Phoebus Apollo, in giving his response, had told him that it should be, in sacred Pytho, when he passed over the threshold of stone to inquire of the oracle. For then the beginning of the woes was rolling upon Trojans and Danaans through the will of great Zeus.
>
> (*Od.* [Murray] 1: 263–65; emphasis mine)

Ancient commentators on the Odyssean passage tell us about the nature of this altercation: the two heroes were arguing over how Troy would be taken—by force (Achilles) or by stratagem (Odysseus). Because of the excellence each manifested in his characteristic mode of action, these heroes vied for the distinction of being called "the best" (*ho aristos* in Greek), which status each achieved in his respective epic.

The epithets used to characterize Achilles and Odysseus reflect their different approaches to action: Achilles's epithet, "swift-footed," focuses on a physical trait that is essential in the completion of his heroic feat; he chases Hector three times around the walls of Troy to force him into the decisive duel. Odysseus's epithet, "wily," underscores his ability to scheme, and in fact he devises and executes a number of different stratagems on his return to Ithaca and especially in his defeat of the suitors. Thus, in the *Iliad* Achilles is the best because of his physical strength; in the *Odyssey* Odysseus is the best because of his brilliant strategies. Moreover, each hero rises to his best in order to achieve a personal goal. Achilles kills the great warrior Hector as vengeance for the loss of his friend Patroclus, not because he wants to sack Troy (something he thought of giving up) or because of any Panhellenic sentiments; Odysseus is determined to regain his wife, child, and home.

In the *Argonautica*, the third century BC epic poet Apollonius of Rhodes redefined the nature of the hero to suit contemporary tastes and times. When the Argonauts meet for the first time on the beach at Pagasae prior to their departure for Colchis, Jason invites the men to choose the best man as leader of the expedition:

> But, my friends, our return back to Greece is a matter of common concern and our journey to the palace of Aeëtes is also of common concern. Accordingly, sparing no one's feelings, elect now the best man among you as leader. To him will fall the consideration of all the details: the initiation of conflicts and treaties with foreign peoples.   (1.336–40; Clauss 62)

Although the Argonauts immediately choose Heracles, deeming him best on the basis of his strength, Heracles himself refuses the responsibility and for a good reason. Jason asked not for the strongest man but for the one who could manage details, in particular the handling of conflicts and treaties with foreign peoples. Instead of a hero of strength or a hero of strategy, we find that the Argonautic hero is a hero of details, diplomacy, and, as we come to see, love. By featuring a limited and more realistic hero, whose epithet is "helpless" (*amēchanos*), the poet offers us the opportunity to see how an ordinary young man, though physically attractive and manipulative, might take on an adventure fit for a Heracles. Such a hero is presented as the best for an age that was losing confidence in, or at least touch with, the archaic heroic ideal. Like Achilles and Odysseus before him, Jason does not lay the foundation for, or serve the interests of, a new Panhellenic society. In fact, all he ever claims to want is to get the fleece and go home. For Aeneas, the situation is different.

Like the *Iliad*, *Odyssey*, and *Argonautica*, the *Aeneid* explores the nature of the hero, the best of the Trojans, as it were. But, in the context of a poem that so obviously retrojects first century BC values into a legendary past, the hero would more appropriately be called the best of the Romans. As seen in the three Greek epics, assignment of the term "the best" involves not merely identification of the hero but also, more important, the quality or means by which he achieves his goal and the nature of that goal. We should ask, then, in what way might Aeneas be called the best of the Romans.

Aeneas's epithet is "pious." Right away we encounter a major difference between the Greek and Roman hero. The Greek was distinguished by physical and intellectual traits; what characterizes Aeneas is an ethical quality: his piety or devotion to his family, gods, and country. From as early as the fourth century BC, as is evidenced by terra-cotta figurines, the Romans had a tradition that Aeneas personally carried his father and household gods out of Troy. So, when he introduces himself to his mother in disguise in book 1 as "pious Aeneas" ("I am pious / Aeneas, and I carry in my ships / my household gods together with me, rescued / from Argive enemies; my fame is known / beyond the sky. I seek out Italy, / my country, my ancestors born of Jove" [Mandelbaum 1.534–39; in Latin 378–80]), the poet has in mind this time-honored tradition. To us, the statement, based on Odysseus's claim "I am Odysseus, son of Laertes, who am known among men for all manner of wiles, and my fame reaches unto heaven. But I dwell in clear-seen Ithaca" (*Od.* [Murray] 1: 303; in Greek 9.19–21), comes across as odd, because Homeric heroes did not use their epithets in introducing themselves. Even if the statement is ironic, as some have argued, uttered by Aeneas to underscore that he feels, on the basis of his experiences, he has been devoted to no avail, it is nonetheless interesting, perhaps significant, that, like Jason in the *Argonautica* (1.336–40 above), Aeneas himself, a character in the epic, defines the nature of his heroic quality.

Book 2 is crucial in the evolution of Aeneas's heroic status in the epic. After the Trojan horse is brought within the walls of Troy, the Greeks pour out of it at night and proceed to sack the city. In the first of three supernatural appearances in the book, Hector comes to Aeneas in a dream, warning him to leave Troy. Vergil's choice to accentuate the gruesome disfiguring of Hector's body at the hands of Achilles and the other Greek warriors (2.268–79; cf. *Il.* 23.284–92, 367–75, 24.18–21) ignores Homer's statements that Aphrodite and Apollo had protected that body from physical defilement by Achilles (*Il.* 23.184–91; 24.18–21) and that, when Priam went to fetch his son's body, Hermes told him that it was clean and undecayed and that all its wounds were closed (*Il.* 24.411–23). Hector's ghastly appearance in the context of his words of warning underscores the impending destruction not only of Troy but even of the Homeric hero, who is now, contrary to tradition, encouraged to flee and, what is more, to assume the responsibility of establishing an empire.

> Ah, goddess born, take flight [. . .] and snatch
> yourself out of these flames. The enemy
> has gained the walls; Troy falls from her high peak.
> Our home, our Priam—these have had their due:

could Pergamus be saved by any prowess,
then my hand would have served. But Troy entrusts
her holy things and household gods to you;
take them away as comrades of your fortunes,
seek out for them the great walls that at last,
once you have crossed the sea, you will establish.
        (Mandelbaum 2.395–404; in Latin 289–95)

Aeneas's first reaction, however, is to fight and die for Troy; that is, he still instinctively thinks like a Homeric hero. So off he goes and engages in a disastrous battle with the Greeks, in the course of which his men don Greek armor. Not only does the ruse of wearing the enemy's armor backfire—as would not have been the case were Odysseus involved in the ploy—but also the ghostly image of Hector, which precipitated this course of action, calls to mind that the appropriation of another's armor can be inappropriate and even fatal. Following this unsuccessful skirmish, Aeneas wends his way to the palace of Priam and witnesses the pitiful death of the old king. This event is critical, because the death of Priam signals the death of Troy.

Moreover, the king's demise reminds Aeneas of his own father, Anchises, to whom he races back. On his way home, Venus appears to her son and reveals the gods at work in the destruction of Troy. She states:

My son, what bitterness has kindled this
fanatic anger? Why this madness? What
of all your care for me—where has it gone?
Should you not first seek out your father, worn
with years, Anchises, where you left him; see
if your own wife, Creusa, and the boy
Ascanius are still alive? [. . .] Look now—for I
shall tear away each cloud that cloaks your eyes
and clogs your human seeing [. . .] Son, be quick
to flee, have done with fighting. I shall never
desert your side until I set you safe
upon your father's threshold.
        (Mandelbaum 2.802–08, 836–39; in Latin 594–620)

The scene is based on Athena's assistance offered to Diomedes at *Iliad* 5.124–28.

Be of good cheer now, Diomedes, to fight against the Trojans, for in thy breast have I put the might of thy father, the dauntless might, such as the horseman Tydeus, wielder of the shield, was wont to have. And the mist moreover have I taken from thine eyes that afore was upon them, to the end that thou mayest well discern both god and man.

        (*Il.* [Murray] 1: 203–05)

There Athena intervenes to urge the Greek warrior to enter the fray and, by removing the cloud that obscures mortal vision, allows him to see and even attack the gods Aphrodite and Ares. Vergil's inversion of the Iliadic scene is striking. Venus's advice is not to engage the enemy but to flee; Diomedes's prowess in war, inherited from his father, drives the hero on, while Aeneas's fear for his father sends him away from the fight. Unlike Diomedes, Aeneas does not fight the gods but helplessly observes Neptune and Juno dismantle the walls of Troy.

When Aeneas eventually finds his father, Anchises refuses to go and chooses instead to stay and die. Aeneas states, "My father, had you thought I could go off and leave you here? Could such unholiness [*nefas*] fall from a father's lips?" (Mandelbaum 2.887–89; in Latin 657–58). Aeneas prepares to reenter the battle a second time, when an auspicious event occurs: a flame appears over the head of his son, Iulus, which Anchises recognizes as a sign that they should leave. Unfortunately, in their frantic passage out of the city, Aeneas's wife, Creusa, is lost and Aeneas goes back to find her. For a third time, the hero's immediate reaction is to return to battle, and he is about to do so, until Creusa, now dead, appears and reiterates his fated course of action:

> O my sweet husband, is there any use
> in giving way to such fanatic sorrow?
> For this could never come to pass without
> the god's decree; and you are not to carry
> Creusa as your comrade, since the king
> of high Olympus does not grant you that.
> Along your way lie long exile, vast plains
> of sea that you must plow; but you will reach
> Hesperia, where Lydian Tiber flows,
> a tranquil stream, through farmer's fruitful fields.
> There days of gladness lie in wait for you:
> a kingdom and a royal bride.
>   (Mandelbaum 2.1046–57; in Latin 776–84)

What we discover in the course of book 2 is that Aeneas did die during the sack of Troy but in a figurative sense: he died as a Homeric hero. That Vergil may have seen this experience as a kind of death is hinted at by the ghostly appearances of Hector and Creusa, which give this book its funereal quality. Unlike Achilles and Hector, Aeneas does not have the luxury to die brilliantly on the battlefield and thereby win eternal glory in the songs of the epic poets. Rather his heroic challenge is to survive and forgo personal satisfaction and glory for public service; in this epic, as in Roman political and social philosophy in general, the interests of the state surpass those of the individual. Subjugation of the self is the form of heroism that Aeneas must learn in his odyssey. Only in this way can he become the best of the Romans.

On his way toward Italy, he is diverted to Carthage, where he has a romantic encounter with the queen, Dido. As the relationship develops, the hero
appears to be settling into a new home and future, when Jupiter finally sends
Mercury with a message:

> Are you
> now laying the foundation of high Carthage,
> as a servant to a woman, building her
> a splendid city here? Are you forgetful
> of what is your own kingdom, your own fate?
> [. . . . .]
> remember
> Ascanius growing up, the hopes you hold
> for Iulus, your own heir, to whom are owed
> the realm of Italy and land of Rome.
> (Mandelbaum 4.353–57, 366–69; in Latin 265–76)

Like Odysseus on Circe's and later Calypso's island and like Jason on Lemnos
with Hypsipyle, Aeneas is temporarily derailed from his mission by his affair
with Dido. Through Mercury's intervention (in the *Odyssey* it was Hermes
who delivered the order from Zeus mandating the hero's release from
Calypso), the hero discovers that he must forsake not only personal glory but
also the right to seek personal relationships. Love and passion are simply no
longer his to choose. It is perhaps not insignificant that when Aeneas, despite
his strong feelings for Dido, refuses to entertain Anna's pleas to put off departure, Vergil calls him "hero" (4.447–48), one of only twenty-three times he does
so in the poem and only here in book 4. Given that the term is used by the poet
and not another character in the epic and that it applies to Aeneas as he makes
the painful decision to leave Dido and follow the will of Jupiter, I find its
appearance here not ironic, as some have suggested, but defining.

When Aeneas finally gets back on course, he eventually makes his way to Italy
and encounters death yet again, this time in his journey to and from the Underworld at Cumae. The differences between Odysseus's (*Od*. 11) and Aeneas's
(*Aen*. 6) Underworld experience reflect the difference in the lessons to be
learned from the dead. Odysseus discovers what he must do to get home safely
and appease Poseidon's anger; more significant, he discovers what death means.
He sees in the condition of his mother (an incorporeal form) and the statements
of Achilles (who would rather be the servant of a poor man than the king of the
Underworld) that death is a depressingly grim state, and yet he forgoes Calypso's
offer of immortality. His choice is truly heroic yet personal in that it involves only
himself and his family, and it is freely made—there are no infernal visitations
from his mother or messengers from Zeus compelling him to choose death over
immortality. Aeneas enters a different kind of hell. Vergil's vision of the Underworld, a combination of the Odyssean "Nekuia" and Plato's "Myth of Er" (fea-

tured at the end of the *Republic*), focuses on the public and not the personal task that the hero undertakes. When Aeneas goes to Elysium and meets his father, he sees not only the souls of his Greek and Trojan past but also, more important, those of the Roman future. Instead of discovering what he must do to save his life (as Odysseus did), Aeneas learns of his part in the future destiny of Rome and hears Anchises's message of social responsibility and manifest destiny:

> For other peoples will, I do not doubt,
> still cast their bronze to breathe with softer features,
> or draw out of the marble living lines,
> plead causes better, trace the ways of heaven
> with wands and tell the rising constellations;
> but yours will be the rulership of nations;
> remember, Roman, these will be your arts:
> to teach the ways of peace to those you conquer,
> to spare defeated peoples, tame the proud.
>   (Mandelbaum 6.1129–37; in Latin 847–53)

At the end of book 6, we learn that there are two gates of sleep that lead to the upper world from below: the one made of horn is for true shades; the other, of ivory, is for false dreams (6.893–96). The image is borrowed from Penelope's description of where dreams come from:

> For two are the gates of shadowy dreams, and one is fashioned of horn and one of ivory. The dreams that pass through the gate of sawn ivory deceive men, bringing words that find no fulfilment. But those that come forth through the gate of polished horn bring true issues to pass, when any mortal sees them.   (*Od.* [Murray] 2: 269; in Greek 19.562–67)

That Vergil has Aeneas come through the gate of ivory has long puzzled readers. We should recognize that Vergil did not need to incorporate the idea of the twin gates, inasmuch as he borrowed the image from a passage in the *Odyssey* that has nothing to do directly with Odysseus's journey to the land of the dead. So the poet is clearly problematizing Aeneas's departure from the Underworld. Given that Aeneas has now completely lost whatever personal goals he might have had or entertained, he is also in the process of losing that which makes him an individual; he is becoming more form (an icon of complete dedication) than flesh, a projection of *Romanitas* whose former self must now appear like a false dream. Rather than claim his humanity, as Odysseus did, Aeneas, in his journey to the land of the dead and subsequent rebirth as the founder of the Roman state, seals his transition from human being to public virtue and, beyond the conclusion of the epic, from mortal to god.

Once in Latium, Aeneas introduces himself to the local king, Latinus, who offers him the hand of his daughter, Lavinia. Aeneas is close to settling down and founding a new Troy, when Juno intervenes by sending the Fury Allecto to infect Amata, the king's wife, with hysteria and Turnus, Lavinia's erstwhile fiancé, with implacable anger. Allecto then directs Ascanius's dogs toward a sacred deer, whose death at the hands of the Trojan prince will prompt the skirmish that leads to all-out war. The slaughter of the deer recalls an important event at the beginning of Trojan War: the killing of the deer at Aulis that led to the sacrifice of Iphigeneia. The war is described in the second half of the *Aeneid*, in which the hero is cast in the role played by Achilles in the *Iliad*. I now turn to two elements that form part of this overarching allusion: Aeneas's new shield and the killing of Turnus.

After Hector stripped the body of Patroclus, who had fought in Achilles's armor, Achilles was at a loss as to how he might return to battle in order to avenge the slaughter of his close friend. Thetis asked Hephaestus to make him new armor, and Homer provides an elaborate description of the scenes on the shield in book 18 of the poem. The first scene establishes the setting for those that follow:

> Therein he wrought the earth, therein the heavens, therein the sea, and the unwearied sun, and the moon at the full, and therein all the constellations wherewith heaven is crowned—the Pleiades, and the Hyades and the mighty Orion, and the Bear, that men call also the Wain, that circleth ever in her place, and watcheth Orion, and alone hath no part in the baths of Ocean.   (*Il.* [Murray] 2: 323–25; in Greek 18.483–99)

The shield thus represents the entire world, particularized in the lines that follow by scenes of a city at war, a city at peace, and various images of daily life. In this way, the audience is encouraged to see the tragic events of several days in the tenth year of the Trojan War as a part of this larger frame of reference, one that is universal, not limited by race, time, or geography.

Vergil narrows the scope of the scenes that decorate his shield. Just as Achilles's mother, Thetis, asks Hephaestus for new armor for her son, so Venus, Aeneas's mother, asks her husband, Vulcan (the Roman equivalent of Hephaestus), to do the same for her son. The shield that Vulcan makes carries a representation not of the world but of Roman history from Romulus and Remus to Augustus's triple victory celebrated in 29 BC:

> For there the Lord of Fire had wrought the story
> of Italy, the Romans' victories, since he was not unskilled in prophecy
> or one who cannot tell the times to come.
> There he had set the generations of
> Ascanius, and all their wars, in order.
>   (Mandelbaum 8.810–15; in Latin 626–29)

The reactions that the heroes have to their new shields are also worth noting. The Myrmidons tremble at the sight of the armor:

Howbeit, when Achilles saw the arms, then came wrath upon him yet the more, and his eyes blazed forth in terrible wise from beneath their lids, as it had been flame; and he was glad as he held in his arms the glorious gifts of the god.   (*Il.* [Murray] 2: 337; in Greek 19.15–18)

When Aeneas picks up the shield, Vergil states:

Aeneas marvels at his mother's gift,
the scenes on Vulcan's shield; and he is glad
for all these images, though he does not
know what they mean. Upon his shoulder he
lifts up the fame and fate of his sons' sons.
(Mandelbaum 8.951–55; in Latin 729–31)

The sight of the shield elicits from Achilles the emotion that initiated the series of tragic events celebrated in the epic and that motivates the hero's actions—the overwhelming anger aroused by his personal losses. Moreover, he does not appear to make an attempt at interpreting the meaning of the scenes. Aeneas actually studies the engraved narrative on his shield, though he has no idea what it means. He implicitly and symbolically accepts the shield and the responsibility for the future of Rome that it foretells, and in this action he evinces his characteristic devotion to the rebirth of his nation. Comparison with the Iliadic model reveals that the sphere in which the Roman hero operates is considerably narrower than that of his Greek counterpart. Aeneas's actions are set not against the background of the whole world but as a necessary link in the predestined course of Roman history.

In his search for allies, Aeneas receives help from Evander, a Greek émigré from Arcadia, whose community lives at the site of the future Rome. In addition to giving him troops, Evander puts his son, Pallas, into Aeneas's care. But Pallas, like Patroclus, his model in the *Iliad*, will die at the hands of the hero's chief rival, Turnus, and the resulting duel between rivals will form the climax of the poem. In the *Iliad*, however, the death of Hector, while a climactic moment, is not the conclusion of the poem or of Achilles's anger, which the hero continues to exert even against the corpse of his fallen rival. It is only after Priam, Hector's father, goes to Achilles's tent to ransom his son's body and reminds Achilles of his own father that the celebrated anger abates. Vergil ends his epic with the battle between Turnus and Aeneas.

After the usual preliminaries to the duel are played out, Aeneas wounds Turnus in the thigh, but the wound is not fatal. Turnus, recognizing that he has lost the duel and the war, says:

I have indeed deserved this; I do not
appeal against it; use your chance. But if
there is a thought of a dear parent's grief

that now can touch you, then I beg you, pity
old Daunus—in Anchises you had such
a father—send me back or, if you wish,
send back my lifeless body to my kin.
For you have won, and the Ausonians
have seen me, beaten, stretch my hands; Lavinia
is yours; then do not press your hatred further.
(Mandelbaum 12.1242–51; in Latin 931–38)

With the memory of Achilles and Priam's conversation in mind, we might expect Aeneas to comply, especially since he has shown himself to be a respectful leader, humane person, and a son devoted to his father. And he begins to, for Vergil tells us, "Turnus' words began to move him more and more" (12.1254–55; 940–41). But then he see Pallas's belt, which Turnus stripped from the body of his dead comrade, and Vergil continues:

And when his eyes drank in this plunder, this
memorial of brutal grief, Aeneas,
aflame with rage—his wrath was terrible—
cried: "How can you who wear the spoils of my
dear comrade now escape me? It is Pallas
who strikes, who sacrifices you, who takes
this payment from your shameless blood." Relentless,
he sinks his sword into the chest of Turnus.
His limbs fell slack with chill; and with a moan
his life, resentful, fled to the Shades below.
(12.1262–71; 945–52)

In this final moment the hero's *pietas* is once again engaged; for the murder of Turnus is an act of devotion to Pallas's father, Evander, who had sent the following message to Aeneas after learning of his son's death:

[. . .] if I drag along my hated life
though Pallas now is dead, it is because
of your right hand—which, as you see, still owes
Turnus to father and to son. This is
the only thing that still is left undone
by your own worth and fortune. I do not
implore this joy of you for my own life —
that would be wrong—but that I may yet carry
these tidings to my son in the deep Shades. (11.231–39; 177–81)

Yet the killing of Turnus at this point is senseless. Turnus has conceded, and Aeneas has accordingly won. What then are we to make of this final act?

In the course of the epic, we have observed how Aeneas comes to relinquish his individual needs, wants, and emotions in the service of Rome. One might well ask if at this moment he is even capable of feeling his own wrath in the wake of the many experiences that have stripped him of the ability to make personal choices. The hero's words suggest that the answer is no: "It is Pallas / who strikes, who sacrifices you, who takes / this payment from your shameless blood." Unlike Achilles, who loses his closest friend and is furious with the one who killed him, Aeneas has lost not an intimate friend but a young man in his charge, whose father created a formal bond between himself and the Trojan hero. At the end of the poem, Vergil provides us with two views of Aeneas, separated by the sight of Pallas's belt: the Aeneas who still possesses a tenuous— and seemingly final—link with his former, more humane, self, the one who might spare Turnus, and the Aeneas who, forced to override every personal desire and inclination, kills Turnus, an incapacitated suppliant, in the dutiful and by now almost mechanical fulfillment of a perceived responsibility. The epic then comes to an abrupt stop, leaving us with the shocking yet poignant image of a hero who has crossed a personal threshold from which there will be no return. Following the trajectory of Aeneas's gradual and irrevocable loss of self, we might well conclude that the senseless slaughter of Turnus results not (though a more judicious reader might say, "results less") from the hero's own anger but ("than") from the *furor* and *ira* (in Latin 12.946) that rightly belong to Pallas and Evander. Achilles's anger ultimately abates after his encounter with Priam; he regains his humanity when he returns the body of a son to his father. By contrast, Aeneas loses his, in the course of learning to respond automatically and immediately to what he feels is his duty, irrespective of the cost. At the end of the *Iliad*, we know that Achilles will soon die in battle; at the end of the *Aeneid*, we see the spiritual death of Aeneas, who is forced to serve a future for reasons he never understands.

What then does it mean to be the best of the Romans? Achilles won personal fame because of his irresistible strength, Odysseus because of his unbeatable cunning, Jason because he was handsome and knew how to make deals with foreign women. In each case, the hero was deemed the best on the basis of his actions that reflected the kind of person he was. But Aeneas's experiences in the epic suggest that Aeneas achieves his defining heroic status when he succeeds in annihilating who he is, an honorable and humane prince of Troy, and becomes the personification of a concept, the concept that Romans throughout their history found so admirable and so inspiring in the working out of their manifest destiny: dedication to the family, to the gods, and most of all to the state.

The annals of Roman history offer many examples of soldiers and statesmen who subordinated and surrendered their lives to the *Res Publica* in a number of dramatic, sometimes questionable, ways, including obedience to orders at all costs, suicidal charges, and even the murder of one's own children, all in the name of Rome and *Romanitas*. In the *Aeneid*, Vergil magnified this idealized notion of the self-sacrificing Roman to epic proportions. Disquieted or even embarrassed by Aeneas's decision to kill Turnus, some have argued that the final scene reflects Vergil's negative or disapproving view of Aeneas and that this view in turn is an indirect criticism of Augustus, whom Vergil so clearly and closely links to his Trojan ancestor. If we change our focus slightly, and in place of negative or disapproving we view Aeneas's choice as quintessentially Roman and its result as tragic, we may more readily see that Vergil, neither subtly critical nor disappointingly sycophantic, as others have charged, has created an entirely new level on which to observe Roman *pietas*. While in other historical and legendary examples of self-immolation the result is typically physical death, Aeneas loses not his life but his individuality. As such, the *Aeneid* is the artistic representation of a collective ideation of the Roman national character, and Vergil's contribution to the ethical discourse on duty and responsibility constitutes the creation of a hero who is driven to relinquish his most intimate possession, his personal uniqueness, in the service of Rome, a choice as tragic for the individual as it is beneficial to the state. I could well imagine that Augustus refused to fulfill the poet's desire that the unfinished epic not survive the poet, not only because of the flattering references to the emperor and his family but particularly because he might have imagined his own experiences reflected in those of Aeneas—the surrender of a personal life, assumption of the responsibility for the survival of the Roman state, and the grim necessity to kill, even when he might have preferred to spare, in the name of duty.

Homer, *Pietas*, and the Cycle of Duels in *Aeneid* 10 and 12

Randall Colaizzi

Readers who encounter the *Aeneid* today often face an abridgement meant to fit the demands of a college literature survey: Troy, wanderings, Dido, the Underworld—the exotic Odyssean *Aeneid* of the first six books. The poem's second half, if read at all, might offer only scenes from book 8 (etiology and shield), Nisus and Euryalus from book 9, sometimes Camilla in book 11, Turnus's death at the end of the poem. But since the first cut in such selections usually includes most of the warfare, Vergil's subtlety (and difficulty) can be misunderstood, especially if the poem's close is to be considered. In the combat scenes, in particular a series of duels in *Aeneid* 10 and 12, the poet exchanges Homeric fatalism for Vergilian pathos by constructing scenes that develop the complexities of *pietas*. Vergil begins his poem with a paradox about this exchange:

> Tell me the reason, Muse: what was the wound
> to her divinity, so hurting her
> that she, the queen of gods, compelled a man
> remarkable for *goodness* [*pietate*] to endure
> so many crises, meet so many trials?
> Can such resentment hold the minds of gods?
> (Mandelbaum 1.13–18 [emphasis mine]; in Latin 8–13)

And as he begins the second half of his poem, he asks the muse Erato for her help, because, as he says,

> [. . .] I shall tell
> of dreadful wars, of men who struggle, tell
> of chieftains goaded to the grave by passion,
> of Tuscan troops and all Hesperia
> in arms. A greater theme is born for me; I try a greater labor.
> (7.50–55; 37–45)

This greater theme and labor of *Aeneid* 7–12 concern not only the difficulty of telling a story less wondrous than the Odyssean spectacle of *Aeneid* 1–6 but also the complications of further adapting a Homeric model.

A chain of three great deaths connects the narrative in the last third of Homer's *Iliad*: Sarpedon, Patroclus, Hector. Homer's line is direct: Sarpedon's death, the pinnacle of Patroclus's *aristeia*, leads to Patroclus's death, the climax of Hector's *aristeia*. Hector's death crowns Achilles's *aristeia* and all the battle scenes of the poem. Each death leads directly to the next; although we may account for divine interference, the antagonists are nevertheless well-matched and mature fighters. Vergil enlarges the series to six encounters and insists on inequality in his matchups. *Pietas* seemed a straightforward virtue, both to the reader and perhaps to Aeneas himself, in the first half of the poem: carrying Anchises through Troy's conflagration, leading the refugees through seven years of wandering, even abandoning Dido at a divine injunction. It now becomes a much more complicated ideal, not least because of these six pairings in books 10 and 12:

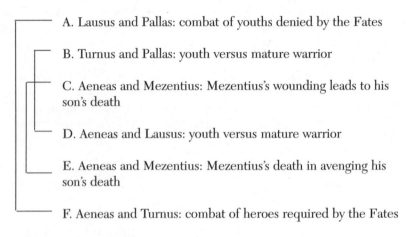

A. Lausus and Pallas: combat of youths denied by the Fates

B. Turnus and Pallas: youth versus mature warrior

C. Aeneas and Mezentius: Mezentius's wounding leads to his son's death

D. Aeneas and Lausus: youth versus mature warrior

E. Aeneas and Mezentius: Mezentius's death in avenging his son's death

F. Aeneas and Turnus: combat of heroes required by the Fates

A. Lausus and Pallas
(Mandelbaum 10.602–08; in Latin 433–38)

The characteristic Vergilian sympathy and the complications of *pietas* compel the poet to present the significant combatants of the poem engaged in overmatched fights. Thus the only equal match in the Vergilian series would have been the one that does not occur. Following Pallas's *aristeia* (501–92; 365–425) and the briefer description of Lausus's deeds (593–98; 426–33), the poet describes Pallas and Lausus:

> [. . .] both close in their years,
> and both most handsome; both denied by fortune
> return to their homelands. Nevertheless,
> the king of high Olympus did not let
> them duel; soon enough their fates await them,
> each fate beneath another, greater hand.   (603–08; 433–38)

Vergil thus makes clear that Jupiter himself favors this imbalance of fate. The Homeric "awareness of mortality, from which none in the *Iliad* is exempt" (Gransden, *Virgil's* Iliad 104) becomes instead a Vergilian problem of competing obligations when fighter meets fighter. The poet's troubling precision directs the reader's response into unexpected reactions. This device becomes all the more obvious when we recall Aeneas's entry into the warfare of book 10:

> Aeneas is the first to attack the Italians and produce an omen of victory by killing Theron (310ff.) [Mand. 10.430-34]. As he continues forward, six more victims of his prowess fall, variously wounded. Vergil describes each killing realistically, but dispassionately, so that we appreciate Aeneas' valor and success without feeling great sympathy for the fallen.
>
> (Anderson, *Art* 82)

In the ensuing duels, there is no such lovely, sad balance of Pallas and Lausus, and no such plain, heroic glory of Aeneas and Theron.

B. Turnus and Pallas
(Mandelbaum 10.609-702; in Latin 439–509)

The first actual combat of this series sets up *pietas* as a problematic virtue, which will be examined with increasing complexity in the following five encounters. The poet marks this first example in two ways. First, he comments on Turnus's behavior: "O mind of man that does not know the end / or further fates, nor how to keep the measure / when we are fat with pride at things that prosper!" (690–92; 501–02). Second, he separates this duel from the other major ones with a long series of lesser encounters. This duel makes a clear contrast with the match between Pallas and Lausus that never takes place. Turnus's sister urges Turnus to attack Pallas; in response he orders his allies to stop fighting, claiming that "[. . .] I alone / meet Pallas; he is owed to me, my own. / I could have wished his father here to watch" (613–15; 441–43). The inaccuracy of his perception matches the impious nature of his remarks; Aeneas, not Pallas, should be Turnus's objective. Though overmatched, Pallas nevertheless faces Turnus bravely and piously (617–25; 444–51). In all the mismatches, the doomed combatant makes the first cast; in all the mismatches, the doomed combatant also demonstrates his *pietas*. Pallas's prayer to his patron, Hercules (638–43; 460–63), offers a pious contrast to Turnus's behavior; his sad death after his *aristeia* recalls the death of Patroclus after his *aristeia* (*Il.* 16). Patroclus's greatest feat is his killing of Sarpedon, son of Zeus—to prevent which (even though it is destined [*Il.* 16.433]) Zeus considers stealing his son from the fighting; Zeus must be dissuaded by Hera. She states the gods' opposition to rescuing a doomed mortal (16.442–43) and suggests that Death and Sleep remove Sarpedon's body to Lycia for "due burial / with tomb and gravestone. Such is the privilege of those who have perished" (*Il.* [Lattimore] 16.456–57). Zeus weeps tears of blood (459) at the thought of Sarpedon's coming death, which is a major event in the *Iliad* for two reasons: First, [Sarpedon] is Zeus' son and provides a test case as to whether Zeus will go so far as to save him from death. But human mortality, in this tragic epic, is stronger than the power of the gods. Secondly, Sarpedon's death carries a further tragic irony in that he dies at the hands of Patroclus, who is himself doomed, the last victim of the death-littered promise of Zeus to Thetis—the greatest and most fatal act of Hector's *aristeia*.

(Gransden, Virgil's Iliad 141–42).

In the *Aeneid*, Hercules, another son of Zeus-Jupiter, reacts to Pallas's prayer with "tears that were useless"; Jupiter then consoles his son:

> Each has his day; there is, for all, a short,
> irreparable time of life; the task
> of courage: to prolong one's fame by acts
> [. . . . .]
>   [. . .] even great Sarpedon,
> my own child, lost his life together with them.
> And Turnus, too, is called by his own fates;
> he has reached the border given to his years.
>   (Mandelbaum 10.648–50, 652–55; in Latin 467–72)

Although Vergil's Jupiter expresses Iliadic sentiments here (and takes Hera's place as the comforting deity), his reaction is not the painful and fated powerlessness of a divinity to save his own son but an acknowledgment of the limitations of *pietas*. Vergil's Hercules complicates this allusion to Homer. Rather than mourn because he cannot save his own son (the Iliadic example), he grieves because he cannot save the pious son of Evander (the son of Mercury), to whom he owes, and who owes to him, a debt of *pietas* for his stay in Evander's settlement (narrated in book 8).

Pallas's high point in battle is grazing Turnus on the first spear cast; Turnus's lance pierces the center of Pallas's shield and kills Pallas immediately (656–75; 474–89). With sarcastic magnanimity, with mock *pietas*, Turnus returns Pallas's body for funeral rites after removing Pallas's belt; he will later request from Aeneas just such a return of his own corpse. This scene thus makes two important thematic allusions to the *Iliad*: Jupiter's more cosmic Vergilian remarks enlarge on Zeus's personal Homeric grief, and the stripping of Pallas recalls the stripping of Patroclus—with similar dangers for the victor. In this first duel, which Turnus wins, Jupiter foretells the last, which Turnus will lose. Above the fallen Pallas, harshly noting what Evander has scarcely "deserved" (*qualem meruit*) and addressing the Arcadians, Aeneas's new allies, Turnus refers by name to Aeneas, mocking both his victim's father and his victim:

> O Arcadians,
> remember, take my words back to Evander:
> just as he has deserved, I send him Pallas!
> Whatever comfort lies in burial
> I freely give. His welcome to Aeneas
> will not have cost your King Evander little.
> (676–81; 491–95)

He then immediately strips the belt.

Fallen later before Aeneas, humbly noting what he truly deserves (*merui*) and addressing Aeneas, Turnus refers by name to the Ausonians, Aeneas's future allies, invoking the victor's father—and the victim's:

> Then humble, suppliant, he lifts his eyes
> and, stretching out his hand, entreating, cries:
> "I have indeed deserved this; I do not
> appeal against it; use your chance. But if
> there is a thought of a dear parent's grief
> that now can touch you, then I beg you, pity
> old Daunus—in Anchises you had such
> a father—send me back or, if you wish,
> send back my lifeless body to my kin."
> (12.1240–48; 930–36)

Aeneas then immediately notices the stripped belt.

Aeneas's frenzied response to Pallas's death—killing many who stand between him and Turnus—draws to a narrative close only with the poet's interlude in which Juno wins a concession from Jupiter. This interlude allows Vergil to postpone the Aeneas-Turnus duel and enables him first to arrange the other major encounters. It also begins the most intense period of Aeneas's *aristeia*, which will have its climax in Turnus's death in the poem's very last line. Throughout the series of lesser combats leading to the four remaining matches of book 10, Aeneas responds bitterly to claims of *pietas* before killing ten named warriors (10.717–827; 521–605). This long section isolates the Turnus-Pallas encounter from the series; involving Aeneas, Mezentius, and Lausus, it responds to that encounter. With these incidents, most of which have significant Homeric precedents, Vergil shows Aeneas reacting darkly to the troubles offered to one so *pius*; these tests will make his encounters with Mezentius and Lausus even more emotionally complex.

Because Turnus does not pursue Aeneas, because Jupiter grants to Juno "a breathing space for that doomed youth" (856; 623), the two great antagonists do not meet until the poem's end. Turnus's response to the invasion is to seek Pallas (not Aeneas) alone. Aeneas, however, responds to Pallas's death by seeking Turnus. He "grabs four youths alive, / four sons of Sulmo, then four raised by Ufens, / to offer up as victims to the Shade / of Pallas" (713–16; 517–19). These eight sons of Sulmo and Ufens recall Achilles's capture of twelve youths to offer to Patroclus's shade (*Il*. 21.26), but Vergil works significant changes on the deed. Achilles's victims are unnamed; Homer comments repeatedly on his cruelty and the terror of the twelve victims, adding the piteous detail of their belts:

> He, when his hands grew weary with killing,
> chose out and took twelve young men alive from the river
> to be vengeance for the death of Patroklos, the son of Menoitios.
> These, bewildered with fear like fawns, he led out of the water
> and bound their hands behind them with thongs well cut out of leather,
> with the very belts they themselves wore on their ungirt tunics [. . .]
> (*Il*. [Lattimore] 21.26–31)

Four complete books (about 2,400 lines, nearly one-sixth of the poem), separate Patroclus's death from Achilles's actions here. In the meantime Achilles has killed many men and faced in battle both Aeneas and Hector, who were saved by Poseidon and Apollo, respectively. Vergil is more immediate: as soon as Aeneas hears that Pallas has died, he captures his victims.

Homer's episode of the captives precedes the story in which Lykaon supplicates Achilles, reminding him that he has already captured and ransomed him handsomely. Lykaon proclaims that he is not from the same womb as Hector, "who killed your powerful and kindly companion" (21.93–96). Achilles refuses the request because Patroclus is dead—and because Achilles too will die (110). He then tells all before him to die, in payment for Patroclus and the "slaughter of the Achaians / whom you killed beside the running ships when I was not with them" (122–35). Thus the only scene of captured prisoners in the *Iliad* precedes a noteworthy denial of pity to a suppliant.

The only scene of captured prisoners in the *Aeneid* also precedes a denial of *pietas* to a suppliant, but Vergil compresses these longer Homeric episodes to a horrifying concentration, only a few lines after Pallas's death. The twelve unnamed youths seized by Achilles in the *Iliad* become the eight sons of two named fathers in the *Aeneid*. The Vergilian suppliant Magus, as the Homeric Lykaon does, refers to the wealth he can offer his captor. But Vergil adds the demands of *pietas*, both when Magus appeals and Aeneas sarcastically refuses:

> He grips Aeneas' knees and, suppliant,
> he begs him: "By your father's Shade and by
> your hopes in rising Iülus, I entreat,
> do spare this life for my own son and father.
> I have a splendid house; there, hidden deep,

are many talents of chased silver; I
have heaps of wrought and unwrought gold; the victory
of Trojans cannot turn on me; one life
will not make such a difference"—so Magus.
Aeneas answered him: "Those heaps of talents,
the gold and silver that you tell of, Magus,
save them for your own sons; such bargaining
in war was set aside by Turnus first,
just now when he killed Pallas. This is what
Anchises' Shade decides, and so says Iülus."
(10.721–35; 521–34)

When Vergil adapts Achilles's remarks about Patroclus and applies them to the
avenging of Pallas, Aeneas refers not to himself but to Anchises and Iulus. For
Lykaon's claimed nonconnection to Hector, Vergil substitutes Magus's claimed
irrelevance to the battle. But his pretext recalls the sacrifice of Palinurus in
book 5, when Poseidon says, "one life will be offered for many" (5.1077; "*unum
pro multis dabitur caput*" [815; emphasis mine]): "the victory [. . .] cannot turn
on me; one life / will not make such a difference" (10.727–29; "non hic victoria [. . .] vertitur aut *anima una dabit* discrimina tanta" [529; emphasis mine]).
Thus all three changes wrought on the Lykaon episode emphasize *pietas*: the
appeal in the names of father and son, the practical reason offered for sparing
("one life will not make a difference"), and the rejection in the names of father
and son. *Pietas* toward Evander prompts Aeneas's capture of the sons of Sulmo
and Ufens and the rejection of Magus; the death of Evander's son immediately
moves Aeneas to destroy two remarkable families and claim his own family in
denying a suppliant. And although he chases Turnus, before they meet he
must, in his major combats, first wound a father (Mezentius), kill the son
defending him (Lausus), and then kill the father.

Yet Aeneas's cruel rejections (and claims) of *pietas* in all these scenes have
an end that is not merely an emotional response to Pallas's death (Achilles's
response to the death of Patroclus is merely emotional):

Such were the deaths dealt by the Dardan chieftain
across the plains while he raged like a torrent
or black whirlwind. The boy Ascanius
and all the warriors break out at last
and quit their camp site; now the siege is pointless.
(828–32; 602–05)

This too is *pietas*, in the relentless way in which Vergil arranges his narrative.
Aeneas's actions have saved his threatened son and the other besieged Trojans.
The darker necessities of this quality prepare the reader for the remaining
duels, in every one of which Aeneas prevails.

C. Aeneas and Mezentius
(Mandelbaum 10.1047–84; in Latin 762–88)

One-fifth of book 10 intervenes between the death of Pallas and Aeneas's first meeting with Mezentius. This "cruel despiser of the gods" (7.855; 648) is nonetheless "spurred on by Jupiter," (10.943; 689). His *aristeia* lasts for more than a hundred lines before Aeneas meets him. Evander told Aeneas the story of Mezentius's cruel nature and the shelter given Mezentius by Turnus (8.626–45; 481–96); thus long before Allecto inflamed him (7.603–21; 456–70) and thereupon added a divine explanation for his behavior, Turnus welcomed and protected Mezentius. The expulsion of Mezentius recalls, in its language and imagery, Evander's earlier instructive tale told to Aeneas: Hercules's defeat of the monster Cacus (8.248–350; 184–272), around whose cave "The ground was always warm with recent slaughter / and fastened to the proud doorposts, the faces / of men hung pale with putrefaction" (8.259–61; 195–97). As Hercules once piously saved Evander's people, so now must Aeneas: "in just anger." Only Turnus has a greater buildup than Mezentius as an enemy to Aeneas.

Aeneas's two encounters with Mezentius (C, E) frame his meeting with Lausus (D), and although the Aeneas-Lausus duel answers the Turnus-Pallas fight (B), the entire cluster of meetings with Mezentius and Lausus (CDE) provides a complex answering episode to Turnus and Pallas. In B, Turnus wishes impiously for Pallas's father to watch the death of his son (10.615; 443); in CDE, Mezentius helps cause (C), must suffer (D), and then atones for (E) the death of his own son. The Mezentius cluster also anticipates the final duel with Turnus (F), especially in the way both Mezentius and Turnus face Aeneas in the end.

Mezentius stands "unfrightened, steady, and awaiting his / great-hearted enemy" (10.1059–60; 770–71). Just as he gave to his son, Lausus, the spoils from an earlier victory (960–62; 700–01), so he claims, in an ironic perversion of *pietas*, that he will win Aeneas's armor for his son:

> My own right hand, which is my god, and this
> my shaft that I now poise to cast, be gracious:
> I vow that you yourself, Lausus, my son,
> shall be the living trophy of Aeneas,
> dressed in the spoils stripped from that robber's body.
> (1062–66; 772–76)

Turnus stripped Pallas; Aeneas will not be stripped, nor will he strip Lausus. Mezentius's javelin misses, as do all the first casts in this series, but Aeneas, called *pius* as he throws, wounds Mezentius in the groin, at which sight "Lausus, for the love of his dear father / groaned deep" (1067, 1076, 1085–86; 777, 783, 789–90). The son, who must watch his father suffer, becomes the victim of a reluctant Aeneas; Aeneas is the mirror opposite of Turnus, who wished his victim's father present to see his son's death.

D. Aeneas and Lausus
(Mandelbaum 10.1085–141; in Latin 789–832)

Vergil prompts the reader to pay special attention to this episode by his address of Lausus:

> And here I surely shall not leave untold—
> for such a deed can be more readily
> believed because it was done long ago—
> the trial of your harsh death and gallant acts
> and you yourself, young man to be remembered.
>
> (1087–91; 791–93)

This duel completes the arc from A (Pallas and Lausus) to D (Aeneas and Lausus). A more complicated nexus of *pietas* can scarcely be found in the entire *Aeneid*: Mezentius, repellent torturer who scorns the gods but loves his son, is defended by that splendid boy; Aeneas, *pius* defender of Mezentius's people, upbraids the son for his *pietas* but easily dispatches him:

> [. . . Aeneas] taunts Lausus, menacing:
> "Why are you rushing to sure death? Why dare
> things that are past your strength? Your loyalty [*pietas*]
> has tricked you into recklessness." And yet
> the youth is wild and will not stop; at this,
> harsh anger rises in the Dardan chief;
> the Fates draw the last thread of Lausus' life.
>
> (1112–18; 810–15)

The contrast with B is telling: Turnus desired only to kill Pallas; Aeneas attempts to dissuade Lausus from battle. Turnus wanted Pallas's father to witness his son's death; Aeneas kills Lausus nearly in front of Mezentius but unwillingly. Pallas wounds Turnus slightly (the only defeated combatant to wound his killer); Lausus dies with no real attempt on Aeneas.

Although (in A) Vergil regards Pallas and Lausus as equals and although Lausus is "such a bulwark in that battle" (593; 427), the balance of greatness tips somewhat to Pallas. While Lausus has only one named victim, Abas (595; 427), Pallas has a detailed *aristeia* (501–92; 362–425) with eight victims named; he urges his men to "attack where the mass is thickest" (515; 373). The parallel between Pallas and Patroclus is clear: both are killed after an *aristeia*, both have close ties to the hero, both are stripped of their armor, and both provide an added incentive for the hero's rage. Even though Pallas is called a "youth" at the beginning of B (617; 445), nothing subsequent to this word detracts from his status as a warrior. He faces Turnus calmly; dismisses his threats; hopes for the greatest Roman military prize, the armor of the opposing general (*spolia opima*); prays to Hercules ("let his dying eyes see me a conqueror"); and dies, pierced in his "enormous chest" (625, 623, 642, 670; 450, 449, 462, 485).

In contrast, Vergil reduces everything about Lausus. He never answers or challenges Aeneas: "the youth is wild and will not stop" (1116; 813). Though he dies almost in his father's presence, the details are softer, smaller, gentler, and feminine:

> The blade passed through the shield, too thin
> for one who was so threatening, and through
> the tunic Lausus' mother spun for him
> of supple gold. His chest was filled with blood;
> across the air his melancholy life
> passed on into the Shades and left his body.
> But when he saw the look and face of dying
> Lausus—he was mysteriously pale—
> Anchises' son sighed heavily with pity [. . .].
> (1121–29; 817–23)

Lausus's pallor recalls two women in the poem, Dido and Cleopatra, both "pale with approaching death" (4.891; 644) (8.925; 709). No challenge is made, no weapon is cast; even his armor is "thin." His "supple gold" tunic brings his mother into the picture. Only after death—when brought by his comrades back to his father, not when he must face the hero of the *Aeneid*—does Lausus become "a giant corpse undone / by giant wounds" (10.1154–55; 842). Only after death, when brought by his comrades back to his father, will Pallas be softened:

> They set
> the soldier high upon his rustic bed:
> just as a flower of gentle violet
> or drooping hyacinth a girl has gathered;
> its brightness and its form have not yet passed,
> but mother earth no longer feeds it or
> supplies its strength. And then Aeneas brought
> twin tunics, stiff with gold and purple, which
> Sidonian Dido, glad in that task, had
> once made for him with her own hands [. . .].
> (11.88–97; 62–75)

Turnus stripped Pallas (B), and in mock magnanimity boasted to the Arcadians (above, section B). Aeneas refuses to strip Lausus, and in genuine magnanimity proclaims:

> *Poor boy* [*miserande puer*], for such an act what can the pious
> Aeneas give to match so bright a nature?

Keep as your own the arms that made you glad;
and to the Shades and ashes of your parents
I give you back—if Shades still care for that.
But, luckless, you can be consoled by this:
you fall beneath the hand of great Aeneas.
             (10.1132–38; 825–30; emphasis mine)

His words recall the words of his own father in the Underworld; Anchises
praises the shade of Marcellus, the emperor Augustus's designated successor
and son-in-law, who died young: "*O boy whom we lament* [*miserande puer*]
[. . .]" (6.1177; 882; emphasis mine). Vergil uses the phrase only one more time,
when he addresses the dead Pallas, paying him "useless honors" (11.69; 52)
before returning his body to Evander. Thus the phrase, spoken only by Aeneas
and his father, makes a final link between Pallas and Lausus. Turnus defiled the
dead Pallas ("his left foot pressed upon the body" [10.682]); Aeneas acts quite
differently: "He even calls the hesitating comrades / of Lausus, and he lifts the
body off / the ground, where blood defiled the handsome hair" (1139–41;
830–32).

E. Aeneas and Mezentius
(Mandelbaum 10.1198–1247; in Latin 872–908)

With his son's death, the worst villain of the poem grows somewhat in stature—
just in time to die:

Am I, a father, saved by these your wounds?
Do I live by your death? For now at last
I understand the misery of exile,
and now at last my wound is driven deep.
More, I myself have stained your name, my son,
with sins; for I was banished—hated—from
the throne and royal power of my fathers.
I owed my homeland and my angry people
their right revenge; I should have given up
this guilty life to death from every side.
But I still live, have still not left the light
of day, the land of men. But I shall leave them.
             (1163–74; 848–56)

With the possible exception of Dido, Mezentius might be the most introspec-
tive character of the poem—at least in facing death. Episode E (the effect)
forms a frame (with C, the cause) around the scene of Lausus's death (D).
     Aeneas welcomes the chance to face Mezentius, but Vergil has again

adjusted the view of the reader. Mezentius's words are brave, subdued, impious still, blunt. Aeneas becomes, in this scene, the harsher one:

> You savage one, why try to frighten me
> now that my son is torn away? That was
> the only way to ruin me. For I
> do not fear death or care for any god.
> Enough; I come to die. But first I bring
> these gifts to you.   (1205–10; 878–82)

As in all the unsuccessful duels (except for the duel of Lausus, who never casts), the wounded Mezentius throws first and misses three times. The contest is "unequal" (1221) not because Mezentius is wounded and thus threatened but because he is on horseback and thus favored. Only in this respect, and in this instance alone, does Aeneas suffer any disadvantage during these combats.

Mezentius is the first of the fallen combatants to address his victor. Aeneas taunts, with a lower tone:

> "Where now is brave Mezentius, and where is
> his ruthless force of mind?" The Tuscan drank
> the air and watched the sky and came to life
> and then replied: "My bitter enemy,
> why do you taunt and threaten me? There is
> no crime in killing me; I did not come
> to war with any thought of quarter, nor
> did Lausus ever draw such terms with you.
> I ask you only this: if any grace
> is given to the vanquished, let my body
> be laid in earth. I know my people's harsh
> hatred that hems me in. I beg of you
> to save me from their fury, let me be
> companion to my son within the tomb."
>   (1232–45; 897–906)

If earlier he recalled to the reader Achilles (where Achilles addresses his horse; cf. Achilles's address to Xanthos [*Il.* 19.400–23] with Mezentius's address to Rhoebus [1181–89; 861–66]), here Mezentius, anticipating Turnus at the end of the poem, recalls Hector in asking for burial though not for mercy (*Il.* 22.338– 43). His final words, driven by *pietas*, consider his son. His taunting, "savage," "bitter enemy" makes no reply; Aeneas's *pietas* (to Evander and the allied Etruscans) is in sacrificing Mezentius: "with full awareness, / he gives his throat up to the sword, and pours / his life in waves of blood across his armor" (1246–48; 907–08). Mezentius's death closes the book without response from Aeneas; Turnus's death will so end book 12. In each case the poet deprives the reader of the hero's response to his deed; only with Lausus does Aeneas respond. With the long interlude of book 11, which concentrates on the side story of Camilla, and with the expanse of book 12, the poem's longest book, nearly one-fifth of the poem intervenes before Aeneas will face the final duel with Turnus. But the difficulties of that encounter have been prepared by the events of *Aeneid* 10: "In his first day of hard combat, Aeneas has displayed the complex qualities—sanity, valor, strength, hot indignation, cruelty, pitilessness, compassion (not all, by any means, lovely virtues in isolation)—which are demanded of a victorious general" (Anderson, *Art* 75).

F. Aeneas and Turnus
(Mandelbaum 12.1178–271; in Latin 908–52)

This is no place for an extended discussion of the poem's ending; let me merely connect that scene with the preceding series of fights. The final duel of the poem recalls not only the Homeric precedents—the deaths of Sarpedon, Patroclus, and Hector—but also the previous series of combats in the tenth book. Aeneas and Turnus (F), the matched heroes whose duel the Fates demand, balance Pallas and Lausus (A), the matched youths whose duel Jupiter forbids. In this contest Turnus pays for his actions in B; Aeneas himself makes Pallas the victor:

> How can you who wear the spoils of my
> dear comrade now escape me? It is Pallas
> who strikes, who sacrifices you, who takes
> this payment from your shameless blood.
> (1265–68; 947–49)

Like Mezentius (C), Turnus misses his cast, a rock, and receives a wound, in the thigh (1208, 1235). Although Aeneas's conduct toward the dead Lausus (D) seems to anticipate his conduct toward the suppliant Turnus (F), he finally acts instead as he did toward Mezentius (E). Mezentius and Turnus both admit defeat, though with a different emphasis: Mezentius the father asks only burial with his dead son; Turnus invokes his living father in requesting mercy:

> I have indeed deserved this; I do not
> appeal against it; use your chance. But if
> there is a thought of a dear parent's grief
> that now can touch you, then I beg you, pity
> old Daunus—in Anchises you had such
> a father—send me back or, if you wish,
> send back my lifeless body to my kin.
> (1242–48; 931–36)

In Vergil's tone, *pietas* reduces Pallas from warrior (B) to child. The sight of "the luckless belt of Pallas, of the boy / whom Turnus had defeated" (1257–58; 941–44) brings to mind the "dear parent's grief" of Evander, whom Turnus desired as witness to Pallas's death. Invoked by Turnus to gain clemency, parental grief demands from Aeneas retribution.

Yet Vergil imposes a disquieting perspective. In every previous duel the reader's sympathy at some point turns toward the victim: to Pallas (B), because of his bravery and Turnus's arrogance; to Lausus (D), out of pity for his youth— and because Aeneas rewards his sacrifice; to Mezentius (E), when he offers his neck to the sword. With Turnus at the poem's close, Vergil literally changes the reader's viewpoint with the poem's final simile. When Turnus fails in his cast, he

> [. . .] does not know if it is he
> himself who runs or goes or lifts or throws
> that massive rock; his knees are weak; his blood
> congeals with cold. The stone itself whirls through
> the empty void but does not cross all of
> the space between; it does not strike a blow.
> Just as in dreams of night, when languid rest
> has closed *our* eyes, *we* seem in vain to wish
> to press on down a path, but as *we* strain,
> *we* falter, weak; *our* tongues can say nothing,
> the body loses its familiar force,
> no voice, no word, can follow [. . .].
> (1203–14; 903–12; emphasis mine)

Even this unsettling shift to the first-person plural may have a Homeric precedent modified by Vergil. The most singular and egotistical of the Iliadic heroes, Achilles, responds to the fallen Hector:

> Hektor, surely you thought as you killed Patroklos you would be
> safe, and since I was far away you thought nothing of me,
> o fool, for an avenger was left, far greater than he was,
> behind him and away by the hollow ships. And it was I;
> and I have broken your strength.   (*Il.* [Lattimore] 22.331–35)

Not only does he reject Hector's entreaty "by your life, by your knees, by your parents" (338) for burial, he also gives the final expression of how personal is this combat: "I wish only that my spirit and fury would drive me / to hack your meat away and eat it raw for the things / that you have done to me" (346–48). After this statement comes the astounding change in Achilles's words, from the raging first-person singular to the plural:

> But now, you young men of the Achaians, let *us* go back, singing
> a victory song, to *our* hollow ships; and take this with *us*.

We have won *ourselves* enormous fame; *we* have killed the great Hektor whom the Trojans glorified as if he were a god in their city.

(391–94; emphasis mine)

Homer's plurals after the death of Hector mark Achilles's complete and momentous return to his society; the reader regards Achilles differently (and Achilles could be said to regard himself somewhat differently). Vergil's plurals before the death of Turnus likewise force the reader to regard Aeneas differently.

This dream simile recalls the stunned and dreamlike state of Patroclus just before Hector kills him (*Il.* 16.786–92)—a blurring of Hector and Patroclus in Turnus's actions, like the blurring of Patroclus and Sarpedon in Pallas. But Vergil once more changes the Homeric orientation:

> For this last long simile in his poem Vergil once again invents a radical transformation of his model. Homer is interested, in the simile, in emphasizing the all but equal strength and valor of his two opposing figures, and if there is a slight imbalance in this near equilibrium, it is to be discovered in the frustrations of the pursuer who dreams, not with the pursued. I say "dreams" because the equilibrium that obtains between the pursuer and the pursued, while it may be frustrating and unpleasant for the pursuer, does not become horrible. Homer's dream is not a nightmare, as it might be if it were the pursued who was dreaming. In Vergil's simile, of course, it is the pursued who dreams, and his dream is one of the great nightmares of poetry; this nightmare is a suitable recapitulation of what has immediately preceded it, and is a transition to, and adumbration of, the closing moments of the poem, for both the nightmare and the closing action of the poem are presented from the viewpoint of Turnus. So it is fitting that his growing terror, his despair, and his sudden and final inability to act should be crystallized in this simile.
>
> (Johnson, *Darkness* 97–98)

The simile also means that when Turnus "trembles at the coming spear" (12.1220; 916) the reader, who has been drawn literally into Turnus's perspective because of such "dreams of night," looks up helplessly at Aeneas's threatening spearpoint. "We" who have weighed all the demanding requirements of *pietas* in the preceding five duels, "falter, weak" and feel directed at us the *pietas* of Aeneas's final savagery. This perspective proves even more stunning because of the changing expectations aroused in the previous combats.

NOTE

I dedicate this essay in memoriam to Barbara Fowler, who first taught me how to read Latin poetry. I am indebted to William S. Anderson, Lorina Quartarone, and Michael Kandel for their comments and suggestions.

Vergil's *Aeneid* and the Evolution of Augustus

Michael C. J. Putnam

There are few masterpieces of literature for which historical background is more important as an aid to interpretation than Vergil's *Aeneid*, and few for which that background is more intricate and controversial. On the surface of the poem we are engaged with the adventures of Aeneas, a prominent figure in the *Iliad*, adventures that take him and us from the moment of Troy's demise through some seven years of wandering on the way to landfall in Italy, where he battles his way to supremacy over native rulers. In other words Vergil offers us a variation of the *Odyssey* followed by a reprise of the *Iliad*, with the difference that we move over the course of epic time to Latium and to the site of future Rome. A Roman contemporary of Vergil, who was writing his epic during the 20s BCE, would calculate its events as having occurred a millennium earlier, that is, some three hundred years before the founding of the city, which conventional tradition places at 753 BCE.

But Vergil complicates such facile distancing in ways both general and specific. It is a salient part of his larger intellectual schema to have his readers view the action of the last half of the epic as encapsulating a civil war. We begin with the challenge Aeneas's arrival brings to King Latinus and to Turnus, who considers himself betrothed to Aeneas's destined wife, Lavinia, the king's daughter; we conclude with Aeneas furiously killing Turnus, now helpless and a suppliant. In fact the final book is dotted with intimations that what we are witnessing is a civil conflict. At its beginning, for instance, the aged monarch himself announces to Turnus, "I have taken up impious arms" (*arma impia sumpsi* [12.31]),[1] the implication being that his decision has had the effect of pitting brother against brother. As the book progresses and the treaty, which would have brought an immediate end to the battling through a single combat between the rivals, is broken, Aeneas shouts to the newly embroiled troops, "Where are you charging? What is this sudden surge of discord? Control your wrath!" ("Quo ruitis? quaeve ista repens discordia surgit? / o cohibete iras!" [313–14]). *Discordia*, as we see in an even grimmer context later in the book, is a catchword here for civil war. Aeneas seeks to bring it to a stop. His subsequent actions tell a different tale.

By thus having the plot of the last half of his epic take on characteristics of civil strife, Vergil also compresses a thousand years of history and centers his reader's attention on the events of the decades immediately preceding the poem's composition, that is, on the concluding years of Rome's century of fraternal struggle, specifically from the death of Julius Caesar, on the ides of March, 44 BCE (Vergil himself was twenty-six at the time), until 2 September 31, when Octavian, Caesar's great-nephew and adopted son, defeated Antony at Actium to bring the warring to an end.

Mention of Octavian takes us back to Vergil's condensation of history, this time to a specific, focal character in the final decades of that history who at the age of nineteen succeeded in large measure to Caesar's power. By the time he accepts the cognomen Augustus in 27, four years after Actium and seventeen after Caesar's murder, we are in the *Aeneid*'s future, anticipating, in the words of Anchises to his son in *Aeneid* 6, the era of "Augustus Caesar, offspring of a god, who will found again the golden generations in fields once reigned over by Saturn" ("Augustus Caesar, divi genus, aurea condet / saecula qui rursus Latio regnata per arva / Saturno quondam" [792–94]). We see the emperor again on the shield of Aeneas, proleptically given the title of Augustus as he leads his forces into battle at Actium and returns in triple triumph to his capital to review his subject peoples before the gleaming marble of his new temple to Apollo (8.678–728).

There is no direct mention of Octavian in the battle books of the *Aeneid*'s foreground, nor could there be, but that these books document a civil conflict and that Octavian was not only a major protagonist in Rome's last bout of fraternal strife but ultimately the emergent victor urges the reader to link the epic's central, conquering hero with him and to ask how far and in what ways Vergil intimates that we should press a semblance between the two. It is to the problematics that arise from pursuing such intimations of allegory, and to the value of their analysis for interpretation of Vergil's masterpiece, that I devote the following pages.

The difficulties that face us as we pursue a connection between Aeneas and Octavian are compounded by the biases that inform our sources about Octavian. First and foremost of these sources is the *Res gestae*, the "Achievements" of Augustus himself, promulgated in the penultimate year of his life after a rule of over four decades (Augustus). Written in the clipped, direct style of Caesar's *Commentarii*, it summarizes in one sentence Augustus's treatment of Roman citizens during his reign:

Bella terra et mari civilia externaque toto in orbe terrarum saepe gessi,
victorque omnibus veniam petentibus civibus peperci.   (3.1)

I undertook many civil and foreign wars by land and sea throughout the
world, and as victor I spared the lives of all citizens who asked for mercy.

The key phrase is the last, but the wording as a whole briskly glosses over the
events of the early years of the emperor's rise to power. These events include
the immediate and more long-run aftermath of Philippi (42 BCE), distinguished by brutality on the battlefield and by the subsequent proscriptions, as
well as details of the siege of Perusia (40 BCE), which became notorious for its
cruelty. Here and in what we can glean of Augustus's unpreserved *Memoirs*,
which covered his career up to the Cantabrian campaign in 26–25, the
emperor naturally enough skews the presentation of his deeds to present his
conduct in a morally favorable light. For an example, the third century CE
jurist Ulpian says that Augustus, in the *Memoir's* tenth book, claims always to
have given back the bodies of those executed under his command to their relatives for burial (from the *Digesta* of Justinian, 48.24.1, in Malcovati).

But the sources that have been preserved cast the happenings of 42–40 in a
more ambiguous light, allowing us to follow Tacitus's leads in the famous
overview of the Augustan principate that opens his *Annales* (1.9–10) and evaluate them in both positive and negative lights. The events at Perusia are an
example (for modern discussions, see Scott 27–28; Syme 211–12; Harris
300–02; Weinstock 398-99; Kienast 39; Pelling 16). It was in that city that, during the winter and early spring of 41–40, Octavian pinned Lucius Antonius,
brother of the triumvir, and Fulvia, Antonius's wife. The city was besieged into
submission, plundered, and burned to the ground.

Certain details of this sequence are clear. Antonius's veterans were spared
along with their leader, who was posted to the governorship of Spain, and Fulvia was allowed to flee to Athens. Other details are cloudy, and their interpretation concentrates primarily on the depth and intensity of Octavian's
viciousness. Both Suetonius, writing around 112 CE, in his life of Augustus
(14), and the Greek Dio Cassius, in his early third-century history of Rome
(48.14), speak of how Octavian starved the city into surrender. But as early as
Lucan, whose epic, *Bellum civile*, dates from the later years of Nero's principate, *Perusina fames* (1.41), the "hunger at Perusia," had become quasi-prover-
bial. The starvation of the besieged is also mentioned several times (5.34–36)
by the chief apologist for the future emperor's actions, Appian, at work on his
narrative of the civil wars at a date slightly later than Suetonius.

Appian, however, fails to refer to the most notorious deed ascribed to Octavian after the town's capitulation, namely his offering of human captives as sacrifice on an altar or altars dedicated to the divinity of Julius Caesar on the ides
of March, 40, fourth anniversary of his assassination. Appian says that only the
town councillors, with one exception, were put to death; all the other inhabitants

were pardoned. Suetonius relates a harsher tale, telling us, first in general terms, that Octavian sought vengeance against many by replying to their pleas for pardon, "You must die" (*moriendum esse* [15]). To this detail he immediately adds, "Some write [*Scribunt quidam*] that three hundred of both orders [senators and knights] were selected from the prisoners of war and sacrificed like victims [*hostiarum more mactatos*] on an altar raised to Deified Julius [. . .]." The opening proviso is important, suggesting either Suetonius's disbelief in the implications of his words or his acknowledgment of the anti-Augustan prejudice of his source or sources. The same stipulation initiates Dio's account of the matter (48.3–4): after stating that most of the senators and knights were put to death, he adds that "the story goes" that three hundred knights and other senators were led to an altar consecrated to "the former Caesar" and there sacrificed. Unlike Suetonius, however, Dio lends credence to his statement by naming a particular senator, Tiberius Cannutius, as among those who were executed.

It is apropos of Octavian's conduct that Seneca the Younger, displaying the same sententiousness with which his nephew Lucan was gifted, can speak of the "Perusine altars" (*Perusinae arae*) along with the proscriptions. The philosopher does not resist adding, for the benefit of his addressee, the young Nero, a précis of the cruelty of Nero's great-grandfather, even after the horrors of his rise to power had long passed: "I certainly do not call weariness of cruelty [*lassam crudelitatem*] mercy [*clementia*]" (1.11.1–2) (*De clementia*).

Finally we have the burning of the city. Velleius Paterculus, writing under Augustus's successor Tiberius, and Appian (5.49) state that the city was burned through an accident, that a certain Cestius Macedonicus, in a moment of wildness, set his house on fire and that the flames spread throughout the city. Like Suetonius's apologetic "Some write," such a detail smacks of special pleading, this time on behalf of Octavian, especially since Velleius, in the sentence preceding the story of the conflagration, argues that "If there was savagery exerted [*saevitum*] against the inhabitants of Perusia, it was due more to the anger [*ira*] of the soldiery than to the wish of their leader" (2.74.4). Partisan Velleius would have us believe that Octavian's military forces were, in this instance, free agents and not extensions of their commander, not effectuators of his brutality. Dio is more matter-of-fact: the city burned (save for the Temple of Vulcan and a statue of Juno). Propertius, native of Asisium, some twenty-five kilometers east of Perusia, in a poem dated roughly fifteen years after the events, can speak of the "overturned hearths of the ancient Etruscan race" ("eversos [. . .] focos antiquae gentis Etruscae"), where the symbolism of "focus," as the center of home and thence of city and people, takes on special poignancy because of Perusia's fiery annihilation (2.1.27).

If some sources exonerate Octavian from blame or, at the least, extenuate his savagery, their very protestations of his innocence suggest the opposite. The last two brilliant epigrammatic poems (21 and 22) of Propertius's first book of elegies, published only a dozen or so years after 40, offer the closest to contemporary witness that we possess of the Perusine affair. They allow us to believe we are evaluating the writer's firsthand experience. Propertius does not speak of starvation, of human sacrifice, or of the city's incineration. What he does outline, in the final poem, is the results of civil discord (*discordia*) and, in particular, the dust, tombs, and unburied bones that follow in its wake. It is a concluding ("seal") poem that defines a poet's birth through suffering and death. The preceding epigram is yet more specific. Nearly an epitaph, it is addressed by a presumably dying warrior, who has been "snatched through the midst of Caesar's swords" (*per medios ereptum Caesaris ensis* [1.21.7]), to another soldier, wounded and attempting to avoid a "similar fate" as he hastens (*properas*) from the "Etruscan ramparts." We experience more closely the immediacy of wounding, death, and corpses without burial that resulted from the Perusine campaign. We also have a sense, implicit not only in the need that possessed the victims to escape from Caesar's massed weaponry but also in the hazards they encountered, of Caesar's obsession with vindictiveness and of the vigor with which it was pursued.

I return to Suetonius's account of Octavian at Philippi and thence to Vergil and Aeneas's conduct in the tenth book of his epic. In commenting on Octavian's lack of moderation ("nec [. . .] moderatus est" [13]) in the aftermath of victory over Brutus and Cassius, his biographer tenders a series of examples. First is the sending of the head of Brutus, who had committed suicide, to Rome to be thrown at the foot of Caesar's statue. Second is the savagery of Octavian himself: "he raged [*saeviit*] with insulting language against each of his most distinguished captives." (Vergil allots an intensified form of the same verb, *desaevit* [10.569], to Aeneas on the rampage after the death of Pallas.) But the next two instances take us more specifically into the events of *Aeneid* 10. "To one person humbly praying for [*suppliciter*] burial," says Suetonius, "[Octavian] is said to have responded, 'The birds will soon decide that question'" (*iam istam volucrum fore potestatem*). Turning to *Aeneid* 10, we think of the sequence of suppliants toward whom Aeneas is merciless: of Magus, who clasps his vanquisher's knees in supplication (*supplex* [523]) and, while he beseeches (*orantis*), receives the sword into his body up to the hilt, or of the brothers Liger and Lucagus, killed, to paraphrase Aeneas's bitter charge, so that brother need not desert brother (600). Suetonius's words remind us specifically of the treatment of Tarquitus, whose head, still also in the act of prayer (*orantis* [554]), Aeneas thrusts to the ground and, rolling over the body's trunk, curses him: "Lie there now, you fearful creature! No best of mothers will lay you in earth or load your limbs in the tomb of your ancestors. You will be left to birds of prey or, sunk beneath the flood, the wave will bear you on, and hungry fish will lick your wounds" (in Latin 557–60).

Last in Suetonius's list of Octavian's atrocities at Philippi come the deaths of a father and son: "Others, father and son, begging for their lives, he [is said to have] ordered to draw lots or to play mora, to decide who should be spared, and to have looked on while each dies, since the father was executed because he offered himself [in place of his son] and the son thereupon took his own life." No father-son team in *Aeneid* 10 is cruelly forced to play mora as their victor executes, or has executed, the one while the other commits suicide. The last two hundred lines of the book do, however, tell the extraordinarily moving tale of Mezentius and his son, Lausus; the bond between them, as Aeneas notices too late, exemplifies the most striking instance in the poem of *pietas* experientially at work. Aeneas first wounds the father, then kills the son as he protects his father, then finishes off the father, as the book comes to a close.

However affecting the story, Vergil on one level is merely expanding on what the exempla of Suetonius, writing more than a century later, would suggest. Both authors imply that their subjects, in the heat of battle and spurred on by a desire for vengeance, fail to practise clemency, which was one of Caesar's salient characteristics and which Aeneas's father, Anchises, at the climax of his disquisition on future Rome to his son in the Underworld, urges him to make habitual (6.851–53). In neither set of instances would it have been lost on a Roman reader that failure to exercise clemency brought about the death of a series of pairs who demonstrated *pietas*, Aeneas's most conspicuous attribute, be they father and son or brother and brother. Both Octavian and Aeneas in different ways ignore their fathers. In so doing Aeneas, at least, kills more than one paragon of the noble attribute that his deportment supposedly epitomizes.

If we observe the beginning of Aeneas's violence in book 10 in the context of Octavian's career, we move forward two years in time while returning to the events at Perusia. The most prominent moment in this catalog of rage, prominent because Vergil places it first and because its action is the most ethically dubious on which Aeneas here embarks, is the seizure of eight youthful captives, who are given particularity by the naming of their fathers, for human sacrifice, their blood to be poured on Pallas's funeral pyre (517–20). Though we do not actually witness their deaths, the captives are readied for slaughter as part of the cortege in book 11 (81–82).

Ever since Richard Heinze (210n2 and in English 187–88n44; Farron, "Sacrifice" 26-29), scholars have made a connection between Aeneas's deed and Octavian's putative massacre of some three hundred citizens of Perusia as an anniversary offering on an altar to Divus Iulius. As we saw, our ancient authorities are divided on the severity of Octavian's conduct, and this lack of unanimity is the basis for the repudiation of his possible endorsement of human sacrifice as "certainly false" by the most recent editor of *Aeneid* 10, who adds a further judgment worthy of our consideration: "[. . .] even if [the story of human sacrifice] were true an allusion to it in a poem which otherwise lauds the princeps seems fundamentally unlikely" (Harrison, Aeneid 203). My view is opposite. We do indeed anticipate aspects of Augustus's golden time in three prophecies scattered through the epic. But the poem's foregrounded action, in the last six books, smacks of civil war. If we continue to pursue the correspondence between Aeneas and Octavian as the central figures in a civil conflict, then Aeneas's deeds, and Vergil's words, offer evidence that corroborates the harshest interpretation placed by our ancient sources on Octavian's behavior at

Perusia. Vergil's richness of presentation allows his readers to make the connection and then ask what the parallelism tells us not only about Aeneas's vengeful spate of brutality but also about a similar moment in the rise to power of the future Augustus.

But allegory permits us to seek resemblances, not to make rigid equations, and there is a line of argument that might defend Aeneas while displacing any analogy with Octavian. In two of Aeneas's actions in book 10—taking human victims for sacrifice and telling a defeated but suppliant hero that birds and dogs will provide for his burial—there are parallels in the conduct of Achilles, protagonist of the *Iliad*, the greatest single literary influence on Vergil as he wrote his epic. All the similarities come from the final books of Homer's epic and, with one exception, all center on Achilles's rage after the death of Patroclus at the hands of Hector. Craving vengeance as Aeneas does after Turnus vanquishes Pallas, Achilles promises he will seize human victims (18.336–37), does the capturing (21.26–33), and carries out the slaughter and cremation (23.175–81). He curses the dying Hector that "dogs and birds will devour you completely" (22.354; my trans.), and after he has offered the human sacrifice on Patroclus's pyre, he says of Hector that he will not give his corpse to the fire to eat "but to dogs" (23.183).

But there is no specific counterpart in the *Iliad* to Aeneas's killing of first son, Lausus, and then father, Mezentius (or to Octavian's demand that father and son decide their death by playing mora), and there is no parallel in Homer to our final analogy between Aeneas and Octavian, namely, the burning of Latinus's city vis-à-vis the conflagration of Perusia. We are now more than halfway through the epic's final book. Aeneas's "most beautiful mother" (*genetrix* [12.554]), foundress of the Julian gens and the object of special veneration by Caesar, who made Venus's temple the cynosure of his forum, puts into her son's mind the idea of razing the old king's city because the king had sided with Turnus against the Trojans' fated advent. Aeneas puts his threat succinctly: "unless they agree to accept my rule and, conquered, to obey, I will overthrow [the city] and place its smoking rooftops [*fumantia culmina*] level with the ground" (12.568–69). Fire figures prominently in Aeneas's last words of command to his soldiery: "hurry and bring torches and demand back the treaty with flames" ("ferte faces propere foedusque reposcite flammis" [573]). Later, Saces, wounded and pleading with Turnus to face the final duel with Aeneas, tells him how "torches [*faces*] are now flying to the city's rooftops" (656).

Vergil's vocabulary gives the episode a particular slant. Before he delivers his final orders, Aeneas addresses his soldiers as "citizens" (*cives* [572]), and those in the town who respond to his threats are given the same designation (583). We are witnessing one of the most blatant manifestations of civil strife in the *Aeneid*'s final books, a designation that Vergil underscores in two ways. First is the juxtaposition of the noun *discordia* with Latinus's *cives*. The phrase *discordia cives* occurs in Propertius (1.22.5) to distinguish the conflict between citizens at Perusia, which in turn serves to define the poet's birthplace. It occurs also in Vergil's first eclogue (line 71), a poem written contemporaneously with the event itself, once more to indicate civil strife. Vergil, as I have elsewhere shown ("*Aeneid* 12" 228), also carefully connects *Eclogue* 1 with this concluding moment in *Aeneid* 12 by reiterating the phrase "smoking rooftops" (*culmina fumant*) in that poem's penultimate verse (line 82). To the lucky shepherd, who utters the phrase in Vergil's first poem and who still lays claim to the pastoral landscape, the smoking houses appear to represent one aspect of a peaceful countryside at nightfall. To the reader, schooled in the final reaches of Vergil's epic, and perhaps also to the exiled shepherd Meliboeus in the poem, though we are not told so directly, smoking rooftops connote civil conflict and the suffering and hurt that it brings to those caught in its turmoil.

Vergil offers no direct comparison between Aeneas's instigation of the burning of Latinus's city and Octavian's fiery destruction of Perusia, nor should we expect him to. But both the connections we have earlier drawn between Octavian's behavior at Philippi and Perusia with Aeneas's savage reaction to the death of Pallas and Vergil's pointed definition of Aeneas's onslaught against Latinus's stronghold as the pitting of citizen against citizen help advance a linkage between the two. As far as Aeneas is concerned, the attack on Latinus comes ironically at the hand of one who had experienced the fiery collapse of his own native city. As for Octavian's burning of an Italian city to the ground and executing its citizens, Roman citizens, whatever the circumstances and whatever their number—whether they consisted merely of the members of the town council, as Appian would have it, or whether they were the three hundred senators and knights that Suetonius and Dio speak of as offered in sacrifice to Caesar's memory—it is the ritual aspects of the killing that forge a close connection between the words of Suetonius and Dio (and not of Appian) and *Aeneid* 10 and 12.

Both epic hero and Roman warrior are caught up in the throes of angry vengeance. Even after Octavian became Augustus and inaugurated a time of peace that his greatest poet styles golden, the idea of his vengeance remains paramount. However much his poets may have urged otherwise, Augustus never monumentalizes clemency. On the contrary, even as late as 2 BCE, it is to Mars Ultor, Mars the avenger of the death of his adoptive father, that he dedicates the temple that was vowed on the eve of Philippi and that formed his forum's principal center of attention.

Aeneas's time frame is more circumscribed, but as Aeneas readies to kill Turnus, conquered and suppliant, at the epic's final moment, the verb Vergil puts into his mouth is "to offer sacrifice" (*immolare* [12.949]), the same word the narrator uses in book 10 as Aeneas anticipates his ritual offering of the eight captives in sacrifice (591). His ultimate, vengeful words addressed to Turnus slide responsibility for the final killing onto Pallas, Aeneas serving as Pallas's instrument of retaliation. But the deed is Aeneas's own, as, "set aflame by furies and terrible in his anger," he performs the epic's final act of retribution. The spirit of vengeance, not the espousal of clemency, marks not only Augustus's continued remembrance of Caesar's death even later in his career but also the aura of cruelty with which Vergil stamps his hero, as the soul of Aeneas's last ritual victim slips indignant to the shades below.

NOTE

[1]In this essay, the English translations are mine unless otherwise indicated.

The Anger of Juno in Vergil's *Aeneid*

Patricia A. Johnston

The opening lines of Vergil's *Aeneid* make it clear to the reader that Aeneas's most basic problem is "the unforgetting [literally, 'remembering'] anger of cruel Juno" (*saevae memorem Iunonis ob iram* [1.4]).[1] Juno's anger is the driving force behind the countless misfortunes and endless labors of Aeneas and his Trojan companions as they struggle to fulfill their destiny. Vergil attributes Juno's anger to the traditional Homeric motivations—the disastrous beauty contest (*iudicium Paridis* [1.27; "the judgment of Paris"]) that led to Helen's abduction and the Trojan War; Juno's general grudge against the Trojans (*genus invisum* [1.28; "the hated race"]), and the favors shown to Ganymede, who was assumed bodily into Olympus to be Jupiter's cupbearer (*rapti Ganymedis honores* [1.28; "the honors for stolen Ganymede"])—but especially to Juno's concern for the future of Carthage (15–16), which is destined to be destroyed one day by "a leader who [will] rise from the Trojan race" (19)—that is, by a descendant of Aeneas. This phrase refers to the destruction of Carthage during the three Punic Wars, which will be waged during the third and second centuries BC (13–22).

But another, less obvious cause for Juno's anger emerges in the course of the poem. This anger is based in her role as an early Italic goddess and is reflected in the narrative by the fact that her hostility is most in evidence in the first half of the poem, when the Trojans physically approach the mainland of Italy. In the second half of the poem the hostility is obvious in her support of the Latin forces that oppose the Trojan settlers. Juno was not merely a Roman adoption of Homer's goddess but also a powerful Italic goddess in her own right, worshiped widely throughout central Italy under a variety of attributes.

The narrative begins with Juno's catching sight of the Trojan fleet as it is about to reach the mainland of Italy: "Sicily's coast was just out of sight, when they joyously spread their sails and directed their keels through the salty foam. But Juno, guarding the unhealing wound in her heart, said: 'Shall I now yield, defeated?'" (in Latin 1.34–37). The first evidence of her loss of prestige is found in this opening soliloquy, where she laments, as she observes the Trojans approaching the mainland, that her power is not even that of Pallas Athena, who was able to exact vengeance from Oilean Ajax (37–41). What particularly galls Juno is that they are so close to the mainland of Italy. She still has the ability to persuade Aeolus to stir up the great storm that dominates much of the first book, although Neptune makes it clear that Aeolus has overstepped his bounds by carrying out the request. Once the storm has been subdued, Juno's hostility is not again evident until the prophecy of Helenus at the end of the third book.

Chronologically, the events of the second and third books precede those of book 1. Thus, in the account of the fall of Troy in book 2, where Venus reveals to her son that all the gods are participating in destroying the city, Juno is not singled out as being any more bent on the destruction of Troy than are Neptune, Pallas Athena, and even Jupiter himself. But if the narrative is viewed in its chronological sequence, it soon becomes obvious that the growth of Juno's hostility corresponds to the lessening distance between the Trojans and the Italian mainland, despite the fact that Vergil periodically makes conspicuous reference to the disastrous beauty contest and the rape of Ganymede, and even the threat to Carthage increases as the Trojans approach the Italian mainland.

The third book recounts the wanderings of the Trojans as they search for a new home. First they sail to Thrace but learn, through the Polydorus episode (3.13–68) that this land is now hostile to them. They then sail to Delos, the birthplace of Apollo, for guidance. There the history of the formerly floating island is told: Juno had forbidden any land to allow Latona, pregnant with Jupiter's offspring, to give birth on its soil. At that time the island Delos was not attached to the earth but was "floating from shore to shore" (3.75). Thus it was able to receive Latona and provide a place for her to give birth to the twins Apollo and Diana. In gratitude, Apollo later fixed the island's position with his arrows. In describing this deed, Vergil refers to Apollo with the epithet so often given to Aeneas, "pious": "Apollo, the pious archer-god, anchored it fast to lofty Myconos and Gyaros" (75–76).

This myth conveys a basic antagonism between Juno and Apollo. It shows how Apollo imposes his presence where he is not accepted. In the context of book 3, it also suggests a parallel between the current rootless situation of the Trojans and the past rootlessness of the island. It is implicit that Apollo, having established a permanent setting for the island, will help the Trojans attain a similar stability, despite Juno's opposition.

Early in book 3, the Trojans land at Actium, which in Vergil's time will be the site of Augustus's victory over Antony (31 BC), and mark the beginning of Augustus's rise to power in the empire. At Actium, Vergil nails the shield of Abas to the temple of Apollo (278–88) (see J. Miller). To this shield, which had previously hung in the temple of Juno at Argos, Aeneas adds a taunting epigram: AENEAS HAEC DE DANAIS VICTORIBUS ARMA ("Aeneas [dedicates] these weapons [taken] from the victorious Greeks") The transference of weapons from Juno's temple and their subsequent dedication to Apollo provide another example of Juno's displacement by the young god. Aeneas's lack of comprehension that his antagonist is this great goddess is again evident at the close of the third book, when, concluding the account of his wanderings to the Carthaginians, he refers to his antagonist in the masculine gender: "Then a god [*deus*] drove me off course to your shores" (714–15).

The first explicit warning for Aeneas to worship Juno occurs in the third book, which documents the wanderings of him and his fellow survivors as they search for a new home. The Trojans land on the western coast of Greece at Buthrotum, in Epirus, where they find a small group of Trojan survivors led by Helenus, a son of Priam, and Andromache, eternally in mourning for her dead husband, Hector. Before Aeneas and his men resume their quest for their new home, Helenus, who is also a seer, provides them with some guidance as to the dangers lying ahead in their search for Italy. In this episode, the only other allusion to Juno in book 3, Helenus—who is associated not with Juno but with Apollo—identifies Juno as the most important deity with whom Aeneas must contend. He indicates that, while it is the Fates (Parcae) who limit what he can know, it is Juno who controls what he can reveal. After revealing the dangers in store for the Trojans before they finally reach Italy, Helenus concludes by emphatically stating and restating Juno's importance to Aeneas: "If you believe Helenus as a seer, if Apollo fills my mind with truth, this one thing above all to you I say, O son of a goddess, repeating it once and again to you as strongly as I can" (433–36). The thing that he repeats again is the need to invoke in prayer the divine power of Juno, to sing to her, and to conquer her with offerings; this is the only way Aeneas will at last complete the journey from Sicily to Italy: "Worship before all else the goddess, Juno: sing to her gladly in prayer; win the powerful queen of gods with gifts and offerings. Thus at last will you come to your ultimate destination, Italy" (437–40).

Leaving Buthrotum, the Trojans sail to Acroceraunia, where they land and make offerings to Juno of Argos (*Iunoni Argivae* [547]). (Argos is the site of one of the major temples to Hera and in some versions is said to be her birthplace; Samos, another major sanctuary of the goddess, acknowledged at the beginning of book 1, is the other site said to be her birthplace.) The Greek epithet reflects the aspect of the goddess most familiar to Aeneas at this point—her affiliation with Argos—but also reminds the reader of his recent offense at Actium, where he dedicated to Apollo the shield taken from her temple. As soon as the Trojans set sail from Acroceraunia, they catch sight of the bay of "Herculean Tarentum" and another temple of Juno—but on the Italian side of the sea. It is the temple of Juno Lacinia (*diva Lacinia* [3.552]; see Livy 28.46.16). *Lacinia* suggests the promontory on which the famous temple was placed, like many of Juno's temples. It is perhaps significant that Juno's temple and the bay named after Hercules should mark the Trojans' first sight of the Italian mainland, since Hercules, like Aeneas, is tormented by Juno.

The Trojans then manage to avoid (but still observe) the great dangers and cities of Sicily, and they finally land at Drepanum (707), where Anchises dies. Aeneas's account of his wanderings ends here. The reader knows what came next: the passage to Italy, interrupted by the great storm of book 1, which drove the Trojans back to Carthage, and the hospitable welcome by Dido and her Tyrians. Drepanum, at the northwestern corner of Sicily, is the closest point between Sicily and Carthage; the distance is not great, so it is natural that the Trojans are driven from there to Carthage at the end of book 3 and that they should return there immediately after leaving Carthage at the beginning of book 5.

Juno's hostility to Aeneas and Venus's determination to protect him lead to Dido's tragedy in book 4. The trust that Dido and her sister, Anna, place in

Juno becomes evident when, after Anna (unwisely) assures Dido that the Trojan fleet has come to Carthage "under the auspices of the gods and with the support of Juno" (45), the queen yields to her passion. It is not surprising that Dido would turn to Juno, not only because Juno is the goddess of marriage but also because she is frequently identified with Tanit, the chief goddess of Carthage. Dido's trust in Juno, however, is sadly betrayed, as Juno mercilessly allows Dido to be destroyed in a fruitless attempt to detain Aeneas at Carthage (and thus prevent him from fulfilling his destiny).

After leaving Dido, the Trojans return in book 5 to Drepanum. There Iris instigates the Trojan women to set fire to the Trojan ships. The Trojans have stopped there, briefly, because a year has passed since Anchises died. The focus of the fifth book is the performance of funeral games for Anchises, mock military exercises that are reenacted in later books in real military exercises. As the men perform the games, the Trojan women separately gather to mourn Anchises. To them Juno sends down Iris in the guise of the aged Trojan woman Beroë; in this role she incites the women, weary with travel, to set the ships aflame. Although her intent is to destroy the fleet, enough ships survive to allow a limited number to sail on to mainland Italy. The problem of limited space on the ships is resolved by the decision to leave the women and the elderly in Sicily.

In book 6, the Trojans first set foot on mainland Italy. There Aeneas approaches the sibyl at Cumae to seek a prophecy about the future. Helenus was the first to warn Aeneas about Juno. Now the sibyl, in her prophecy, gives a second warning. There is only one other reference to Juno in this book, the Juno of the Underworld (discussed below), but the sibyl, too, makes it clear that Juno continues to be a large problem for Aeneas: "A new Achilles has been born in Latium, also a son of a goddess, nor will Juno, an added problem for the Trojans, ever be far away" (90–91). No reaction to the prophecy from Aeneas is indicated in this book. It lurks in the reader's mind, however, waiting to surface.

The other unspoken reference to Juno in this book is the fact, of which Vergil's contemporaries were aware, that although the sibyl is now a spokesperson of Apollo, in the past she was the spokesperson of the great goddess. Here is yet another example of Apollo set in opposition to the worship of Juno. Actual physical evidence of the Cumaean sibyl's early association with Hera was found early in the twentieth century, in a bronze oracular disk from the vicinity of Cumae. The original bronze disk has been assigned to the seventh or sixth century BC and has been translated, "Hera does not permit a supplementary inquiry of the oracle," that is to say, she does not allow the visitor to press the question further, beyond the oracle's initial response. Apollo was not established at Cumae until the later fifth century BC (420 BC); thus the sibyl would not have given oracular responses for Apollo before then. The Greek Hera was clearly established at this site, if not at the time of the fall of Troy (c. 1250 BC) then certainly before Apollo was in evidence at Cumae (see Guarducci; Renehan; Parke; Johnston, "Juno"). Vergil's contemporaries, such as Varro (42; in Lactantius, *Divinae institutiones* 1.6.10) and Tibullus (2.5.68), were clearly aware of this association, inasmuch as they refer to the Cumaean sibyl by the name Herophile ("dear to Hera").

Juno's hostility to the Trojans as they approach the Italian mainland indicates her concern about the future role of the Trojans in Italy, but this time she does not prevent their landing. In Vergil's version, she does not even seem to be aware of their success until book 7. When the Trojans land at Cumae at the beginning of book 6, they have completed their journey to mainland Italy. They directly proceed to the temple of Apollo and the cave of the sibyl. The sibyl, in preparing Aeneas for his trip into the Underworld, directs him to seek out a golden bough (*aureus ramus* [137]) in the depths of the forest, which is sacred to "Juno of the Underworld." *Iuno Inferna* refers to Proserpina, queen of the Underworld, who is often closely linked with Juno. At Paestum in southern Italy, where not one but two of the three temples are dedicated to Hera, numerous pomegranates painted in the tombs suggest both Juno and Proserpina. As Juno Lucina, she was believed to watch over childbirth (a function assigned by the Greeks to Artemis, who in some accounts was said to be, like Proserpina, the daughter of Demeter-Ceres). These goddesses are thus intertwined in their association with fertility; the pomegranates at Paestum are but one of many items found there associated with fertility. *Iuno Inferna* also anticipates Juno's association with Allecto, the Fury summoned from the Underworld in book 7.

The action in book 1 begins with a terrible storm at sea and ends with the peaceful reception of the Trojans at Carthage. Book 7, by contrast, begins with the Trojans' being welcomed peacefully by King Latinus and the betrothal of his daughter, Lavinia, to Aeneas, and it ends with both Trojans and Latins engaged in the terrible storm of war (see Johnston, "Storm"). The tenor of the book changes about a third of the way through, from the happy reception to an angry storm that grows into full-fledged war, and this war in turn dominates the second, Iliadic, half of the poem. The change happens when Juno, returning from Argos, sees from Pachynus (the southeastern promontory of Sicily and the location of Scylla and Charybdis) that the Trojans have reached the Tiber and are already beginning to settle into the mainland: "Look! the cruel spouse of Jupiter was returning from Argos, land of Io, wafting through the air, when she caught sight of Aeneas and the Dardanian fleet all the way from Sicilian Pachynus" (286–90).

Juno's anger reflects her frustration in defeat. The reference to Io marks an earlier defeat, since Io escaped the watchful eyes of Argus (Juno had sent him to guard her). Much of Juno's anger in the last six books can be tied to her waning power and prestige. As in book 1, Juno laments that her divinity is not respected. "If my divine power is not sufficiently great to sway the gods above, I shall arouse Acheron itself!" (7.310–12), she exclaims. Acheron refers to the Underworld, out of which she summons the Fury Allecto to be the agent through whom she will set the Trojan and Latin peoples at war with each other. Allecto carries out Juno's orders: she goads Lavinia's mother, Amata, and then Turnus, Lavinia's rejected suitor, to oppose the wedding of Lavinia and Aeneas. Like Turnus, the Latin farmers are soon aroused to a frenzy, and they ultimately cast aside their peaceful plows and turn to their long-neglected swords (633–36). Allecto finally directs her attention to the hunting dogs of Aeneas's young son, Iulus, whom she incites to pursue a deer that just happens to be a pet of Silvia, daughter of King Latinus's herdsman and gamekeeper. When Iulus fatally wounds Silvia's pet deer, the final blow has been struck, and war between Latins and Trojans becomes inevitable.

Juno then dismisses Allecto, who has done her job, and proceeds to the Temple of Janus (601), where she opens the iron Gates of War, traditionally opened only in time of war. Juno bursts through them and casts them open wide. It is not insignificant that the first letter of lines 601–04 form the acronym M A R S, the god of war.

> Mos erat Hesperio in Latio, quem protinus urbes
> Albanae coluere sacrum, nunc maxima rerum
> Roma colit, cum prima movent in proelia Martem,
> Sive Getis inferre manu lacrimabile bellum [. . .].

> It was the sacred custom in Hesperian Latium,
> which the Alban cities once practiced and now
> Rome, the greatest of states, cultivates, when they
> first begin to engage in war, or to inflict a
> war worthy of tears on the Getae [. . .].

From this point until the end of book 7 there follows a long catalog of the Latin forces, culminating with the best and brightest, Turnus and Camilla. It is as if the forces pass in military formation through the gates, like a huge dam breaking and pouring its contents uncontrollably through the breech, washing away any hope of peaceful resolution. In a structure that reverses the pattern in book 1, this book begins peacefully but ends in the tragedy of war, which continues to the close of book 12.

Between the outbreak of war and its final resolution, Juno and her representatives fight on, stubbornly but hopelessly opposing the inevitable. Before the fighting fully develops, however, Aeneas travels up the Tiber to get assistance from Evander and the Arcadian people, who inhabit the future site of Rome.

In book 8, Aeneas receives his third warning to worship Juno, this time from the river god Tiber (Tiberinus): "Arise, son of a goddess, and duly offer prayers to Juno while the first stars are setting, and overcome her anger and threats with suppliant prayers" (59–61). Aeneas responds initially by praying not to Juno but to the Laurentine nymphs. As soon as he encounters a white sow with newborn piglets, however, as Tiberinus has advised, he sacrifices it to Juno; his first overt offering to her.

When Aeneas arrives at the future site of Rome, the festival of the Ara Maxima is under way, and the story of Hercules and Cacus is told. The second major allusion to Juno found in book 8 lies in the entire Hercules episode. Hercules is seen as an exemplar for both Aeneas and for the future Augustus, in that he accomplished impossible deeds and through his sufferings became a god. Because his struggles were imposed by Juno, references to him and his deeds carry an allusion to her, his persecutor. Hercules's labors cease with the end of Juno's hostility, when he becomes a god and marries Juno's daughter, Hebe. The obvious parallel in the *Aeneid* will be Juno's mollification at the end of book 12, when Juno allows the Trojan and Latin race to become one and thus brings Aeneas's labors to an end.

Following the advice of Tiber, Aeneas journeys up the god's river to the future site of Rome, where he meets Evander and seeks aid from him. Evander, a Greek but "a good man" (the meaning of the Greek elements in his name), entrusts his only son, Pallas, to Aeneas, along with soldiers and weapons. Before this negotiation takes place, however, Aeneas must wait while Evander and his people carry out a ritual that commemorates the presence of Hercules at this site. Hercules is a prominent presence throughout Sicily and southern Italy, often in close proximity to temples of Hera, as in the Bay of Tarentum. Hera's temples at Paestum and Sele are good examples. The metopes from her temple at Sele depict the labors of Hercules; they are now displayed at Paestum, where two of the three enormous temples are dedicated to the great goddess. In Agrigento, Sicily, one finds similar juxtapositions of temples of Hera and Hercules.

Aeneas is given a simple meal, which he eats seated on a lion's skin, the symbol of Hercules's first labor. He then hears the story of Cacus and Hercules from Evander. The tale of Cacus's attempt to steal the cattle is followed by a ritual at the Ara Maxima, dedicated to the great hero in gratitude for his freeing the area of the monster. The priests sing of Juno's cruelty to Hercules and of how he once overthrew the city of Troy, a reference to his sack of that city after he was cheated by Laomedon, an early king of Troy. At the close of book 8, after Aeneas and Evander have arranged for Pallas to bring Arcadian troops to aid the Trojans, Venus presents her son with a magnificent shield, made for him by Vulcan. On the shield are depicted important events in the early history of Rome. Juno's role in Roman activities is notable in at least two of the events shown there. One is the story of the sacred geese that saved the city in 390 BC by alerting the Romans to an attack by the Gauls (655–66). The geese were reared in the sanctuary of Juno Moneta, the goddess who alerts or warns people (see Livy 7.28.6). A second item on the shield is the rape of the Sabines (8.635). The festival of the Matronalia, held in Juno's honor (on the first day of March), traditionally took place on the anniversary of the end of the Roman-Sabine war, when Sabine women threw themselves between their fathers and husbands to prevent them from fighting and thereby reestablished harmony between the two sides. That both these important events in Roman history are associated with Juno suggests that the support of this great goddess will be necessary for the success of the future nation.

Juno's appeasement, at the end of book 12, is thus important not only to bring her persecution of Aeneas and the Trojans to an end but also to make possible harmonious relations among future Romans. The terms of that agreement, that the Trojans must accept the native Latin name, language, and attire ("Let the name of Troy, and Troy itself, perish" [822–28]), make it possible for a single unified people to come into being. Jupiter's assurance, on granting Juno's request, that "no other race will worship you with greater devotion" (840) converts her fury into pride and devotion to her new people.

NOTE

[1]All translations are by P. Johnston.

Vergil and the Monuments

Mary Jaeger

A people's identity depends a great deal on the public memory preserved in its monuments and works of art. This memory can be helpful or debilitating, inspiring a people or trapping it in a self-destructive past. Much of Rome's public memory was preserved in its topography, its hills and valleys, together with the buildings and place-names that covered them (Cançik; Edwards 27–30). This topography changed rapidly during the decade in which Vergil wrote the *Aeneid* (29–19 BCE). For in these years Augustus began to construct a series of monuments that would transform the city into a beneficial reminder, obscuring memories of a century of urban violence and civil war while recovering those of an idealized past—a lost golden age (Galinsky, *Augustan Culture* 141–55; Zanker 167–263). Vergil's representation of Rome in the *Aeneid* responded to these changes in the material city. But influence moved in both directions. While some of Augustus's early building projects and their settings appear at key points in the *Aeneid*, adding contemporary memories to the poem's many layers of meaning, the poem also reinterprets the Augustan landscape, making the objective world appear more complex to Vergil's original audience.

When we study monuments in the *Aeneid*, we have to consider them as part of the commentary on debilitating and empowering memory that runs through the poem (Henry; Quint 50–83). Emphatic references to memory begin and end the *Aeneid*. In the opening lines we learn that Aeneas suffers because of "savage Juno's remembering anger" ("saevae memorem Iunonis ob iram" [1.4]). Mindful of her old conflicts with Troy (again, *memor* [23]), the goddess cannot forget the causes of her pain (25–26). In the last scene of the epic, Pallas's baldric, the "reminder [*monimentum*] of savage grief," transmits Juno's rage to Aeneas (12.945). Pallas's presence in this reminder is so strong that Aeneas tells Turnus it is Pallas who strikes the final blow (948–49). This fresh outbreak of anger triggered by memory undermines the sense of closure conveyed by Turnus's death. The baldric is only one of many reminders (*monimenta, monumenta*) appearing throughout the poem. Others are the pictures on the temple of Juno at Carthage, the spoils Aeneas dedicates at Actium, the records Anchises misreads in book 3, the cloak Andromache gives to Ascanius, the items Aeneas left at Dido's court, the Minotaur, Deiphobus's mutilations, and the remains of previous settlements on the future site of Rome. Such reminders both preserve memory (the mutilated Deiphobus will never forget Helen) and evoke emotional responses from the people who see them (Aeneas's tears at Carthage, his wonder at seeing the traces of earlier men on the site of Rome). When Vergil represents the reminders in Rome's memory-laden topography, he interprets them in a way that determines the memory associated with them and the response that they evoke.

A good example of a place and a reminder transformed by the poem is the

Campus Martius, a level plain north of the city, which Augustus would make into a showpiece of urban design. Here he built the most imposing of his early monuments, his mausoleum (Zanker 72–77; Favro). The geographer Strabo calls the mausoleum "a great mound near the river on a lofty foundation of white marble, thickly covered with ever-green trees to the very summit" (Jones 2: 409; 5.3.8). By placing his mausoleum on the Campus Martius, Augustus (then Octavian) declared his commitment to Rome as the center of empire. Rumor had it that Julius Caesar had planned to rebuild Troy and relocate the capitol there, while Antony had stated in his will—at least Octavian's propaganda declared so—that he wanted to be buried next to Cleopatra, in Alexandria. The mausoleum, then, gave Romans physical proof of Rome's predominance and reminded them of the contrast between Antony and Octavian. The mausoleum's shape, that of a tumulus, had both Trojan and Italian (Etruscan) antecedents; moreover, the tumulus shape had already been used in the Campus for the tombs of Sulla and of Caesar (Richardson 248–89). In shape and location, then, the mausoleum respected tradition, even while it dramatically changed the Roman landscape by adding what was virtually a new hill.

It was in this mausoleum that Marcellus, Augustus's nephew, was buried in 23 BCE, and it is this tumulus and its setting that Anchises pictures at the end of book 6, when he concludes his eulogy of Marcellus, last in his catalog of Roman heroes:

> [. . .] how many groans
> Will be sent up from that great field of Mars
> To Mars' proud city, and what sad rites you'll see,
> Tiber, as you flow past the new-built tomb.
>   (Fitzgerald 1184–87; in Latin 872–74)

With his evocative words Anchises represents himself as an eyewitness at the funeral, and his emotional cry draws a connection not only between Rome's mythic past and the Augustan present but also between the Elysian Fields of book 6 and the Roman landscape (Austin, *Sextus* 272). For Vergil's contemporaries several features of Anchises's lament must have called to mind epitaphs on actual Roman tombs: the stress on family, the glorification of ancestors, and the emphasis on war (Brenk 223). In addition, any member of Vergil's audience who had been (or for that matter has been) to Rome, could (can) also conjure up a remembered image of the actual Augustan mausoleum and its setting. Thus, just as references to monuments conclude episodes in the historical narrative of Vergil's contemporary, Livy, this reference to a real monument provides a sense of closure to Anchises's catalog of prominent figures in Rome's history.

Yet Vergil's representation affects how the audience, whose vision is focalized through Anchises's words, sees the actual place. The Augustan mausoleum was isolated from the city proper by its location at the north end of the Campus Martius and by its extensive grounds. Anchises's exclamation pulls together a complete landscape around the tomb: "that great field of Mars," "Mars' proud city," the river Tiber. Looking at the actual tomb and recalling Anchises's words, Vergil's audience would now see it not in isolation but in the framework of these major topographical features. Thus the *Aeneid*, like two contemporary works, Horace's *Odes* and the second book of Livy's history (2.5.2–3), integrates into the Roman urban landscape the place that Augustus would develop most extensively (Jones 2: 407–09 [Strabo 5.3.8]; Favro; Jaeger, "Reconstructing"; Zanker 139–56).

In addition, Anchises's address places Marcellus's funeral in the context of the *Aeneid*'s other burials and the mausoleum in the context of the *Aeneid*'s other tombs. Coming at the end of the catalog of heroes, at the close of a detailed description of the Underworld, and at the close of the first half of the epic, Anchises's evocation of the mausoleum recasts it into a reminder of all the deaths and burials of *Aeneid* 1 through 6, including those of Orontes, Creusa, Priam, Hector, Polydorus, Dido, Palinurus, Misenus, and Marcellus.

Anchises's words, moreover, extend the mausoleum's literary associations beyond the *Aeneid*. The passage also recalls the prophecy of an earlier poem, Catullus 64, which anticipates the life, career, and death of Achilles: "no hero will go to clash with him in war," sing the Fates ("non illi quisquam bello se conferet heros" [343]). Brilliant in warfare and dying young, Marcellus is very like the Greek hero: "no enemy / could have come through a clash with him unhurt," says Vergil (Fitzgerald 6.1193–94), in Latin that recalls Catullus's words ("non illi se quisquam impune tulisset / obvius armato" [879–80]). Catullus's prophecy personifies the landscape of Troy, claiming that the river Scamander will bear witness to Achilles's greatness (347). Vergil's poem personifies the Roman landscape: the Tiber will see the funeral rites; the plain will send up groans. Vergil's educated audience would not miss this invitation to compare the mausoleum to the tomb of Achilles and the bloody sacrifices at Troy (the maiden Polyxena slaughtered over Achilles's grave [Catullus 368]) to the less violent offerings imagined by Anchises ("scarlet flowers" [Fitzgerald 1200; in Latin 884]).

Achilles's tomb has a literary life that extends the associations of the Augustan mausoleum even further. In a speech whose central point is the power of poetry, Cicero says that Alexander the Great, looking upon Achilles's tumulus, was said to have cried out, "O happy youth, who found a Homer to sing your praises!"—words truly spoken, adds Cicero, since without Homer Achilles's tomb would have buried the great man's fame along with his body (*Pro Archia* 24). Thus, while the mausoleum contributes to the form of the *Aeneid* by strengthening the sense of closure at the end of book 6, Vergil's Roman landscape, by recalling that of Troy, helps measure a Roman of Augustus's family against the highest standards of epic heroism. For all his status as a member of the imperial house, Marcellus has captured the imagination of generations of readers largely because of this passage. A message appears subtly in book 6 and will reappear overtly later, in book 9: poetry spreads fame farther and preserves it longer than even the most pretentious monument (Galinsky, *Augustan Culture* 352–53; Jenkyns, *Virgil's Experience* 640).

When Aeneas and Evander tour Pallanteum, the site of future Rome, in book 8, the poet again sets up a dynamic relation between the narrative and the physical city (Edwards). Sketching the backdrop for events commemorated later in the description of Aeneas's shield (626–728), the tour takes the form of a simple and straightforward narrative. Aeneas and the audience alike see one thing after another. Aeneas asks about the places he sees, and Evander explains them:

> Marveling,
> Aeneas gladly looked at all about him,
> Delighted with the setting, asking questions,
> Hearing of earlier men and what they left [*monimenta*].
> (Fitzgerald 408–12; 310–12)

Vergil organizes Evander's storytelling so that movement through the landscape runs parallel to chronology: while approaching the city, Evander tells of the site's early history, beginning with nymphs and fauns, going on to the arrival of the refugee Saturn, and concluding with his own flight to Italy in response to his mother's warnings. He then points out an altar and a city gate; the Romans, we are told, will name it after his mother, Carmentis, who foretold "the future glory of Pallanteum and Aeneas' / great descendants" (Fitzgerald 450–51; 340–41). The gate marks the boundary and provides a metaphoric point of transition between the site's past history and future, for Evander goes on to point out monuments and places that would be important in early Rome as well as in the Augustan city:

> Then he showed the wood
> That Romulus would make a place of refuge,
> Then the grotto called the Lupercal
> Under the cold crag, named in Arcadian fashion
> After Lycaean Pan. And then as well
> He showed the sacred wood of Argiletum,
> "Argus' death," and took oath by it, telling
> Of a guest, Argus, put to death. From there
> He led to our Tarpeian site and Capitol,
> All golden now, in those days tangled, wild
> With underbrush—but awesome even then.
> A strangeness there filled the country hearts with dread
> And made them shiver at the wood and Rock.
> (Fitzgerald 451–63; 342–50)

The narrative creates a double perspective, that of Aeneas, for whom this landscape holds no memories, who has to be told these stories, and who therefore can view it with pleasure and wonder, and that of the poem's audience, which sees a landscape rich in the memories of Rome's past, some of them violent. The forum had been the site of armed violence for the last three generations, including, for example, the mob scene after Clodius's death, when the people cremated his body and burned down the senate house for good measure. A Roman reader who had lived through years of civil war might well look on this landscape and weep, as Aeneas wept at the images of the Trojan War on the temple of Juno at Carthage. But in 29 BCE Augustus completed a new senate house and the Temple of the Divine Julius in the forum; in 28 BCE he dedicated the great Temple of Apollo next to his own relatively modest house on the Palatine; he restored the Lupercal and the Capitoline Temple in 26 BCE (Augustus 19; Eden 112–13). The topographical references invite comparison between the city's distant past and Augustan present. Indeed Vergil explicitly compares the Capitoline now to the Capitoline once upon a time: "All golden now, in those days tangled, wild / with underbrush [. . .]." This leap from the distant past to the present leaves unmentioned the recent violent events in these places.

Moreover, the passage contains numerous etiologies, invocations of the distant pre-Roman past (O'Hara, *True Names*): the names Latium, Tiber, Carmentis, Lupercal, Argiletum, Ianiculum, and Saturnia are all explained through stories:

> Here, too, in these walls
> Long fallen down, you see what were two towns,
> Monuments [*monimenta*] of the ancients. Father Janus
> Founded one stronghold, Saturn the other,
> Named Janiculum and Saturnia.   (Fitzgerald 469–73; 355–58)

The elaborate account of Hercules's battle with Cacus that preceded all these names and etiologies represents the detailed story that could be prompted by each place mentioned. While Vergil's audience does not hear in full the story of Argus (prompted by the wood of Argiletum), it learns that Aeneas heard it, presumably, in as much detail as he heard the story of Hercules.

All these places, their stories, and the reminders of their stories, bring to light many layers of the past at once. In a brief sixty-three lines (Fitzgerald 405–90; 306–69) Evander's tour traverses centuries, from the earliest occupation of the site to his own time, to the Rome of Augustus's time and beyond, even to the Rome of modern readers, who recall their own image of the city ruins complete with traffic on the Via dei Fori Imperiali and the backdrop of the Colosseum. The poem creates what Catherine Edwards calls a "palimpsestic landscape" where "past time was conflated and places became vehicles for a kind of non-sequential history" (42–43). The attributes of the place may change, but its identity remains stable. From the poem's teleological, Augustan perspective the Capitoline, tangled or golden was, is, and will always be the

Capitoline, as the forum is the forum even when cows graze in it, and the Carinae the Carinae. Evander knows the Capitoline's intrinsic importance: "Some god," he said, "it is not sure what god, / Lives in this grove, this hilltop thick with leaves" (Fitzgerald 464–65; 351–52).

The density of memory conveyed by the description of Pallanteum becomes all the more striking when we compare it to that of Buthrotum, Andromache's replica of Troy, in book 3 (Anderson, *Art* 41; Putnam, "Third Book" 273; Quint 58). Aeneas comes upon a sacrifice taking place in the grove, only instead of finding the locals sacrificing to Hercules, he meets Andromache offering sacrifice to Hector at an empty tomb. Like Pallanteum, Buthrotum is a small town, but Aeneas calls it a "Troy in miniature" (Fitzgerald 477). Its citadel only resembles the one at Troy, unlike the Capitoline with its unique identity and divine aura. The river that flows through this Troy is a "thin replica of Simoïs" (Fitzgerald 408; 302), and even the stream named after the Trojan river Xanthus is dry. Vergil's audience might well compare these rivers to the Tiber, which identifies itself authoritatively to Aeneas: "I am that river in full flood you see / Cutting through farmland, gliding past these banks, / The sea blue Tiber, heaven-delighting stream" (Fitzgerald 83–85; 62–64). Evander's Pallanteum suggests that any refugees' memories of past lives and abandoned homes must adjust themselves in order to fit into the already densely mnemonic landscape of the future Rome (unlike Aeneas, Evander tells his story in only a few lines [Fitzgerald 439–45; 333–36]). In contrast, Andromache and Helenus's settlement imposes the significant topography of Troy onto a foreign landscape without taking into consideration that landscape's history. Aeneas needs no Evander to interpret Buthrotum, for it has meaning only in reference to the lost Troy. Its memories belong elsewhere.

In his emotional outburst at the deaths of Nisus and Euryalus, the narrator measures the commemorative power of his poetry against the existence of Rome itself:

> Fortunate both! If in the least my songs
> Avail, no future day will ever take you
> Out of the record of remembering Time,
> While children of Aeneas make their home
> Around the Capitol's unshaken rock,
> And still the Roman Father governs all.
>   (Fitzgerald 633–38; 446–49)

The memory preserved by poetry endures as long as an inhabited landscape. Moreover, as transmitters of cultural continuity, landscape and poetry depend on each other: the changing landscape provides material to the poem, but the poem determines how this landscape will appear. The parade of souls, the funeral of Marcellus, the topography of the future Rome, all have meaning for Aeneas because Anchises and Evander interpret what he sees. Even Aeneas does not see Rome for himself. Much less does the audience, which sees a complicated physical landscape and the metaphoric landscape of Rome's history, sometimes through Aeneas's eyes, sometimes through those of Anchises or Evander, but always through those of the poem, which shapes both the place and its painful and inspiring memories.

Future Perfect Feminine:
Women Past and Present in Vergil's *Aeneid*

Sharon L. James

The role of women in the *Aeneid* poses problems for students reading in translation, as women either play short but crucial roles, like Dido and the sibyl, or receive virtually no screen time, like Creusa and Lavinia. There is little consistency to the presentation of women, except for their thematic association with irrational passion and fire and their resulting tendency to retard the hero's progress. Yet the poem does not treat women with contempt; in fact, it often expresses compassion for them. So, how to explain the *Aeneid*'s women to undergraduates reading the poem in English? A major key is the relation of women to Aeneas's military-dynastic mission, a project in which they can only lose, since in every case they must give up either their homes or their way of life, or both. Vergil shows women resisting their inevitable defeat in a way that both consistently associates them with the epic past and demonstrates the tragedies of the poem's movement from Troy to Rome, for that journey is a battle with numerous losers who must not be overlooked or taken lightly.

From its beginning, the *Aeneid* connects women with the past—emotional, concerned with family and private life, wishing to settle down rather than struggle on to Italy—while Aeneas must learn to move toward the future; to contain his feelings; and to press on, at all costs, toward the unknown land and the unseen wife.[1] Women are thus also associated with the doomed cities that Aeneas must either abandon or destroy. Dido, Amata, Juno, Silvia, and Camilla all stand in the way of his marriage to Lavinia and establishment of the proto-Roman city. Vergil complicates matters by frequently ascribing Juno's agency to their actions: she, with Venus, infects Dido; she sends Iris to incite the Trojan women to burn the ships in book 5; she sends Allecto to infect Amata. In other words, the women are not entirely to blame for their interference with Aeneas and his mission (about which he too is frequently ambivalent). Ironically, the only women who don't actively interfere are Aeneas's two wives, Creusa, who obligingly dies in Troy, and Lavinia, but then neither has much choice in the matters of death and marriage (Oliensis notes that these two women "prove their virtue precisely by submitting to the masculine plot of history" [303]). The poem's ambiguity thus allows, even encourages, its readers to recognize the human costs of the necessary and inevitable translation of empire from Troy to Rome. Women oppose the poem's forward motion and dynastic mission and provide a powerful voice of mourning for those who lose the battle for Italy's future, and for many readers their laments linger in the mind's ear longer and more effectively than the countervailing male prophecies of future Roman rule (on the power of lament in the *Aeneid*, see Perkell, "Lament").

Although the *Aeneid* narrates the tale of Aeneas's progress toward Italy and the future Roman Empire, it does not do so in simple fashion or with unmixed feelings. In fact, the poem's emotional register is at odds with its plot, for its most memorable characters and episodes are those connected with the vanishing past. As the poem progresses from the mythic Trojan past to the proto-Roman historic past and points toward the Roman imperial future, it suggests that the tragedies of history fall on individuals and families, the realm of women. It further shows the change in social and cultural structures and values, from the domestic monarchies of Troy and early Italy, which value women, to the primarily masculine regimes of the fated Roman Republic and Empire. (See Oliensis on women as "linked [. . .] to origins" and men as "oriented toward ends" [303].) Strikingly absent, however, are the kinds of women historically seen as important in the establishment and progress of Rome: there is no mention of Lucretia, for instance, although she catalyzed the establishment of the Roman Republic. Nor is there room, in Aeneas's trip to the Underworld, for a pageant of heroines like that of *Odyssey* 11. Indeed, in Aeneas's sneak preview of Roman history, the only women mentioned are Lavinia and Ilia—the mothers of Rome. In the *Aeneid*, women, including the goddesses, lose the heroic dimension available to them in the Homeric world and even, available to a much lesser extent, in the world of Roman mythic history. Thus the *Aeneid* enacts a sort of erasure of women, a disappearing act (see Nugent, "Women") that leaves, for many readers, a troubling dissonance between the poem's affecting depiction of the private life of the family and its sometimes erratic insistence on Aeneas's mission.

The Women of the Past

The *Aeneid* is filled with disappearing and dead women, members of a past era in which they exercised irrationally their excessive free will, power, and influence. Throughout the first half of the poem, Aeneas loses women left and right: in book 2 he is restrained by his mother from killing Helen, who then vanishes from his sight and the reader's; Creusa dies and subsequently evaporates before his eyes in the same book. He leaves Dido in book 4 and last sees her dead, mute, and angry in book 6; he leaves the Trojan women in Sicily in book 5. In book 6, he is guided through the Underworld by a female figure closely associated with death. Finally, at the poem's midpoint stands the last dead Trojan woman: Aeneas's nurse Caieta—even a piece of the landscape is marked with the name of yet another of the lost women of Aeneas's past (6.900–01, 7.1–4; Mandelbaum 6.1202, 7.1–7);[2] this dead woman structurally bridges the poem's two halves (Hinds 107–11). From that point, Aeneas appears to have no contact with women. Certainly he does not meet with any women to whom he is emotionally connected or who have any influence over him: Lavinia he never even sees, so that he cannot actually care about her in any personal fashion, and he is not present for the speech of Euryalus's nameless mother, whose scene in book 9 brings the association of Trojan women and death into Italy. To Italy Aeneas brings a protonationalist agenda that threatens the families and the way of life of every woman there. Thus his journey costs not only the lives of the men who fall on the battlefield but also the way of life of every woman in the poem. Though this cost could be said to apply to every man as well, the *Aeneid* shows that the women have more to lose: they will have to give up the important roles they have played in the monarchies of Troy and Italy and, to put Congreve's Mrs. Millimant into the plural, dwindle into wives.

Dido

Dido is the *Aeneid*'s most memorable and noteworthy female figure, and she is either physically or spectrally, as it were, present in nine of the poem's twelve books: she receives Aeneas in 1, is the audience of 2 and 3, and is the main focus of 4. Book 5 begins with the flames from her pyre and Aeneas's meditations on her; in 6, of course, he pursues her in the Underworld. Her gifts are mentioned in books 5, 9, and 11 (5.571–72, 9.266, 11.74; 5.750–53, 9.356, 11.94–98). In book 7, she is repeatedly invoked through episode and imagery: Silvia's deer recalls the image of Dido as a wounded, wandering deer at 4.68–73 (90–97); Amata's rampage through the city, under Allecto's influence, recalls Dido's maddened nighttime patrols; the maenadic mothers likewise invoke Dido. As Pierre Grimal points out, no female dominates either of the Homeric epics as Dido does the *Aeneid* (52). She is also the woman most obviously associated with a doomed city, a city Aeneas endangers both by staying in it (the building program ceases at 4.86–89 [113–18]) and by leaving it (the city walls catch fire from Dido's pyre at 5.3–5 [4–6]). Vergil concentrates his richest imagery and densest allusions on Dido, as she brings together all the themes associated with women throughout the poem: the epic past in which women can be rulers; the passion, fury, and irrationality of love; female opposition to, and destruction by, Aeneas's westward journey toward dynastic marriage; wounded deer; maenads; grief; mourning.

Even before her first appearance, Dido's exceptional nature and accomplishments are obvious: she took her people away from her brother and established a city so impressive that Aeneas envies it on sight (1.437; 619–20). In person she is striking (most gorgeous: *pulcherrima* [496; 700]), followed by a retinue, compared with Diana. She settles in the temple, rules her people, establishes laws and rights, and gives the men their work orders (505–08; 714–17), seeming closer to a king than a queen. In his speech Ilioneus approaches her like a suppliant. Her gracious response—that she will help the Trojans and that they may settle in her kingdom, to be treated equally with the Tyrians—underscores her power, confidence, and generosity. Aeneas himself praises her and makes her promises almost more appropriate to a divinity (595–610; 836–55). Her palace is filled with exceptional luxuries (637–42; 889–97), a further mark of her accomplishments and her status. But Dido's control is short-lived: Venus plans to destroy her by sending Cupid to inflame "the raging queen" (659–60; 921–23), a foreshadow of Dido's eventual destruction. Forthwith Dido converts from joyous (*laeta*) to wretched (*infelix*), as Cupid erases the memory of her dead husband. Even Aeneas's story—an odd seduction speech—further inflames the ailing queen, who asks him to repeat it again and again (4.77–79; 102–04). Her resistance to the new passion is sincere (9–29; 10–36) but brief, since her sister's speech causes her to hope. Significantly, however, Anna's persuasion is based primarily not on a defense of love but on the defense of Carthage: she mentions love only twice (33, 38; 41–42, 49), focusing instead on the advantages to Carthage of an alliance with the Trojans. The happy liaison of Dido and Aeneas lasts only 126 lines, from 169 to 295 (218–395), or one winter season. From 296 to 705 (396–971), Dido rages, not even recognizable as the powerful and gracious queen of book 1.

Dido's exceptional power is already, of course, resented and threatened by hostile neighbors; thus it is perhaps to be short-lived in any case. But certainly her passion for Aeneas brings ruin to her city and makes her lose control, so that she effectively abdicates her throne to roam, frenzied, about the city. She is an anachronism even before Aeneas meets her—a powerful queen, exactly the sort of woman not to be allowed in the Roman future (particularly given that Vergil's Roman readers will recall Cleopatra at every point of Dido's story), since Rome, as both republic and empire, will require the containment of women and the overthrow of foreign monarchies.

The Trojan Women

Throughout ancient myth and literature, the Trojan women are associated with death and with their ruined city; their primary activities are to weep, lament, and perform funeral rituals. The *Aeneid* gives little other activity even to those women who leave Troy with Aeneas. Though like every other Trojan refugee they are "ready in spirit and resources / to go by sea into whatever lands" Aeneas chooses (2.799–800; 1074–78), their main activity continues to be funeral rituals. (Their first described act, after leaving Troy, is to perform the rites for Polydorus [3.65; 85–86]; their final described act is to perform the rites for Pallas [11.34–35; 47–48].) The only human female to speak in *Aeneid* 3 is Andromache, who perhaps more than anyone else represents the pure association of the Trojan woman with death, for although she is alive and remarried to a Trojan, she looks only backward in time, envying Cassandra's death (3.321–24; 417–21).

Even in book 5, the Trojan women have little to do but weep, perform funerary rituals for Anchises, and oppose the forward motion of the poem. The funeral games offer the Trojan men opportunity for happy competition, which Aeneas resolves in such fashion that no competitor goes without some prize, thus violating the purpose of contest but making everyone happy (it is worth noting that the only woman in the games is the slave woman named Pholoë, given as a consolation prize to the loser of the boat race [284–85; 375–77]). The male competitions and the horse show of the boys are enjoyable events, with much laughter, boasting, and applause; they take place out in the open. The women, in striking contrast, observe Anchises's death far away, in secret, and in grief (613–614; 807–09; see Nugent, "Voice" 267–68). Where the men see the ocean as an arena for games, the women see it as a source of trouble and struggle (614–16; 810–11). The narrator describes the women as worn out by lengthy ocean voyages and as desiring to stay in their present location (615–16, 655–56; 813, 863–64). Thus they pray for one thing, a city, for they are weary of the toils of the sea (616, 617; 812, 813). This prayer occurs even before the disguised Iris stirs them up. Though her speech is designed to derange the women, she articulates their feelings clearly, particularly with the telling phrase *Italiam sequimur fugientem* ("we keep chasing fugitive Italy") (629; 829): they want to stay put. Iris easily convinces them to destroy the mechanism of their dreaded continued travel. But even the solution—that they should stay and establish a new town in Sicily—reconsigns these Trojan women to their paradigmatic fate, for Acesta can hardly be a self-sustaining city: its citizens are so senior that they are unlikely to be able either to support their town or to bear a next generation to support it and themselves. Thus, again, the Trojan women are associated with a dead city, a city doomed even before it is built. They leave the poem as they entered it: associated with loss, fated to have no part in the future.

The Italian Women

As Charles Babcock notes, in the second half of the poem Vergil focuses surprisingly on the costs of the war to the Italian women (49). The women have begun disappearing even before Aeneas arrives (a process accelerated by his arrival): among the Italians, Amata is the only surviving named mother, and she does not last long; Evander's wife is dead, and so is Mezentius's. Turnus's "goddess" mother never appears. Silvia, important enough to start the war, disappears once that war begins. The remaining Italian women are shown as belonging to a world already gone, now that Aeneas has entered it: Camilla and the mothers who want her as a daughter-in-law; the Latin mothers who rush off with Amata in book 7; the Italian mothers who attempt in book 11 to protect their city; Juturna, who labors vainly to save her brother. All are seen as inhabiting a vanishing moral universe, in which they have played important roles and whose extinction they attempt vainly to prevent. In the history of Rome, the Italian women will suffer the same fate as the Trojan women: loss of their city, home, and way of life. (Indeed, in the imperial future of Rome, as designed and desired by the emperor Augustus, the importance of women will be almost exclusively reproductive.) Significantly, however, Vergil shows the Italian women resisting that loss actively and effectively, for unlike Hecuba and her daughters huddling like doves when the Greeks enter Troy (2.515–16; 693–94), they take to the ramparts to fight off the invaders (11.891–95; 1180–86).

The primary strategy for women, Trojan and Italian alike, is to influence the men in their families and the citizens in their towns. Silvia's grief incites the men to take up arms. Amata affects everyone in the city and brings its functions to a halt; she is well prepared for Allecto's assault: "female concerns and angers were boiling her up, as she was burning over the arrival of the Trojans and the wedding of Turnus" (7.344–45; 455–47). Allecto fans these preexisting flames, so that Amata bursts out at her husband in an emotional speech opposing the marriage of Lavinia to Aeneas (359–72; 474–95). When Latinus holds out against her, Amata becomes a maenad, kidnaping her daughter and taking her to the mountains outside the city. Her calls reach the Laurentine mothers, who leave home to join in her bacchic frenzy. These mothers play out their eventual fate in advance, for they are, like every other woman in the poem, displaced from their city. Here that displacement does not occur because of the city's ruin but rather prefigures and precipitates it. The transformation of the Laurentine mothers into maenads—a dangerous force indeed—suggests the influence of women in this civilization: Amata helps turn the city against both the Trojans and Latinus himself, for not only does she remove the city's mothers from their houses, she also provides a cause for war among her people. After the skirmish over Silvia's deer, the relatives of the missing mothers gather around Latinus and urge him to make war: "for also the name of Amata was no light consideration," says the narrator (581; 765–67). Latinus gives in.

Thus the women incite the men to war—Amata drawing the Laurentine mothers out of town and Silvia calling on her countrymen to avenge the deer—both by making emotional appeals to kinship and by disrupting the life of the city. Once the city appears doomed, in the assault of the Trojans at the end of book 11, the mothers themselves go to the tops of the walls to join the desperate battle: "true love of their homeland instructed them, as they had seen Camilla— / trembling they hurl weapons [. . .] / headlong, they burned to be the first to die for their city walls" (11.892–93, 895; 1180–86). Camilla and Juturna also join the fighting—Camilla in the front of the battle, Juturna at her brother's side—but likewise to no avail. Juturna must leave her brother, lamenting his death and her pointless, painful immortality, and Camilla dies on the field (she is particularly doomed, because her refusal to marry and procreate means that she can have no place in the proto-Roman state). The "Italian excellence" ("Itala [. . .] virtute") (12.827; 1099) that is to make Rome powerful can be seen in these determined women, who use every method available to fend off their enemies (see Zarker 21). Regardless, theirs is a doomed effort, and their defeat in war will become a defeat of another sort in Roman history, as they will suffer a diminished role in the life of their country.

Women of the Future: Goddesses and Mothers of the Roman State

According to the *Iliad*, mythical Troy, though certainly no matriarchy, demonstrated greater respect for, and participation by, women than did either historical Rome or Greece. Even the Greek heroes of the Homeric epics treat the women in their lives with respect (on the relationships of Hector to Andromache and Odysseus to Penelope, see Perkell, "On Creusa" 357). To turn Aeneas into a Roman thus requires Vergil to remove all influence of women from him. Nothing about the Homeric Aeneas endows the character with any notable traits—in the *Iliad*, his primary distinguishing characteristics are his propensity to need rescue (5.314–18, 430, 436, 20.158–317 [lines in both Greek and the Lattimore translation]) and his divine mother. That mother, one of two divine ancestors for Rome (the other being Mars, father of Romulus and Remus), is hardly the sort of deity that Augustus wishes to feature in his program of rebuilding Rome. One simple solution is to identify not the mother (as for Achilles) but the father as the source of Aeneas's primary qualities, which must be recognizable as foundational Roman character traits, and to turn the mother into an agent of the Roman state. Thus Vergil both tames the troublesome goddess of love and establishes the father-son relationship so crucial to Rome's automythology. Anchises takes on the work, and the importance, of the mothers of Aeneas's Homeric models: he offers the emotional sustenance that Aeneas desires but does not find in his mother (as Thetis did for Achilles in *Iliad* 1); he gives his son instruction in the Underworld (as Anticleia did for Odysseus in *Odyssey* 11). Notably, the loss of Creusa means that Ascanius too grows up without a mother, though both Dido and Andromache behave maternally toward him. Thus even in the first family of the *Aeneid*, the mother is significantly missing and the father takes over many of her functions. This family structure is repeated in most of the primary Italian families as well; as I noted above, Turnus, Pallas, and Lausus have no mothers.

Even the Olympian divinities suffer the consequences of the *Aeneid*'s imperial imperatives and play out its westward movement toward the Roman future: Juno begins by delaying the Trojan mission and ends, as Jupiter predicts at 1.281–82 (391–92), by becoming an agent of Rome. Venus, that destroyer of cities Greek and Trojan, devotes herself more to the establishment of Rome than to her own son. The conversion of Juno and Venus into Roman goddesses signals the final destruction of the Homeric past, for at the end of the poem even the two most capricious deities have become august sponsors of Roman religion and empire.

Juno of course begins the poem in a state of rage fueled, significantly, by memory, the part of the mind that keeps the past alive; she employs multiple delaying strategies to oppose the poem's forward motion. But at the end of the poem she answers Jupiter's ultimatum (12.803–06; 1066–70) by seeking the final erasure of Troy. She asks that the joined Italians and Romans remain Italian in name, language, dress, and customs so that Troy will finally perish (828; 1100). Jupiter goes her one better: the Trojans will be mixed only physically with the Italians, and the resulting race will honor her more than any other people (830–40; 1102–17). At this promise Juno, rejoicing, literally "twists her mind back" (*mentem laetata retorsit*) (841; 1118–19), now presumably looking forward to the future rather than backward at the past. Though this agreement undoes Aeneas's mission of reestablishing Troy with his household gods, it places Juno in a position of sponsorship for Rome (indeed, she was the presiding divinity of Roman marriage). Only Juno's conversion to the future allows Aeneas to defeat Turnus (ironically with a remembering anger of his own, when he sees Pallas's sword belt) and bring the poem to a close.

Venus in the *Aeneid* resembles less the *Iliad*'s Aphrodite than the famous Spartan mother who told her son to return from battle with his shield or on it. Though the goddess of love is never easy to understand or predict, she is more confusing in the *Aeneid* than elsewhere, partly because she is uncharacteristically focused not on love but on public matters of nation, empire, government— in other words, on Rome itself. Her first speech virtually merges her with the Trojans, not as her former favorites but as her future offspring, the Romans. She uses first-person plural pronouns and verbs (1.250–53; 349–54) in asking Jupiter to stop the prolonged sea travel of the Trojans. Her dedication to the project of establishing Rome is such that she seems too busy to give her son the emotional closeness that he wants from her: he complains at 407–08 (581–84) that she often deceives him with false shapes and never speaks with him face-to-face and hand in hand. In this scene, as at the fall of Troy, Venus's concern is for Aeneas's physical safety (a reasonable maternal concern) rather than for his emotional well-being; her motives for protecting Helen are unstated, but she shows no further interest in her former protegée. The one time Venus embraces Aeneas, when she has just brought him Vulcan's armor (commissioned at her request rather than at his), he seems more interested in the armor than in her. Elsewhere she exhibits more concern for Ascanius than for Aeneas, as in her sarcastic speech at 10.18–62 (24–85); shortly after, the narrator calls Ascanius "Venus' most righteous care" (132; 188–89), as if to mark her dynastic interest as primary to her maternal concerns. Thus she becomes an institutional divinity suited to the Augustan program—she is the *alma genetrix*, fostering mother, of Rome itself rather than either the dangerously seductive goddess of the Homeric poems or a protective mother to the *Aeneid*'s hero, her son. As Eleanor Leach argues, throughout the poem Venus acts like a Roman mother of the elite class—indeed, she becomes a Roman before Aeneas does ("Venus").

Vergil's Lavinia is similarly diminished, in striking contrast to Livy's version of her (Greenough), for in the *Aeneid* she is little more than a means to an end. Though she is betrothed to Turnus and, if R. O. A. M. Lyne is correct (*Voices* 114–22), loves and wants to marry him, she is handed over to Aeneas instead. Aeneas seeks her only for dynastic purposes and, in fact, never even lays eyes on her. The *Aeneid*'s version of the mother of the future does not even speak: she blushes once, and she shrieks when she finds her mother dead. Oddly, the poem gives no indication at all of her character, or even of her appearance; though she is the *Aeneid*'s Helen, her Trojan suitor pursues not her beauty but her dynastic function. Where Livy describes her as exceptional (Greenough 1.3–5)—a woman of such character (*tanta indoles* [1.3.1]) that she ruled Lavinium while Ascanius was young, protecting it so effectively that the town not only survives but thrives despite its hostile neighbors (like the Dido of *Aeneid* 1)—the *Aeneid*'s Lavinia is nothing more than the mother of Aeneas's posthumous son. The poem erases a woman of character and accomplishment, placing in her stead a woman important only for her reproductive function. Even so, Vergil manages to make many of his readers wonder, Can Lavinia want to marry Aeneas? What does she want? And he perhaps encourages them to ask, At what price are women converted from agents of their own lives to passive producers of sons?

Though the *Aeneid* appears to erase women, its female characters stand out and their erasure from involvement in public life leaves its mark, for the future family life of Rome loses the intimate and loving aspects of past family life in Italy and Troy. And if the *Aeneid* presents its hero's mission as both inevitable and necessary, it also dramatizes the costs of that mission, particularly through the female characters who block it—from Dido in books 1 through 4, to the Trojan women in book 5, to the Latin women who run off with Amata in book 7, to the Italian mothers and wives at the end of book 11, who go to the tops of the walls and the city gates to join in the battle to save their home. The poem insists that those costs not be overlooked or forgotten (see Nugent, "Women," esp. 269–70). "Tantae molis erat Romanam condere gentem" ("so great a struggle was it to establish the Roman people") (1.33; 50), says the poem's narrator. Through the figures of its women, the *Aeneid* shows that this struggle was two-sided and that in some ways both sides lost.

NOTES

[1]For another view of women in the *Aeneid*, see P. Miller; Keith.

[2]The English translation of the *Aeneid* referred to throughout this essay is by Mandelbaum.

Pietas, Furor, and Ecofeminism in the *Aeneid*

Lorina N. Quartarone

Aeneas carrying his father on his back and holding his son by the hand as he escapes the flames of Troy (2.721–25; Mandelbaum 974–79):[1] the image—which appears in Greek, Etruscan, and Roman art, in vase and wall paintings, on coins and in votive figurines—is familiar to both modern and ancient readers of the *Aeneid*. In many ways, this icon conveys Aeneas's significance to Roman history: he symbolically carried the Trojan past, embodied in his father, Anchises, and ushered the future, represented by his son, Ascanius, forward along the path to empire. This image of the family and Aeneas's long-admired *pietas* adumbrate the centrality of the family in Italian culture; various depictions include the Penates or household gods carried by either Anchises or Aeneas, further attesting that *pietas* is central to the Aeneas legend.

The conspicuous absence of the female in Vergil's image speaks volumes through silence. Readers know that Creusa, Aeneas's wife, follows behind as he rescues father and son and that she becomes a casualty of the city's destruction. Readers should also realize that Vergil is adapting this image from traditional Italian art and lore to suit his poetic purposes. He must remove Creusa from the picture to allow Aeneas's relationship with Dido and with his new bride in Italy. Vergil's choice to represent Aeneas as simultaneously leaving behind Creusa and Troy gives the text a shape and character that illustrate the principal tenets of ecofeminism. In what follows, I discuss ecofeminism, first with respect to the image of Aeneas just presented, second in a more general application to the poem. I then analyze the poem from an ecofeminist perspective through the traditional themes of *pietas* and *furor*.

The central premises of ecofeminism are twofold: that the female and nature are integrally connected and that the androcentric forces that have shaped Western culture are responsible for the oppression of both the female and nature. Many ecofeminists recognize the tendency in Western thought and speech to perceive the world in the dualistic terms of nature/culture, female/male, and body/mind, and they address the need to eradicate such dualism. The *Aeneid*, an important text in the Western tradition, displays these notions.

Vergil's representation of Aeneas leaving behind his wife and homeland crystallizes the image of the male as the center of progress and culture. This image relegates the female and the native land to a position of replaceability. In this regard, the *Aeneid* differs greatly from its Homeric predecessors. In the *Odyssey*, native land, home, and wife remain the stable center of life to which Odysseus longs to return throughout the epic. Had Penelope or Ithaca been replaceable, he would have remained with Circe or Calypso. In the *Iliad*, if Helen had been replaceable, the war would never have occurred. This is not to say that these societies were not patriarchal or oppressive to women in other manners; Homer's two poems simply portray specific women as possessing certain traits that make them individual and irreplaceable. Aeneas does not want to lose Creusa and Troy; he would rather remain there, fight, and die. He is compelled to move forward, and as he leaves behind his loving wife and nurturing homeland (the distinction should be made here between Troy the culture and Troy the native land), he leaves behind part of himself. He does not set out to replace what he has lost, but when Creusa's ghost informs him that he will obtain *regnumque et regia coniunx* ("a kingdom and a royal bride") (2.783; 1057), we learn that he will replace Troy with Italy and Creusa with Lavinia. Unlike Odysseus, Aeneas has no emotional attachment to the kingdom and wife that await him; in a figurative sense, his home travels with him in his father, son, and gods. It is significant that this portable home has no female. This omission symbolically devalues the mother and fertility. The lack of individuality with which Vergil portrays Lavinia and that Aeneas marries her for political reasons reinforce the idea that one woman may substitute for another.

Vergil associates both Creusa and Lavinia with the land and fertility. He frames the episode in which Aeneas loses Creusa with references to the temple of Ceres, described as *desertae* at the start of the scene and *antiquae* toward its end (2.714, 742). These adjectives suggest a departure from the earlier worship of the nurturing earth goddess. Aeneas's reference to *deserta Creusa* (562) and her shade's assertion that "me magna deum genetrix his detinet oris" ("It is the gods' / great Mother who keeps me upon these shores") (788; 1062–63) associate her with Ceres. Creusa's statement that "this could never come to pass without / the gods' decree" (777–78; 1048–49) implies divine sanction of her abandonment and, in keeping with the epic, grounds the rise of Rome in divinely ordained destiny. From the start of the poem, Vergil reminds those familiar with the legend that Lavinia will lend her name to the land (*Lavinaque venit / litora* [1.2–3]), which will be called Lavinium, and in this way the epic underscores the implicit connection between the earth and the female. That the people will be called Latins (after Latinus) and later Romans (after Romulus) illustrates the primacy of males as rulers and progenitors. The female remains linked primarily to fertility (the natural and physical); the male remains the central factor in the progress of history and the conveyance of culture (the intellectual and cultural).

Ecofeminism recognizes that the male views himself as the standard or norm and comes to view the female as his opposite, the other, whom he considers different or inferior. By similar opposition, the Trojan or Roman male, maintaining himself as the standard, views males of different cultures as the other. As Anchises instructs Aeneas in the Underworld, "yours will be the rulership of nations, / remember, Roman, these will be your arts; / to teach the ways of peace to those you conquer, / to spare defeated peoples, tame the proud" (6.851–53; 1134–37). In effect, the native Italians, Carthaginians, females, and the earth or nature all function in the poem as the other. As Greta Gaard states:

In [. . .] analyses of oppression [. . .] ecologists, and feminists each distinguish between privileged and oppressed groups where the privileged are upper- or middle-class, human, technologically and industrially "developed," male, and the oppressed are poor or working-class, non-human animal, "undeveloped" nature, and female, respectively. Ecofeminism describes the framework that authorizes these forms of oppression as patriarchy, an ideology whose fundamental self/other distinction is based on a sense of self that is separate, atomistic.

("Interconnections" 1–2)

It is understandable that Aeneas frequently experiences isolation and remoteness; although it is not his choice, he must distance himself from most of the indigenous Italians, other non-Trojan peoples, and women. The conflicts that arise between him and these groups often engender *furor*. As he attempts to restrain *furor*, in both others and himself, he appears to be grappling with or stifling his emotions; often, he must subdue personal desires and demonstrate *pietas*. In teaching the ways of peace to those he conquers, he must also conquer himself. This is the central paradox of patriarchy.

Vergil depicts the hero, from his initial appearance in the poem, as struggling to contain his emotions: "though sick with heavy cares, / he counterfeits hope in his face; his pain is held within, hidden" (1.208–09; 290–92). In this repression of emotion, Aeneas stands in opposition to Juno and Dido, who are effusive without reserve. The text suggests that Aeneas presents the acceptable or proper way of handling emotion; while Juno and Dido threaten to disrupt order, he maintains or restores it. These characterizations demonstrate Gaard's observation:

The way in which women and nature have been conceptualized historically in the Western intellectual tradition has resulted in devaluing whatever is associated with women, emotion, animals, nature, and the body, while simultaneously elevating in value those things associated with men, reason, humans, culture, and the mind.   (5)

In the *Aeneid*, Vergil's opposition of males (primarily in the figures of Aeneas, Jupiter, and Neptune) to females (Dido, Juno, and Allecto) exemplifies this ideology. Vergil frequently links these females with violent forces of nature (e.g., raging winds, fire) that threaten the established order (as Allecto does generally). Although he writes with great sympathy and sensitivity, elements of the text display the tendency of Western culture to parallel women, animals, nature, and cultures that patriarchy deems inferior. The poem also presents different types of feminine behavior. As Carolyn Merchant observes, "The virgin nymph offered peace and serenity, the earth mother nurture and fertility." Venus, Creusa, and Lavinia represent this category. But "wild uncontrollable nature was associated with the female. [. . .] Disorderly woman, like chaotic nature, needed to be controlled" (127). Juno, Dido, and Amata play this role.

Ecofeminism offers a number of templates to employ when interpreting the *Aeneid*: the characterization of males or females, the animalization of both females and conquered males, the parallels between women and nature, the feminization of subdued males and other cultures, and the opposition between reason and emotion. In the first half of the poem Vergil uses *pietas* and *furor* gender-specifically: he attributes *pietas* to the male, *furor* to both women and destructive natural forces. In the second half of the poem he expands the influence of *furor* to men and complicates the clearly delineated gender-specificity of the earlier books. This portrayal of *furor* as a force that affects both sexes reflects the complexity and ambivalence that scholars find in the poem's conclusion: like the benefits of empire that come at significant cost, *furor* both founds and destroys civilization.

That Vergil associates *pietas* with the male is evident from his initial description of Aeneas as a man distinguished for piety—*insignem pietate virum* ("remarkable for goodness") (1.10; 16). In fact, more than half of the sixty-one occurrences of the adjective *pius* or the substantive *pietas* characterize Aeneas: twenty-eight describe him and his actions, another eight occur in his speech. By making *pietas* the distinctive trait of Aeneas, Vergil establishes its importance to the foundation of the Roman city and empire. Furthermore, most of the remaining appearances of *pius* or *pietas* denote men and male behavior. The terms occur ten times in the speeches of Anchises and other men such as Priam and five times to describe the actions of Trojan or proto-Roman men. In sum, fifty-two of the sixty-one occurrences of *pius* or *pietas* directly portray men and their behavior.

Vergil never applies *pietas* to female behavior. Although *pius* and *pietas* do occur in women's speeches, in four of the ten occurrences the females describe the pious behavior of men (two describe Aeneas). In the remaining instances, the *pietas* that women purport to recognize is undercut by the *furor* of their behavior. Euryalus's mother, in her lament, ironically begs the Rutulians, "If you have any pietas, Rutulians, / then run me through, hurl all your shafts at me, / and let me be the first you kill" (9.493–94; 655–58). Describing her as *amens* ("mad") (9.478; 636), Vergil emphasizes her state as she rushes toward the fray, mindless with grief. Likewise, Amata, possessed by *furor*, addresses the frenzied Latin matrons and their "pious hearts" (*piis animis* [7.401; 534]). In this passage, seven forms or cognates of *furor* (*furibunda, furentem, furiale, furit, furorem, furiis,* and *furores* [348, 350, 375, 377, 386, 392, 406]), illustrate that this female behavior is the antithesis of *pietas*. *Ululatibus* ("with quivering cries") (7.395; 526) further associates their actions with those of Euryalus's frantic mother, who also runs "with a woman's wailing" (*ululatu*) (9.477; 634). In fact, even though women do pray and demonstrate loyalty in the epic, Vergil never employs *pietas* to describe them. As the distinguishing feature of Aeneas, who carries his father and household gods out of the conflagration at Troy, *pietas* is the sense of duty and control that is central to the establishment and maintenance of patriarchal society.

Vergil opposes *pietas* and *furor* from the poem's beginning. After characterizing Aeneas as *insignem pietate virum*, he describes Juno and her wrath. When Juno seeks the help of Aeolus, who is responsible for keeping these potentially destructive forces in check, he unleashes "the raging South winds" (*furentibus Austris*) (1.51; trans. mine). Though released by a male, these natural forces symbolize Juno's anger. When the resultant storm evokes primordial chaos, Neptune quells it, rebuking the winds for inciting such a tempest: "So, Winds, you dare to mingle sky and land, / heave high such masses, without my command?" (133–34; 188–89). As he describes the restoration of order, Vergil compares Neptune to a man of public office subduing a raging mob. This man, "remarkable for righteousness and service" (*pietate gravem ac meritis*) (1.151; 213–14), controls a crowd enflamed by passion ("saevitque animis [. . .] / furor arma ministrat [. . .] / ille regit dictis animos et pectora mulcet" ["the rabble rage in their minds (. . .) / fury finds its weapons (. . .) / he controls / their passion by his words and cools their spirits" (149–53; 210–16)]). Opposing the male, *pietas*, and social order to the female, *furor*, and unpredictable natural phenomena, Vergil illustrates how the former controls or subordinates the latter. Long before the term *ecofeminism* emerged, both Viktor Pöschl (*Art* 16–18) and William Anderson (*Art* 13) observed the opposition of the male and reason to the female and emotion in this scene, in effect anticipating what ecofeminists like Janis Birkeland later observed: "Women and nature have been juxtaposed against mind and spirit, which have been associated in Western cosmology with the 'masculine' and elevated to a higher plane of being" (18).

Pöschl notes that the opposition of Juno and Jupiter symbolizes "the struggle between light and darkness, mind and emotion, order and chaos" (18). As John Patrick Sullivan observes, Juno is the linchpin in the text, the crux of the female *furor* that obstructs Aeneas in his mission. Since it threatens the foundation of Rome, it must be subdued. Vergil's repeated references to Juno's *furor* function in two manners: first, they provide a structural framework for the poem that associates her anger with wild natural forces; second, they heighten the distance between her, who resists the patriarchy, and Venus, who supports it. In the storm in book 1, instigated by the *furentibus Austris* ("raging south winds"), the "surge [. . .] seethes with sand" (*furit aestus harenis*) (107; 152). In book 2, Venus herself describes Juno as *furens* ("raging"; trans. mine) against Troy, where Juno's anger is once more unleashed through *furentibus Austris* (613, 828). In book 5, Venus again labels Juno's impassioned behavior as *furor* and accuses her of attempting to re-create chaos ("she mingled all the seas with heaven" [788–91; 1043]). In book 10, she complains of Juno's anger and her *ventosque furentis* ("raging winds" [37; 50]). When Jupiter finally dictates that Juno relinquish her *furor*, which is *inceptum frustra* ("begun in vain" [12.832; trans. mine]), the text indicates the futility of her struggle against patriarchal control.

It is apparent from these references that Venus serves as a vehicle to criticize Juno's *furor*. Vergil depicts two types of women, those who support the patriarchy and those who oppose it (see Merchant). Although not virginal, Venus represents the nurturing or helpful type of female, while Juno is the disorderly one whom the male must subdue. Venus never acts out of *furor* and often rebukes it. Although Vergil never actually ascribes *pietas* to Venus—he remains consistent in portraying it as a male trait—he depicts her as a proponent of the coming empire through her protection of Aeneas and opposition to Juno. Significantly, when she retrieves Aeneas's spear (12.787), her support of the patriarchy also condones its oppressive tendencies. The spear, which Aeneas had cast at Turnus, was stubbornly embedded in the trunk of a tree. This tree was sacred to the woodland deity Faunus and honored by the Laurentians, but the Trojans had irreverently (*nullo discrimine* ["heedless of this custom"] [770; 1020]) cut it down. This action demonstrates their lack of respect for the traditions and religion of the native Italians. Emphasizing the disrespect, Turnus prays to Faunus and the Earth to retain the spear: "I pray you, Faunus, pity me; and you, / most gracious Earth, hold fast that steel, if I / have ever kept your rites—those that Aeneas's / men have irreverently profaned by war" (777–79; 1030–33). When Juturna returns Turnus's sword, the indignant Venus frees Aeneas's spear, overturning the fulfillment of Turnus's plea by Faunus and the Earth and essentially prefiguring the victory of the patriarchy. Venus's intervention protects Aeneas, restores to him the means of subduing Turnus, and supports the coming empire's defeat of the native Italian culture. Gerda Lerner would argue that such tangible support by Venus for the patriarchy represents the female's complicity in her own subordination.

In his introduction of Venus, Vergil describes her as *tristior* ("rather sorrowful" [1.228; trans. mine]). This characterization lends depth and gravity to a goddess who in Greek myth is known for frivolity and capriciousness (as her Greek epithet *philommeides,* "laughter-loving," suggests). Through this portrayal and her concern for *pietas,* the mother of Aeneas and ancestress of the Romans is rendered more respectable than the troublesome Aphrodite of Greek myth. When Venus accuses Jupiter of abandoning his support of Aeneas, she asks, *hic pietatis honos?* ("Is this your reward for piety?") (253; trans. mine—the phrase is oddly omitted by Mandelbaum). Jupiter responds that to Aeneas's descendants *imperium sine fine dedi* ("I have given empire without end" [279; trans. mine]) and refers to Juno's anger in its connection with natural forces: "Then even bitter Juno shall be changed; / [. . .] she, who now harasses lands and heavens / with terror [. . .]" (279–80; 391–92). He closes his speech with the compelling image of *Furor impius* (294), speaking of peace as the time when "unholy Rage / shall sit on his ferocious weapons, bound / behind his back by a hundred knots of brass; / he shall groan horribly with bloody lips" (294–96; 414–17). Thus far, the reader has encountered *furor* in the wrath of Juno and Neptune's simile; this passage completes the portrayal. In the personification of *furor,* the adjective *impius* confirms that *furor* lacks *pietas*—or, more precisely, is diametrically opposed to *pietas*—and justifies the oppression of women and natural forces, whose *furor* is potentially harmful to society. Although this embodiment of civil strife as *furor* suggests that it may also overwhelm the male, as will occur in the second half of the poem, Vergil primarily shows *furor* in men as emerging from female *furor* (e.g., Allecto's infecting Turnus) or from the necessity of subduing *furor* to protect societal order (e.g., Hercules *furens* subduing Cacus in book 8).

On the divine plane, Vergil associates *furor* with Juno; in the mortal realm, he associates it most with Dido. Dido illustrates that *furor* emerges as a reaction to oppression and is not a natural uncontrollability in women. Venus, the advocate of the patriarchy, bears the responsibility for the fate of Dido. In book 1 she encourages Aeneas to seek Dido's assistance and contrives to make her fall in love with him (an apparently unnecessary beguilement, since Dido already welcomed Aeneas and his people [561–78; 791–815]). The hapless Dido can no more overcome the power of Venus and *amor* than she can transcend the patriarchally imposed concept of the *univira* (a woman who remains faithful to her husband even after his death). Overwhelmed with passion for Aeneas, she sullies her vow to remain faithful to the dead Sychaeus. When the divine machinations of patriarchy beckon Aeneas to Italy, her transgression prompts her to suicide. Her behavior shows that, in patriarchal society, a woman's worth is measured by devotion to her husband. The distinction between respectable and nonrespectable women is determined by the number of sexual partners: "a married woman's sexual behavior, such as adultery or an unmarried woman's loss of chastity, could declass her in a way in which no man could be declassed by his sexual activity" (Lerner 140). When Dido loses her mark of respectability—her faithfulness to Sychaeus—as well as her new lover-husband Aeneas, she behaves in a manner befitting a woman steeped in patriarchal ideology, who knows that there can be no remedy for her shame.

From this perspective, Dido's behavior is rational and comprehensible; yet Vergil's choice to portray Dido as overwhelmed by *furor* emphasizes unrestrained feminine emotion. He thereby demonstrates his sympathy for the plight of women, recognizing that patriarchy allows women few choices and may impel them toward *furor*. Book 4 contains more occurrences of *furor* and its cognates than any other, sixteen: fourteen describe Dido, who is characterized even outside book 4 as *furens* (1.659, 5.6; 1.922, 5.7). Vergil compares the lamentation that consumes Carthage at Dido's death to the destructive power of flames ("femineo ululatu [. . .] / [. . .] flammaeque furentes" [4.667–70; 919–24) and underscores her *furor* by having Dido recognize it herself (*furiis incensa feror* ["I am whirled along / in fire by the Furies!"] [376; 513–14]) and by eliciting a verbal tension between *pietas* and *furor* in what follows. First, the raging Dido, in a far from rational state, angrily refers to the gods as *pia numina* ("pious divine powers") (382; trans. mine). Second, having attributed *furor* to Dido three times in close proximity (*furentem, furias, furores* [465, 474, 501]), Vergil ironically describes her as offering sacrifice "with pious hands" (*manibusque piis* [517]). Finally, still raging, Dido urges her nurse to encircle her temples "pia [. . .] vitta" ("with a pious fillet" [637]). By heightening this tension, Vergil indicates the difference between the *furens* Dido and the *pius* Aeneas, a difference that opposes their initial similarities (both are refugees-exiles, both are widowed, and both are respected rulers of their people). The opposition of Dido and Aeneas first occurs in the deer simile at 4.68–79 (90–101), which establishes the roles of hunter/hunted or aggressor/victim; it diminishes Dido's responsibility in her death and likens her to an unfortunate animal destined to be subdued: that "she roams / the forests and the wooded slopes [. . .] / the shaft of death still clinging to her side" (72–73; 95–97) symbolizes man's irresponsible injuries toward both nature and women. This portrayal of Dido demonstrates the tenet of ecofeminist theory that "in the self/other dualism of patriarchal thought, 'others' are feminized or animalized [. . .] in order to make their subordination seem more natural" (Gaard, "Interconnections" 8). What Vergil's simile stresses, however, is the shepherd's unintentional harm to the doe; he may not set out to cause this damage, but he is its source. When Dido later wishes that she could have spent her life "never knowing marriage, like a wild / beast, never to have touched such toils" (550–51; 764–65), she inveighs against the institution; she understands the restrictions placed on women by society and ironically envisions her escape in the form of a wild creature. Vergil conveys the tragedy of her oppression by describing her death as one "not merited or fated" (696; 959), when Juno—not the more responsible Venus—takes pity on Dido's suffering.

Vergil pairs women and the power of fire in book 5, when the Trojan women, wearied by their lengthy voyage, longing for a home, and incited by Juno's "old / resentment" (*antiquum dolorem* [608; 801–02]), set fire to the ships. After Iris inflames them with *furor*, they are "driven mad" (*actaeque furore*) and start a fire that "rages" (*furit*) on the ships (659, 662; 870, 874). Ascanius, as if recognizing the *furor* behind the fire, shouts, *quis furor iste novus?* ("what strange madness is this?" [670; 883]). As in book 1, masculine piety quells the *furor*. *Pius Aeneas* (685; 903) prays to Jupiter, who sends a rainstorm to quench the fire. The storm, initiated by *pietas*, responds to female *furor* in kind: the tempest rages ("tempestas [. . .] furit" [694; 916]). Shortly thereafter, Neptune confirms that the male restrains formidable natural forces, particularly those incited by feminine *furor*: "I have earned this trust, / for I have often checked the frenzy [*furores*] and great anger of the sea and sky" (801–02; 1057–59). The sea and sky are often the locales of Juno's *furor* (e.g., 1.279–80 and 5.790). His statement assumes that females, their emotions, and natural forces are all rightfully subject to masculine control. This is the attitude that ecofeminism recognizes as central to patriarchal society.

As mentioned above, Vergil does not associate *furor* exclusively with women —his poetry remains too complex for such universal bias, and he often creates distinctions only to blur them later. After book 7 *furor* takes a new trajectory. Through book 7, the tension between *pietas* and *furor* is maintained, and *furor* is associated primarily with women and natural forces. Of the fifty-six occurrences of *furor* to this point, Vergil employs thirty-four to describe women, ten to portray the wildness of natural forces—nine of which are instigated by females—and three to characterize civil strife. The nine remaining instances do describe men, but seven of these occur in book 2, where men are consumed by Juno's *furor* during the fall of Troy. Thus, Vergil establishes that *furor* is something that overwhelms males only in exceptional circumstances. (Even under dire conditions, however, *furor* in men does not invite approval, as Venus illustrates in her reproach of Aeneas when he considers slaying Helen: *quid furis?* ["Why this madness?"] [2.595; 803]). Vergil maintains this line of distinction through book 7, when Juno rouses Allecto to infect the native Italians with *furor*. The poet compresses six appearances of *furor* into fewer than fifty lines (348–92) as Allecto corrupts Amata and the Latin matrons; when she infuses Turnus with *furor*, the poet compares him to water bubbling out of its cauldron: "the liquid dances with the heat; within, / the water rages [*furit*], violent, and pours / a stream of smoke and foam" (464–65; 613–15). The effect is appropriate: Turnus is compared to water, not in a natural environment, such as a river or sea, but in a cauldron, a man-made device that contains a potentially changeable and harmful element.

Later in book 7, Allecto incites the shooting of Sylvia's pet stag:

> And here the hellish virgin casts a sudden
> frenzy upon his dogs, touching their nostrils
> with scent they know too well, inflaming them
> to chase after a stag: this hunting was
> the first cause of the troubles, and for this
> the rustic minds of Latium were driven
> to war.   (479–82; 633–39)

This docile creature, reared by a native Italian woman, becomes an innocent victim and the ostensible cause for war between the native Italians and Trojans. Vergil's description of the deer illustrates the close relationship between it and the Latins: they enjoy a peaceful coexistence with an animal they have tamed without violence. Ascanius's arrow shatters both this harmony and the Trojans' welcome by the native Italians. Although Juno's *furor* instigates war on the divine level, the attack on an animal is the catalyst on earth; the causes of conflict are women, emotion, and nature. The circumstances evoke Dido as the wounded deer, further suggesting that the injuries done to her, like those done to Juno, will one day erupt in warfare. This animalization of the other also occurs with Turnus, whom Vergil frequently likens to animals: a stallion (11.492–97; 651–57), a wolf (9.59–66; 74–84), and a lion (9.792–98; 1055–64) (see Putnam, "Anger" 172–94, on the irrational, nonhuman aspect of *furor*). By comparing Turnus, who will be vanquished, to an animal, Vergil implies that his *furor* represents the uncontrollable aspect of human behavior that the civilizing forces of patriarchy must harness.

In book 8, Vergil adjusts his previous depiction of *furor*. Through Evander's tale of Hercules, he suggests that *furor* is a justifiable tool in subduing primitive, bestial forces. When the *furens* ("in frenzied anger") Hercules pursues Cacus, who embodies a primal *furor* natural to monsters ("at furiis Caci mens effera" ["But then the mind of Cacus / was driven wild with frenzy"]), Vergil emphasizes Hercules's *dolor* or "resentment": "At this, / the wrath of Hercules was hot with black / gall and with grief" (228, 205, 219–20; 299, 270–71, 286–88). *Dolor* links Hercules's *furor* not only to Juno (it is the source of her *furor* at 1.25, 5.608, and 10.63–64) but also to Dido (4.434, 419, 474), Amata (12.599), and ultimately Aeneas himself (12.945). For all these figures, *dolor*, normally "pain" or "distress," evolves into a "resentment," often justified, that engenders *furor* (as Otis, Virgil, and Putnam, "Possessiveness," have demonstrated). That it is often this *furor*, not *pietas*, that subdues *furor* is illustrated by the tale of Mezentius, who is both impious (*contemptor divum* ["despiser of the gods"]) and "a madman" (*furentem*) and whose extreme cruelty caused "furiis [. . .] iustis" ("just anger") and "iustus [. . .] / dolor" ("just resentment") in his people (7.648, 8.489, 494, 500–01; 7.855, 8.636, 641, 650). Vergil thus shows that *furor* not only may but perhaps must be assumed by men who struggle to effect social change or justice (as Galinsky, "Hercules," suggests).

In book 9, the metamorphosis of the ships offers a nexus of elements that lend themselves to ecofeminist interpretation. First, the poet identifies the earth, the "Great Mother," as female. Second, he portrays her, the "mother of the gods" ("deum [. . .] genetrix" [82], the same phrase used at 2.788) as subordinate in power to the male Jupiter, despite the fact that she calls him her son (*nate*) and Vergil refers to him as her *filius* (83, 93). Finally, an injury at the hands of the male compels her to action. Vergil's reference to the behavior of Turnus as *iniuria* ("outrage") (108; 141) recalls the injury done to Juno at the poem's start (where she experiences *dolor* and *iniuria* through the actions of Paris and Jupiter [1.25–28]). In this passage, Vergil's attribution of *furor* to Turnus (rather than to the injured female) through the simile comparing him to a wolf that "rages in anger" (*ira / saevit* [9.62–63], an echo of *irarum saevique* [1.25]) demonstrates the thorough transfer of female *furor* to the male. Turnus's depiction as a wild and predatory animal also presages his eventual subordination.

The chaos heightens as *pietas* collapses into *furor* in book 10. After the death of Pallas, Vergil portrays Aeneas as angry, irrational, possessed by *furor*. In sixty lines, Vergil uses *furor* twice to describe Aeneas (*furit* ["storms"] and *furens* ["he raged"]) (545, 604; 753, 829). Moreover, "so does Aeneas / rage on" (569; 783–84) contains *desaevit*, a verb that occurs only twice in the epic (the other instance is in a description of a raging winter storm [4.52; 70–01]). Aeneas is now like a wild force of nature; his *furor* erupts, and he cannot control it. He "storms" again as he rushes at Lausus (10.802; 1102) and ironically taunts him for displaying *pietas*: "fallit te incautum pietas tua" ("your loyalty / has tricked you into recklessness") (812; 1114–15). Lausus is likewise described in terms of irrationality. He is *demens* (813), an adjective Vergil applies three times to

Dido ("insane," "madly," "seized by frenzy" [4.78, 374, 469; 102, 511, 647]), once to characterize *Discordia* in the Underworld ("mad Strife" [6.280; 371]), and will employ again to describe the frenzied Amata ("mad" [12.601; 807]). The adjective *incautus* also evokes Dido in the deer simile; it symbolizes her lack of awareness of the danger that will destroy her (4.70; 94). These links undermine Lausus's alleged *pietas*. Is his motivation truly *pietas*, or is it *furor*? Or is the enraged Aeneas now unable to distinguish between the two? The "saevae [. . .] irae" ("harsh anger" [10.813; 1117]) that emerges in both Lausus and Aeneas (for commentary on 10.813, see R. Williams, Aeneid) also recalls Juno, who is *saevae* ("savage"), possesses *irae* ("resentment"), and experiences *saevique dolores* ("savage hurt") (1.4, 11, 25; 7, 18, 40). Although Aeneas appears to regain his sense of *pietas* after killing Lausus, this scene truly signals the disintegration of his self-restraint. *Pietas* and *furor*, previously distinct, are now blurred, and as they lose their clearly delineated lines, so too do gender distinctions (as Oliensis discusses).

In book 11 Vergil describes the role reversals of Camilla, who becomes a warrior, and her father, who carries his infant at his breast (544; 714–15). Is Camilla's *furor* that of a female who was nourished on the milk of wild animals (570–72; 754) or that of a skilled warrior who struggles to defend her freedom? Likewise, is Turnus's *furor* born out of defense for what is rightfully his or is it completely infused by Allecto? Vergil's portrayals of these characters obfuscate his earlier and more limited association of *furor* with the female as the chaos of war, elicited by the *furor* of Juno, infects the behavior of both males and females.

In the final duel, when Aeneas sees Pallas's sword belt, that *saevi monumenta doloris* ("memorial of brutal grief"), he becomes "aflame with rage" (*furiis accensus*) (12.945, 946; 1263, 1264). He wavers momentarily as he considers his *pietas* toward Pallas and that which he could show toward his enemy Turnus. That he acts out of *furor* and kills Turnus because of his *dolor* (as Putnam has convincingly argued ["Possessiveness" 41–42]) demonstrates that *furor* is not an exclusively female trait but a human characteristic. Indeed, as Merchant observes, "there are no unchanging 'essential' characteristics of sex, gender, or nature" (xvi); rather, individuals form such notions through cultural and social experience. That Aeneas acts from emotion rather than *pietas* illustrates the paradox that, in order to exert control, *pietas* at times resorts to *furor*. Both Hercules and Aeneas demonstrate the irony that society, to a certain extent, rests on a foundation of *furor*. In this ironic ending, Vergil confirms that *furor* is human, not only feminine; he also denies that the male and *pietas* can completely subdue *furor*, by portraying the male struggle to contain *furor* as a struggle not only with the other but also with the self. Vergil effectively mends the rift—between the male, reason, and control on the one hand and the female, emotion, and uncontrollability on the other—that he describes in the first half of the poem. In the second half, his attribution of *furor* to both male and female underscores the similarity of the sexes rather than their separateness and reminds us that emotions are an integral part of being human. William Anderson may have said it best when he observed that the initial question *tantaene animis caelestibus irae?* ("can such [great] resentment hold the minds of gods?") (1.11; 18) evolves by the poem's conclusion into "can such great resentment hold the minds of human beings?" (*Art* 23). Whereas Juno, despite her previous *furor,* quickly surrenders her will and ceases to struggle against destiny, the pious Aeneas becomes overwhelmed by *furor.* In these two moments, the distinction between male and female, reason and emotion breaks down, revealing that complexity rather than reductionism is at the core of human affairs.

NOTES

I would like to thank William S. Anderson, John Breuker Jr., and Linda Gillison for their many helpful comments and suggestions.

[1]The English translation of the *Aeneid* referred to throughout this essay is by Mandelbaum, unless indicated as mine.

Feminae Furentes: The Frenzy of Noble Women in Vergil's *Aeneid* and the Letter of Cornelia, Mother of the Gracchi

Judith P. Hallett

At the close of *Aeneid* 6, during the reunion in the Underworld between Aeneas and his father, Anchises parades before his son a series of men destined to lead the Roman state, each of them as yet unborn. Included in this illustrious company are "the family of the Gracchi [and] the twin Scipiones, two thunderbolts of war, the destruction of Libya" (842–43; trans. mine). In this elliptical manner, Vergil refers to several of the Sempronii Gracchi and a pair of the Cornelii Scipiones. Commentators assume that these Sempronii Gracchi are Tiberius Sempronius Gracchus, consul in 177 BCE, and his two sons Tiberius and Gaius Sempronius Gracchus, each of whom was assassinated by enemies while serving as tribune of the people, in 133 and 121 BCE respectively (Austin, *Sextus* 258). The twin Scipiones, our commentaries state, are the two men responsible for Rome's greatest victories over the north African city of Carthage. The first, Publius Cornelius Scipio Africanus, ended the second Punic War by defeating Hannibal at Zama in 202 BCE; the second, Africanus's adoptive grandson Publius Cornelius Scipio Aemilianus, destroyed Carthage and ended the third Punic War in 146 BCE (259).

Vergil does not have Anchises list any women in this roster of future Roman leaders. But by juxtaposing these references to the Sempronii Gracchi and the Cornelii Scipiones in book 6, he obliquely recalls the woman who linked the two families: Cornelia, daughter of Scipio Africanus. First cousin, then adoptive aunt, and eventually mother-in-law of Scipio Aemilianus, Cornelia was married to the consul of 177 BCE. She earned acclaim from future generations as a paragon of matronal and maternal excellence and for her devotion to her two tribune sons after she was widowed at a relatively early age (Horsfall, *Cornelius Nepos* 125–26). The first century CE Roman author Pliny, for example, describes a celebrated statue of Cornelia at 34.31 of his *Historia Naturalis*. The inscription at its base—"Cornelia, daughter of Africanus, [mother] of the Gracchi"—survives to this day. Pliny reports that the statue was originally placed in the portico of Metellus, built during Cornelia's lifetime. In his era, however, it stood in the portico of Augustus's sister Octavia, constructed around the time that Vergil wrote the *Aeneid*.

I would contend that the *Aeneid* may call this illustrious noblewoman to mind in another oblique way as well. A letter from Cornelia to her son Gaius Gracchus shares various verbal and thematic details with speeches that Vergil assigns to three memorable and noble female figures, all of them depicted as in a frenzied state, *feminae furentes*. Two of these women are also mothers, from nations that Vergil represents as ancestors of the Roman race: the mother of Euryalus, a Trojan warrior who loses his life in battle, and the Latin queen Amata. The third woman, however, is childless and rules over a long-standing foe of the Roman people: Dido, queen of Carthage. The similarities among the speeches assigned to these three women are in themselves significant but become more comprehensible if Vergil drew on this one Roman literary model for all three. Even if he is not specifically echoing Cornelia's letter, an examination of her language and concerns illuminates the cultural and literary context in which he wrote. It allows us a close glimpse of a historical Roman woman whom Vergil and his Roman readers were likely to have regarded as a counterpart to, if not the inspiration for, these fictional female characters.

Cornelia's letter is preserved for posterity in the manuscripts of the historian and biographer Cornelius Nepos, who died a few years before Vergil wrote the *Aeneid*. It survives in two excerpts, refers to her elder son, Tiberius, as already dead, and represents her addressee, Gaius, as merely considering a run for the office of tribune. As Gaius assumed the position in 123 BCE, this letter must have been composed earlier, most likely during the preceding year. Cornelia, born between 195 and 190 BCE, would have been in her late sixties at this time (Horsfall 125).

No other extant Roman source quotes this letter directly. Some scholars view it as a male forgery, unlikely to have been written by the much esteemed mother of the Gracchi because it uses impassioned language and describes frenzied female behavior (Horsfall 41–42, 125–26). Yet resemblances between the letter and speeches assigned to impassioned, frenzied female characters in Latin literary works such as Vergil's *Aeneid* may furnish proof, albeit of an indirect nature, for the authenticity of this text or at least for the perception of the text as Cornelia's. Before we look at Cornelia's words in this letter, let us turn to the three impassioned and frenzied female figures in the *Aeneid* whose words resemble those of one another as well as hers. Like Cornelia, these women are of mature years and lofty birth. Like Cornelia, too, they voice powerful emotions, expressing their unhappiness at (and usually to) males they regard as showing insufficient heed and honor to them and their wishes.

One of these women, a widowed, noble-blooded Trojan exile, has come to Italy with Aeneas. We meet her only at 9.473, when she hears that her son Euryalus has fallen in battle against the Rutulians. After rushing forth in a crazed state (*amens*)—oblivious to the men, dangers, and weapons around her—she sees her dead son's head impaled on a pike before the Trojan camp. She addresses him in a series of rhetorical, and what Susan Ford Wiltshire calls "unanswerable" (*Public* 52), questions:

> Must I see you
> Even like this, Euryalus? You that were
> In these last days the comfort of my age
> Could leave me, could you, cruel boy, alone?
> Sent into danger so, had you no time

For your poor mother's last farewell? [. . .]
[. . . . .]
                                    But where
Shall I go now? Where is the earth that holds
Your trunk dismembered, all your mangled body?
                (Fitzgerald 9.680–85, 692–94)

    The phrase *senectae / sera meae requies* (481–82; "in these last days the com-fort of my age"), which Euryalus's mother applies to her newly dead son fore-shadows the words that the Latin queen Amata employs in a highly emotional speech at 12.57–58. There, pleading with her prospective son-in-law, Turnus, she calls him *senectae / tu requies miserae* ("my stay in grim old age") (see Wilt-shire 53). Earlier, at 7.359–72, Amata engages in an impassioned confrontation with her husband, King Latinus, protesting his decision to betroth their daugh-ter to Aeneas rather than to her sister's son, Turnus (Fordyce 130). She demands that family ties and family feeling be given pride of place in forging political alliances. In the process, she fires off a string of rhetorical if not unan-swerable questions, makes a powerful appeal to the king that he consider her needs, stresses his responsibilities to others, and invokes divine authority:

             These Trojan refugees,
Father, are they to take away Lavinia
In marriage? Have you no pity for your daughter,
None for yourself? No pity for her mother,
Who will be left alone by the faithless man,
The rover, going to sea at the first north wind
With a girl for booty? Was that not the way
The Phrygian shepherd entered Lacedaemon
And carried Helen off to Troy's far city?
What of your solemn word, your years of love [*cura*]
For your own people, your right hand so often
Given to Turnus, our blood-kin? Suppose
A son of foreign stock is to be found
For Latins, and this holds, and the command
Your father, Faunus, gave weighs hard upon you,
Then I maintain that every separate country
Free from all rule of ours, is foreign land,
And this is what the gods mean. Turnus, too,
If we seek origins, had Inachus
And Acrisius as forebears at Mycenae.   (Fitzgerald 7.495–514)

    When we first encounter Amata in book 7, Vergil depicts her as brought to a boiling point (*coquebant* [344]) by women's concerns and angers and as ren-dered *furibunda* ("full of frenzy") by the fury Allecto. Amata's frenzied and

fury-possessed state is stressed; Vergil calls her *furentem* (350), and the evil
that has seized her is *furiale* (375). She rages in a crazed state (*furit* [379]), and
the Latin mothers she stirs up are set aflame by furies (*furiis accensas* [392]).
At 406, Allecto sharpens Amata's initial *furores*. Vergil's account of Amata's suicide at 12.593–611 also emphasizes her possession by *furor*: she is crazed
through sorrowful frenzy ("per maestum demens [. . .] furorem" [601]) and in
a crazed state (*furit* [607]) as the crowd of women mourn her rage.

To be sure, Euryalus's mother is merely described as insane (*amens*) and not
specifically said to display *furor*, but Vergil portrays her in a hysterical state. He
also calls her unhappy (*infelix* [9.477]), a word he applies twice to Amata
(7.401, 12.598). Furthermore, the sufferings of both women are associated
with *Fama*, the personification of rumor. At 9.473–75, *Fama* conveys to
Euryalus's mother the news of Euryalus's death. Fitzgerald translates: "In the
meantime, / Rumor [*Fama*], on strong wings flying [*volitans*], went about / the
settlement in dread, until it whispered / close by Euryalus's mother's ears"
(669–72). At 7.392, Vergil reports that *Fama volat* ("rumor flies") to the effect
that Amata has stirred up Latin mothers into frenzied bacchic worship; at
12.608 he relates that the *infelix fama* ("unhappy rumor") of Amata's suicide
spreads throughout the city.

Through these and other details, moreover, Vergil links the two emotionally
overwrought mothers not only with each other but also with an earlier figure
in the epic: Dido, queen of Carthage. At 4.298, in reporting how *Fama* conveys
to Dido the news of Aeneas's sudden departure, he uses the adjective *furens* to
describe her response. At 465 and 548, he employs this adjective for Dido
again: first when depicting her imagined state in a terrifying dream, later when
portraying how she characterizes herself in her poignant and deceptive appeal
to her sister Anna. At 474, he describes Dido as having imagined *furiae* in her
hallucinating mind; at 501, he states that Anna does not think her sister is possessed by such great *furores*; at 646, he speaks of Dido as *furibunda* when she
mounts her funeral pyre and prepares to end her life; at 670, he likens her
death to the fall of a city such as her own Carthage and Tyre, consumed by
flammae furentes ("raging flames").

Vergil also repeatedly applies the adjective *infelix* to Dido: when she is
inflamed by ill-fated passion for Aeneas (1.712, 4.68) and when she suffers over
Aeneas's abandonment of her (4.450, 529) (see Austin, *Quartus* 45). Dido calls
herself *infelix* when she witnesses Aeneas's departure (4.596); she says she
would have been the opposite of "infelix—felix, heu nimium felix—" if
Aeneas's ships had never touched her shores (657). When Aeneas meets her in
the Underworld, he addresses her immediately as *infelix Dido* (6.456). Finally,
the personification of rumor, *Fama*, plays a major role in Vergil's narrative
about Dido's tragic love affair. *Fama* makes her entrance at 4.173 and occupies
center stage for the next twenty-three lines: as in the passage where she brings
the news of Euryalus's death to his mother, she is said to be feathered and flying. *Fama* returns, provoking Dido to engage in the frenzied behavior of a bac-

chic celebrant (4.298); she rages like a bacchante herself at the moment of Dido's death (666) (see Austin, *Quartus* 71–72, 96, 191).

Dido, of course, differs from Euryalus's mother and Amata in many respects. She is not a mother, she voices her powerful emotions not about a son or son surrogate but a lover, and her people are not Rome's ancestors but Rome's archenemies. Yet she concludes a distraught speech to Aeneas with the wish that she had conceived a son. "If only," she cries, "before your sudden flight there had been a child by you for me to rear, if some little Aeneas were to be playing in my palace, who would recall you in his features, I would not seem so utterly defeated and deserted" (4.327–30; my trans.). Wiltshire has observed, as well, the special relationship between Dido and Aeneas's son, Ascanius, described in books 1 and 4, further documented when we are told that Ascanius rides a horse given him by Dido as a "reminder and pledge of affection" (5.572) (Wiltshire 45–47).

The speech during which Dido voices this wish is composed of a series of rhetorical and unanswerable questions, in the fashion of the speeches that Vergil assigns to both Euryalus's mother and Amata. In it, however, Dido exhibits feelings that are more inflamed than those attributed to these two women, and she powerfully voices concerns that do not figure, or do not loom quite as large, in their words. She angrily calls the man she loved and still loves her enemy, displays an increasing preoccupation with her impending death, and repeatedly threatens vengeance. These feelings and concerns are illuminated by, and may well evoke, the letter from Cornelia to her son Gaius.

My translation of the Latin text follows:

> These words are excerpted from a letter of Cornelia, mother of the Gracchi, from the book of Cornelius Nepos about Latin historians.
>
> You will say that it is a beautiful thing to take vengeance on enemies [*inimicos ulcisci*]. To no one does this seem either greater or more beautiful than it does to me, but only if it is possible to pursue these aims without harming our country. But since that cannot be done, our enemies [*inimici*] will not perish for a long time and for the greater part, and will remain as they do now in preference to having our country destroyed and perish.
>
> The same letter in a different passage. I would dare to take an oath swearing solemnly that, because of all these events, except for those who murdered Tiberius Gracchus, no enemy [*neminem inimicum*] has foisted so much difficulty and so much distress upon me as you have. You should have shouldered the responsibilities of all those children whom I had in the past. You should have taken care [*curare ut*] that I might have the least anxiety possible in my old age [*senecta*]; that, whatever you did, you would wish to please me most greatly; and that you would consider it sacrilege [*nefas*] to do anything of rather serious significance contrary to my feelings, especially as I am someone with only a short portion of my

life left. Cannot even that time span, brief as it is ["ne id quidem tam breve spatium"], help me keep you from opposing me and destroying our country?

What end will there finally be? When will our family stop behaving insanely ["ecquando desinet familia nostra insanire"]? When will we cease insisting on troubles, both suffering them and causing them? When will we begin to feel shame about disrupting and disturbing our country? But if this simply cannot take place, seek the office of tribune when I will be dead [ubi ego mortua ero]; as far as I am concerned, do what will please you, when I shall not perceive what you are doing. When I have died [ubi mortua ero], you will sacrifice to me as a parent and call upon the god of your parents. Does it not shame you to ask for the prayers of those as gods, whom when they were alive and on hand you treated as abandoned and deserted [relictos atque desertos]? May Jupiter not for a single instant allow you to continue in these actions nor permit such madness to come into your mind. If you persist, I fear that, by your fault, you may incur such trouble for your entire life that at no time would you be able to make yourself happy.

Admittedly, Cornelia and Dido differ in their interactions with and terms for the men they represent as hostile as well as in their relationships to these men. When calling her son her enemy, Cornelia is speaking of a fellow Roman and doing so to his face, albeit indirectly (by telling him that, with the exception of his brother's murderers, no hostile individual has made her life as miserable as he has). Dido is speaking of a foreigner and doing so behind his back, talking to her sister Anna: first with "go, intercede with our proud enemy" ("hostem [. . .] superbum" [4.424]), then with "you [. . .] burdened a mad queen [furentem] with sufferings and thrust me on my enemy [hosti]" [548–49]). By the same token, Cornelia uses the word inimicus, personal political enemy, rather than Dido's hostis, enemy of the state. But Dido, right before her death, refers to a fellow Tyrian and blood relation, her brother Pygmalion, as her inimicus and a rightful recipient of her vengeance (656). When Aeneas encounters the silent Dido in the world of the dead, she is referred to as inimica when she flees from his sight (6.472).

Cornelia emphatically characterizes herself as on the verge of death, twice with the perfect participle mortua and future tense of the verb "to be" (ero), once by referring to the small portion and brief span of life left to her. When Dido decides to end her life on Aeneas's departure, her allusions to her death are neither vague premonitions nor idle threats. Vergil states that she "prays for death" (4.651). But he depicts her, even before she has made her fatal decision, as repeatedly describing her approaching death. Vergil has Dido describe herself as "about to die," using the word moritura, the future active participle of the verb that gives us mortua (308, 604). She speaks of herself as moribundam ("about to die" [323]). She warns Aeneas that "when cold death has parted body from soul, I shall be everywhere, a shade to haunt you [. . .] the news [*Fama*] will reach me even among the lowest of the dead!" (385–87).

Cornelia, in the first excerpt of her letter to Gaius, voices approval of vengeance against one's enemies as an abstract principle. Yet she proceeds to warn her son against allowing an unchecked desire for vengeance to destroy their country. The dying Dido promises future vengeance on Aeneas's Roman descendants through her Carthaginian descendant Hannibal (621–29), the very man defeated at Zama by Cornelia's father, Publius Cornelius Scipio Africanus. But Dido places no limits on her desire to avenge herself on Aeneas and laments that she dies unavenged; as she utters her final words, moreover, she destroys the city that she founded. Words derived from the verb *ulcisci*, which Cornelia employs to describe the act of vengeance in her letter, abound at the end of *Aeneid* 4: Dido speaks of Hannibal as an avenger (*ultor*), "arising from our bones" (625); takes credit for having taken vengeance (*ulta*) on her brother (656); and says, "I die unavenged [*inultae*] but let me die" (659–60).

There are further similarities between Cornelia's letter and Dido's speeches. Like Cornelia, Dido employs the strong word *nefas* ("sacrilege") to condemn the conduct of the man who has wronged her. Her description of herself as "utterly defeated, utterly bereft" (*capta ac deserta* [4.330]) resembles Cornelia's characterization of the gods that her son neglects as "abandoned and deserted" (*relictos atque desertos*). Cornelia's plea that Jupiter not allow Gaius to continue in his actions is paralleled when Dido invokes the same god on realizing that Aeneas has departed (590).

Cornelia confronts Gaius with a series of rhetorical, unanswerable questions. She hence resembles not only Dido raging at Aeneas (4.305–30, 365–87) but also the mother of Euryalus lamenting before the head of her slain son and Amata beseeching both her husband, Latinus, and her prospective son-in-law, Turnus. And Vergil portrays both the mother of Euryalus and Amata as uttering words and voicing thoughts that recall Cornelia's letter. Both women, for example, refer to their "old age" by using the Latin word that Cornelia employs: *senecta*, rather than the more prosaic *senectus* (Glare 1734). Neither displays Cornelia's (or Dido's) obsessiveness about her approaching death. Still, Euryalus's mother terms her death both imminent and desired; Amata is described, like Dido, as *moritura* ("about to perish" [12.55]) and pledges to end her life if Turnus is killed.

Euryalus's mother recalls Cornelia in other ways. She speaks of both her son and her life without him as "cruel" (*crudelis* and *crudele*), "exacerbating," in Wiltshire's words, "the sense of separation" (53). She expresses outrage, if not rage, at her dead son for failing to inform her that he was undertaking a dangerous and indeed deadly mission, and she invokes Jupiter. Significantly, before Euryalus undertakes his mission, and in response to the anxieties that Euryalus expresses about deceiving and bereaving his mother, Aeneas's son (and Euryalus's kinsman), Ascanius, makes a solemn promise. He vows that if anything terrible befalls Euryalus, Euryalus's mother will become his mother,

lacking only the name of his own dead mother, Creusa ("namque erit ista genetrix, nomenque Creusae / solum defuerit" [9.297–98]). In promising to take
the place of this woman's son, Ascanius calls to mind Cornelia's demand that
her living son Gaius replace her deceased offspring, his brother Tiberius most
prominent among them.

Amata insists that her husband honor his obligations to family, claims to Turnus that the fate of their entire household rests with him, and appeals to her
own powerful emotions, thereby adopting arguments and deploying strategies
that Cornelia attempts with Gaius. Amata further resembles Cornelia in that
her advice to Turnus goes unheeded. She begs him not to engage in combat for
her daughter's hand with Aeneas, but he proceeds to do so anyway. Her indignant expression of family-first sentiments is characterized as *solito matrum de
more* ("in the manner customary for mothers" [7.357]). Thus Vergil implies
that his Roman audience will recognize her fierce display of emotion, insistence on sensitivity to the feelings of family members, and the privileging of
blood family ties over other political goals as typical features of maternal discourse in times of major decision making. These are, of course, key features of
Cornelia's speech as well.

Vergil may not have recalled, or expected his audience to recall, Cornelia in
characterizing these three different *feminae furentes*, frenzied and distraught
women. The similarities they share with her, unlike those they share with one
another, may well be coincidental: valuable merely as information about the
Roman cultural and literary milieu in which Vergil wrote, evidence merely that
he drew on Roman cultural as well as Greek literary models in the *Aeneid*. But
if he was deliberately calling to mind this particular historical figure, we need
to ask why. In the case of Euryalus's mother, Vergil would have rendered this
Trojan ancestor of the Roman people more sympathetic to his Augustan read-
ership by having her evoke the words as well as experience the plight of an
admired Roman matron. In the case of Amata, a Latin forebear of the Roman
race, he may have echoed Cornelia's letter to elicit some measure of sympathy
for her as well, especially because Amata proves so powerless relative to the
men she tries to influence.

By the same token, the resonance of Cornelia's concerns and language in
Dido's speeches would have endowed Dido's circumstances with added
poignancy. Yet Vergil might also be seeking to illustrate the disastrous emotional and political consequences of a rigid, inflexible cast of mind, such as
Dido exhibits in her inability to compromise on the matter of revenge. He
would then be evoking Cornelia's letter to remind his readers that while her
anger at the men who killed her elder son was intense and altogether justifiable, Cornelia nonetheless refused to sanction the destruction of her country
in order to take vengeance on these enemies. In rendering Dido a far more
emotionally unbalanced and politically irresponsible version of Cornelia, therefore, Vergil contributes to her characterization as a tragic, self-destructive
female figure. But whether or not he was influenced by a Roman woman's

voice when he expressed powerful female sentiments in the *Aeneid*, our attention to Cornelia's voice helps place these sentiments in their distinctive Roman context.

NOTE

I dedicate my essay to Marie Hildebrand Bintner, *magistra memorabilissima*, on her retirement.

CLASSROOM TECHNIQUES AND STRATEGIES

Appreciating the Poetry of the *Aeneid*

Scott Ward and Gary S. Meltzer

What is the best way to teach Vergil's epic? Is it to focus on the narrative action, the historical context, or the literary tradition? All of these things are important, and a reader who studies these facets of the poem will understand a lot about the *Aeneid*. To neglect the poetic dimension of Vergil's text, however, deprives one of a crucial aspect of the experience the poem provides. The *Aeneid* is, first and foremost, a poem, and Vergil is an outstanding poet. As poets have always done, Vergil employs poetic figures and devices at crucial moments to heighten the drama, lyricism, and complexity of his narrative.

Most instructors and students of Vergil are doubtless aware that the *Aeneid* employs such poetic conventions as the invocation, epithets, and the epic simile. But the fact that the poem is usually read in translation, and often not even in its entirety, may interfere with one's appreciation of it as poetry. In many survey courses only several books of the poem are taught, and books 7 through 12, which the poet introduces as a "greater history" (Fitzgerald 7.58), are omitted altogether. Teaching Vergil in this way may foster the notion that the poem can be quickly consumed and assimilated. But the *Aeneid* presents a vital and enthralling account of human experience; it tells a story in a monumental form; like all great literature, it must be felt, lived with, read and reread. In order to appreciate fully the poetry of the *Aeneid*, one should ideally read the whole poem in the original Latin. Vergil's style is particularly rich in sound effects and in schemes—poetic devices such as alliteration and chiasmus that depend on the arrangement of words in a line of verse. These are the very features of the poem that are eradicated or at least radically transformed by the act of translation. Any translation necessarily reinvents the original.

But it is clearly better for students to have some exposure to the *Aeneid* than none at all. We prefer Robert Fitzgerald's verse translation (which we use in this essay), but whichever one is chosen, we would urge the instructor to ask students to read passages of the poem aloud. Even in translation, the imagery of the poetry, the sound of the words, the rhythm and tone of the verse have a subliminal effect on the reader, allowing the poem to work at least some of the delightful magic it has in the original.

This essay offers instructors a simple pedagogical method they can employ to elicit discussion and heighten students' appreciation of Vergil's poetic effects. The method focuses on tropes, or poetic devices such as simile and metaphor, since these tend not to be as easily obscured in translation as schemes. The method consists of a set of three model questions that introduce tropes, help students understand how they work, and lead students to discuss their implications:

> What poetic figure (metaphor, simile, personification, image, etc.) does the passage employ?
> How does the figure affect your understanding of the characters and events portrayed?
> Have you encountered similar figures elsewhere in the poem? What effect do these figures have on your understanding of the poem's overall themes?

These questions encourage students to linger over the language of the poem, to consider the role of poetic devices in the narrative, and to trace the epic's interwoven patterns of imagery. Students employing the model will come to appreciate not only the power and beauty of Vergil's poetry but also its complexity. The rest of the essay discusses examples of three poetic devices in Vergil—simile, image, and symbol—to suggest ways in which the model might be employed.

Let us first examine the simile in book 4 in which Aeneas, resisting Dido's pleas to remain with her, is compared to an oak tree:

> And just as when the north winds from the Alps
> This way and that contend among themselves
> To tear away an oaktree hale with age,
> The wind and tree cry, and the buffeted trunk
> Showers high foliage to earth, but holds
> On bedrock, for the roots go down as far
> Into the underworld, as cresting boughs
> Go up in heaven's air: just so this captain,
> Buffeted by a gale of pleas
> This way and that way, dinned all the day long,
> Felt their moving power in his great heart,
> And yet his will stood fast; tears fell in vain.
>   (Fitzgerald 610–21)

The question "What poetic figure does the passage employ?" can lead to an explanation of the epic simile and the terms *tenor* and *vehicle* to provide a vocabulary for discussion. The tenor is the subject of the simile, what "holds" (from the Latin *teneo*) the comparison—in this case, Aeneas. The vehicle is what the subject is compared with, what "carries" (from the Latin *veho*) the subject—here, the oak tree. Putting this information on the board helps ground the discussion in the poem's immediate context.

After ascertaining that Aeneas (the tenor) is being compared to the oak tree (the vehicle), the class has a foundation on which to build a reading of the passage. Students may discover in the simile a reference to the strength of Aeneas's resolve to leave Dido, an impression reinforced by the image of the oak, a tree sacred to Jupiter; this comparison reminds us that Aeneas is fulfilling a divine command in founding Rome and that in so doing he is perhaps inspired by divine strength. The branches go up into "heaven's air," suggesting Rome's future greatness; the roots go down to Tartarus, suggesting both Aeneas's respect for his ancestry and his need to lay down roots in new soil. The image of the leaves shaken off the tree makes clear that, despite his resolve, Aeneas is troubled by the pleas Dido conveys through her sister, Anna; we understand him better in human terms after reading the comparison (see Pöschl, *Art* 45–47). Students may also note the ambiguity in the simile's concluding line, "tears fell in vain," which may apply not only to Dido and Anna but also to Aeneas himself.

The instructor could elicit further discussion of this passage by pointing out that it contains a second simile. If Aeneas is compared to an oak tree, to what is Dido (as tenor) being compared (as vehicle)? What is the effect of this second comparison and how is it apt? If the comparison of Aeneas to the oak highlights the strength of his resolve, the comparison of Dido to the turbulent winds reveals the strength of her passion and her volatile emotional state. Dido's appeals are portrayed as both powerful and dangerous: the winds threaten to "tear away" the tree.

The final step in our model is to address larger thematic concerns. The image of the oak epitomizes the *pietas* of Aeneas, the reverence he holds for the gods, destiny, and the future Roman state. The simile thus dramatizes a conflict between *pietas* and passion that will be revisited at many points in the epic. But Aeneas, who succumbed to his passion for Dido earlier in the book, even helping her build the walls of Carthage, is hardly a perfect embodiment of *pietas*. Through additional questioning, the instructor can—and should—complicate a simplistic reading of both the passage and the poem itself. One could well ask, Is the comparison perfectly consistent? This question might lead students to realize that the comparison undoes itself, generating a productive ambiguity: Aeneas's portrayal as a man who is moved "in his great heart" by Dido's pleas runs counter to the force of the image of the impenetrable oak. This reading emphasizes the suffering and loss that both Aeneas and Dido must endure as part of his struggle to found Rome. Posing a question about the effect of this passage, in all its complexity, should provoke a lively class discussion.

The next poetic device to discuss is imagery: language that appeals to the senses and, like a ship weighted down with cargo, carries a repository of ideas and associations. These associations can change, however, as they do with the image of fire, one of the poem's most pervasive. Let us first consider the image of a "city lost in flames" from the story of the fall of Troy in book 2, as Aeneas recounts the desperate speech he gives to his comrades once he realizes his city is doomed:

> The gods by whom this kingdom stood are gone,
> Gone from the shrines and altars. You defend
> A city lost in flames. Come, let us die,
> We'll make a rush into the thick of it.
> The conquered have one safety: hope for none.
> (Fitzgerald 469–73)

If asked how the image of fire affects their view of this scene, students will probably think mainly of destruction, and the instructor should lead them to consider the full import of that destruction: the loss of almost the whole population of the city; of its wealth; and, except for those artifacts that Aeneas carries away, of its entire culture. The lines also convey the sense of desolation felt by Aeneas as he recognizes the conflagration as a sign that the gods have abandoned his city.

A little earlier in book 2, the poet describes the hero as "burning" to enter the fray of combat: "Only I burned [*ardent animi* (316)] to gather up some force / For combat, and to man some high redoubt" (Fitzgerald 423–24). What is the effect of the depiction of Aeneas as burning as the city of Troy burns? Students might discuss how the metaphor of an inner fire conveys Aeneas's turbulent state of mind, dramatizing his identification with his city. By incorporating the fires of Troy in Aeneas's inner landscape, the poet intensifies the sense of his plight and the desperation of his response to it.

No sooner, however, does Vergil establish the destructive aspects of the image of fire with regard to setting and character than he imbues it with new and positive associations. Just a little later in book 2, when Anchises refuses to leave his house, the gods send a sign in the form of fire on the head of Iulus: "A point on Iulus' head seemed to cast light, / A tongue of flame that touched but did not burn him" (Fitzgerald 891–92). In book 7, the same "divine fire" appears over the head of Lavinia:

> It seemed her long hair caught, her head-dress caught
> In crackling flame, her queenly tresses blazed,
> Her jewelled crown blazed. Mantled then in smoke
> And russet light, she scattered divine fire
> Through all the house [. . .].   (96–100)

Two other significant images of fire occur in book 8, both times in close association with battle. In the first, fire appears on the helmet of Aeneas "with its terrifying plumes / And gushing flames" (840–41); in the second, "[t]win flames gushed upward" (920) from the brow of Augustus, who is depicted in his triumph at the battle of Actium on Aeneas's shield.

What is the effect of the poet's use of the image of fire in these examples? A discussion may elicit the notion that fire, which earlier conveyed a sense of devastation and loss, can also serve as a sign of divine favor and destiny (Knox 138–40; Putnam, *Poetry* 40). The line of Aeneas has indeed been touched by the fires of Troy but will not be consumed by them; rather, Iulus and his descendants will come to rule the world under Augustus's leadership, a link symbolically forged by the flames "gushing" upward from both Aeneas's helmet and Augustus's brow. The image of fire thus points the way out of the ruins of Troy for both Aeneas and the reader, helping the poet solve a dilemma: How can Aeneas desert his burning city and still maintain his heroic stature? Part of the answer lies in this transmutation of the image of fire: it is not Aeneas's destiny to die defending "a city lost in flames," as an Iliadic warrior may have done, but to live on in order to ensure the eventual survival and triumph of his line elsewhere (Knox 134–35). Just as the gods willed the destruction of Troy, so they will the foundation of a new city, Rome, a city that will rule the world. Vergil's brilliant use of fire imagery, though it was originally inspired by the *Iliad*, helps advance a different concept of heroism than is found there (see Whitman 128–53).

The last poetic device to discuss is the symbol, a device of central importance in the poem; indeed, Viktor Pöschl argues that the meaning of the epic unfolds on a symbolic level and that Vergil "is far more *consciously* symbolic" than Homer (*Art* 1). The symbol is an object, act, character, or scene that, by virtue of association, evokes qualities beyond itself. Students will easily recognize the shield that Vulcan makes for Aeneas in book 8 as a symbol of Rome's destined greatness. But the symbolic import of actions and events, such as the funeral games held by Aeneas for his father in book 5, may not be so readily apparent. The description of drills led by Ascanius as "sham cavalry skirmishes" and as "mimicry of war" (Fitzgerald 756, 770) lends support for a symbolic reading of the games as warfare. Indeed, the structure of the entire book, which contains many parallels between the "world apart" of game (Putnam 67) and the perilous world of heroic action, suggests that the games serve as a form of ritualized combat (65–68). For Brooks Otis, the games offer "'pre-views' of martial prowess to come and thus anticipate the impending struggle in Latium" (*Virgil* 274). But, more than that, the games serve to convey to the reader a sense of the heroic values that will be essential in that struggle and in the future Roman state (see Putnam 65; Anderson, *Art* 52–55). The boxing match between Darès and Entellus provides a brief but dramatic example of an incident that serves both functions.

To introduce the scene, the instructor may wish to explain that Vergil's games are based on the funeral games for Patroclus that are held in book 23 of the *Iliad*, and that the boxing match is based on a similar contest there (651–99). Asking students to read the two accounts alongside each other (aloud, if time permits) would highlight the symbolic importance of Vergil's account. The instructor might then ask the class to consider how the differences in the two accounts help shape a new heroic ethos in Vergil.

The first similarity a reader may notice is that both Homer's Epeios and Vergil's Darës are described as formidable fighters: Epeios is "well skilled" (*Il.* [Lattimore] 23.664), and Darës is a champion who alone "held his ground with Paris" (Fitzgerald 5.475). Both fighters lay claim to first prize even before an opponent has come forward: Epeios "laid his hand on the hard-working jenny" (666) and Darës "made no bones of grasping the bull's horn" (488). What does this behavior say about both characters and their values? A discussion should elicit the fact that the Trojan Darës is cast in the mold of the Homeric warrior who fights primarily for individual gain and honor. The prize is an essential marker of the Iliadic warrior's status, as is evident from Achilles's decision to withdraw from battle because Agamemnon has deprived him of his.

Students may notice that in both Homer and Vergil, an opponent steps forward only after receiving encouragement from one of his fellows. But whereas Homer devotes only a few lines to a description of Epeios's opponent, Euryalos, Vergil gives Entellus and his comrade, Acestës, several speeches. These speeches suggest that Entellus's reason for entering the contest is very different from Darës's. Acestës speaks first, urging Entellus to defend his own reputation and the honor of their god, Eryx, Aeneas's brother (see 31). Entellus replies that, although he is old and tired, he will indeed fight the "arrogant fellow," Darës, but not to gain glory or win the prize. As he says, "Gifts don't concern me" (517).

At first, both Epeios and Darës seem to make good on their boasts: Epeios knocks Euryalos off his feet, and Entellus falls "mightily to earth" after throwing a punch that misses Darës. Both Homer and Vergil use similes to describe these encounters. But the nature of the similes differs markedly, as does the eventual outcome of the contests. Homer uses only one short simile in the episode, comparing Euryalos's fall to the fall of a fish that "jumps / in the weeds of the beach-break, then the dark water closes above him" (*Il.* 23.692–93). By contrast, the two longer similes in Vergil symbolically connect the contest with the poem's central themes.

The first simile describes Darës's initial, unsuccessful attempts to penetrate Entellus's defenses:

> Darës, like one assaulting a tall city
> Or laying siege to a stronghold on a height,
> Tried this approach, then that, explored the ground
> On all sides cleverly, came on, came in
> From various angles, all to no avail.   (Fitzgerald 5.567–71)

The second simile describes Entellus's falling to earth after his missed punch:

> The mighty man fell mightily to earth,
> As ponderously as, from time to time,
> A hollow and uprooted pine will fall
> On Erymanthus or the range of Ida.   (577–80)

What is the effect of these comparisons and how do they resonate in the narrative? The comparison of Darës's feints and footwork to the siege of a tall city or a stronghold clearly evokes the fall of Troy, which is so poignantly described in book 2. Vergil's use of this simile (where none appears in Homer) lends an epic grandeur to the scene. The second simile, with its allusions to mountains in Greece and Troy, also evokes the setting of Homer's epic. Since Epeios in the *Iliad* wins his match, the reader might suppose that Darës will win, too, especially since he is younger and more aggressive. But the old Entellus recovers and batters Darës with a storm of blows. Aeneas steps in to stop the fight— an intervention altogether absent in Homer. He urges Darës to yield to a "force now more than mortal" and to recognize that "heaven's will has changed" (603–05). As if to underline the wisdom of this advice, Entellus strikes dead the bull that he receives as the victor of the match, dedicating it as a sacrifice to Eryx (626–27).

To help show the significance of Entellus's surprising victory, an instructor may ask what he, in contrast to Darës, is fighting for. If Darës is the symbolic Iliadic warrior who fights for personal honor and glory, Entellus is the defender who protects his city and its culture. Unlike the arrogant Darës, Entellus is quiet and reluctant to do battle; he enters the match not to win the prize but to defend his kinsman and deity, Eryx. Entellus's striking dead the prize bull dramatizes the disdain he holds for personal glory, to be sure; but, more important, his sacrifice demonstrates his devotion to his patron deity and the honor of his ancestors. Divine destiny favors the fighter who exhibits the quality of *pietas*, in both the boxing match and the future war in Latium. Indeed, the stages of Entellus's combat—first being under siege, then being uprooted, and finally prevailing—correspond to the stages of Aeneas's heroic journey.

When invited to think about the larger significance of the episode, students might recall Jupiter's prophecy in book 1 that Aeneas will "[e]stablish city walls and a way of life" in Italy (Fitzgerald 357). The outcome of the boxing match suggests that a new breed of hero—one dedicated to his community, ancestry, and gods—better fulfills this mission than the old Iliadic warrior. The boxing match thus not only anticipates the war that Aeneas will wage against Turnus in Italy but also dramatizes the Roman ideal announced in book 6: "[t]o spare the conquered, battle down the proud" (1154).

Our model should help students discover for themselves something of the force, intricacy, and beauty of poetic language in the *Aeneid*. Considering the patterns of imagery in the poem will also give them a more complex understanding of Aeneas as a Roman hero and of the nature of his accomplishment in founding Rome. Students who use the model will be less tempted to skip or skim over Vergil's poetic devices and more able to appreciate the essential role they play in shaping his narrative art.

NOTE

The authors would like to thank Cliff Roti, John Petruccione, and the editors of this volume for their helpful insights and suggestions.

Look Who's Talking: A Narratological Approach
Nancy Ciccone

When my upper-division seminar begins the second half of the *Aeneid*, student enthusiasm dramatically wanes. They have domesticated the love story of book 4. Book 6 elicits wonder and invites discussion. But those dissatisfied with the wanderings of book 3 and the funeral of book 5 are basically predisposed toward odd-numbered book boredom. I rely on the beginning of book 7 to illustrate one of Vergil's narrative strategies: the repetition of syntactic constructions to align speakers, to convey ambivalence, and to undercut imperialism.

These students read the *Aeneid* in Mandelbaum's translation, usually for the first time and at a public, urban university. Given their concurrent professional commitments and taxing family responsibilities, even an abbreviated lecture falls dead. My most successful pedagogy relies on problem-based learning. Rudimentary terms borrowed from narratology supply an interpretative methodology, because they level the discussion field among students from different disciplines. However disserviceable to narratology's theoretical aims, simplification of its distinctions enables me to exploit the literacy students bring to the seminar. With attention to syntax and structure, I focus on the ways the *Aeneid* signifies story (plot), narrative (signifying discourse), narrator (who speaks), narratee (addressee), focalization (who sees), and focalized (object of sight) (Bal 75–108; Rimmon-Kenan 71–116). Narratology specifically foregrounds distinctions between narrator and focalizer and between story and narrative. It inhibits the conflation of voice and point of view that traditional literary terms induce. By providing a pedagogical shorthand, its terms key students to the possibilities and constraints of the literary epic.

A brief writing exercise provides a transition into the class meeting. I ask students to imagine, in a written response of about ten minutes, how they would begin book 7. As students share their invented beginnings to *Aeneid*, part 2, discussion focuses on narrative choice—Why continue one way and not another?—and on how the imagined piece fits the epic structurally, stylistically, and thematically. I stay especially alert to point out Vergilian imitation of any kind.

To test various expectations against the actual first lines, I distribute among groups of three to four students various translations of the beginning of book 7:

> In death, you too, Aeneas' nurse, Caieta,
> have given to our coasts unending fame;
> and now your honor still preserves your place
> of burial; your name points out your bones
> in broad Hesperia—if that be glory.   (Mandelbaum 1–5)

> Tu quoque litoribus nostris, Aeneia nutrix,
> aeternam moriens famam, Caieta, dedisti;

et nunc servat honos sedem tuus, ossaque nomen
Hesperia in magna, si qua est ea gloria, signat.   (1–4)

I then ask students to compare the assigned text with the one they have just received. The pedagogical goals of this exercise are twofold: to ferret out the essential matter, despite stylistic and lexical differences, in order to address the concept of translation and thereby to distinguish between story and narrative; and to introduce students to the *Aeneid's* translation heritage (e.g., Dryden, Henry Howard, Thomas Phaer and Thomas Twyne, John Conington, Christopher Pearse Cranch, C. Day Lewis, C. H. Sisson, Humphries, Fitzgerald).

Since the second half of the *Aeneid* curiously begins by invoking a woman unheard of before this point and invokes her in the context of her renown, reference to Caieta elicits further discussion of story alone. Her death thematically follows the conclusion of book 4 and the funeral rites neglected by Aeneas, whose knowledge of Dido's death has just been confirmed in book 6. Like Caieta, Dido nursed Aeneas but from his wretched position as a complaining victim to an adept leader able to leave love for destiny. In the absence of funeral rites for women, Caieta also substitutes for Creusa, if Creusa's apotheosis can be treated as death. Some students interpret Caieta as another "vicarious sacrifice" (Anderson, *Art* 52); her death foreshadows the victims of war in the last six books.

The example of Caieta recalls previous casualties from whom geography takes names. Half the class compares Caieta's death with that of Misenus (6.224–50; in Latin 156–76), the other half with that of Palinurus (6.445–89; 375–83). I post their findings in narratological categories so as to shift class focus from story as the signified, narrative content or plot (Genette 27) to narrative as the signifying discourse. For no matter how Caieta complements the story, she remains an anomaly.

Students' analyses steer discussion to who's talking. In beginning book 7, the narrator not only speaks (narrates) but also focalizes (sees); he directly addresses the narratee Caieta and focalizes on her burial place. Other examples of the narrator's direct address lead to the invocations, and we explore the implications and delay of that address in book 7. Revealing Aeneas's thoughts, simultaneous events, and mortal and immortal conversations, the narrator has so far claimed a temporal and panoramic omniscience and, with it, authority. He is superior to the story and a nonparticipant in it. But the narrator also restricts information: What exactly does Aeneas say in the cave (book 4)? I invite students to locate other episodes where the narrator frustrates them by means of silence.

Returning to Caieta, I ask students to configure another sentence with the same syntax but different content. For example: "You, too, [student's name], received an A in the course as a result of arduous study and rereading, so that a plaque will direct all future Vergilian scholars to your recuperative hospital room where your comments will model their endeavors, if that's mentoring." I turn the condition into a question to elicit their responses: Does the invalid mentor? Technically, the *si* clause, the conditional if, inserts information that modifies the declaration. The qualification undermines the invalid's achievement as it does Caieta's renown. Alert to an ambivalent element of valorization once they see themselves as invalids, students understand that Vergil's clause questions the quality and the value of glory. The formally conditional sentence semantically implies an indirect question as to whether or not glory exists in the securing of eternal fame gained by dying and giving one's name to a promontory. I contextualize this point by mentioning Achilles's choice between eternal renown dependent on early death, on the one hand, and peaceful, long-lived obscurity, on the other. Then I ask students to compare Achilles's and Caieta's situations.

The syntax of 7.1–4 admits a complexity and depth in the notion of glory and heroism that either part of the sentence in itself disallows. A voice of conditional doubt undermines encomium. If the syntax implies ambivalence, the narrator evades a precise statement of the ambivalence. But his subjective emotion seemingly measures a fixed, objective ideal and effectively questions the assumptions of empire, which the epic ostensibly praises.

For comparison, we turn to other passages exemplifying the distinction between public and private voices (Wiltshire, *Public*). For example, Aeneas publicly exhorts his comrades to optimism although he privately admits pessimism (1.276–92; in Latin 198–209). The narrator's description of Aeneas's thoughts counters Aeneas's narration. The object of focalization shifts from his comrades to his perceptions. It reveals him as a leader who controls the situation in public and despairs of it in private. Although inclusive of distinctions between public and private voice, the beginning of book 7 differs from Aeneas's narration and focalization. So far, the narrative has distinguished between fictional speakers and omniscient narrator so as to instill the narrator with muse-inspired authority. The conditional sentence enables double talk, an evasion staked high because it issues from the narrator and not from Aeneas.

Another example occurs after the ship burning (5.923–82; 700–60). The narrator focalizes Aeneas's "shaken" (*concussus* [700]) reaction. Nautes urges leaving women and old men behind, but this advice leaves Aeneas disturbed (948–53; 719–20) until Anchises's shade resolves his ambivalence. The narrator's voice in the beginning of book 7 subsequently articulates the emotional loss Aeneas feels but forfeits in order to follow Anchises's advice in book 5 to leave the weary behind. As the second half of the *Aeneid* begins, Vergil refocalizes the uncertainty attributed to Aeneas in books 1–6: it is now implied by the narrator.

Suggesting a tone other than that of wholehearted praise, the beginning of book 7 alerts students to a complex polyphony. The external, unpersonified narrator emotionally evaluates authoritative ideology in a direct discourse that endows him with the qualities of a character, however momentarily. Is the focalization past or present? Does the narrator speak in the confines of the

Aeneid's present or from the vantage point of an author's present? When else is narrative time indiscrete? The supportive material students use to maintain their positions highlights historical framing no matter what their final decision. Modern indications of time in literary and cinematic narratives (e.g., "Tomorrow was Thursday"; see Quentin Tarantino's *Pulp Fiction*) further alert students to narrative techniques available and unavailable to Vergil.

Addressing Caieta, the narrator imitates Aeneas, who habitually talks to shades but in particular to Misenus and Palinurus, Caieta's forerunners (6.254–58, 486–89; in Latin 257, 448). Returning to the previous charting of these episodes, students elaborate on the representations of Trojans who die and give their names to places. Although Misenus's death sends Aeneas to gather wood for the pyre and thereby to notice Venus's signal of doves, the narrative undercuts death's propitiousness. Focalized through Aeneas, Misenus's death is "not merited"; he challenged the gods, "if the tale is to be believed" (*uidet indigna morte peremptum; si credere dignum est*) (Mandelbaum 6.226, 239–40; in Latin 163, 173). In relating simultaneously the events of and Aeneas's reaction to Misenus's death, the narrative discredits the story. In respect to Palinurus's death, the narrative gives contradictory causalities. It records Venus and Neptune's conversation, Neptune's demand for one more death, and Sleep's impersonation of Phorbas (5.1075–139; 779–871). But Palinurus denies the hand of a god whom Aeneas and readers of book 5 blame for Palinurus's death (6.455–61; 337–62). Misenus and Palinurus reflect opposite sides of the same mouthpiece. Whereas Misenus relies on his voice to challenge the gods, Palinurus refuses to blame them. The two claim agency for themselves but, with it, foolishness. In both situations, the narrative undermines what the story necessitates.

With Caieta, the narrator steps forward to articulate an ambivalence disseminated throughout the first six books and implied in episodes such as those focusing on Palinurus and Misenus. Moreover, the object of focalization, Caieta, doesn't answer. In the second half of the *Aeneid*, the dead don't speak. Caieta's silence paves the way for the authorial narrator to emerge and co-opt heroic focalization. It indicates a systematic shift in the articulation of ambivalence from the juxtaposition of story elements to the story's individual speakers.

Students realize that Caieta's silence defies the divine voices (prophecies, dreams, impersonations) that get Aeneas where he needs to go. Discussions of narrator and focalization highlight the representations of ambivalence in the first six books so as to foreground the narrator's increased presence in the last six. The shift suggests Vergil's awareness of his literary performance. Like the impersonating gods, he practices polyphony for all his characters. But the narrator's emergence in the narrative curtails Vergil's alignment with the immortals. He squarely sides with the mortal situation and the land the mortals occupy. The reference to Caieta focalizes narrative authority on the silenced and the dispossessed. The narrator joins with other characters to speak of civilization's costs.

As the course proceeds, students maintain the terminology to note narrative focalization as distinct from narration. Generally speaking, extended narration in the second half of the *Aeneid* occurs publicly and bespeaks both public and private concerns in councils of the immortals, the Latins, and Evander's Arcadians or on the battlefield between challenging heroes. Gilbert Highet's study of the *Aeneid*'s speeches provides a starting point for this discussion. But whether Juno disobeys Zeus's orders or Latinus listens to prophecy instead of his wife or the Trojans whisk Euryalus's mother offstage, words maintain little purchase on deeds and indicate the breakdown of social order. Focalization accounts for the cost of actions. We see Euryalus put on a helmet, Pallas rush to battle, Turnus fixate on a belt, Camilla go for the gold. We don't hear them. Significant action excludes a narrator. Even when Aeneas speaks in *furor* of his need to kill Turnus at the epic's conclusion, the action remains inexplicable in the plethora of interpretations it generates (12.1262–65; 947–49).

I devote a class meeting to applying students' analyses of 7.1–4 to syntactic constructions linguistically similar to one another but different from any others in books 7–12: the spoken thoughts of Aeneas over the dead Lausus (10.1132–38; 825–28) and those of Mezentius to his horse (1181–89; 861–62). Direct speech merges focalizer and narrator in all three examples, and they imply a relationship among characters confronting death. All collapse a public-private dichotomy. The following chart gives the examples of syntactic *if* clauses; discussion points follow the chart:

Passage	Narrator	Narratee	Focalizer	Focalized
7.1–5; 1–4	narrator	Caieta	narrator	death-glory
10.1132–38; 825–28	Aeneas	Lausus	Aeneas	death-honor
10.1181–89; 861–62	Mezentius	horse-Rhoebus	Mezentius	death-time

When Aeneas decides to return Lausus's body, he undercuts his conformity to decent battle protocol by means of a conditional construction: "if Shades still care for that" ("si qua est ea cura") (1136; 828). That is, he wonders whether or not the honor he confers matters. The ambivalence of his statement suggests human limitation in the face of death. But if we consider that Anchises pointed out the heroes from the past and those yet to be in the preceding book, Aeneas's ignorance suggests ethical frustration rather than lack of factual information. Given the relative paucity of Aeneas's speeches in the second half of the epic (Highet 33), the narrative foregrounds his reflection, voice, and perspective. At this moment, the internal focalization unfolds an Aeneas questioning not just his momentary actions but also his cultural values. A handout of Menelaus's debate with himself about Patroclus's corpse in *Iliad* 17 provides an additional means of comparison. Menelaus questions his next move within a definitive set of practical choices. Aeneas's reason for his action remains indefinite. The comparison suggests that mortality limits his capacity not to act but to know the value of action.

When Mezentius echoes the narrative syntax beginning book 7, he speaks to his horse. Class discussion focuses on interpretations of "if anything / that mortals have is long" ("res si qua diu mortalibus ulla est") (1181–82; 861). Student response generally boils down to "No, nothing lasts for mortals; yet most lifetimes last long enough to allow attachments to things, people, a horse." Loss thematically binds all three examples. But Mezentius—"despiser of the gods" (*contemptor divum*) (7.855, 8.8; 7.648, 8.7)—embodies quintessential evil. The authoritative ideology that objectifies and condemns him in book 7 turns to subjectivity in book 10. Perhaps the bravery and fidelity of his son Lausus, perhaps his suicidal grief voicing a crucial question in the epic—"do I live by your death?" (10.1164)—partially redeems his atrocities. But in that question Mezentius's syntax follows the same conditional form in which Aeneas (10.1132–38; 825–28) and the narrator (7.1–5; 1–4) address Lausus and Caieta, respectively; Mezentius adopts the idiom of human pathos that they share. The technique of internal focalization inserts him into a heroic discourse from which his savage cruelty has excluded him. While suggestive of a common bond, the conditional form shared by three such different speakers also reveals a mortal instability beyond the capability and culpability of any of the individual characters.

Analyses of narration and focalization keep students from reducing fictional speakers to Cliff's Notes cardboard. The conditional constructions from books 7 and 10 disclose private voices in public situations and, in so doing, disable a good guy / bad guy dichotomy. Their internal focalization, in turn, reveals alternative ideologies claiming equal authority, if not viability. The narrator (as witness), Aeneas (as winner), and Mezentius (as loser) merge and collude in their expression of demoralization. By means of their representation, Vergil diligently fails to maintain the objectification of contradictory ideologies and thereby undermines monolithic authority.

Concentration on specific narrators prepares students for the complexity of the epic's conclusion. As the narrative records the shade leaving the body, the final focalization on Turnus matches that on Caieta (12.1270–71; 951–52). The narrative withholds the dead's voice. It invites speculation modeled in 7.1–5. But falling silent along with the shade, the narrator leaves the continuation of his story-history up to the reader. Exposing literariness, narratology humanizes the epic for those overwhelmed by the epic's daunting achievement. It likewise discloses complexity for those dismissive of epic as archaic, imperialistic propaganda. Charting narration and focalization foregrounds Vergil's deployment of historical relativity and mortal fragility.

INTEGRATING THE *AENEID* INTO LARGER ACADEMIC CONTEXTS

Tragedy and Vergil's *Aeneid*

Ann Engar

Maro cothurnatus Martial called Vergil [Bailey], "Vergil in buskins" or Vergil the writer of tragedies like those in Athens (5.5.8, 7.63.5–6). Since ancient times parallels between Vergil's *Aeneid* and Greek and Roman tragedies have been recognized by commentators from Servius and Macrobius to, more recently, Richard Heinze and Philip Hardie. Though the *Aeneid* is an epic rather than a tragedy, one of Vergil's greatest achievements is his infusion of the tragic element into the epic genre, an infusion Hardie claims reinvigorated "the flagging tradition of the Graeco-Roman epic" ("Virgil and Tragedy" 322). Students can gain a better understanding of tragedy and appreciate the extent of Vergil's genius by comparing and contrasting the *Aeneid* with earlier Greek plays and by identifying tragic elements propounded by Aristotle and later writers on tragedy.

There are numerous tragic episodes and instances in the *Aeneid*: the fall of Troy, the death of Creusa, the premature death of Marcellus, the killing of Turnus, and so on. Hardie has identified as one of the most obvious tragic features of the poem the series of promising young people who die before their time (320). But foremost is the story of Dido and Aeneas, and this story is the main focus of my teaching of the tragic elements in the *Aeneid*.

I teach an honors course entitled Intellectual Traditions of the West, in which my students spend a semester reading major texts of the ancient world. We spend two weeks on drama and a week on the *Aeneid*. In these three weeks we look at Euripides's *Medea* and *Hippolytus* as forerunners of the Dido and Aeneas story and test against their story Aristotle's definition of tragedy in the *Poetics*.

The story obviously has similarities to the *Odyssey* and Odysseus's encounters with detaining women such as Circe and Calypso. But my students also identify a number of important similarities between Medea and Dido. Both are royal, powerful women, and both risk much for love. Dido puts her kingdom in jeopardy, while Medea sacrifices her brother and rebels against her father. Both are women to whom reputation is important: Dido because she must remain strong in the face of the warlike African chieftains who surround her nation, Medea because she wants to be feared and admired as an intelligent person. Both are alien women and so do not come under the protection of the Greek or Trojan cultural laws. Thus, Medea's marriage to Jason does not keep him from seeking a Corinthian bride in a politically advantageous marriage; Medea becomes a foreign mistress. Likewise, what seems to Dido a marriage to Aeneas, Aeneas can declare is not one. Finally, their lovers' abandonment of them leads both women to raging grief and murder or suicide.

In these similarities, however, students recognize important differences that reveal a more complex political situation in the *Aeneid* and more sympathy for both Dido and Aeneas. Medea loves Jason, but she also loves herself and her reputation. Like any Greek warrior, she wants recognition: she says she would much rather be on a battlefield than bear a child (*Medea*, lines 250–52). Her moral code is similar to that of Achilles and Odysseus: she seeks to benefit friends and harm enemies (808–11). Like Odysseus, she is an intelligent trickster: she tries to figure out the consequences of each action she takes and wins by stratagem, killing King Creon and his daughter with a poisonous, fiery garment. Like Agamemnon, she has the "heart" to kill her own children. Euripides is interested in male-female roles, and Medea's pride seems more at stake than her love for Jason. Also, the audience's assessment of Jason shifts toward the end of the play. At first he is insufferably arrogant and insensitive, but his tenderness for his slain children at the end seems genuine and elicits sympathy. The ending, too, is shocking and morally ambiguous. While students have sympathized with Medea in her abandonment, that sympathy turns to horror as she sacrifices her children to punish their father. As she triumphantly escapes in a heavenly chariot sent by her grandfather, Helios, students question gods who bring no retribution to a child-killing mother.

Vergil similarly plays with the sympathies of his readers, but students come to recognize that he is interested more in the political implications of his tragic love story than in male-female roles or questions about the gods. Students first see Dido as a successful ruler building a city. While she, too, tries to think through consequences—for example, as she talks to her sister, Anna—her motivations are both personal and political: with a leader like Aeneas by her side, her city will prosper and be strengthened against its neighboring adversaries. But by the time of the next scene, in which she is shown thinking things through—as Aeneas is leaving, she ponders whether to turn to earlier suitors, follow his fleet, or kill herself—she has abandoned her political responsibilities and thinks only of herself.

Dido is not concerned with recognition as a warrior but as a *univira*, a matron of high moral character who is faithful to one husband. After she casts aside this reputation in her passion for Aeneas, she feels great guilt. Her only trick is to deceive Anna that the funeral pyre she prepares is only a bonfire to destroy the things Aeneas has left. Finally, the only killing Dido does is of herself; thus, the reader sympathizes with rather than turns against her. Instead of killing her children, she wishes she had a child by Aeneas to retain something of him. Aeneas, too, is no Jason. His abandonment of Dido occurs only after ghostly appearances of his father, guilt over his son's future, and a divine visit from Mercury. Dido and Aeneas's love is thus a tragedy not of ego and power but of individuals subject to forces larger than themselves: gods, duty, and destiny. Venus disguises Cupid as Ascanius to make Dido fall in love with Aeneas, Juno and Venus create the marriage scene in the cave, and Mercury commands Aeneas to go. While Medea's actions do have political consequences for the kingdom of Corinth and hint at a future threat to Athens, there is no background to her story of a hundred years of Punic Wars or of an Antony and Cleopatra giving up the world for love.

Students similarly compare Euripides's *Hippolytus* with the *Aeneid*. As Aeneas's life takes place on the battleground between his mother, Venus, and his enemy, Juno, so the action of *Hippolytus* depicts the warfare between Aphrodite and Artemis, love versus chastity. Dido echoes both Hippolytus and Phaedra. Having vowed chastity in honor of her dead husband, Dido, like Hippolytus, is besieged by Venus. In the prologue of *Hippolytus*, Aphrodite says Hippolytus must be killed by his father, Theseus; that Phaedra will die is of secondary importance. The main action of the *Aeneid* decreed by Jupiter and Venus is that Aeneas will found Rome; Dido's death is of secondary importance. Phaedra, while possessed by the goddess of love, is like both Dido and Medea in her love ravings, her concern about her reputation, her thinking through of alternatives, and her desire for death. She tells her nurse that by keeping silent about her troubles she will win honor and glory. She tells the chorus the three alternatives she considered when love first wounded her. The conversation between Phaedra and the nurse is very similar to Dido's conversation with Anna: both the nurse and Anna urge Phaedra and Dido to accept the love that has seized them. In her wild wanderings Phaedra longs to be a hunter (like the goddess Artemis-Diana), to go to the woods with hounds and hurl a Thracian spear. Dido does go hunting with Aeneas, but she spears herself (Vergil likens her to a doe hit by an arrow [4.68–70; Mandelbaum 91–92]) rather than a wild beast in this realm of Diana. Both Phaedra and Dido cherish their reputations (though Dido has political as well as personal reasons to preserve hers), risk their reputations for love, and betray vows to their husbands by loving another. Both are vindictive when disappointed in love. Phaedra plans to bring calamity on Hippolytus and deflate his hubris with her suicide, while Dido curses Aeneas with wars and untimely death. Her cursing of Aeneas also resembles Theseus's cursing of Hippolytus: each speaks of the accused as an exile and prays that his life will be bitter. Finally, both literary works use the imagery of love as a sickness.

There are, likewise, important differences between the characters of *Hippolytus* and Dido and Aeneas. Aeneas may not draw our sympathy and attention to the extent that Dido does, but he is not as priggish as Hippolytus—Hippolytus's priggishness is evident in his worship of Artemis, rejection of Aphrodite, and boast that he is the most virtuous of men. Nor is Aeneas irrational like Hippolytus, who fears, hates, and condemns women. Never does Aeneas say, as both Jason in *Medea* and Hippolytus do, that the human race should produce children by some source other than females (*Medea* 573–76; *Hippolytus* 617–25). The closest antifeminine sentiment in the *Aeneid* is Mercury's warning that a woman is a various, changeable thing (4.568–70; Mandelbaum 786–87). Also, Dido's love for Aeneas is not that of a stepmother for her stepson. Her husband, Sychaeus, is dead, and her vow of chastity can excusably be broken (even Sychaeus shows he forgives her in Hades). Her love is not "unholy," as Phaedra's is (*Hippolytus* 765). Though it alters Dido's reputation as a woman of the highest moral character, her love for Aeneas is understandable given his reputation and her need to strengthen her city. Furthermore, the curse that Dido utters leads not just to the death of one pious man but also to a long series of wars over generations between two empires. For her there is not the forgiveness that Hippolytus nobly renders to his father.

Next, students see how well the story of Dido and Aeneas fits Aristotle's definition of tragedy in his *Poetics*. They respond to the following:

> Which elements of Dido and Aeneas's story elicit pity and fear? How does Vergil stimulate these emotions with the reader?
> Give examples of Vergil's use of language with pleasurable accessories. What literary devices does he use?
> Find examples of peripeteia, discovery, and suffering in book 4.
> How well does Dido fit Aristotle's requirements for a tragic hero? How well does the concept of hamartia fit with her character and judgment?

Students recognize that the tragedy of Dido and Aeneas meets many of Aristotle's requirements. It involves serious action and the imitation of happiness and misery: Aeneas's arrival in Carthage, his entrancing storytelling, the hunt, their lovemaking in the cave, his departure, and her suicide. The story also elicits pity for Dido (Saint Augustine responded strongly to Dido [*Confessions* 10–11] and centuries later the composer Hector Berlioz described his inability as a young boy to hear the last few lines of book 4 read) and for Aeneas as love racks his heart and he groans deeply (395; Mandelbaum 542). Vergil includes fearful descriptions: the appearances of Anchises's ghost; Mercury's appearance, which makes Aeneas's hair stand on end and freezes his voice (279–80; 373–75); Dido's sacrificial offering, at which the holy water turns black and the wine pours out in clots of gore; and Dido's hearing her husband's voice and the owl sing songs of death.

Students can find many examples of Aristotle's requirement of language with pleasurable accessories. Prominent among these are the use of fire imagery, the fire of love in Dido devouring her soft heart's flesh (2–3; 2–3) and the funeral pyre that will literally consume her, and the use of epic similes, where Aeneas is likened to an ancient oak tree blasted by winds but holding firm (441–49; 607–19) and Dido is likened to a wounded deer (68–70; 91–92). Students can also look at other specific literary devices Vergil uses: his images of love as a wound and a sickness; the brilliant colors he chooses to describe the hunt; the irony of Dido breaking her vow of chastity in the realm of Diana, goddess of chastity and the hunt; and his personification of *fama* as a horrifying female winged monster (173–83; 229–42).

Aristotle's injunctions that good tragic plots include peripeteia, discovery, and suffering, with the best combining all three, are realized in the tragedy of Dido. Dido goes from being a happy, successful queen of unimpeachable moral character who commands her people and her city to the opposite: a miserable, abandoned woman no longer in control of herself. Aristotle first defines discovery as a change from ignorance to knowledge, a stipulation that does not exactly apply to Dido, but adds to this definition a change to either love or hate in personages marked for good or evil fortune. This definition fits well with Dido's great love for Aeneas that becomes the hatred and scorn she demonstrates in Hades when she hears his excuses. Lastly, suffering as an action of a destructive or painful nature certainly is evident in Dido's suicide.

In his investigation of the tragic hero, Aristotle says that the hero must be a person not preeminently virtuous and just, whose misfortune comes about through hamartia, which is sometimes translated as an error in judgment rather than vice or depravity. Jean-Pierre Vernant has described it more precisely as "blindness. That is, something which surpasses man, which comes crashing down on him, which keeps him from seeing things as they are, so that he takes good for evil, commits a crime and is then punished by this crime" (285–86). Dido fits the requirement. She is a beautiful leader who inspires loyalty from her people and has already had one happy marriage. Her error in judgment, her blindness, is to break her vow of fidelity to Sychaeus and allow herself to fall completely in love with Aeneas, to subsume herself in him and neglect her kingdom. Her attraction to Aeneas impedes her from asking important questions about this man who arrives on her shore. How was he able to survive the destruction of Troy? Since he did survive, what forces are at work and why? What is his destiny? Was he really saved from Troy only to arrive in Carthage and become her consort? At this point, another of Vernant's elements of hamartia enters: hubris. Dido oversteps her bounds by allowing her passions rather than reason to rule her. In general, then, the Dido-Aeneas story displays the psychological motivation, focused dramatic action, and striking reversals demanded by Aristotle's analysis of tragedy.

With the Dido-Aeneas story as a tragic tale, are there elements of tragedy that Aristotle's definition does not reach? Dido's half of the story is clearly Aristotelian, but is not Aeneas also a tragic figure? He does suffer, yet he does not exactly experience anagnorisis: he begins the Dido episode as a lonely middle-aged widower bound by destiny to found Rome and ends the episode in the same way. He does undergo a reawakening of his sense of responsibility to his father, son, and destiny. But his story is tragic in that he, like the character Job in the poetic, dramatic section of the Book of Job, is subject to forces outside his control. Aeneas's mistakes in judgment include continuing to fight in Troy when it is clear the battle is lost and allowing Dido to distract him from his purpose of founding Rome. He is both virtuous and just, and his tragedy is part of his nobility. Because he is obedient to the gods, he leaves his beloved Troy when he would prefer to die in battle. Because he feels responsible to his son and father, he leaves Dido although he loves her deeply. Tragedy in his case is born not from error but from the conflict of public and private forces and the necessity to subdue private desire for public good. Though Aeneas will found Rome and achieve everlasting fame, he sees this great destiny only when his father reveals it to him in the Elysian Fields. In life he experiences loss after loss: his country, his wife, his father, his love, his friends. The tragedy that Aeneas experiences is better defined by Georg Lukács, who writes that the essence of tragedy is selfhood, the force of which "overleaps everything that is merely individual," which "elevates all things to the status of destiny," and simultaneously brings self-affirmation and self-cancellation in the face of the "All" against which the tragic man is "shattered" (160). Aeneas's self and life are destiny: his public self as founder of Rome is reawakened and affirmed in the episode with Dido, but his private self as a man who can choose his love and his life pattern is canceled.

Aeneas also fits Friedrich W. J. Schelling's discussion of the tragic hero as the guiltless guilty person (251–55). Aeneas must choose to follow destiny but then becomes guilty in the destruction of Dido, a guilt he manifests when he tells her in Hades that he did not know his departure would cause her such grief. William Storm writes that the "implicated" status of the guiltless guilty hero brings up the concern of personal responsibility and thus freedom. It is a "component of the tragic figure's character to rigorously test the limits of both responsibility and freedom—that is, spheres of personal implication in cosmic processes" (63). Aeneas is personally responsible for loving Dido and not rebuffing her—he asserts his freedom and individuality in doing so—but is neither free nor responsible for leaving her in the necessity of his surrender to the powers of the cosmos. Thus, he is both guilty and guiltless.

Dido, too, falls into the category of the guiltless guilty person. She is guilty of loving Aeneas, breaking her vow, and ignoring her kingdom. But is love a crime? And is Aeneas, from her point of view, the wrong person to love? Dido does assert her freedom but then avoids personal responsibility for Carthage and for herself. Philip Hardie writes in agreement with Storm that the "essence of tragedy is conflict" but adds that it is conflict "not only of wills but of rights" ("Virgil and Tragedy" 313). Aeneas and Dido have separate points of view, both are guiltless and guilty, and students sympathize with both.

George Steiner in his *The Death of Tragedy* also explores the kind of tragedy experienced by Aeneas and Job, men of virtue, obedience, and duty who are subject to forces outside their control. He calls a view like Aristotle's a "Judaic vision" of disaster that comes about through a "specific moral fault or failure of understanding." Dido's actions in breaking her vow and not comprehending Aeneas's devotion to destiny would fall into this category. But she also fits Steiner's more extensive view of tragedy, which he identifies as a "dramatic testing of the view of reality in which man is taken to be an unwelcome guest in the world. [. . .] But absolute tragedy exists only where the substantive truth is assigned to the Sophoclean statement that 'it is best never to have been born' or where the summation of insight into human fortunes is articulated in Lear's fivefold 'never'" (xi). Dido is thrust out of her homeland by her brother's evil machinations, is unwelcome in Africa, and is rejected by Aeneas. Her punishment is far out of proportion to her desire to be loved. According to Steiner, the Homeric heroes knew they could "neither comprehend nor master the working of destiny. [. . .] Call for justice or explanation and the sea will thunder back with its mute clamor. Men's accounts with the gods do not balance" (6). The Greek poets, then, assert that the forces that govern, shape, or destroy our lives lie outside reason's governance. Students recognize this line of thinking as a fuller explanation of the tragedy of Dido from her point of view. Her error in judgment in loving Aeneas is an error only in the sense that Aeneas is subject to destiny: he loves her in return and would make a fitting partner to rule Carthage. His leaving Carthage makes no sense to her. To her, the world is unrelenting and absurd, with the exception of her guilt over her broken vow. According to Steiner's definition, Dido's suffering ennobles her.

Still another modern definition of tragedy that sheds light on the power of the story of Dido and Aeneas is presented by Storm in his *After Dionysus*. Storm lists the common themes of tragedy as "achievement of wisdom through suffering [. . .] the limits of aspiration, the possibility of freedom in the context of destiny or 'necessity,' and the implications of individual guilt or responsibility" (36). Students can trace all these themes in the story of Dido and Aeneas. The themes seem to make Aeneas somewhat more the tragic hero than Dido. Dido's only wisdom gained through suffering is judgment of Aeneas's character and despair over her broken vow. Aeneas's suffering, however, leads to his greater understanding of *pietas*, of his particular role in the greater scheme of destiny. Both Dido and Aeneas learn the limits of their aspirations to make personal choices, and Aeneas in particular learns how little freedom he has in the context of destiny or necessity. As far as individual guilt or responsibility is concerned, Dido takes little responsibility for falling in love and neglecting her city; but she does feel enormous guilt over breaking her vow of faithfulness. Aeneas is torn by guilt and responsibility. As he encounters Dido in Hades, he expresses his guilt over hurting her. Guilt also is one of the prime motivations for his departure, guilt over the inheritance he is stealing from his son, Ascanius, by not going to Rome. His responsibility is to his family, the gods, and the future.

Storm follows Hegel in delineating an important structural and philosophical pattern that further elucidates the operations of tragedy and that can be applied to the tragic in the *Aeneid*. Storm writes that "two of tragedy's most notable philosophical behaviors [. . . are] ironic and dialectical patterns of thought and argument" (39). A little later in his discussion, he writes that the tragic "involves a collision in terms that are utterly irreconcilable, with no possibility of union. The exertion of the tragic is one of determined separation, and the result of this effect is a condition that is unmendable" (43). Students can explore how well this definition fits Dido and Aeneas's story, its irony and the characters' dialectical movements with each other. The irony arises in their similarity—both are rulers, both have lost their spouses, both have been forced to leave their homelands and build new empires—and yet their lack of synchronization. The dialectic occurs as they come together (attempt synthesis) but discover that their destinies do not coincide. While Aeneas demonstrates his ability to control his emotions and act (with much prompting) in accordance with reason and destiny, Dido enslaves herself to her passions and takes her life before destiny had decreed it to end. It is the dialectic in their relationship that supposedly leads to the Punic Wars.

Storm also contrasts the "chaos" and "cosmos" present in tragedy: the disorder stemming from gods struggling against one another, social structures collapsing, and the madness of characters; the order stemming from discovery and change in circumstances. This pattern, too, prevails in the Dido-Aeneas story as Venus and Juno contend over the establishment of Rome, Carthage's building slows, and Dido is driven mad, while the forces of destiny and rationality triumph in Aeneas's departure.

Yet another example of dualism in the events of the story is how the same act may, as Hardie suggests, embody two antagonistic principles. Like Orestes and Antigone, Aeneas faces competing family duties. According to Hardie, his heroic acts of *pietas* can also be acts of the "greatest moral repugnance" (314). His *pietas* toward his father and Ascanius in leading them from the flames of Troy is accompanied by his neglect of his wife, which leads directly to her death. His leaving Carthage in obedience to his *pietas* toward his son and the gods also leads to his abandonment of Dido.

Thus, students can benefit from a study of Vergil and tragedy in seeing the influence of Greek tragedy, particularly Euripides, on the story of Dido and Aeneas and identifying Vergil's emphasis on the larger forces at work behind the love story. They can examine the extensiveness of Aristotle's commentary on tragedy and, using more modern definitions of tragedy, recognize the richness of Vergil's storytelling and exploration of themes: freedom, destiny, and responsibility; guilt and guiltlessness; irony and the dialectic; and rationality and absurdity.

Dante's Vergil
Rachel Jacoff

> What happens when a new work of art is created is
> something that happens simultaneously to all the works
> of art which preceded it.
>
> —T. S. Eliot

Dante's resurrection of Vergil and Vergil's *Aeneid* is one of the most powerful acts of the sympathetic imagination in literary history. Not only was Dante influenced by Vergil as Vergil had been by Homer, but he dramatized the relation of his poem to the *Aeneid* by making its author a major figure in his poem. The *Aeneid* is the major nonbiblical subtext of the *Commedia* and its author the focus of the poem's greatest poignancy. In his role as guide to Hell and Purgatory, Vergil is granted exceptional if qualified authority and becomes the model of the ideal teacher for later generations. At the same time, his exclusion from Christian salvation makes his fate "the tragedy in the *Comedy*" (Hollander), a source of tender pathos that seems quite Vergilian in nature.

Teaching the *Commedia* and the *Aeneid* together raises a number of issues concerning literary genealogy, epic tradition, and the Christian appropriation of classical culture, all made particularly acute by the high degree of literary self-consciousness evident in Dante's relationship to his models and predecessors. Since Dante had no direct access to Homer, the *Aeneid* served as his model epic, and the *Commedia* is punctuated by extravagant homage to Vergil as "the glory of the Latins" (*Purgatorio* 7.16) and "our greatest Muse" (*Paradiso* 15.26). The *Commedia* gives continuous evidence of the "long study and great love" with which Dante read his "master and author" (*Inferno* 1.84, 85). Dante had access to medieval allegorizations of the *Aeneid*, but his intimate knowledge of the text itself is what gives rise to his own poem's ongoing dialogue with it. At one point he has Vergil allude to his knowledge of the *Aeneid* as total ("tutta quanta" [*Inferno* 20.114]), a claim borne out by the extent and detail of Dante's borrowings and allusions. Dante's Hell, particularly upper Hell (cantos 1–9), is filled with such Vergilian figures as Charon, Minos, Cerberus, and the Furies. Perhaps because Aeneas does not enter Tartarus, the lower reaches of Dante's Hell are less replete with Vergilian figurations even though they allude to episodes and contain characters from the *Aeneid*. The extremely systematic and geographically specific quality of Dante's Hell, its precise concordance of sin and punishment, is far more elaborate, of course, than that of any of his models, Vergil included.

In the *Purgatorio*, too, the *Aeneid* supplies episodes and characters; several of the examples on the purgatorial terraces are drawn from the *Aeneid*, and it comes into play in Dante's encounter with Statius and later in his meeting with Beatrice. Although Vergil as a character is not present in the *Paradiso*, his poem is brought to mind at several key moments. Dante's idealized history of empire in *Paradiso* 6 contains several allusions to the *Aeneid*, one of which makes the sacrificial death of Pallas the founding event of empire (6.36). Dante's meeting with his great-great-grandfather Cacciaguida explicitly recalls Aeneas's meeting with his father in Elysium: "with like affection did the shade of Anchises stretch forward [. . .] when in Elysium he perceived his son" (15.25–27). The last Vergilian allusion occurs in the *Commedia's* final canto, where the dispersal of the sibyl's "light leaves in the wind" (33.65) becomes a figure for the sensation of loss after the final vision.

References to the *Aeneid* operate on many levels. Sometimes merely an epithet or a phrase, at other times a character or an episode is brought to mind. Book 6 is important not only for the details it supplies but above all for the idea of a descent to the Underworld as a confrontation with a past both public and private and with a promise of a future that will justify the hero's struggles in the present. Vergil's brilliant conflation of temporalities in book 6 was crucial for Dante's understanding of the potential of such a journey. Just as Aeneas encounters key figures from his past such as Palinurus, Dido, and Deiphobus, so Dante meets with a series of figures who represent allegiances or temptations in his own earlier life. Many of the figures Dante meets also serve as versions of his own history; encounters with such significant characters as Francesca da Rimini, Pier della Vigna, Brunetto Latini, or even Ulysses are made self-confrontations as well. Anchises's roll call of future Roman history becomes, in Dante's encounter with Cacciaguida, a promise of his poetic future; instead of taking up arms, Dante is to take up the task of his poem, "making manifest all his vision" (*Paradiso* 17.128).

Dante's meticulous and intimate knowledge of the *Aeneid* underscores his revisions and rewritings of it. His allusions are often double-edged, offering an implicit critique as well as explicit compliment. In canto 3 Dante invokes Vergil's comparison of the souls of the unburied to falling leaves (6.309–12) in describing the souls waiting to cross into Hell, but he makes several small changes that shift its meaning. Vergil emphasizes the number of the souls ("Quam multa [. . .]" [309]), while Dante sees the leaves falling "one by one" (116); Vergil sees their fate as part of a natural cyclical process, comparing them to migrating birds, while Dante underlines the role of individual volition rather than seasonal process in changing the migrating birds to a bird that has been trained to respond to a call. These and other changes point to a "shift in time, from the cyclical time of organic nature to the linear time of the soul" (Freccero 149). The underlying circularity of Vergil's poem, its concern with the tragic repetitiveness of history and its elegiac undersong are, for Dante as well as for many contemporary readers of the *Aeneid*, in counterpoint to the poem's positive claims for Rome's historical significance and the destined momentum of its progress toward peace and empire.

Dante's rewriting of the *Aeneid* is even more provocative in *Inferno* 20, when he has Vergil tell a different version of the story of the founding of his native city, Mantua, than the one in the *Aeneid* and then makes Vergil tell him not to pay attention to any other version. By demystifying the Vergilian original, Dante seems to be insisting on a natural rather than a supernatural foundation myth. This is the same canto where Dante has Vergil praise his total knowledge of the *Aeneid* just after mentioning something that doesn't actually take place in Vergil's poem as if it did. These violations of the *Aeneid*'s integrity occur in the context of comparable violations of the other ancient epics, as if Dante's critique of the sin of divination (the sin punished in this canto) were also a critique of the dignity and truth status of ancient prophecy. At the same time that Dante wants his vernacular poem to be seen as the direct heir of the classical epics, he also finds ways of making himself their arbiter.

There are other forms of rewriting where Dante supplements the Vergilian original, for example, in an imagined speech of Lavinia (*Purgatorio* 35–39) in response to her mother's death. The most powerful revisions, however, are those in which Dante takes Vergil's lines and places them in a context in which their original meaning is transformed or even inverted. His rewriting of the epic topos of the failed embrace in the Underworld is a case in point. Tears are the response to Aeneas's failure to embrace both his wife and his father, tears that underscore the finality of loss and death. Dante stages a failed embrace at the opening of *Purgatorio*, in his first encounter with a penitent who turns out to be his old friend, the musician Casella. Because the episode is so Vergilian in its language, we are surprised that a smile rather than tears accompanies Dante's failure to embrace Casella's unsubstantial shade. In the context of the promise of salvation, there is nothing to weep about here, and Casella insists on the continuity of his affection: "even as I loved you in my mortal body, so do I love you freed from it" (2.88–89). A comparably surprising smile accompanies Manfred's showing of his wounds to Dante (3.112), so different in tone from Deiphobus's painful display in *Aeneid* 6.494–99.

Most striking is the extraordinary constellation of Vergilian allusions that accompany the arrival of Beatrice just as Vergil is disappearing from the poem. In this tour de force of intertextuality, Dante rhymes the Latin of the Vulgate ("Benedictus qui venis" [30.19]) with the Latin of the *Aeneid*, as the angels accompanying Beatrice's triumphal chariot sing, "Date, o, manibus lilia plenis" ("give lilies with full hands" [30.21])—Anchises's funereal gesture for the early death of Augustus's nephew Marcellus at the conclusion of his catalog of future Roman heroes (6.883). The contrast between the context of the line in the *Aeneid* and that in canto 30 could hardly be greater: it invites us to meditate on the differences between the two texts and between the two worldviews that subtend them. While Vergil mourns the defeat of hope and faith by the stark finality of death, Dante transforms Anchises's vain (*inani munere* [6.885]) gesture into a joyous greeting, a sign of the triumph of hope and faith (and love) over death. Both Marcellus and Beatrice died before their promise was fulfilled, but Beatrice's promise continues on after death. She speaks of her death not as an end but as a threshold, a "change of life" (*mutai vita* [30.125]). For

Dante it is the hope and the fact of the Resurrection that authorizes the trans-figuration of Vergil's lilies of mourning into lilies of welcome. In a larger sense, it is the hope of the Resurrection that is the core of Dante's faith (see *Paradiso* 25), the great promise of Christian revelation that allows Dante to think of pre-Christian culture as vitiated by its lack of hope; "without hope we live in desire" (*Inferno* 4.42), Vergil explains in Dante's Limbo, the place to which he and other virtuous non-Christians are relegated.

The other Vergilian allusions in the scene of Vergil's disappearance offer similar contrasts between their fatal original contexts (the death of Dido, then of Eurydice from *Georgic* 4) and the joyous reunion scene at the top of the mountain of Purgatory. As several critics have noted, the allusions constitute a fade-out or effacement of Vergil's voice as they progress from direct quotation to translation to allusion. While Vergil's name is given five times in the space of ten lines (30.46–55), Dante's name, Beatrice's first word in the scene, is given for the only time in the whole poem; Vergil's farewell is thus coordinate with Dante's overt assumption of authorship in this signature canto. So intense is the sense of Vergil's loss at this juncture that many readers feel disappointed by the arrival of Beatrice, although it is the event that the poem has eagerly antici-pated since its opening.

To understand the complexity of response generated by the figure of Vergil, we need to look closely at another episode, the encounter with the Silver Latin poet Statius in *Purgatorio* 21–22. Dante, on no known authority, invents the story that Statius was a secret Christian. In two cantos Statius presents a tri-partite autobiography whose three aspects—poetic, moral, and spiritual—are unified in that each turns on his reading of Vergil. He credits the seminality of the *Aeneid*, his "mother and nurse" ("mamma / fummi, e fummi nutrice" [21.97–98]), with his poetic inspiration. Just as Statius's *Thebaid* concludes with an homage to "the divine *Aeneid*" (12.816), so Dante's Statius speaks of the *Aeneid* as the "divine flame" (*Purgatorio* 21.95) from which he has been lit. The extravagant praise of the *Aeneid* reminds us of its role in Dante's own poetic formation and his greeting to Vergil ("You are my master and author") in the *Commedia*'s initial canto (*Inferno* 1.86). Subsequently Statius explains that he was converted from the sin of prodigality by reading a line in the *Aeneid* that he interpreted as an injunction against that sin. Finally, he attributes his con-version to Christianity to the consonance between the words of the Christian preachers and Vergil's fourth *Eclogue*, whose celebration of the birth of a mirac-ulous child was appropriated and interpreted by Christians as a prophecy of the coming of Christ. In this tradition Vergil is understood as an unknowing or inadvertent prophet who tells the truth without understanding its meaning, as he is imagined when Statius says, "You were like one who goes by night and car-ries a lantern behind him, not helping himself, but making wise those that fol-low" (*Purgatorio* 22.67–69). His gratitude to Vergil—"Through you I was a poet, through you a Christian" (73)—informs the whole episode. Dante's inven-tion of Statius's Vergilian conversion maximizes the salvific potential of Vergil's poetry while deeply engaging our sympathies for Vergil himself, who is at the center of the episode and yet excluded from its most important consequences.

A similar dynamic is at work in other episodes where Dante departs from tradition. The first is his invention of Limbo as the home not only of unbaptized infants (as it is in orthodox theology) but also as a special place for virtuous non-Christians. Clearly modeled on Vergil's Elysium, it is a *locus amoenus*, both on the margin of and yet in Hell, permeated by a wistful sadness, "where laments sound not with cries, but with sighs" (*Purgatorio* 7.29–30). Dante's honoring of the great figures of antiquity is protohumanistic in its valuation of classical culture; but its exemplars remain forever excluded from "the good of the intellect" (*Inferno* 3.18), which those who have not been baptized can never know. Nonetheless, Dante complicates this ground rule of his poem by inventing exceptions to it. Cato, the great paragon of Roman Stoic virtue, greets Dante and Vergil as they arrive in Purgatory; Cato is saved despite being a pagan, a suicide, and an enemy of Caesar (and for Dante, of empire). For the emperor Trajan Dante is following a legend that claims that Pope Gregory's prayers on Trajan's behalf allowed Trajan to be brought back to life in order to be converted and saved. He is found in the circle of just rulers in the Heaven of Jupiter alongside such figures as King David and Hezekiah. It is in this heaven that Dante makes one of his most daring moves, placing beside such famous figures a minor character mentioned only briefly in *Aeneid* 2. Among the first Trojans to fall in the battle described in book 2 is Ripheus, "most just among the Trojans and most zealous for the right" (426–27). For Vergil "the gods thought otherwise" (428), but for Dante Ripheus's zeal for righteousness becomes the theme of a fictive biography he invents to justify Ripheus's salvation in a Christian heaven. The salvation of an obscure companion of Aeneas in a poem where neither Aeneas nor Vergil are saved underscores both the inscrutability of divine justice and the paradoxical role of Vergil in Dante's poem.

For Dante the *Aeneid* was Rome's scripture, the equivalent of the Old Testament as a document of the providential prehistory of Christian revelation. He places the Roman epic and the Hebrew scripture in direct parallelism when, for example, he compares the Jews who crossed the Red Sea but did not make it into the Promised Land with the Trojans who dropped out of the journey of "Anchises's son" to Italy (*Purgatorio* 18.133–38). He rewrites the significance of Aeneas's mission, extending it beyond any telos Vergil could have imagined, claiming at the very opening of his poem that Aeneas was chosen ("eletto") in the empyrean as "the father of glorious Rome and of her empire," both of which were established as the holy place where the successor of great Peter has its seat" (*Inferno* 2.20–24). The continuity between Rome's Vergilian prehistory and the central events of Christian history is explicitly stated in the last book of the unfinished *Convivio* and book 2 of *Monarchia*; Dante asserts that David was born at the time Aeneas came from Troy to Italy and that Christ chose to be born during the Pax Romana, when the world was most perfectly disposed under the rule of the commander of the Roman people (*Convivio*

4.5). The proof text of this sacral understanding of Roman history is the *Aeneid*, which is liberally cited in both texts as well as in the *Commedia*.

In the imperial vacuum of his own historical moment, Dante looked to the idea of Roman imperial power as a solution to the internecine conflicts that he saw in the political vacuum around him, among whose vicious consequences was his exile. He must have felt that he was living through an experience like the civil wars whose destructive violence Augustus's victory and assumption of power brought to an end; his idealization of Roman *imperium* reveals the degree to which his desire for peace allowed him to deny the inevitable problems of political power attained and maintained by force. Dante anticipated contemporary readings of Vergil in his awareness that Vergil is not only the celebrator of Augustan values and the empire but also a tragic poet, a poet of incompleteness and regret. Although he has no desire to rend the ideological veil of empire, he remains sensitive to Vergil's melancholy and historical pessimism, bringing them to bear on his haunting characterization of Vergil.

Suggested Reading

Barolini, Teodolinda. *Dante's Poets: Textuality and Truth in the* Comedy. Princeton: Princeton UP, 1984.

Brownlee, Kevin. "Dante and the Classical Poets." *The Cambridge Companion to Dante*. Ed. Rachel Jacoff. Cambridge: Cambridge UP, 1993. 100–19.

Comparetti, Domenico. *Vergil in the Middle Ages*. Trans. E. F. M. Benecke. Princeton: Princeton UP, 1997.

Davis, Charles Till. *Dante and the Idea of Rome*. Oxford: Clarendon, 1957.

Freccero, John. *The Poetics of Conversion*. Ed. Rachel Jacoff. Cambridge: Harvard UP, 1986.

Hollander, Robert. *Il Virgilio dantesco: Tragedia nella* Commedia. Florence: Olschki, 1983.

Jacoff, Rachel, and Jeffrey T. Schnapp, eds. *The Poetry of Allusion: Virgil and Ovid in Dante*. Stanford: Stanford UP, 1991.

Mazzotta, Giuseppe. *Dante, Poet of the Desert*. Princeton: Princeton UP, 1979.

Schnapp, Jeffrey T. *The Transfiguration of History at the Center of Dante's* Paradise. Princeton: Princeton UP, 1986.

Teaching the *Aeneid* with Milton's *Paradise Lost*

Patrick J. Cook

Stanley Fish writes that the reader of *Paradise Lost* is "met at every turn with demands his intellect cannot even consider" (37). Perhaps foremost among demands is assembling the poem's significations that depend on allusion or, as Claes Schaar puts it in the finest study of Milton's intertextual practice, on the reader's construction and interpretation of "vertical context systems." The situation is particularly daunting for teachers, who can acquire through years of study the knowledge required to experience many Miltonic effects created through complex verbal and situational echo but who cannot easily prepare today's students to do the same. My solution is to assign in my undergraduate course on Milton extensive sections of the Bible and Robert Fitzgerald's translation of the *Aeneid* in its entirety. The latter seems to me as useful as the former, because Milton assumed that his most "fit audience [. . .] though few" (*Paradise* 7.31) would be intimately familiar with Vergil's prestigious epic and because there is scarcely a single concern of the *Aeneid*, large or small, that is not also a concern of *Paradise Lost*.

Instructors wishing to teach the two epics together should know that there is an abundance of scholarship available to assist in drawing connecting lines between the two poems on specific topics: the values and costs of empire (Quint; Sims), the nature of heroism (Steadman), Roman *pietas* and Christian piety (Garrison), dynastic lineage (Fichter), fathers and sons (Butler), formal structure (Condee), the Muses (Gregory), allegory (Murrin), the epic-pastoral relation (Knott; Rosenberg). Broader studies of Milton's relation to classical and other epics are also helpful and can efficiently direct interested readers to further scholarship (Addison; Blessington; Burrow, *Romance*; Cook; DiCesare, "*Paradise*"; Gransden, "*Paradise*"; Greene; Harding; Kates; Lewis; Martindale, *Milton*; Porter; Webber). In addition to providing analyses of an enormous number of passages, Schaar's *The Full Voic'd Quire Below* contains one of the finest available discussions of the nature and functions of literary allusion. The two indispensable compendiums of verbal parallels are the index to the Columbia edition of Milton (Patterson 10: 2026–29) and Andre Verbart's *Fellowship in* Paradise Lost (261–302).

In addition to providing what Thomas Greene calls "the norms of epic," reading Vergil with Milton allows a student-driven process of active exploration through the discovery and interpretation of allusions, an experience that to most is unfamiliar and therefore extremely valuable. To stimulate discovery of meaningful connections between the two epics, I ask students to make note of passages in each reading assignment of Milton that appear to recall Vergil in any way, to find and reread the corresponding sections of Vergil, and to comment briefly on whatever similarities and differences they notice. In the parts of class discussions devoted to this aspect of *Paradise Lost*, we consider both the allusions that have caught the attention of many and a few others that many have missed but that appear especially provocative. This exercise is of course a learning experience for the instructor as well, since students will uncover aspects of the two texts that I have overlooked and since the process reveals much about how Milton might have expected that fabled creature, the classically educated seventeenth-century reader, to respond to his densely allusive poem.

Having belabored Vergil's opening list of "causes" (*causas* 1.8)—a plural frequently reduced to the singular by translators but admirably maintained by Fitzgerald—of his hero's misfortunes, I can expect the Miltonic narrator's asking the Muse for a provocatively singular "cause" (1.28) of the Fall to garner considerable attention. The class has closely scrutinized Vergil's list of Juno's grievances, noted the intertwined emotions of wrath and pride underlying what at first appears to be a random series, and observed the association that the *Aeneid* develops between a hero dangerously prone to the same combination of emotions and the goddess who punishes him, in an important sense, for resembling her. Expecting causality no less complex in Milton, students will rise to the challenge of his implausibly singular cause. Milton adds further provocation by posing his question in a poem over which presides an omnipotent and putatively all-virtuous deity and amidst language that links this deity to the Aristotelian prime mover. Milton thus introduces the logical implication that God himself is in some sense the singular cause of everything, an implication that the poem will later labor mightily to deny. The inevitability that the epic poem they are now entering will contain irreconcilable points of view and pose unresolvable conundrums presents itself to students most forcefully at this point, and they will expect Milton to develop the multivocal complexity that Vergil bequeathed as a central feature of the genre. Aware of the Vergilian precedent that unfolds from Juno's initial characterization, they will also be watchful for subtle forms of identification between characters otherwise opposed. Many will recognize, for example, the *Aeneid*'s opening question about Juno, *tantaene animis caelestibus irae?* (1.11), when variations of it are applied to the Son by the Father (*Paradise Lost* 3.216), to the rebellious angels by Raphael (6.788), and by Satan to God (9.729–30), and they will develop the associations and then make the distinctions that the connected allusions prompt. (See Porter 119–27; Rudat, "Milton's Satan"; Martindale, *Milton* 3–4; and Verbart, "Milton" 115–16. Fitzgerald's translation "can anger black as this prey on the minds of heaven?" should be modified to make Milton's allusions more evident; I offer "In heavenly minds could such great anger dwell?")

Few students fail to notice that the opening books of *Paradise Lost* cast Satan in the heroic role of Aeneas (as well as of Moses), who seeks to establish a new home for his exiled people, at once inviting the familiar charge that Milton is of the devil's party and prompting them into further consideration of the morally troubling aspects of Vergil's hero. This obvious situational parallel is reinforced and nuanced by very specific textual echoes that generate repeated ironies at Satan's expense. For example, Satan's first words lamenting the physical change in his fallen comrade Beelzebub (1.84–85) echo Aeneas's address to Hector's ghost (2.274), encouraging the reader to observe in Satan equivalents of the obtuseness shown by Aeneas in this scene, to note how the futility of his continuing to fight in Troy after receiving the new mission of translating empire comments on the futility of Satan's dream of reconquest, and to find irony in the fact that in Milton's epic both parties are disfigured and infernal. Because I have emphasized in class the repression of emotion and instinct as a component of Aeneas's heroism, when Satan composes his countenance to boost the morale of the fallen angels as they rise from the burning lake (1.522–27), students will often recall an instance where Aeneas similarly "feigns hope with his face" (e.g., *spem vultu simulat* [1.209]) (trans. mine here and throughout). A first impression might be that the comparison lends dignity to Satan. But the opening books of *Paradise Lost* also contain ample signs that Satan's hypocrisy is less benevolent and constructive than it seems. He tearfully addresses his troops "in spite of scorn" (1.619) following a passage that encourages one to read this scorn as directed toward his hapless followers as much as toward God—in marked contrast to the heroic self-abnegation employed by Aeneas to bolster morale on the Carthaginian shore. The infernal debate of book 2 of *Paradise Lost* turns out to be a sham, yielding at last to Satan's preconceived plan for a revenge that is always, despite his protests about the public good, fiercely personal. His initial appearance (1.193) alluded to Neptune's rising above the waves in *Aeneid* 1.127. He now foists his plan on the infernal assembly in cooperation with the only apparently statesmanlike Beelzebub, whose "grave aspect" (2.300–01) ironically invokes the *Aeneid*'s memorable first simile, where sea-calming Neptune is compared to a grave statesman (1.147–56).

It does not take students, focusing on such passages, long to appreciate Milton's provocative realignment of forces. The Neptune figure in Milton's hell remains allied with the Aeneas figure, but both are now opposed to the poem's moral agents; the sea god in effect reverts to the stormy Homeric role that Vergil so conspicuously revises. How then, one must inevitably ask, does Juno fit into Milton's realignment? The answer most students immediately offer is that Satan takes on Juno's role as well, since the stoic and order-inducing roles he assumes in these early allusions to Aeneas and Neptune are but masks covering his true role as embodiment of the vindictive *furor* and *superbia* ("haughtiness") that are among Juno's defining characteristics (on Juno-Satan, see Rudat, "Milton's Satan"). This answer points to the inextricable links among these vicious qualities in Milton, in Vergil, and indeed in the European epic tradition. Many insights and interpretive challenges issue from Milton's concentration in his devil of Vergil's forces of pride and wrath. For example, readers who see aspects of wrathful Jehovah in the Father will wonder if he is not proud too, like Juno, Neptune, and Aeneas on his bad days (on Aeneas's *superbia*, see Cook 46–50). To address this issue I ask students to reconsider the Father's wrathfulness by looking at all the poem's attributions of wrath to God, a task now easily accomplished through access to online texts and concordances. Wrath, it turns out, is assigned to God only by fallen characters, who thereby reveal their fallenness. Even the first instance in the poem, "But his doom / Reserv'd him to more wrath" (1.54), which will cause most readers to assign this wrath to God, is worded so as to allow us to assign it to Satan, once we have been surprised by our sin and corrected ourselves. The Father, it seems, is by implication absolved of pride.

Outside the narrative of the war in heaven, where, as has long been acknowledged, Satan draws Turnus into his repertoire of allusive roles, the celestial realm offers fewer opportunities than his hell to refocus Miltonically on the *Aeneid*. Although Milton removes from his council in heaven the Olympian gods' personal bickering and one-upmanship, Vergilian allusion enriches Milton's depiction of God for the most part in a negative way. Students will productively compare the downward glance of the Father and the Father-Son dialogue in book 3 with the parallel episode in *Aeneid* 1. Some will notice the vast difference between the Father's contradictory vision, which is represented as sequential despite our understanding that his vision of past, present, and future is simultaneous (3.78, 7.176–77), and the relatively unproblematic gaze of the more consistently anthropomorphic Jupiter. Despite the difference, the problem of delineating human and divine agency is basically the same in both poems. The Father's defensive disclaimer of responsibility for sin is troubling to many readers, since he cannot really deny the logical implications of his nature. The disclaimer troubles even more when it is recalled that even for the "less omnipotent" (the paradoxical phrase seems unavoidable) Jupiter "foresight appears to be not simply a matter of knowledge, for the fates ('fata') which he reveals are his will; by a bald etymological play, Jupiter gives us to understand that the *fata* ('things said') are what he says ('fabor' [261])" (Feeney, *Gods* 139). More positively, some students will observe the parallel created between the Son and Venus, which highlights the Son's role as a god of love, including sexual love, an idea to which the class will return when considering the active sexuality of Edenic life. The parallel leads as well to further inquiry into the gender system of Milton's poem. The apparent change of sex is more complicated than it seems. One of the poem's endless series of traps designed to catch and reform the unwary reader, the Son's nominal maleness is illusory; it is a reminder of the inadequacy of our fallen conceptions, for Milton's heavenly spirits transcend gender (1.424).

In the human world the most intertextual interest clusters around the parallels between Adam and Eve and Aeneas and Dido, which have long attracted critical attention, though without substantial illumination before articles by Wolfgang Rudat ("Milton's Dido") and Verbart ("Milton"). Beyond these relations the *Aeneid* intersects most meaningfully with *Paradise Lost* on earth through the poems' shared use of vertical imagery to symbolize ethical imperatives. As background to Vergil's vertical imagery, I compare Anchises's description of the Roman mission of sparing the subjected and battling down the proud ("parcere subiectis et debellare superbos" [6.853]) with Aristotle's description of the magnanimous man, who is "haughty toward men of position and fortune, but courteous toward those of moderate station, because it is difficult and distinguished to be superior to the great, but easy to outdo the lowly" (*Ethics* 223). As his father's formula suggests, magnanimity, with an adjustment or two in emphasis in the Aristotelian description, is among the most important trappings of empire that Aeneas is destined to translate. He is, in fact, the only character in the *Aeneid*'s present time to be labeled "magnanimous," and the epithet is first applied, significantly, when Jupiter promises to raise him to the skies (1.259–60). Milton revises the tradition of epic magnanimity in a passage linking it at once to humankind's ennobling upright posture and the need to acknowledge humbly our dependence on the descent of divine grace (7.506–16). This is but one among countless instances in the poem of the familiar Christian paradox of lowering that leads to rising and rising that leads to lowering. Satan's fall is the result of an improper attempt to rise to the level of God, in contrast with the exemplary behavior of the Son, whom "humiliation shall exalt" (3.313). The same principles apply to Adam and Eve, who are restored to grace between the end of book 10, when they throw themselves humbly "prostrate" (1099), and the beginning of book 11, when we find that "they in lowliest plight repentant stood" (1). Although the unshown change of posture has produced charges of inconsistency, it effectively demonstrates the working of divine magnanimity.

The extent to which Milton interweaves Christian and Vergilian materials grows clearer when we recognize that this Christian spatial paradox is closely related to Vergil's vision of empire, which combines glory with self-abnegation. Indeed, it is worth noting, especially given the dearth of scholarship on the subject, that the early Christian development of this paradox owes much to Vergil. Aeneas's stooping to enter Evander's lowly dwelling (8.363, 455) is much more than a gesture intended to court a needed ally. In the poem's pervasively spatialized ethical framework it is a condition for apotheosis and for the eventual raising of the eternal Capitol on Evander's hill. Aeneas must as well "overcome" Juno's anger by becoming a suppliant (from *sub-* + *plico* or "fold"). Helenus tells him to "overcome with suppliant gifts" (*supplicibus supera donis* [3.439]), and Tiberinus nearly repeats the advice: "overcome with suppliant vows" (*supplicibus supera votis* [8.61]). It is the *Aeneid*'s long implicit argument about the perils of *superbia* and the rights of the humble suppliant, conveyed through this vertical lexicon, that makes its hero's failure to be magnanimous in the final confrontation with Turnus so resonantly tragic. Similarly, it is through asserting the providential application of divine magnanimity that Milton justifies the ways of God to men in his divine comedy.

APPENDIXES

Appendix A: Homeric Parallels

It is commonly noted that *Aeneid* 1 through 6 uses the *Odyssey* to throw light on Aeneas's wanderings from Troy and that *Aeneid* 7 through 12 is Vergil's *Iliad*; yet there are many Iliadic episodes in the poem's first half (e.g., the fall of Troy, the funeral games for Anchises) and Odyssean passages in the second (e.g., Aeneas's arrival in Italy, his kind welcome by Evander, the metamorphosis of the ships). This appendix provides references, accompanied by brief descriptions, of passages in the *Aeneid* that strongly resemble passages from the epic poems of Homer. The list is by no means complete; we have selected only those passages where Vergil's debt to Homer is apparent and in which Vergil adapts Homer in ways that elicit tension between the texts. We have concentrated on those passages in which Vergil complicates his portrayals of character by adapting Homer's description in what may at first appear to be incongruous ways. We have also chosen to include references to the *Homeric Hymns*, even though not composed by Homer, because they were written in Homeric style and in a few instances serve as important models for Vergil. This appendix should enable instructors to select those passages that highlight specific themes or illustrate Vergil's use of adaptation and poetic composition; we hope it will encourage active class discussions.

The line numbers for the *Aeneid* refer to the Latin text; we have not privileged any translators or translations. Likewise, the references to Homer refer to the Greek texts. Since English translations normally include references, even if only by page, to the original Greek or Latin, we expect that readers of any translation will find the appropriate passages without difficulty. The abbreviations used are *Aen.* for *Aeneid*, *HH* for *Homeric Hymns*, *Il.* for *Iliad*, *Od.* for *Odyssey*.

Book 1

In book 1 Vergil establishes the character of Aeneas with frequent allusion to Odysseus. Unlike Achilles and Odysseus, both of whom are motivated by personal gain and glory and display heroic wrath, Aeneas is motivated by obligation or duty (*pietas*). Tensions emerge in Vergil's portrayal of the role of Juno, whose divine wrath functions as a structural or motivational force in the poem; it combines the anger of Poseidon in the *Odyssey* and the wrath of Achilles in the *Iliad*. Like Poseidon, Juno is angry over injuries committed against both herself and those she holds dear (Dido and Carthage); like Achilles, her wrath stems from injured honor. Vergil's characterization of Venus is a loose combination of Thetis in the *Iliad* and Athena in the *Odyssey*, both of whom serve as protectresses of the hero, with significant differences in the relationships. Thetis, Achilles's mother, displays great tenderness toward him and comforts him; Athena selects Odysseus as her favorite because of their like-mindedness. Venus is a strained conflation of these two models: she may be Aeneas's mother, but she is not as compassionate and tender as Thetis is toward her son; like Athena, she is more detached and removed but does not share any like-mindedness with Aeneas. His relationship with Venus does not provide the satisfaction we find in either of the Homeric precedents; her function seems to be to help him achieve his destiny and secure the future of the Trojans-Romans. This role diminishes her function as protectress-patroness to the hero, which Thetis and Athena strongly portray. Finally, Vergil's descriptions of Dido are rich and complex, since he likens her, at different times, to Nausicaa, Alcinous, and Artemis from the *Odyssey*.

> *Aen.* 1: *arma virumque* ("arms and the man"). The poem's first line incorporates two words, each of which refers to a Homeric epic: *arma* ("weapons") evokes the *Iliad*, *virum* ("man") Odysseus. ▪ *Il.* 1.1: μῆνις (*mēnis*). "Wrath" is the first word of the *Iliad*; not a precise parallel to *arma*, but certainly a theme that Vergil elicits from the poem's start. ▪ *Od.* 1.1: ἄνδρα (*andra*) ("man"), the first word of the *Odyssey*, refers to Odysseus.
>
> *Aen.* 81–101: the description of the storm and Aeneas's first words. ▪ *Od.* 5.295–312: the storm and Odysseus's speech. This first view of Aeneas, tossed about on the sea and wishing he had died in Troy, can encourage us to view him as a weakling. However, he not only echoes Odysseus, he surpasses him: whereas Odysseus wishes he had died a hero's death at Troy, Aeneas wishes he could have died at Troy defending his home and loved ones; Aeneas also reaches his destination with most of his company alive, unlike Odysseus, who is alone when he makes this speech.
>
> *Aen.* 184–95: shooting the stags. ▪ *Od.* 10.156–71: Odysseus kills a stag and brings it back to his men. Aeneas's first act mirrors one of Odysseus's: bringing down a stag to feed comrades. Odysseus kills one, Aeneas seven.

Aen. 198–203: Aeneas's speech. ▪ *Od.* 12.208–13: Odysseus's speech. Both exhort their men as no strangers to suffering who one day will remember these difficulties, but Aeneas is forcing himself to sound optimistic.

Aen. 314–417: Aeneas meets Venus. ▪ *Od.* 7.19–81: Odysseus meets Athena ▪ *Od.* 6.135–315: Odysseus meets Nausicaa. ▪ *HH* 5.81–142: Aphrodite encounters Anchises. This scene of the *Aeneid* borrows elements from three Homeric scenes: Vergil creates a complex tension by comparing Aeneas to both Odysseus and Anchises; Venus to Athena, Nausicaa, and Venus's Greek counterpart, Aphrodite.

Aen. 411: Venus conceals Aeneas in a cloud on his entrance to Carthage. ▪ *Od.* 7.14: Athena conceals Odysseus in a mist on his entrance to Phaeacia.

Aen. 437–38: Aeneas marvels at Carthage. ▪ *Od.* 7.43–45: Odysseus marvels at Phaeacia.

Aen. 446–49: the splendor of the temple to Juno. ▪ *Od.* 7.84–90: the splendor of Alcinous's palace.

Aen. 450–63: Aeneas weeps at the pictures on the temple doors. ▪ *Od.* 8.73–92: Odysseus weeps at Demodocus's song during the banquet. Both heroes respond emotionally to artistic representations of their trials during the war; Aeneas's emotions again misinterpret the situation.

Aen. 498–504: simile of Dido to Diana. ▪ *Od.* 6.102–08: simile of Nausicaa to Artemis.

Aen. 589–93: Venus beautifies Aeneas. ▪ *Od.* 6.229–35: Athena beautifies Odysseus.

Aen. 731–33: Dido pours a libation to Jupiter. ▪ *Od.* 7.179–91: Alcinous pours a libation to Zeus.

Aen. 740–41: Iopas (the bard) sings at the banquet. ▪ *Od.* 8.73, 261–66: Demodocus (the bard) sings at the banquet.

Book 2

If the images of Hector mutilated (not as he appeared in the *Iliad*, anointed with ambrosia and preserved by the gods) and Priam decapitated (treated with the sort of cruelty visible in Achilles after the death of Patroclus but not characteristic of him) do not completely manage to thrust the specters of death and destruction on the reader in book 2, surely the final encounter of Aeneas with his wife Creusa's ghost and its unmitigated allusion to Odysseus's encounter with his mother, Anticleia, in the *Odyssey* invest the book with an aura of death and irretrievable loss. While much derives not from scenes in the *Iliad* and *Odyssey*, much is tragic. Vergil alludes to Homer mainly through similes, often imposing an element of tension that increases the overall sense of tragedy, destruction, and violence.

Aen. 3–12: Aeneas begins his tale with an emphasis on personal involvement and suffering. ▪ *Od.* 9.12–15: Odysseus emphasizes his pain and suffering as he narrates his adventures.

Aen. 304–08: simile of fire and water devouring a field. ▪ *Il.* 4.452–56: waters rage from the mountains, a shepherd hears. Aeneas watches the destruction of Troy from his rooftop. Vergil adds fire, the primary destructive element of book 2, to Homer's simile and depicts Aeneas as the helpless observer, intensifying this comparison of the war din that devours Troy to a natural force.

Aen. 379–82: description and simile: Androgeos draws back as one who has stepped on a snake. ▪ *Il.* 3.30–37: Paris, seeing Menelaus, draws back like a man who has seen a snake. Snakes are a significant, recurring image in book 2. Note the ethnic reversal: the cowardly Paris in the *Iliad*, the hapless Greek Androgeos in the *Aeneid*.

Aen. 416–19: simile: winds clash and seas churn; so the Greeks fall on Troy. ▪ *Il.* 9.4–8: simile: winds meeting and clashing like hearts in the Achaeans' chests. The Homeric simile precedes the speeches and council of the Greeks, which occur before the embassy to Achilles. In the *Aeneid*, an attempt to rescue Cassandra precedes the slaughter in the palace of Priam.

Aen. 469–75: simile of Pyrrhus like a snake fed on evil herbs. ▪ *Il.* 22.93–97: Hector, like a snake fed on evil poisons and guarding his hole, awaits Achilles. Pyrrhus is not a sympathetic character in the *Aeneid*, unlike his counterpart in this simile, Hector.

Aen. 496–99: simile: Greeks rush into the palace like a foaming river. ▪ *Il.* 5.87–94: simile: Diomedes like a winter torrent. During his *aristeia* ("most impressive or memorable martial exploits"), Diomedes, like an unstoppable force of nature, removes all in his path.

Aen. 601–18: Venus's words: it is the gods who are responsible, not Helen, not Paris. ▪ *Il.* 3.164–235: Priam to Helen: you are not blameworthy to me, but the gods (are blameworthy). Venus, Aeneas's divine mother, speaks to prevent Aeneas from slaying Helen and then reveals to him the gods behind the scenes—Neptune, Juno, Pallas, Jupiter—who ultimately destroy the city. From the walls of Troy (the Teichoscopia ["viewing from the walls"]), Priam, the very human father figure, asks Helen to identify various Greek fighters—Agamemnon, Odysseus, Ajax—who will be largely responsible for destroying Troy.

Aen. 604–06: Venus removes the clouds from Aeneas's vision so that he may witness the divine forces at work. ▪ *Il.* 5.127–28: Athena removes the mist from Diomedes's eyes so that he can tell man from god during his *aristeia*.

Aen. 626–31: simile: Troy falls like a tree. ▪ *Il.* 4.473–89: simile: Ajax brings down Simoisius, who is compared to a poplar tree. In contrast to a young, unwed warrior, Troy is old and resists for a time. It takes many to bring it down. The young Simoisius falls easily.

Aen. 792–94: Aeneas attempts to embrace Creusa's shade three times. ▪ *Od.* 11.206–08: Odysseus tries to embrace Anticleia's shade in the Underworld. Vergil employs nearly a direct translation of Homer. Troy is now a land of the dead, like the Underworld. Neither Aeneas nor Odysseus knows of the death of his loved one until this encounter. Note the parallel of wife and mother, both of whom are irretrievably lost.

Book 3

In book 3, as Aeneas tells of the Trojans' wanderings, Vergil alludes to the *Odyssey* but employs much less direct interplay than we might expect. There is a reference to the island of the Phaeacians at 291, and at 386 Helenus prophesies that the Trojans will pass Circe's isle. In lieu of actual encounters with monsters, he describes to Aeneas and company some of the dangers that lurk on their coming journey. As he offers the most detailed account of Scylla and Charybdis, Achaemenides, a Greek abandoned on Sicily, retells the story of Odysseus and his men in Polyphemus's cave. Vergil invests this book with more reality than fantasy through these suggested encounters with characters and places from Odysseus's travels; Vergil's debt to Homer is clear but not as tangible as in other parts of the *Aeneid*.

Aen. 97–98: a voice from Apollo's temple prophesies that Aeneas and his descendants will rule the world. ▪ *Il.* 20.307–08: Poseidon prophesies that Aeneas will rule the Trojans. Vergil expands the prophecy in Homer.

Aen. 109–10: the story of Teucer. ▪ *Il.* 20.216–17: the story of Dardanus founding Troy.

Aen. 192–95: description of being out at sea with no land in sight and a storm brewing. ▪ *Od.* 12.403–06: the same. Vergil repeats this phrase almost exactly at 5.8–11.

Aen. 374–462: Helenus's prophecy. ▪ *Od.* 12.37–141: Circe's prophecy. Helenus's speech generally echoes the Homeric precedent in character and import.

Aen. 424–32: description of Scylla. ▪ *Od.* 12.85–100: the same.

Aen. 490–91: description of Ascanius. ▪ *Od.* 4.149–50: description of Telemachus. Andromache focuses on Ascanius's resemblance to her son, Astyanax; Menelaus remarks on Telemachus's resemblance to his father, Odysseus. Both speakers mention similarities in eyes, hands, and face.

Aen. 515: Palinurus at sea watches the night sky. ▪ *Od.* 5.271–75: Odysseus on his raft watches the night sky. Both observe the same constellations.

Aen. 570–71: description of the harbor at the Cyclopes' island. ▪ *Od.* 9.136–37: Odysseus describes the harbor at the Cyclopes' island. Both descriptions introduce the famous scenes.

Aen. 623–38: Achaemenides's account of Polyphemus eating Odysseus's comrades. ▪ *Od.* 9.289–394: Odysseus's account of Polyphemus eating his comrades. Vergil's account compresses Homer's.

Aen. 659: Polyphemus uses a lopped pine trunk for a cane. ▪ *Od.* 9.319: the same.

Book 4

Vergil's depiction of Dido is complex. Although in function she recalls Calypso, who detains Odysseus and wishes to keep him as her husband, Vergil does not evoke Calypso in his portrayal of Dido, nor does he compare her to Nausicaa or Circe. Interestingly, the one Homeric woman to whom he likens Dido is Penelope, at line 322; he also alludes to Homeric men, for example, Patroclus and Hector, and even the monster Polyphemus. The closest literary parallels to Dido occur not in Homer but in tragic plays; Vergil employs echoes of Euripides's Medea, Phaedra, Pentheus, and Alcestis; Sophocles's Ajax; and Aeschylus's Orestes in his dramatic depiction of Dido's circumstances. Giving additional dimension to her character, he also uses as models Apollonius's Medea from the *Argonautica* and Ariadne from Catullus's poem 64. Thus, in book 4, the Homeric parallels emerge mostly in small details, which frequently give rise to complex tension.

Aen. 4–5: description of Aeneas. ▪ *Od.* 2.288–89: Mentor's description of Odysseus. ▪ *Il.* 9.443: Phoenix's description of Achilles. Dido falls in love with the Homeric version of the hero, who is "a doer of deeds and a speaker of words."

Aen. 69–73: simile of Dido to the wounded deer. While this simile may not have a direct Homeric parallel, it reflects one in character. Viktor Pöschl (*Art* 80–82) briefly discusses the difference between the function of this simile and that of those in Homer; Brooks Otis (*Study* 71–83) offers a more detailed discourse on the primary (Apollonius's Medea as a doe pursued by dogs in *Argonautica* 4.12–13) and secondary (*Il.* 11.473–81, where Odysseus is compared to a wounded stag attacked by jackals) models.

Aen. 173–96: Rumor personified. ▪ *Od.* 24.413–14: Rumor as messenger. *Il.* 4.442–43: the personification of Strife. Vergil closely imitates the Iliadic depiction of Strife, who begins as small but then reaches the heavens with her head.

Aen. 222: Mercury, as messenger of Jupiter, tells Aeneas to leave Carthage. ▪ *Od.* 5.28: Hermes, as messenger of Zeus, tells Calypso to let Odysseus leave. Jupiter emphasizes Aeneas's public destiny and responsibility, Zeus Odysseus's personal fate. The catalysts to sending a messenger also differ greatly: Iarbas's prayer to Jupiter (incited by Rumor), Athena's prompting of the gods. Before the approach of the messengers, Aeneas has been staying in Carthage willingly, Odysseus has been wanting to leave Calypso.

Aen. 239–44: description of Mercury with sandals and wand. ▪ *Od.* 5.44–49 and ▪ *Il.* 24.340–44: the same. Like Mercury, Hermes is described as the "psychopomp" (leader of souls to the Underworld) at *Od.* 24.1–14.

Aen. 254–55: simile: Mercury like a bird. ▪ *Od.* 5.51–54: the same.

Aen. 285–86: Aeneas "turns his mind this way and that." An often repeated Homeric line, first occurring at *Il.* 1.189.

Aen. 287: "this plan seemed best in his heart." Another often repeated Homeric line, first occurring at *Il.* 2.5.

Aen. 322–23: Dido's honor, her hope of reaching the stars. ▪ *Od.* 19.108: Odysseus speaks of Penelope's reputation reaching the broad heavens.

Aen. 365–67: Dido's refutation of Aeneas's parentage. ▪ *Il.* 16.33–35: Patroclus's refutation of Achilles's parentage. Each speaker emphasizes the hero's pitilessness.

Aen. 441–49: simile of Aeneas to an oak tree. ▪ *Il.* 12.765–71: simile of Polypoetes and Leonteus to oak trees. ▪ *Il.* 12.131–36: simile of the Achaeans and Trojans like east and south winds assailing oak and ash trees.

Aen. 584–85: description of Dawn. ▪ *Il.* 11.1–2: the same.

Aen. 615–20: Dido's curse on Aeneas. ▪ *Od.* 9.532–35: Polyphemus's curse on Odysseus. Both speakers predict details that are later realized.

Aen. 669–71: description of lamentation for Dido. ▪ *Il.* 22.410–11: description of lamentation for Hector. Both occur "just as if the city were falling and being consumed by fire."

Book 5

The principal model for the games in honor of Anchises is *Iliad* 23, the funeral games for Patroclus. Vergil subtly parallels the fallen, beloved Patroclus, the older companion of Achilles, with Aeneas's father; simultaneously, Aeneas as presider over the games plays the role of Achilles in the earlier epic. Both Aeneas and Achilles are in control, poised, generous, and kind. Vergil reduces the eight games in Homer to four and interposes the shorter scenes of the foot race and archery contest between the longer episodes of the ship race and boxing match. All the contestants receive material rewards, as do their Homeric predecessors. After many parallels in detail to the games in the *Iliad*, Vergil returns to the world of the *Odyssey* by alluding to two characters from Odysseus's journey to the Underworld, thus setting the stage for book 6.

Aen. 8–11: description of being at sea with no land in sight and a storm brewing. ▪ *Od.* 12.403–06, 14.301–04: the same. Vergil's earlier echo of this phrase when Anchises, alive and accompanying Aeneas, gently recalls his importance (3.192–95).

Aen. 109–13: description of the prizes. ▪ *Il.* 23.259–61: the same.

Aen. 114–285: description of the ship race. ▪ *Il.* 23.262–650: description of the chariot race. Vergil's changing of the contest to a ship race is appropriate to this "Odyssean" portion of the poem, just as the chariot race was fitting for the *Iliad*.

Aen. 132: drawing lots for position. ▪ *Il.* 23.352–57: the same.

Aen. 137–38: description of the men's excitement. ▪ *Il.* 23.370–71: the same.

Aen. 144–47: simile of ship race to chariot race. Vergil alludes to the scene's primary model, the Homeric chariot race.

Aen. 189–96: Mnestheus's speech of encouragement to his oarsmen. ▪ *Il.* 23.402–16: Antilochus's speech of exhortation to his horses. Mnestheus then passes Sergestus; Antilochus passes Menelaus.

Aen. 235–38: Cloanthus's prayer to the gods. ▪ *Il.* 23.768: Odysseus's prayer to Athena during the foot race. Both prayers are successful: Cloanthus doesn't yield to Mnestheus; Odysseus surpasses Ajax.

Aen. 241: the sea god pushes with his great hand. ▪ *Il.* 15.694: Zeus pushes Hector with his mighty hand.

Aen. 270–72: Sergestus, coming in last, brings in his crippled ship. ▪ *Il.* 23.532–33: Eumelus, who lost control of his horses, drags in his chariot last.

Aen. 286–361: description of the foot race. ▪ *Il.* 23.740–97: Vergil's account includes many named runners as well as many unnamed contestants; Homer has only three named runners.

Aen. 327: Nisus slips in a pool of blood left by the sacrificial animals. ▪ *Il.* 23.774–76: Ajax slips in dung left by the sacrificial animals. Unlike the heroic and graceful Ajax, Nisus uses his mishap to interfere with Salius and allow his beloved Euryalus to win the race.

Aen. 340–61: dispute among the competitors. ▪ *Il.* 23.540–650: the same.

Aen. 362–86: description of the boxing match. ▪ *Il.* 23.653–99: the same. The braggart Dares volunteers, like the boastful Epeus in the *Iliad*. At 468–71 Dares, like Epeus at 695–97, spits out blood as his mates lead him away. Friends must collect the prizes for the incapacitated contestants in either account.

Aen. 394–98: Entellus's speech. ▪ *Il.* 23.627–29: Nestor's speech. Both mention the lost capacities of youth. Entellus fights and brings down Dares; Nestor doesn't fight but receives a prize.

Aen. 463: Aeneas stops the boxing match. ▪ *Il.* 23.734: Achilles stops the wrestling match.

Aen. 485–518: description of the archery contest. ▪ *Il.* 23.850–83: the same.

Aen. 487: Aeneas sets up the mast. ▪ *Il.* 23.852: Achilles sets up the mast.

Aen. 495–96: the reference to Pandarus recalls his breaking of the truce at *Il.* 4.72. He was a skilled archer.

Aen. 564: the young Priam, who is an age mate of Iulus, recalls his grandfather and namesake. Priam, the father of Creusa, is also Iulus's grandfather. Thus the unnamed and parallel grandfather is Anchises, the honoree of the games.

Aen. 741–42: Aeneas wants Anchises's shade to remain. ▪ *Il.* 11.210: Odysseus wants Anticleia's shade to remain.

Aen. 785–87: Venus's description of Juno's hatred of the Trojans. ▪ *Il.* 4.34–36: Zeus's description of Hera's hatred of the Trojans.

Aen. 817–26: description of Neptune driving his sea chariot and followed by his retinue. ▪ *Il.* 13.23–31: description of Poseidon. The list of nymphs at 826. ▪ *Il.* 18.39–40.

Aen. 835–71: death of Palinurus. ▪ *Od.* 3.278–83: death of Phrontis, the helmsman of Menelaus; he is slain by Apollo as he steers the boat. ▪ *Il.* 14.231–91: portrait of the god Sleep. ▪ *Od.* 11.51–80: Elpenor. Like Elpenor's shade when he meets Odysseus, Palinurus will beg for burial when he encounters Aeneas in the Underworld at 6.365–67.

Book 6

The principal Homeric counterpart to *Aeneid* 6 is *Odyssey* 11, where Odysseus describes his descent to the Underworld; Elpenor in the *Odyssey* serves as predecessor to both Palinurus and Misenus; Teiresias, in function, precedes the sibyl; and Agamemnon, in his message, prefigures Deiphobus. Patroclus (*Il.* 23) is also a model for Misenus. Like Odysseus, Aeneas encounters figures from his past (e.g., Palinurus, Dido, and Deiphobus, moving from the most recently departed to the most remote); but Vergil depicts Aeneas's journey as pivotal between past and future more directly than Homer portrays Odysseus's: Odysseus learns very little of his future, but Aeneas sees notable persons from Roman history to come. In this episode, Aeneas comes to terms with his past, releases it, and develops a greater and more tangible relation with his future and the destiny of Rome.

Aen. 1: *sic fatur* ("so he speaks") ▪ *Il.* 7.1: ὣς εἰπὼν; ▪ *Od.* 13.1: ὣς ἔφαθ: a typical Homeric closure to a speech. Although some scholars find this phrase a logical part of Aeneas's farewell to Palinurus at the close of book 5, it echoes Homer's opening of two different books and thus establishes the line as the start of book 6. Interestingly, the wording at *Od.* 13.1 signals the completion of Odysseus's narration of his travels; simultaneously, it points to the beginning of his journey homeward. Likewise, book 6, from its initial words, indicates a new direction for

Aeneas: his attachment to the past and his resolution to press forward are altered in the course of this book.

Aen. 89: "alius [. . .] Achilles" ("another Achilles"): so the sibyl refers to Turnus; but thus far in the epic, Vergil has alluded to Aeneas's similarities to the Greek hero. Both Aeneas and Achilles have goddess mothers (Aeneas's mother is Venus, Achilles's Thetis, Turnus's the nymph Venilia) who assist them in their pursuits. Achilles's name has been mentioned several times up to this point, in contexts frequently recalling his destruction of the Trojans (e.g., 1.30, 458, 475, 484), but his heroism has also been noted (1.752, 2.540). Applying the name to Turnus here, Vergil evokes tensions between Greek and Trojan (Achilles and Aeneas), Italian and Trojan (Turnus and Aeneas): while Aeneas is in the role of foreigner-invader, like the Greeks when they invaded Troy, Turnus is parallel to Achilles because he will challenge Aeneas (counterpart to Paris) on behalf of Lavinia (counterpart to Helen). The triangle is shifting and strained, because Turnus defends his homeland, as did Aeneas at Troy; Turnus more closely resembles Menelaus, since his bride-to-be will be taken by a foreigner; the invading Aeneas more closely resembles Achilles in that his arrival leads to the conveyance of the bride, who had been wrongly engaged to Turnus, to her proper (in the sense of destined) husband. Heightening these tensions, Vergil later compares Aeneas to Achilles through the words of Turnus at 11.438.

Aen. 179–82: description of the felling of trees for Misenus's funeral pyre. ▪ *Il.* 23.114–22: description of the felling of trees for Patroclus's funeral pyre.

Aen. 212–35: description of the funeral rites for Misenus. ▪ *Il.* 23.163–70, 250–53: description of the funeral rites for Patroclus. Homer's longer account includes speeches, but details of the burials are similar.

Aen. 245–46: burning hairs from the sacrificial victim's head. ▪ *Od.* 3.446: the same.

Aen. 249–57: Aeneas sacrifices a black lamb to the Eumenides and the great mother. ▪ *Od.* 11.32: Odysseus sacrifices a black lamb to Teiresias (the Greeks also sacrifice two lambs—one black, one white—to the Sun and Earth to seal their truce with the Trojans at *Il.* 3.103). *Aen.* 251: Aeneas sacrifices a barren heifer to Proserpina. ▪ *Od.* 11.30: Odysseus sacrifices a barren cow to the shades.

Aen. 290–94: Aeneas draws his sword. ▪ *Od.* 11.48–50: Odysseus draws his sword. Whereas the sibyl reminds Aeneas not to attack the insubstantial shades, Odysseus uses his sword to keep the shades away from the blood until he can speak with Teiresias.

Aen. 300: Charon's flaming eyes. ▪ *Il.* 13.474: Idomeneus's flaming eyes. This description alludes to Aeneas's encounter with Idomeneus in the *Iliad*, where Aeneas and Deiphobus lead a charge against the Greeks.

Aen. 304: the "green old age" of Charon. ▪ *Il.* 23.791: Antilochus jokes about Odysseus's "green old age."

Aen. 305–08: description of the shades. ▪ *Od.* 11.36–43: the same.

Aen. 309–14: similes of the shades to falling leaves. ▪ *Il.* 16.146: Glaucus compares the lives of men to the generations of leaves on trees, compares the shades to birds. ▪ *Il.* 3.2–7: the Trojans, as they attack the Achaeans, are like birds fleeing a winter storm.

Aen. 325–28: unburied shades find no rest. ▪ *Il.* 23.71–76: Patroclus's shade asks for burial, to end his wandering. ▪ *Od.* 11.71–76: Elpenor, who had been left "unwept and unburied," asks for burial.

Aen. 413–14: Charon's boat groans under the weight of Aeneas (*ingentem Aeneam* ["huge Aeneas"]). ▪ *Il.* 5.838–39: Diomedes's chariot groans under the weight of Athena and Diomedes himself, who is "the best of men." The adjective modifying Diomedes, ἄριστον, is that commonly applied to heroes. Aeneas is parallel here to both hero and deity.

Aen. 436–37: the sentiment that souls would "prefer to be in the upper air and endure poverty and harsh labors" rather than be dead. ▪ *Od.* 11.488–91: Achilles's speech to Odysseus: "I'd rather be a thrall serving a poor master on earth than be king over all the dead."

Aen. 445–76: the procession of heroines. ▪ *Od.* 11.225–330: the same. Odysseus sees his mother first, Aeneas sees Dido last. Odysseus interrupts the intensity of the narrative to remind the Phaeacians that it is time to sleep, but after a brief conversation he resumes his tale. There is no such reprieve in the *Aeneid*—Aeneas's address to Dido, unanswered, only heightens the difficulty and sadness.

Aen. 469–74: Dido turns away in silence. ▪ *Od.* 11.563–64: Ajax turns away in silence. In their speeches to these figures, both Aeneas (461–64) and Odysseus (558–60) lay blame on the gods for the events that have occurred.

Aen. 489–93: the sight of Aeneas frightens the shades of the Greek soldiers; they flee with cries. ▪ *Od.* 11.601–06: the dead flee at the sight of the shade of Heracles. Some only eke out a sound, as in *Od.* 24.5, where the souls squeak like bats.

Aen. 509–30: Deiphobus's speech. ▪ *Od.* 11.405–34: Agamemnon's speech. Each tells the living visitor the story of his wife's betrayal and his own death. Agamemnon's wife, Clytemnestra, and Deiphobus's wife, Helen, are sisters in Greek folklore.

Aen. 577–79: description of Tartarus. ▪ *Il.* 8.13–16: the same.

Aen. 595–600: description of Tityus's punishment. ▪ *Od.* 11.576–79: the same.

Aen. 625–27: "I could not name them all [. . .] not if I had a hundred tongues, a hundred mouths." ▪ *Il.* 2.488–89: "I could not name them all [. . .] not if I had ten tongues, ten mouths." Vergil echoes Homer's invocation to the Muse before the catalog of ships.

Aen. 637–65: description of Elysium. ▪ *Od.* 4.561–68: the same. Vergil expands Homer's description but preserves the sense that Elysium is a much brighter place than the rest of the Underworld.

Aen. 700–02: Aeneas attempts to embrace Anchises's shade three times. ▪ *Od.* 11.206–08: Odysseus tries to embrace Anticleia's shade three times. Vergil employs nearly a direct translation of Homer. See also the parallel at *Aen.* 2.792–94.

Aen. 707–09: description of souls hovering around Lethe's banks like bees. ▪ *Il.* 2.87–90: the armies are like bees.

Aen. 893–98: the Gates of Sleep, one of horn, one of ivory. ▪ *Od.* 19.562–67: Penelope's description of the two gates of dreams. Why Anchises sends Aeneas and the sibyl through the gate of ivory, which gives passage to "false dreams sent by the spirits," and not the gate of horn, through which "true shades" pass, is still a debated issue. In the *Odyssey,* Penelope doubts that her dream came through the gate of horn, but it does come true: Odysseus (the eagle) does slaughter the suitors (the geese). In Homer, the meaning is clear, but the way of exit is uncertain; in Vergil, the way of exit is clear, but the meaning uncertain.

Book 7

As Vergil begins the Iliadic half of the *Aeneid,* his principal Homeric allusions are predictably to the *Iliad.* Yet they are spare and, when they do occur, often serve to characterize important figures, such as Turnus and Camilla, in a light that evokes appreciation or sympathy.

Aen. 10: reference to Circe's island as the Trojans sail past signals the end of the Odyssean half of the epic.

Aen. 11–12: "where the rich daughter of the Sun makes the remote groves resound with her tireless song." ▪ *Od.* 10.221: the Greeks hear Circe singing on her island.

Aen. 28–83: the horses from an immortal line stolen by Circe from the Sun and mated with her mortal mare. ▪ *Il.* 5.261–72: the story of Aeneas's horses, bred from the immortal line that Zeus had given to Tros and stolen by Anchises.

Aen. 286–89: Juno spies Aeneas at sea. ▪ *Od.* 5.282–85: Poseidon spies Odysseus at sea.

Aen. 321: "Paris [. . .] alter" (Aeneas = "another Paris"). As Turnus is a second Achilles in his function as a force destructive to the Trojans (see note above on *Aen.* 6.89), so Aeneas is another Paris for the destruction Juno hopes he will bring on his people; Amata echoes this phrase at 7.363.

Aen. 378–84: simile of Amata to a top. ▪ *Il.* 14.413: simile of Hector to a top. Vergil embellishes Homer's simple phrase, where a blow from Ajax sends Hector whirling like a top.

Aen. 444: "men will wage wars and peace." ▪ *Il.* 6.492: "war will be the men's concern." These words of Turnus to the disguised Allecto echo those in Hector's levelheaded speech to his wife, Andromache. This allusion to a very moving scene in the *Iliad* should evoke the reader's sympathy for Turnus in this scene, which immediately precedes his affliction with *furor*.

Aen. 462–66: simile of Turnus to water bubbling in a cauldron over a fire. ▪ *Il.* 21.362–65: simile of the river Xanthus boiling when attacked by the fires of Hephaestus. This allusion to the helplessness of the river (a force of nature in its own right) should also elicit sympathy for Turnus's circumstance: he is the victim of a merciless attack by supernatural forces.

Aen. 586: simile of Latinus to a cliff assaulted by the ocean surf. ▪ *Il.* 15.618–22: simile of the Greeks who, like a cliff, withstand the Trojan onslaught led by Hector.

Aen. 641–46: invocation to the Muse. ▪ *Il.* 2.484–93: the same.

Aen. 647–817: catalog of the warriors. ▪ *Il.* 2.494–877: catalog of the ships.

Aen. 650: "Lausus, most handsome, save Turnus." ▪ *Il.* 2.671–74: "Nireus, most handsome, save Achilles."

Aen. 699–702: simile of soldiers like swans. ▪ *Il.* 2.459–64: the same.

Aen. 722: "earth thunders beneath the trampling feet" of the armies. ▪ *Il.* 2.466, 784: the same.

Aen. 808–09: Camilla could have flown over the fields and never bruised the stalks below. ▪ *Il.* 20.223–29: the foals, offspring of the North Wind, never bruise the stalks when they frolic.

Book 8

Vergil's primary model for book 8 is *Iliad* 18's long ecphrasis on the shield. In this serene book, which may be the most optimistic in the poem, Vergil presents the counterpart to the *Aeneid*'s book 2: book 8 details the humble origins of Rome, the agents of her rise, and a hope in new beginnings to contrast with the pitiable destruction of Troy in book 2. The Homeric model for Aeneas's journey to Pallanteum and visit with Evander is Telemachus's journey to Pylos and meeting with Nestor; Eumaeus's kind welcome to Odysseus also influences the portrait of Evander.

Aen. 102–51: the arrival of Aeneas. ▪ *Od.* 3.4–101: Telemachus's arrival in Pylos. A sacrifice is taking place when either hero arrives. Nestor is assisted by his son, Pisistratus, Evander by his son, Pallas.

Aen. 152–56: Evander recognizes Aeneas through his resemblance to his father. ▪ *Od.* 3.123–29: Nestor recognizes Telemachus through his resemblance to his father. Nestor speaks admiringly of Odysseus, as does Evander of Anchises. ▪ *Od.* 4.140–45: Helen recognizes Telemachus through his resemblance to his father.

Aen. 154–63: Evander reminisces about hosting Anchises. ▪ *Od.* 3.204–11: Antenor reminisces about hosting Odysseus and Menelaus.

Aen. 182–83: Aeneas feasts on the chine. ▪ *Od.* 14.437–48: Odysseus feasts on the chine, the guest's portion of honor.

Aen. 184: "after their hunger had been removed." ▪ *Od.* 3.67: a formulaic Homeric line.

Aen. 209–10: "lest there be any tracks." ▪ *HH* 4.75–77: Hermes makes the cattle of Apollo walk backward when he steals them; this description highlights the thievery of Cacus but recalls Hermes's position in the Homeric hymn. This theft is the catalyst through which Hermes obtains his realm and place of honor among the gods; it also necessitates Zeus's intervention and establishment of fairness and justice. The Homeric account has much humor, the Vergilian much violence.

Aen. 243–46: description of Cacus's cave. ▪ *Il.* 20.61–65: Hades fears that Poseidon's earthquake will lay open the Underworld.

Aen. 315: "a race of men sprung from trees and strong oak." ▪ *Od.* 19.163: Penelope asks the disguised Odysseus who he is: "you're not sprung from a rock or oak of ancient fable."

Aen. 353–54: "the darkening shield." ▪ *Il.* 4.166: Zeus's black shield, which summons the storms. Vergil infuses details from Greek myth and legend into his account of ancient Italians.

Aen. 370–413: Venus asks Vulcan to make armor for her son. ▪ *Il.* 18.428–67: Thetis asks Hephaestus to make armor for her son. Venus's seduction of Vulcan is also reminiscent of Hera's seduction of Zeus (*Il.* 14.292–351). Venus refers to Thetis at 383.

Aen. 408–15: simile: Vulcan tends to his task like a woman spinning in the early morning hours. ▪ *Il.* 12.433–35: soldiers are compared to a woman spinning in the early morning hours.

Aen. 424–53: description of Vulcan's workshop. ▪ *Il.* 18.468–77: description of Hephaestus's workshop.

Aen. 448–49: the seven layers in the shield. ▪ *Il.* 7.245: Ajax's seven-layer shield.

Aen. 455–60: description of Evander putting on tunic, sandals, and sword. ▪ *Il.* 2.42–45: description of Agamemnon putting on tunic and sandals. ▪ *Od.* 2.1–4: description of Telemachus putting on sword and sandals.

Aen. 461–62: Evander's two watchdogs. ▪ *Od.* 2.11: Telemachus's two watchdogs.

Aen. 560–61: Evander's speech about the days of youth. ▪ *Il.* 7.132–33: Nestor's speech about the days of youth.

Aen. 587–91: simile of Pallas to the morning star. ▪ *Il.* 5.1–7: Athena sets Diomedes ablaze like a star.

Aen. 626–728: Aeneas's shield. ▪ *Il.* 18.478–613: Achilles's shield. Whereas Achilles's armor has been lost and he needs a replacement, Aeneas is in no urgent need. Rather, Vergil uses the shield as another opportunity to describe the destiny for which Aeneas is fighting and poignantly places it here, before the battles of books 10 through 12. Achilles's shield contains depictions of the world, communities at war and at peace, with scenes pertinent to the *Iliad* (a wedding, death, ransom, armies); Aeneas's shield bears scenes of the coming founding of Rome and Roman history.

Book 9

Perhaps the most Iliadic in the second half of the poem, book 9 includes a number of scenes influenced by not only the *Iliad* but also the *Odyssey*. Vergil's use of these scenes as models illustrates his talent at adaptation: instead of slavishly imitating, Vergil composes a complex work that repeatedly challenges our understanding of both his poem and its models. Although heavily influenced by Homer, book 9 remains distinctly Roman in sentiment and ambiance. He complicates his portrayal of Turnus by comparing him frequently with both Homeric heroes who have lapses in judgment (e.g., Hector and Patroclus) and those whose reputations remain mighty (e.g., Menelaus and Ajax).

Aen. 1–24: Iris, sent by Juno, spurs Turnus to battle. ▪ *Il.* 2.786–810: Iris, sent by Hera, spurs Hector to marshal the troops. ▪ *Il.* 18.165–202: Iris, sent by Hera, urges Achilles to fight for the fallen Patroclus. Vergil establishes Turnus as a hero and formidable opponent for Aeneas by modeling him now on Hector, now on Achilles. In this episode, Turnus, like Achilles, recognizes Iris and asks who sent her; but she has already flown away and does not reply.

Aen. 57–66: simile of Turnus to a wolf. ▪ *Od.* 6.130: simile of Odysseus to a lion. Both creatures brave the elements (wind and rain) and seek domesticated animals, but Vergil's simile is harsher and much more violent. Homer's simile describes Odysseus as he approaches the maidens on the Phaecian shore, and he is naked and vulnerable; Vergil's simile describes Turnus's mercilessness as he attacks the Trojan ships.

Aen. 77–122: metamorphosis of the Trojan ships. ▪ *Od.* 13.125–64: metamorphosis of the Phaeacian ships. In Vergil, the Great Mother prays to Jupiter to honor the trees that once grew on sacred Ida; through his agreement, she rewards the ships by turning them into nymphs. In the *Odyssey*, Poseidon appeals to Zeus for honor and at Zeus's suggestion punishes the Phaeacians by turning their ship into stone. Earlier, the magical qualities of these ships, which steer themselves and read the minds of their captains, are described at *Od.* 8.550–63.

Aen. 77–79: invocation to the Muse: "Which god saved the ships from Turnus's firebrands?" ▪ *Il.* 16.112–13: invocation to the Muse: "How did fire first fall upon the Achaean ships?"

Aen. 128–58: Turnus leads the charge with fire against the Trojan ships. ▪ *Il.* 8.172–83: Hector leads the charge with fire against the Achaean camp. Turnus refers to Hector in his speech at 155. A portent immediately precedes each charge; Turnus misinterprets the one he witnesses (the metamorphosis of the ships).

Aen. 159–67: twice seven Rutulians, with a hundred men each, light fires and guard the battlements. ▪ *Il.* 9.85–88: seven Greek chiefs with a hundred men each stand guard, light fires, eat.

Aen. 176–458: Nisus and Euryalus sneak into Rutulian territory. ▪ *Il.* 10: the Doloneia: Odysseus and Diomedes sneak into Trojan territory.

Aen. 181: Euryalus's downy cheek, the first sign of young manhood. ▪ *Od.* 10. 278–79: Hermes with his first beard, in the prime of youth.

Aen. 194–95: Euryalus wants no material gain, only the glory. ▪ *Il.* 10.212–17: Nestor speaks of glory, then material reward, for those who succeed in this mission. If Achilles had not considered his material gain to be an emblem of his honor and glory, there would have been no *Iliad*. This phrase separates Euryalus—whether through foolishness or nobility and honor—from the Homeric hero. Ironically, it will later be the material booty, the helmet that he takes from the slain Messapus, that leads to Euryalus's death.

Aen. 269: if they succeed, Ascanius will give Nisus Turnus's horse. ▪ *Il.* 10.322: Dolon asks for Achilles's horses. Dolon the scout, whom Odysseus and Diomedes kill, asks for this reward for his success; Nisus does not ask for the prize but also does not succeed.

Aen. 303–10: presentation of weapons before the mission. ▪ *Il.* 10.255–71: the same. Iulus, Mnestheus, and Aletes bestow sword and helmet on Nisus and Euryalus; in the *Iliad*, Thrasymedes and Meriones give sword and helmet to Diomedes and Odysseus. Vergil's presentation is more emotional as it follows Euryalus's plea to comfort his mother.

Aen. 339–41: simile of Nisus to a lion. ▪ *Il.* 10.485–88: simile of Diomedes to a lion.

Aen. 435–37: simile of dead Euryalus to a flower. ▪ *Il.* 8.306–08: simile of dead Gorgythion to a poppy.

Aen. 459–502: Nisus's and Euryalus's heads carried around the Trojan walls; the grief of Euryalus's mother. ▪ *Il.* 22.395–515: Hector's body dragged around the walls of Troy; the grief of Andromache.

Aen. 476–77: Euryalus's mother drops the shuttle. ▪ *Il.* 22.448: Andromache drops the shuttle: Euryalus's mother also mentions his body as prey to the dogs (485) and that her weaving should have been his funeral shroud (486–89); she wails (477). Andromache mentions the dogs who will feed on Hector's body (509–10) and the women's weaving that will be his funeral shroud (510–14); she and the women wail (515).

Aen. 503–735: attack on the Trojan camp; Turnus enters the camp. ▪ *Il.* 12.35–471: attack on the Achaean wall; Hector breaks the wall.

Aen. 563–64: simile of Turnus to an eagle. ▪ *Il.* 15.690–94: simile of Hector to an eagle.

Aen. 617: Numanus taunts Ascanius, calls Trojans "Phrygian women." ▪ *Il.* 2.235: Thersites taunts the Greeks, calls them "Achaean women."

Aen. 646–60: Apollo as Butes, Anchises's armor bearer, addresses Ascanius. The Trojans recognize the god. ▪ *Il.* 17.322–34: Apollo as Periphas, Anchises's herald, addresses Aeneas, who recognizes the god.

Aen. 672–90: Pandarus and Bitias defend the Trojan gates. ▪ *Il.* 12.127–94: Polypoetes and Leonteus defend the gates of the Greek camp.

Aen. 674: simile of Pandarus and Bitias to pines and mountains. ▪ *Il.* 12.132: simile of Polypoetes and Leonteus to oaks in the mountains. ▪ *Od.* 9.191: simile of Polyphemus to a mountain peak. All are powerful images of immensity and immovability.

Aen. 709: Bitias falls; his shield thunders. ▪ *Il.* 5.42: Odius falls; his armor clangs.

Aen. 719: Flight and Terror accompany Mars. ▪ *Il.* 4.440: Deimos ("Terror") and Phobos ("Flight") accompany Ares; at *Il.* 13.299 Phobos is also referred to as Ares's son.

Aen. 731: Turnus gleams frighteningly in his armor. The Trojans recognize him and are troubled. ▪ *Il.* 22.131: Achilles gleams in his armor. Hector recognizes him and is afraid.

Aen. 745–46: Juno turns Pandarus's spear away from Turnus. ▪ *Il.* 20.438–39: Athena turns Hector's spear away from Achilles.

Aen. 756–61: Turnus would have taken the camp. ▪ *Il.* 16.698–701: Patroclus would have taken Troy.

Aen. 756–61: simile of retreating Turnus to a trapped lion. ▪ *Il.* 11.544–57: simile of retreating Ajax to a trapped lion. ▪ *Il.* 17.108–13: simile of Menelaus to a lion giving ground as he defends Patroclus's body. The description-simile is repeated at 17.657–64.

Aen. 802–05: Jupiter sends Iris to keep Juno from helping Turnus. ▪ *Il.* 8.397–432: Zeus sends Iris to keep Hera and Athena from helping the Greeks.

Aen. 806–14: Turnus under attack. ▪ *Il.* 16.102–11: Ajax under attack. Even in his weaker moments, Turnus is compared with a great Homeric hero.

Book 10

In this book of intense warfare, Vergil develops his heroes as quasi Homeric through descriptions and similes recalling the *Iliad*. The effect is a high degree of tension, added to the general intensity, because these heroes are clearly not Homeric but part of a different world and culture. For example, we feel an enormous strain when observing the actions of Mezentius; Vergil complicates the portrait of this *contemptor divum* ("despiser of the gods")—which certainly sets him opposed to Aeneas—by encouraging a Homeric view of him through several descriptions and similes reminiscent of the *Iliad*.

- *Aen.* 1–117: the council of the gods. Jupiter warns the Olympians not to interfere. ▪ *Il.* 8.1–40: the council of the gods. Zeus warns the Olympians not to interfere.
- *Aen.* 1: "the palace of Olympus lies open." ▪ *Il.* 5.749: "the palace of Olympus is opened."
- *Aen.* 163: invocation to the Muse (preceding the catalog of forces). ▪ *Il.* 2.484: invocation to the Muse (preceding the catalog of ships).
- *Aen.* 264–66: simile of soldiers' cries to the noise of cranes. ▪ *Il.* 3.2–7: the Trojans' cries are like the noise of cranes.
- *Aen.* 273–75: description of the blazing dog star. ▪ *Il.* 22.26–27: Achilles's armor blazes like the dog star, signaling destruction.
- *Aen.* 280: Turnus's speech: "Mars is in brave men's hands." ▪ *Il.* 16.630: Patroclus's speech: "The fulfillment of battle is in one's hands." Turnus's further encouragement to his men, to think of their families at home, also recalls Nestor's speech at *Il.* 15.662.
- *Aen.* 361: armies clashing at close range, "foot to foot, face to face." ▪ *Il.* 13.131–32: armies clashing "spear to spear, shield to shield."
- *Aen.* 362–79: Pallas exhorts his men. ▪ *Il.* 15.733–41: Ajax exhorts his men.
- *Aen.* 439–509: duel of Turnus and Pallas; death of Pallas. ▪ *Il.* 16.715–867: duel of Hector and Patroclus; death of Patroclus. Turnus kills Pallas, for whom Aeneas has great affection, taunts him, and takes a trophy. Likewise does Hector treat Patroclus, Achilles's beloved friend, in the *Iliad*. Turnus later dies at Aeneas's hands, as Hector dies at the hands of Achilles.
- *Aen.* 454–56: simile of Turnus to a lion chasing a bull. ▪ *Il.* 16.823–28: simile of Hector to a lion defeating a wild boar.
- *Aen.* 464–65: Hercules weeps for Pallas. ▪ *Il.* 16.459–61: Zeus weeps for Sarpedon. Jupiter comforts Hercules and refers to the Iliadic scene where Sarpedon dies (16.477).
- *Aen.* 487: Pallas plucks the weapon from his wound. ▪ *Il.* 16.505: Patroclus pulls the spear from Sarpedon's wound. At 495 Turnus plants his foot on Pallas and takes the belt; at 16.504 Patroclus plants his heel in Sarpedon's chest.

Aen. 488: "his armor clashed." A typical Homeric phrase. See note on 9.709.

Aen. 519: Aeneas takes eight captives to offer as sacrifice to Pallas. ▪ *Il.* 21.27–28: Achilles takes twelve captives to sacrifice to Patroclus.

Aen. 521–36: Magus's appeal and Aeneas's refusal to spare Magus. ▪ *Il.* 21.64–119: Lycaon's appeal and Achilles's refusal to spare Lycaon.

Aen. 557–60: Aeneas's speech to the dead Tarquitus. ▪ *Il.* 21.122–27: Achilles's speech to the dead Lycaon. ▪ *Il.* 11.452–54: Odysseus's speech to the dead Socus.

Aen. 581–83: Liger taunts Aeneas: "There'll be no escape." Liger refers to *Il.* 5.311, where Aphrodite rescues Aeneas from Diomedes; 446, where Apollo rescues Aeneas from Diomedes; and 20.273, where Poseidon rescues Aeneas from Achilles.

Aen. 636–46: the phantom Aeneas. ▪ *Il.* 5.449–53: Apollo creates a phantom Aeneas so he can escape Diomedes. ▪ *Il.* 20.443–46: Apollo conceals Hector in a cloud, at which Achilles slashes.

Aen. 693–96: simile of Mezentius to a rock. ▪ *Il.* 15.618–22: simile of Greeks to a rock that withstands the Trojan onslaught.

Aen. 707–17: simile of Mezentius to a wild boar. ▪ *Il.* 11.414–20: simile of Odysseus to a wild boar. ▪ *Il.* 13.471–77: simile of Idomeneus to a wild boar; Aeneas is his opponent.

Aen. 723–29: simile of Mezentius to a lion facing Acron. ▪ *Il.* 3.23–28: simile of Menelaus to a lion facing Paris. ▪ *Il.* 12.298–308: Sarpedon is like a lion facing the Greeks. ▪ *Il.* 17.61–67: Menelaus is like a lion facing the Trojans. All these similes in close proximity heighten the heroic behavior of Mezentius during his *aristeia*.

Aen. 736: Mezentius plants a foot and pulls a spear from Orodes. ▪ *Il.* 16.862–63: Hector plants a foot and pulls a spear from Patroclus.

Aen. 739–41: Orodes to Mezentius: "I shall not die unavenged." ▪ *Il.* 16.852–53: Patroclus to Hector: "You shall not live long." ▪ *Il.* 16.852–53: Hector to Achilles: "Paris and Apollo will kill you."

Aen. 743–44: Mezentius to Orodes: "Now die." ▪ *Il.* 22.365–66: Achilles to Hector: the same.

Aen. 762–68: Mezentius is huge like Orion. Orion is huge at *Od.* 11.572, where Odysseus sees him in the Underworld.

Aen. 783–85: Aeneas's spear passes through Mezentius's shield, which has three layers: bronze, linen, the hides of three bulls. ▪ *Il.* 3.357–60: Menelaus pierces Paris's shield of the same description.

Aen. 841–42: description of Lausus: "A mighty warrior laid low by a mighty wound." ▪ *Il.* 16.776: description of Cebriones, around whose corpse Hector and Patroclus battle.

Aen. 860: Mezentius addresses his horse, Rhoebus. ▪ *Il.* 8.184–97: Hector addresses his horses. ▪ *Il.* 19.400–03: Achilles addresses his horses. The notion that horses feel sorrow for their masters is expressed at *Il.* 17.426–40, where Achilles's horses weep for Patroclus. This passage is followed by Zeus's lament for the immortal horses that endure the pain of seeing their mortal masters die.

Book 11

In book 11, Vergil conflates various Homeric scenes. For the truce, the general models are the truce before the hand-to-hand duel of Paris and Menelaus in *Iliad* 3; the truce for the burning of the dead, granted to Priam by Agamemnon in *Iliad* 7; and the twelve-day truce for the funeral of Hector (*Il.* 24). For the council of war, again Vergil stacks his principal models: Antenor proposes the return of Helen in *Iliad* 7 and Polydamas proposes a truce, which is vetoed by Hector, in *Iliad* 17. In his portrayal of Camilla, as with those of other heroes in the epic, Vergil alludes to the actions of great warriors from the *Iliad*, particularly Achilles and Patroclus, and to Penthesilea, a woman warrior in Greek tradition.

> *Aen.* 1: "Meanwhile Dawn rising left the ocean." A near translation of *Il.* 19.1.
>
> *Aen.* 23: Aeneas's speech: "Let us commit their unburied bodies to the earth." ▪ *Il.* 16.45–47: "This is the honor for the dead." Hera's words, referring to the burial of Sarpedon.
>
> *Aen.* 45–52: Aeneas's lament for Pallas. Lines 45–48: ▪ *Il.* 18.324–27: Achilles's lament for Patroclus. Lines 49–52: ▪ *Il.* 22.437–46: Andromache preparing Hector's bath.
>
> *Aen.* 68–71: simile of Pallas to a flower (a description that evokes the death of Euryalus [9.435–57]). ▪ *Il.* 8.306–08: simile of dead Gorgythion to a poppy.
>
> *Aen.* 76–77: Aeneas uses one of two cloaks to shroud the body of Pallas. ▪ *Il.* 24.580–91: Automedon and Alcimus leave out two cloaks to cover Hector's corpse; the maids use only one.
>
> *Aen.* 81–82: Aethon, the steed, weeps. ▪ *Il.* 8.185: Aethon is a horse of Hector. ▪ *Il.* 17.426–27: Achilles's horses weep for Patroclus (see note on 10.860).
>
> *Aen.* 96–98: Aeneas's farewell to Pallas. ▪ *Il.* 23.179–83: Achilles's farewell to Patroclus. Both say good-bye, but Aeneas does not speak of revenge, Achilles does.
>
> *Aen.* 135–38: the felling of trees. ▪ *Il.* 23.110–22: the felling of trees for funeral pyres. (See note on 6.179, the felling of trees for Misenus's funeral pyre.)
>
> *Aen.* 139–81: funeral procession for Pallas enters Pallanteum; Evander laments. ▪ *Il.* 24.692–804: Priam conveys Hector's body to Troy; Andromache, Hecuba, and Helen lead the mourning.
>
> *Aen.* 158–61: grief of Evander. ▪ *Il.* 24.485–506: grief of Priam. Evander's speech focuses on his survival of his son, like that of Mezentius in 10.

Aen. 182–224: burning of the dead. ▪ *Il.* 7.422–32: burning of the dead on both sides. ▪ *Il.* 24.783–87: burning of Hector's body.

Aen. 191: "The earth and armor grow wet with tears." ▪ *Il.* 23.15: the same.

Aen. 207–09: the indistinguishable corpses. ▪ *Il.* 7.424: the same.

Aen. 211–12: the pyre of Pallas. ▪ *Il.* 23.250: the pyre of Patroclus. ▪ *Il.* 24.791–94: the pyre of Hector. After the flames are out, the mourners heap mounds of earth around the pyre.

Aen. 285–87: Venulus: "If the land of Ida had borne two such men, [. . .]." ▪ *Il.* 2.371–74: Agamemnon: "If I had ten men like Nestor, [. . .]."

Aen. 292: "Aeneas, first in piety." ▪ *Il.* 20.298–99: "Aeneas always gave gracious gifts to the gods."

Aen. 378–82: Turnus rebukes Drances for making speeches. ▪ *Il.* 2.246: Odysseus rebukes Thersites for being a speaker, not a fighter.

Aen. 445–97: the council dissolves at word of a pending attack. ▪ *Il.* 2.786–810: Hector dissolves the meeting after Iris, disguised as Polites, brings word of a Greek attack.

Aen. 455–58: simile of noise of armies gathering to birds. ▪ *Il.* 2.459–65: the same.

Aen. 477–85: Amata leads the Latin matrons to the temple of Athena. ▪ *Il.* 6.286–310: Hecuba goes with the Trojan women to pray to Athena.

Aen. 483–85: prayer of the Latin matrons: "break the spear of the Phrygian robber." ▪ *Il.* 6.305–07: prayer of the Trojan matrons: "Break the spear of Diomedes."

Aen. 492–97: simile of Turnus to a horse. ▪ *Il.* 6.506–11: simile of Paris to a stallion.

Aen. 610–11: simile of falling missiles to snow. ▪ *Il.* 12.156: the same.

Aen. 664: Vergil addresses Camilla: "Whom first did you bring down?" ▪ *Il.* 16.692–93: Homer addresses Patroclus: "Who was the one you killed first?" This phrase distinguishes Camilla and establishes her as heroic, even masculine, during her *aristeia*. It also presages her death.

Aen. 691–93: Camilla kills Butes. ▪ *Il.* 22.322–37: Achilles kills Hector. Both spear their victim in the neck.

Aen. 694–98: Camilla kills Orsilochus. ▪ *Il.* 20.397–400: Achilles kills Demoleon. Both spatter the brains of their victims.

Aen. 721–24: simile: Camilla kills Aunus's son as a hawk slays a dove. ▪ *Il.* 22.139–40: simile: Achilles pursues Hector as a hawk chases a dove.

Aen. 725–28: Jupiter looks down on the battlefield. ▪ *Il.* 8.51: Zeus looks down on the battlefield. Jupiter spurs Tarchon to action. ▪ *Il.* 15.592–614: Zeus spurs on Hector. Jupiter induces Tarchon to exhort his men. ▪ *Il.* 8.217–19: Hera drives Agamemnon to rouse his men.

Aen. 731: Tarchon calls each man by name. ▪ *Il.* 10.68: Agamemnon tells Menelaus to call each man by name.

Aen. 732–40: Tarchon taunts his men. ▪ *Il.* 4.338–48: Agamemnon taunts his men.

Aen. 785–93: Arruns's prayer. ▪ *Il.* 16.233–48: Achilles's prayer for Patroclus's safe return. Both prayers are only partially successful: Arruns brings down Camilla but does not return to his homeland; Patroclus drives the Trojans from the ships but does not return to Achilles.

Aen. 803–04: Camilla is hit in the right breast. ▪ *Il.* 5.393: Hera is wounded by Heracles in the right breast.

Aen. 806–08: Arruns flees after hitting Camilla. ▪ *Il.* 16.812–15: Euphorbus flees after hitting Patroclus.

Aen. 809–11: simile of Arruns to a wolf in flight. ▪ *Il.* 15.585–86: simile of Antilochus to an animal that has done some damage. Antilochus has just hit Melanippus beside the nipple and brought him down.

Aen. 855–56: Opis to Arruns: "Why so far away?" ▪ *Il.* 20.429: Achilles to Hector: "Come closer."

Aen. 912–14: Night closes the day of battle. ▪ *Il.* 8.485–88: the same.

Book 12

For this final book, Vergil's primary model is *Iliad* 22, the death of Hector. Turnus, who earlier was called "a second Achilles" (6.89) is now more closely modeled on Hector and at times on Patroclus; Aeneas is thus cast in the role of Achilles, the epic warrior who kills his opponent to avenge the death of his friend.

Aen. 4: simile of Turnus to a wounded lion. ▪ *Il.* 5.134–43: simile of Diomedes to a wounded lion. ▪ *Il.* 20.164: simile of Achilles to a lion ready to attack.

Aen. 67–69: simile of Lavinia's flushed cheeks to ivory stained with red dye. ▪ *Il.* 4.141–47: simile of red blood running from Menelaus's wound onto his thigh to ivory dyed red.

Aen. 72–80: Turnus's speech to Amata. ▪ *Il.* 6.486–93: Hector's speech to Andromache.

Aen. 84: Turnus's steeds are "whiter than snow, swifter than wind." ▪ *Il.* 10.437: Rhesus's horses are the same.

Aen. 176–82: Aeneas's prayer for victory. ▪ *Il.* 19.258–65: Agamemnon's vow to Achilles. Both invoke the sun and earth. Agamemnon also invokes the rivers at *Il.* 3.276–77.

Aen. 206–11: Latinus's oath. ▪ *Il.* 1.234–39: Achilles's oath. On the authority of the scepter: ▪ *Il.* 2.100–09, 185–87; *Od.* 2.80–81.

Aen. 224–37: Juturna, as Camers, intervenes. ▪ *Il.* 4.75–103: Athena, as Laodocus, intervenes.

Aen. 247–56: portent: eagle clutching a swan. ▪ *Il.* 12.200–10: portent: eagle clutching a snake.

Aen. 318–23: an arrow breaks the truce; it grazes Aeneas. ▪ *Il.* 4.104–40: an arrow breaks the truce; it wounds Menelaus.

Aen. 331–40: simile of Turnus to Mars. ▪ *Il.* 13.298–303: simile of Idomeneus to Ares.

Aen. 346–52: the story of Dolon. ▪ *Il.* 10.299–571: the same.

Aen. 365–66: simile of Turnus to the north wind. ▪ *Il.* 11.304–09: simile of Hector to the west wind.

Aen. 391–424: Iapyx treats Aeneas's wound. ▪ *Il.* 4.210–22: Machaon treats Menelaus's wound. Vergil adds the intervention of Venus.

Aen. 433–40: Aeneas kisses Ascanius before departing for battle; his prayer. ▪ *Il.* 6.474–87: Hector kisses Astyanax before departing for battle; his prayer. Hector removes his helmet so as not to frighten the child. Aeneas kisses Ascanius through his helmet and mentions Ascanius's uncle, Hector.

Aen. 450–58: simile of Aeneas to a storm cloud sweeping over the plain. ▪ *Il.* 4.275–82: the Greeks are like a storm cloud. Aeneas is now the heart of the force. The singular goatherd in Homer becomes plural farmers in Vergil.

Aen. 469–72: Juturna pushes aside Metiscus and drives Turnus's chariot. ▪ *Il.* 5.835: Athena pushes aside Sthenelus and drives Diomedes's chariot. Athena helps Diomedes battle Ares during Diomedes's *aristeia*; Juturna helps Turnus battle the mortal Aeneas.

Aen. 521–28: simile of Aeneas and Turnus to fires, to rivers. ▪ *Il.* 11.155–62: Agamemnon is like fire. *Il.* 20.490–94: Achilles is like fire. ▪ *Il.* 4.452–56: armies are like rivers. ▪ *Il.* 11.492–97: Ajax is like a river. ▪ *Il.* 16.384–93: Trojan armies are like a river.

Aen. 546–47: Vergil's address to Aeolus after Aeneas kills him. ▪ *Il.* 20.389–92: Achilles's address to Iphition after Achilles slays him.

Aen. 593–616: Reactions of grief. Amata thinks Turnus dead and hangs herself; Lavinia tears her hair and Latinus defiles his head with filthy dust at Amata's death. ▪ *Il.* 22.405–15: Hecuba tears her hair and Priam grovels in filth at Hector's death.

Aen. 632–34: Turnus recognizes Juturna. ▪ *Il.* 5.815: Diomedes recognizes Athena.

Aen. 640: description of Murranus: "A mighty warrior laid low by a mighty wound." ▪ *Il.* 16.776: description of Cebriones, around whose corpse Hector and Patroclus battle. (See 10.841 above.)

Aen. 684–91: simile of Turnus to a falling rock. ▪ *Il.* 13.136–45: simile of Hector to a boulder careening downhill.

Aen. 701–03: simile of Aeneas to a snowcapped mountain peak. ▪ *Il.* 13.754–55: simile of Hector to a snowcapped mountain peak. An image of immensity and immovability. Note the tension created by comparing first Turnus, then Aeneas to Hector.

Aen. 713: "The earth groans." ▪ *Il.* 2.784: the same.

Aen. 725–27: Jupiter weighs the fates of Aeneas and Turnus. ▪ *Il.* 22.209–13: Zeus weighs the fates of Achilles and Hector. Whereas Homer tells us that Hector's fate sank low, Vergil does not say whose is heavier. Zeus also weighs fates at *Il.* 8.68–73, where the Trojans prevail.

Aen. 749–55: simile of Aeneas to a hunting dog pursuing a stag (Turnus). ▪ *Il.* 22.188–93: simile of Achilles to a hound pursuing a stag (Hector). ▪ *Il.* 10.360–64: simile of Odysseus and Diomedes to hounds pursuing a deer or hare (Dolon). Turnus is at once the hero Hector and the self–interested Dolon.

Aen. 764–65: they strive for Turnus's life. ▪ *Il.* 22.159–61: the two race for Hector's life.

Aen. 784–85: Juturna returns Turnus's sword. ▪ *Il.* 22.276–77: Athena returns Achilles's spear.

Aen. 816: Juturna swears by the Styx. ▪ *Il.* 15.37–38: Hera swears by the Styx. ▪ *Od.* 5.185–86: Calypso swears by the Styx.

Aen. 894–95: Turnus realizes that the gods are behind his defeat. ▪ *Il.* 22.297: Hector realizes that the gods are behind his defeat.

Aen. 896–902: Turnus lifts a stone too heavy for twelve men. ▪ *Il.* 12.445–50: Hector lifts a stone too heavy for two men. ▪ *Il.* 5.302–10: Diomedes lifts a stone too heavy for two men; his opponent is Aeneas, whose hip joint he smashes. Vergil exaggerates the Homeric statement; even in defeat Turnus is still remarkable in strength. Both he and Aeneas are like gods. ▪ *Il.* 21.403–06: Athena hurls a boundary stone at Ares.

Aen. 903–04: Turnus does not know himself. ▪ *Il.* 16.805: Patroclus does not know himself.

Aen. 908–14: "As in a dream [. . .] " ▪ *Il.* 22.199–201: the same. In Homer the phrase applies to both Hector and Achilles; in Vergil, only to Turnus.

Aen. 918: Turnus realizes his sister (Juturna) is not there. ▪ *Il.* 22.294–301: Hector realizes his brother (Deiphobus) is not there. Death is near for both.

Aen. 924–25: Turnus's seven-layer shield. ▪ *Il.* 7.245: Ajax's seven-layer shield. Aeneas's shield also has seven layers (see note on 8.448–49).

Aen. 933: Turnus mentions Aeneas's father. ▪ *Il.* 22.420: Priam mentions Achilles's father. ▪ *Il.* 24.486: Priam reminds Achilles of his father.

Aen. 935–36: Turnus: "Return my body." ▪ *Il.* 22.338–43: Hector: "Return my body."

Aen. 951–52: description of Turnus's death. ▪ *Il.* 16.857–59: description of Patroclus's death. ▪ *Il.* 22.361–63: description of Hector's death. In this final image, Vergil recalls two great Homeric heroes. The final line is the same as that which describes Camilla's death (11.831).

Appendix B: Cultural, Historical, and Literary Terminology

Most instructors with even a limited knowledge of Latin and Greek find that the introduction of Latin and Greek terms or concepts that are central to Roman culture is indispensable when teaching the *Aeneid* in translation. We furnish the following list of those terms deemed most fruitful by our survey respondents for introduction to students. Many of the terms are also discussed in this volume's various essays; not all terms mentioned in the essays, however, appear here.

aristeia (ἀριστεῖα)	A hero's most impressive exploits in battle are called his *aristeia*. Cognate with *aristos* ("best") and *aretē* ("virtue"), *aristea* is the way a warrior makes his name or proves his greatness. Both *aristos* and *aretē* appear to derive from the name Ares, which demonstrates that they are linked to the male strength and prowess exhibited in battle. Ares is the god of the brutality of warfare, unlike Athena, who presides over the strategic side of war.
clementia	"Mildness," "benignity," "mercy." An indulgence or forbearance toward the conduct of others. Cognate with English "clemency" but perhaps closer in sense to "amnesty," as it frequently applies to political offenses. Julius Caesar's *clementia* to such former enemies as Brutus cost him his life. According to Augustus's *Res gestae*, in 26 BCE the Roman senate awarded Augustus the "shield of virtue" (*clipeus virtutis*), a traditional Roman emblem of honor, bearing the inscription "on account of his 'virtus' ['courage'], 'clementia,' 'iustitia' ['justice'], and 'pietas' toward the gods and his country" (34).
doloneia	From the name of the Trojan Dolon (related to the Greek for "to trick," "to deceive," δολος), this word most specifically applies to *Iliad* 10, in which Dolon attempts to spy on the Greek camp but is caught and killed by Odysseus and Diomedes as they likewise sneak behind enemy lines. A comparison of the *doloneia* involving Dolon, Odysseus, and Diomedes in *Iliad* 10, and that of Nisus and Euryalus in *Aeneid* 9 throws the major themes and values of either epic into relief.
ecphrasis	From the Greek verb *ekphrazō* (εκφραζω) ("to tell in full"), this noun means "description." It applies most specifically to

a detailed description of a physical work of art in a larger work of art such as a poem. The descriptions of Achilles's shield in *Iliad* 18, Aeneas's shield in *Aeneid* 8, and the murals of the temple of Juno in *Aeneid* 1 are examples of ecphrasis. Such description in the *Aeneid* can be found to explore intricately the major themes of the poem.

fatum   An utterance, prophetic declaration, "destiny," "fate." A law of nature. Death or destruction. In the plural, *fata* can evoke the three Fates: Clotho (the spinner), Lachesis (the disposer of lots), and Atropos (the one who cannot be turned away). At 1.2, Aeneas is described as *fato profugus* ("exiled by fate"), a phrase that indicates the importance of fate to the epic. Fate is protected by the gods (particularly Jupiter), whose responsibility it is to ensure that it occurs as it has been determined. This protection does not mean, however, that things opposed to fate do not take place. That Dido "perished neither through fate nor any deserved death" ("nec fato merita nec morte peribat" [4.696]) shows that mortal actions also can defy fate.

fides   "Trust," "loyalty," "good faith" between people, whether in personal or business affairs. Aeneas violates this trust with Dido, as does Latinus with Turnus. At 4.305 Dido calls Aeneas *perfide* ("untrustworthy") for betraying the trust of their love.

furor   "Rage," "madness," "fury," "passion." Somewhat similar to the Greek term *atē* (ἄτη), which may be rendered "folly" because it steals one's wits away. *Furor* is often the catalyst for a dramatic event or change in a character's life or story. Juno's *furor* pursues Aeneas through the poem. Aeneas struggles to contain *furor*, but at 12.946, *furiis accensus* ("enflamed with passion"), he kills Turnus.

hērōs   "Hero," but without the moral English connotations. In
(ἥρως)   Homer it may refer to any man, not just a warrior. In a more specialized sense, it refers to men superior to the present race, even demigods. In religion and myth it applies to locally worshiped deities or other human beings who are recognized for some extraordinary feats, such as Heracles. Vergil applies the term to Aeneas most frequently but to other warriors as well, including Turnus.

imperium   "Command," "authority," or "power" in earlier Latin, with the Augustan age it comes to mean "empire" or "supreme power." Anchises speaks of it in his famous directive at 6.851.

in medias res	"Into the middle of matters" or "into the midst of affairs." This phrase describes how the *Aeneid* (like the *Iliad* and the *Odyssey* before it) begins, thus making the flashback of Aeneas's narrative in books 2 and 3 necessary.
katabasis (κατάβασις)	A "going down" or "descent." This term applies to the descent of both Odysseus and Aeneas to the Underworld.
mores maiorum	"The manners of one's ancestors," "custom." The tradition of principles and usage, unwritten rules and precedents of duty and behavior, was an outlook on life and conduct. It illustrates the deep sense among the Romans of a connection between public and private responsibilities. At 8.186 Evander tells of the annual feast honoring Hercules, which arose *ex more* ("from custom"), and draws a distinction between actions spurred by superstition and those established by actual events.
nostos (νόστος)	A "return home," "homecoming," or more generally "journey." The destination is typically one's home or family and is associated with the past and memory. Vergil depicts Aeneas's arrival in Italy in book 7 as a *nostos* even though, in contrast to the homecoming of Odysseus, Aeneas is traveling to a new home, one that he slowly discovers after abandoning his native Troy.
penates	"Household gods" or "guardian deities of the hearth," these were the gods that Aeneas rescued from burning Troy and carried to Italy. They are closely associated with the inner chambers of the home, the hearth. Juno refers to Aeneas as carrying his *penates* to Italy at 1.68, and at 2.293 Hector's ghost tells Aeneas "sacra suosque tibi commendat Troia penates" ("Troy entrusts her sacred rites and household gods to you"). On the Ara Pacis ("Altar of Peace") dedicated by the Roman senate (in 9 BCE) to commemorate the peace that Augustus restored to Rome, there is a depiction of Aeneas and the *penates*.
pietas	Deep respect and reverence for one's father, family, country, ancestors, and the gods. Sometimes translated rather colorlessly as "goodness," "devotion," or "loyalty," *pietas* includes "kindness," "compassion," "affection," "dutiful conduct," "scrupulousness," and "gratitude." The Latin word yields two direct English derivatives: "pity" and "piety," both more restricted in sense. Thus *pius*, "reverent," "dutiful," "loyal," or "pious," indicates possession of the quality of *pietas* and is

Aeneas's most frequent epithet. He is described as *insignem pietate* ("distinguished for piety") at 1.10, and *pietas* is most frequently mentioned in book 6. It is *pietas* that will set the Roman apart from others, as Jupiter tells Juno at 12.839. Both *pius* and Aeneas's second most common epithet, *pater* ("father"), illustrate an important difference between the Vergilian and the Homeric heroes: the epithets of Achilles and Odysseus frequently emphasize physical or mental traits (e.g., "swift-footed," "godlike," "wily," or "the great tactician") whereas Aeneas's epithets focus on his relationships to others.

spolia opima   These are the armor and weapons that one leader takes in battle from the corpse of the enemy leader he has killed. Vergil refers to them at 6.855, where he describes Augustus's nephew Marcellus, and at 10.449, where Pallas describes the practice before he battles Turnus.

univira   A "one-man woman," this title applies to Roman matrons who remain faithful to a single husband throughout their lives, even as widows. Vergil never uses the word but depicts Dido as a *univira* through an allusion to Penelope at 4.321–23 and through her vow to remain faithful to the memory of her dead husband, Sychaeus (a vow she realizes she has transgressed at 4.552).

NOTES ON CONTRIBUTORS

William S. Anderson is professor emeritus of classics at the University of California, Berkeley. He has taught classics and comparative literature at Berkeley, the American Academy in Rome, the Intercollegiate Center for Classical Studies in Rome, and Yale University. He also served as Blegen Research Professor at Vassar College, First Robson Lecturer at Victoria College (Toronto), and research fellow at the University of Melbourne. He is the author of several articles and books on Roman poetry, including the frequently cited *The Art of the* Aeneid (1967). His most recent book is *Why Horace?* (Bolchazy, 1999).

Barbara Weiden Boyd, Henry Winkley Professor of Latin and Greek at Bowdoin College, has also taught at the Intercollegiate Center for Classical Studies in Rome. A former NEH fellow and member of the board of directors of the Vergilian Society, she has published *Ovid's Literary Loves: Influence and Innovation in the* Amores (U of Michigan P, 1997), *Brill's Companion to Ovid* (Brill, 2002), and *Vergil's* Aeneid: *Selections from Books 1, 2, 4, 6, 10, and 12*, a textbook with accompanying teacher's guide (Bolchazy, 2001).

John Breuker, Jr., teaches Latin at Western Reserve Academy in Hudson, Ohio. An elected trustee of the Vergilian Society, 1996–98, he is the author of numerous essays on Vergil.

Nancy Ciccone, assistant professor in medieval and classical literatures at the University of Colorado, Denver, has also taught at St. Mary's College in Moraga and Holy Names College in Oakland, California. She has written several articles on classical and medieval literature.

James J. Clauss is professor of classics at the University of Washington, where he is a coleader of the department's Rome Program and has received the university's Distinguished Teaching Award. He also taught at Creighton University. His publications include *The Best of the Argonauts: The Redefinition of the Epic Hero in Book 1 of Apollonius's* Argonautica (U of California P, 1993).

Randall Colaizzi, senior lecturer in classical studies at Wellesley College, has also taught at Boston College, the University of California, Los Angeles, and the University of Wisconsin, Madison. His research focuses on Roman elegiac poetry, ancient comedy, and Vergil.

Patrick J. Cook is associate professor of English at George Washington University. Specializing in Renaissance, medieval, and classical literature, he has recently completed *Milton, Spenser, and the Epic Tradition* (Scolar, 1996).

Ann Engar is Presidential Teaching Scholar in the Honors and Undergraduate Studies Programs at the University of Utah; she has also taught at the University of Washington and Wayne State University. She is a senior bibliographer for the MLA and a contributor to the MLA *Approaches to Teaching Hamlet* volume.

Judith P. Hallett is professor and chair of classics at the University of Maryland, College Park, where she has been named Distinguished Scholar-Teacher. She also taught at Clark, Boston, and Brandeis Universities and served as Visiting Blegen Scholar at Vassar College. She has written *Fathers and Daughters in Roman Society: Women and the Elite Family* (Princeton UP, 1984) and coedited both *Compromising Traditions: The Personal Voice in Classical Scholarship* (Routledge, 1997) and *Roman Sexualities* (Princeton UP, 1998).

Daniel M. Hooley, associate professor of classics at the University of Missouri, has also taught at Allegheny College, Carleton College, and Princeton University. He has published extensively on Latin poetry and English literature. His books include *The Knotted Thong: Structures of Mimesis in Persius* (U of Michigan P, 1997) and *The Classics in Paraphrase: Ezra Pound and Modern Translators of Latin Poetry* (Susquehanna UP, 1988).

Rachel Jacoff is Margaret E. Deffenbaugh and LeRoy T. Carlson Chair in Comparative Literature and professor of Italian at Wellesley College. Having published widely on Dante, she was a contributor to the MLA's *Approaches to Teaching Dante's* Divine Comedy and served as editor for both *The Cambridge Companion to Dante* (Cambridge UP, 1993) and, with Peter S. Hawkins, *The Poets' Dante*. She has taught at the University of Virginia, Cornell and Stanford Universities and served as a fellow at the Bunting Institute, Villa i Tatti, the Stanford Humanities Center, Villa Serbelloni in Bellagio, and the Liguria Study Center.

Mary Jaeger is associate professor in classics at the University of Oregon and former Harvard Mellon Faculty Fellow in the Humanities at Harvard University. She is the author of articles on Cicero, Horace, and Livy as well as *Livy's Written Rome* (U of Michigan P, 1997).

Sharon L. James is assistant professor at the University of North Carolina, Chapel Hill, and also taught at the University of California, Santa Cruz; Hamilton College; and Bryn Mawr College. She is the author of several articles on Latin poetry and *Learned Girls and Male Persuasion: Gender and Reading in Roman Love Elegy* (U of California P, 2002).

Patricia A. Johnston, professor of classics at Brandeis University, also taught at the University of Southern California. Among her numerous publications on Vergil and Roman poetry are *Vergil's Agricultural Golden Age: A Study of the Georgics* (Leiden, 1980), the Latin textbook *Traditio* (with workbook and instructor's manual), and a new translation of Vergil's *Aeneid* (Focus, forthcoming).

Gary S. Meltzer is associate professor of classics at Eckerd College. He also taught at the University of Maryland, College Park, and George Washington University. A contributor to the MLA's *Approaches to Teaching Euripides* volume, he is writing a book on Euripidean drama.

Michael C. J. Putnam, MacMillan Professor of Classics and professor of comparative literature at Brown University, also taught at Smith College and Cornell University and served as the acting director of the Center for Hellenic Studies and the Mellon Professor-in-Charge at the American Academy in Rome. A prolific writer on republican and Augustan Latin poetry, he recently published *Virgil's Epic Designs: Ekphrasis in the* Aeneid (Yale UP, 1998) and *Virgil's* Aeneid: *Interpretation and Influence* (U of North Carolina P, 1995).

Lorina N. Quartarone has taught at the University of Washington; Whitman College; and Loyola University, Chicago, and is currently assistant professor of classics and liberal studies at the University of Montana. Her research interests include Vergil and ancient representations of nature.

Sarah Spence, professor of classics at the University of Georgia, has taught in comparative literature and classics departments at Columbia University; California State University, Long Beach; and Harvard University. She has served as fellow in postclassical humanistic studies at the American Academy in Rome, Mellon Fellow in Comparative Literature at Harvard, and Bunting Fellow at Radcliffe College. She has published widely on classical and medieval topics, including *Rhetorics of Reason and Desire: Vergil, Augustine and the Troubadours* (Cornell UP, 1988) and *Poets and Critics Read Vergil* (Yale UP, 2001). She is the editor of *Literary Imagination: The Review of the Association of Literary Scholars and Critics*.

Scott Ward is professor of creative writing and literature at Eckerd College. His poems have appeared in a number of journals. He is the author of *Crucial Beauty* (1991) and is assistant editor of the journal *Shenandoah*.

Shirley Werner taught at Rutgers University and the University of California, Irvine, and served as American Fellow to the Thesaurus Linguae Latinae in Munich. She has published on Latin poetry and manuscripts and is writing a book on Horace's political odes.

SURVEY PARTICIPANTS

We wish to extend our gratitude to the following survey respondents, whose thoughtful and insightful comments provided the substance of this volume, for their generosity and willingness to share their ideas. Many of them completed several surveys on different courses in which they teach the *Aeneid* (56 respondents furnished information on 108 courses), and their contribution to this project is invaluable.

Henry Alley, *University of Oregon*
James Andrews, *Ohio University*
Pamela Bleisch, *Boston University*
John Bodel, *Rutgers University*
Barbara Weiden Boyd, *Bowdoin College*
John Breuker, Jr., *Western Reserve Academy*
Dana L. Burgess, *Whitman College*
Paul F. Burke, *Clark University*
Leslie Cahoon, *Gettysburg College*
Bonnie A. Catto, *Assumption College*
Nancy Ciccone, *University of Colorado*
James J. Clauss, *University of Washington*
Randall Colaizzi, *Wellesley College*
Patrick J. Cook, *George Washington University*
Raymond Cormier, *Longwood College*
Monica Cyrino, *University of New Mexico*
Stephen G. Daitz, *City College of New York*
Mary Davisson, *Loyola College in Maryland*
Carolyn Dewald, *University of Southern California*
Ann Engar, *University of Utah*
John Finamore, *University of Iowa*
Kirk Freudenburg, *Ohio State University*
Katherine A. Geffcken, *Wellesley College*
Linda Gillison, *University of Montana*
Scott Goins, *McNeese State University*
Ellen Greene, *University of Oklahoma*
Anne H. Groton, *Saint Olaf College*
Thomas Habinek, *University of Southern California*
Judith P. Hallett, *University of Maryland, College Park*
Jamey Hecht, *Castleton State College*
Daniel M. Hooley, *University of Missouri*
Mary Jaeger, *University of Oregon*
Sharon L. James, *University of North Carolina, Chapel Hill*
James F. Johnson, *Austin College*
Patricia A. Johnston, *Brandeis University*
Ross Kilpatrick, *Queen's University*

Robert C. Knapp, *University of California, Berkeley*
Donald G. Lateiner, *Ohio Wesleyan University*
Fr. M. Owen Lee, *Saint Michael's College, University of Toronto*
Gary S. Meltzer, *Eckerd College*
Timothy Moore, *University of Texas*
Mary Anne O'Neil, *Whitman College*
Barbara Pavlock, *Lehigh University*
Michael C. J. Putnam, *Brown University*
Grant C. Roti, *Housatonic Community Technical College*
Charles Saylor, *University of Missouri*
F. M. Schroeder, *Queen's University*
James M. Scott, *University of Montana*
Warren S. Smith, *University of New Mexico*
Sarah Spence, *University of Georgia*
Garth Tissol, *Emory University*
Thomas Van Nortwick, *Oberlin College*
Phiroze Vasunia, *University of Southern California*
Scott Ward, *Eckerd College*
Shirley Werner, *Rutgers University*
Betty Wilkinson, *University of Mobile*

WORKS CITED

Addison, Joseph. *Critical Essays from* The Spectator. Ed. Donald F. Bond. New York: Oxford UP, 1970.

Ahl, Frederick. "Homer, Vergil, and Complex Narrative Structures in Latin Epic: An Essay." *Illinois Classical Studies* 14 (1989): 1–31.

Allen, Archibald W. "The Dullest Book in the *Aeneid*." *Classical Journal* 47 (1951): 119–23.

Anderson, William S. "*Aeneid* 11: The Saddest Book." Perkell, *Reading* 195–209.

———. *The Art of the* Aeneid. Englewood Cliffs: Prentice, 1969. Wauconda: Bolchazy, 1989.

———. "Five Hundred Years of Rendering the *Aeneid* in English." Perkell, *Reading* 285–302.

———. "Vergil's Second *Iliad*." *Transactions of the American Philological Association* 88 (1957): 17–30. Rpt. in Harrison, *Oxford Readings* 239–52.

Appian. *Roman History: The Civil Wars*. Ed. and trans. Horace White. London: Loeb Classical Lib., 1913.

Ariosto, Ludovico. *Orlando Furioso*. Ed. Cesare Segre. Venice: Mondadori, 1976. Trans. as *Orlando Furioso*. Trans. Barbara Reynolds. Harmondsworth: Penguin, 1975.

Aristotle. *The Nichomachean Ethics*. Trans. H. Rackham. London: Heinemann, 1939.

———. *Poetics*. Trans. Gerald Else. Ann Arbor: U of Michigan P, 1967.

Articulating the Curriculum from School to College. Ed. Lee T. Pearcy. Spec. issue of *Classical World* 92.1 (1998): 1–104.

Augustine. *Confessions*. Commentary by James J. O'Donnell. Oxford: Clarendon, 1992.

Augustus. *Res gestae divi Augusti*. Ed. and trans. Peter Brunt and John Moore. London: Oxford UP, 1967.

Austin, R. G., ed. *P. Vergili Maronis Aeneidos liber primus*. Oxford: Clarendon, 1971.

———, ed. *P. Vergili Maronis Aeneidos liber secundus*. Oxford: Clarendon, 1964.

———, ed. *P. Vergili Maronis Aeneidos liber quartus*. Oxford: Clarendon, 1963.

———, ed. *P. Vergili Maronis Aeneidos liber sextus*. Oxford: Clarendon, 1977.

Babcock, Charles. "*Sola . . . Multis e Matribus*: A Comment on Vergil's Trojan Women." Wilhelm and Jones 39–50.

Bailey, D. R. Shackleton, ed. *Martialis epigrammata*. Bibliotheca Scriptorum Graecorum et Romanorum Teubneriana. Stuttgart: Teubner, 1990.

Bal, Mieke. *On Story-telling: Essays in Narratology*. Ed. David Jobling. Sonoma: Polebridge, 1991.

Barchiesi, Alessandro. "Rappresentazioni del dolore e interpretazione nell'Eneide." *Antike und Abendland* 40 (1994): 109–24.

———. *La traccia del modello: Effetti omerici nella narrazione virgiliana*. Pisa: Giardini, 1984.

———. "Virgilian Narrative: Ecphrasis." Martindale, *Cambridge Companion* 271–81.

Barthes, Roland. "The Death of the Author." *Image, Music, Text: Roland Barthes*. Trans. and ed. Stephen Heath. New York: Hill, 1977. 142–48.

Basson, W. P. "Vergil's Camilla: A Paradoxical Character." *Acta Classica* 68 (1986): 57–68.

Bellessort, André. *Virgile, son œuvre et son temps*. Paris: Perrin, 1920.

Benario, Herbert W. "The Tenth Book of the *Aeneid*." *Transactions of the American Philological Association* 98 (1967): 23–36.

Bernard, John D., ed. *Virgil at 2000: Commemorative Essays on the Poet and His Influence*. New York: AMS, 1986.

Beye, Charles R. "Vergil and Apollonius." Perkell, *Reading* 271–84.

Birkeland, Janis. "Ecofeminism: Linking Theory and Practice." Gaard, *Ecofeminism* 13–59.

Blessington, Francis. Paradise Lost *and the Classical Epic*. London: Routlege, 1979.

Bloom, Harold, ed. *Modern Critical Interpretations: Virgil's* Aeneid. New York: Chelsea, 1987.

———, ed. *Virgil: Modern Critical Views*. New York: Chelsea, 1986.

Boardman, John, Jasper Griffin, and Oswyn Murray, eds. *The Oxford History of the Classical World*. Oxford: Oxford UP, 1986.

Bonfanti, Mariza. *Punto di vista e modi della narrazione nell'*Eneide. Pisa: Giardini, 1985.

Bono, Barbara. "The Dido Episode." Bloom, *Interpretations* 103–26.

Bowie, A. M. "The Death of Priam: Allegory and History in the *Aeneid*." *Classical Quarterly* 40 (1990): 470–81.

Bowman, Alan K., ed. *The Augustan Empire, 43 B.C.–A.D. 69*. Cambridge: Cambridge UP, 1996. Vol. 10 of *The Cambridge Ancient History*.

Bowra, Maurice. "Some Characteristics of Literary Epic." *From Virgil to Milton*. London: Macmillan, 1945. 1–32. Excerpted in Commager 53–61.

Boyle, A. J. "*Aeneid* 8: Images of Rome." Perkell, *Reading* 148–61.

———. "The Canonic Text: Vergil's *Aeneid*." Boyle, *Roman Epic* 79–107.

———. *The Chaonian Dove: Studies in the* Eclogues, Georgics *and* Aeneid *of Vergil*. Leiden: Brill, 1986.

———, ed. *Roman Epic*. London: Routledge, 1993.

Brasillach, Robert. *Présence de Virgile*. Paris: Librarie de la Revue Française, 1931.

Braund, Susanna Morton. "Virgil and the Cosmos: Religious and Philosophical Ideas." Martindale, *Cambridge Companion* 204–21.

Braund, Susanna Morton, and Christopher Gill, eds. *The Passions in Roman Thought and Literature*. Cambridge: Cambridge UP, 1997.

Brenk, F. "*Auorum Spes et Purpurei Flores*: The Eulogy for Marcellus in *Aeneid* 6." *American Journal of Philology* 107 (1986): 218–28.

Broch, Hermann. *The Death of Virgil*. Trans. J. S. Untermeyer. Oxford: Oxford UP, 1980. Trans. of *Der Tod des Vergil*.

Brooks, Cleanth. *The Well Wrought Urn: Studies in the Structure of Poetry*. New York: Harcourt, 1947.

Brooks, R. A. "*Discolor Aura*: Reflections on the Golden Bough." *American Journal of Philology* 74 (1953): 260–80. Rpt. in Commager 143–63.

Büchner, K. *P. Vergilius Maro, der Dichter der Römer*. Stuttgart: Druckenmüller, 1955.

Burke, P. F. "The Role of Mezentius in the *Aeneid*." *Classical Journal* 69 (1974): 202–09.

Burnell, P. "The Death of Turnus and Roman Morality." *Greece and Rome* 34 (1987): 186–200.

Burrow, Colin. *Epic Romance: Homer to Milton*. Oxford: Clarendon, 1993.

———. "Virgil in English Translation." Martindale, *Cambridge Companion* 21–37.

Butler, George F. "Fathers and Sons in Vergil's *Aeneid* and Book 6 of *Paradise Lost*." *Classical and Modern Literature* 17 (1997): 265–77.

Cairns, Francis. *Virgil's Augustan Epic*. Cambridge: Cambridge UP, 1989.

Camões, Luíz Vaz de. *Os Lusiadas*. Ed. Frank Pierce. Oxford: Clarendon, 1981. Trans. as *The Lusiads*. Ed. William C. Atkinson. Harmondsworth: Penguin, 1952.

Camps, William A. *An Introduction to Virgil's* Aeneid. Oxford: Oxford UP, 1969.

Cançik, Hubert. "Rome as Sacred Landscape and the End of Republican Religion in Rome." *Visible Religion: Annual for Religious Iconography* 4 (1985): 250–65.

Carpenter, Thomas H. *Art and Myth in Ancient Greece*. London: Thames, 1991.

Carr, Wilbert L., and Harry E. Wedeck, eds. *Latin Poetry*. Lexington: Heath, 1940.

Castriota, David. *The Ara Pacis Augustae and the Imagery of Abundance in Later Greek and Early Roman Imperial Art*. Princeton: Princeton UP, 1995.

Catullus. Poem 64. *C. Valerii Catulli carmina*. Rutgers U Libs. 1999. 19 Dec. 2001 <http://harvest.rutgers.edu/latintexts/catullus/cat64.html>.

Chanson de Roland. Ed. Gerard J. Brault. 2 vols. University Park: Pennsylvania State UP, 1978. Trans. as *Chanson de Roland*. Trans. Dorothy L. Sayers. Harmondsworth: Penguin, 1957.

Cicero. *De inventione*. Trans. H. M. Hubbell. Loeb Classical Lib. 1949. Cambridge: Harvard UP, 1976.

———. *M. Tulli Ciceronis pro A. Licinio Archia poeta oratio*. Latin Lib. *The Classics Page at Ad Fontes Academy*. 12 May 1998. 20 Dec. 2001 <http://patriot.net/~lillard/cp/cic.arch.html>.

Clausen, Wendell V. "An Interpretation of the *Aeneid*." *Harvard Studies in Classical Philology* 68 (1964): 139–47. Rpt. in Commager 75–88.

———. *Virgil's* Aeneid *and the Tradition of Hellenistic Poetry*. Berkeley: U of California P, 1987.

Clauss, James J. *The Best of the Argonauts: The Redefinition of the Epic Hero in Book 1 of Apollonius's Argonautica*. Berkeley: U of California P, 1993.

Clay, Diskin. "The Archaeology of the Temple of Juno in Carthage." *Classical Philology* 83 (1988): 195–205.

Coleman, Robert. "The Gods in the *Aeneid*." McAuslan and Walcot 39–64.

Commager, Steele, ed. *Virgil: A Collection of Critical Essays*. Twentieth Century Views. Englewood Cliffs: Prentice, 1966.

Condee, Ralph Waterbury. *Structure in Milton's Poetry: From the Foundation to the Pinnacles*. University Park: Pennsylvania State UP, 1974.

Conington, John, and Henry Nettleship, eds. *P. Vergili Maronis opera*. 3 vols. London: Whittaker, 1881.

Conlin, Diane Atnally. *The Artists of the Ara Pacis: The Process of Hellenization in Roman Relief Sculpture*. Chapel Hill: U of North Carolina P, 1997.

Conte, Gian Biagio. *The Rhetoric of Imitation: Genre and Poetic Memory in Virgil and Other Latin Poets*. Trans. Charles Segal. Ithaca: Cornell UP, 1986.

Cook, Patrick J. *Milton, Spenser and the Epic Tradition*. Aldershot: Scolar, 1996.

Cotton, Charles. *Scarronides; or, Virgil Travestie*. Durham: Walker, 1807.

Dante Alighieri. *The Banquet (Il convivio)*. Trans. Christopher Ryan. Saratoga: Anma Libri, 1989.

———. *The Divine Comedy*. Trans. with commentary by C. S. Singleton. 6 vols. Bollingen Series 80. Princeton: Princeton UP, 1970–75.

———. *The Inferno*. Trans. John Ciardi. New York: New Amer. Lib., 1982.

DiCesare, Mario A. "*Paradise Lost* and the Epic Tradition." *Milton Studies* 1 (1969): 31–50.

Dio Cassius. *Roman History*. Ed. and trans. E. Cary. London: Loeb Classical Lib., 1917.

Donatus. *Interpretationes Vergilianae*. Ed. H. Georgii. Leipzig: Teubner, 1905–06.

Duckworth, George E. "Recent Work on Vergil (1957–1963)." *Classical Weekly* 57 (1963–64): 193–228.

———. "The Significance of Nisus and Euryalus for *Aeneid* IX–XII." *American Journal of Philology* 88 (1967): 129–50.

Dudley, Donald R., ed. *Virgil: Studies in Latin Literature and Its Influence*. London: Routledge, 1969.

Eden, P. T. *A Commentary on Virgil: Aeneid VIII*. Leiden: Brill, 1975.

Edwards, Catherine. *Writing Rome: Textual Approaches to the City*. Cambridge: Cambridge UP, 1996.

Eliot, T. S. *On Poetry and Poets*. London: Faber, 1951.

———. "Virgil and the Christian World." Eliot, *Poetry* 121–31.

———. "What Is a Classic?" Eliot, *Poetry* 53–71.

Eneas: A Twelfth-Century Romance. Trans. John A. Yunck. New York: Columbia UP, 1974.

Eneit. By Heinrich von Veldeke. Trans. J. W. Thomas. New York: Garland, 1985.

Euripides. *Medea and Other Plays*. Trans. James Morwood. Oxford: Oxford UP, 1998.

Fairclough, H. Rushton, trans. *Virgil*. Loeb Classical Lib. 2 vols. Cambridge: Harvard UP, 1916.

Fantham, Elaine. "Allecto's First Victim: A Study of Vergil's Amata." Stahl, *Vergil's Aeneid* 135–54.

Farrell, Joseph. "*Aeneid* 5: Poetry and Parenthood." Perkell, *Reading* 96–110.

———. *Vergil's Georgics and the Traditions of Ancient Epic*. Oxford: Oxford UP, 1991.

———. "The Virgilian Intertext." Martindale, *Cambridge Companion* 222–38.

———. "Which *Aeneid* in Whose Nineties?" *Vergilius* 36 (1990): 74–80.

Farron, Stephen. "Aeneas' Human Sacrifice." *Acta Classica* 28 (1985): 21–33.

———. *Vergil's* Aeneid: *A Poem of Grief and Love*. Leiden: Brill, 1993.

Favro, Diane. "Reading the Augustan City." *Narrative and Event in Ancient Art*. Ed. Peter Holliday. New York: Cambridge UP, 1993.

Feeney, Denis C. "Epic Violence, Epic Order: Killings, Catalogues, and the Role of the Reader in *Aeneid* 10." Perkell, *Reading* 178–94.

———. *The Gods in Epic*. Oxford: Oxford UP, 1991.

———. "History and Revelation in Vergil's Underworld." *Proceedings of the Cambridge Philological Society* 32 (1986): 145–60.

———. "The Reconciliations of Juno." *Classical Quarterly* 34 (1984): 179–94. Rpt. in Harrison, *Oxford Readings* 339–62.

———. "The Taciturnity of Aeneas." *Classical Quarterly* 33 (1983): 204–19. Rpt. in Harrison, *Oxford Readings* 167–90.

Fichter, Andrew. *Poets Historical: Dynastic Epic in the Renaissance*. New Haven: Yale UP, 1982.

Fish, Stanley. *Surprised by Sin: The Reader in* Paradise Lost. London: St. Martin's, 1967.

Fitzgerald, Robert, trans. *The Aeneid*. By Vergil. New York: Random, 1983.

Foley, Helene, ed. *Reflections of Women in Antiquity*. New York: Gordon, 1981.

Fordyce, C. J. *P. Vergili Maronis Aeneidos libri VII–VIII: With a Commentary*. Oxford: Oxford UP, 1977.

Fowler, Don P. "Deviant Focalisation in Virgil's *Aeneid*." *Proceedings of the Cambridge Philological Society* 36 (1990): 42–63.

———. "Epicurean Anger." Braund and Gill 16–35.

———. "Narrate and Describe: The Problem of Ekphrasis." *Journal of Roman Studies* 81 (1991): 25–35.

———. "Opening the Gates of War." Stahl, *Vergil's* Aeneid 155–74.

———. "Vergil on Killing Virgins." *Homo Viator: Classical Essays for John Bramble*. Ed. Michael Whitby, Philip Hardie, and Mary Whitby. Bristol: Bristol UP, 1987. 184–98.

———. "The Virgil Commentary of Servius." Martindale, *Cambridge Companion* 73–78.

———. "Virgilian Narrative: Story-telling." Martindale, *Cambridge Companion* 259–80.

Fraenkel, Eduard. "Some Aspects of the Structure of *Aeneid* 7." *Journal of Roman Studies* 35 (1945): 1–14. Rpt. in Harrison, *Oxford Readings* 253–76.

Freccero, John. *The Poetics of Conversion*. Ed. Rachel Jacoff. Cambridge: Harvard UP, 1986.

Fredricksmeyer, E. "On the Opening of the *Aeneid*." *Vergilius* 30 (1984): 10–19.

Gaard, Greta, ed. *Ecofeminism: Women, Animals, Nature*. Philadelphia: Temple UP, 1993.

———. "Living Interconnections with Animals and Nature." Gaard, *Ecofeminism* 1–12.

Galinsky, Karl. "The Anger of Aeneas." *American Journal of Philology* 109 (1988): 321–48.

———. *Augustan Culture: An Interpretive Introduction*. Princeton: Princeton UP, 1996.

———. *Classical and Modern Interactions: Postmodern Architecture, Multiculturalism, Decline, and Other Issues*. Austin: U of Texas P, 1992.

———. "Damned If You Do and Damned If You Don't: Aeneas and the Passions."
    Vergilius 43 (1997): 89–100.

———. "Hercules in the *Aeneid*." Harrison, *Oxford Readings* 277–94.

———. "How to Be Philosophical about the End of the *Aeneid*." *Illinois Classical Stud-
    ies* 19 (1994): 191–201.

Garrison, James D. *Pietas from Vergil to Dryden*. University Park: Pennsylvania State
    UP, 1992.

Genette, Gerard. *Narrative Discourse*. Trans. Jane E. Lewin. Ithaca: Cornell UP, 1980.

Gill, Christopher. "Passion as Madness in Roman Poetry." Braund and Gill 213–41.

Gillespie, Stuart, ed. *The Poets on the Classics: An Anthology of English Poets' Writings
    on the Classical Poets and Dramatists from Chaucer to the Present*. London:
    Routledge, 1988.

Glare, P. G. W., ed. *Oxford Latin Dictionary*. Oxford: Clarendon, 1982.

Gottlieb, G. "Religion in the Politics of Augustus." Stahl, *Vergil's* Aeneid 21–36.

Gransden, K.W., ed. Aeneid *Book VIII*. By Vergil. Cambridge: Cambridge UP, 1976.

———, ed. Aeneid *Book XI*. By Vergil. Cambridge: Cambridge UP, 1991.

———. "The Fall of Troy." McAuslan and Walcot 121–33.

———. "*Paradise Lost* and the *Aeneid*." *Essays in Criticism* 17 (1967): 281–303.

———. *Virgil's* Iliad: *An Essay on Epic Narrative*. Cambridge: Cambridge UP, 1984.

———. "War and Peace." Bloom, *Interpretations* 127–47.

Greene, Thomas M. *The Descent from Heaven: A Study in Epic Continuity*. New
    Haven: Yale UP, 1963.

Greenough, J. B., ed. *Livy, Books 1 and 2*. New Rochelle: Caratzas, 1976.

Gregory, E. R. *Milton and the Muses*. Tuscaloosa: U of Alabama P, 1989.

Griffin, Jasper. "Virgil." Boardman, Griffin, and Murray 616–35.

———. *Virgil*. Past Masters. Oxford: Oxford UP, 1986.

Griffith, Mark. "What Does Aeneas Look Like?" *Classical Philology* 80 (1985): 309–19.

Grimal, Pierre. "Les amours de Didon ou les limites de la liberté." Wilhelm and Jones
    51–63.

Grimm, Richard E. "Aeneas and Andromache." *American Journal of Philology* 88
    (1967): 151–62.

Guarducci, Margherita. "Un antichissimo responso dell'oracolo di Cuma." *Bulletino
    della commissione archeologica communale in Roma* 72 (1946–48): 129–41.

Gurval, Robert A. *Actium and Augustus: The Politics and Emotions of Civil War*. Ann
    Arbor: U of Michigan P, 1995.

Habinek, Thomas N. "Science and Tradition in Aeneid 6." *Harvard Studies in Classical
    Philology* 92 (1989): 223–55.

Haecker, Theodor. *Vergil: Vater des Abendlandes*. Leipzig: Hegner, 1931.

———. *Virgil: Father of the West*. Trans. A. W. Wheen. London: Sheed, 1934.

Hall, Jane Harriman, and Alexander G. McKay, eds. *Selections from Vergil's* Aeneid
    Books I, IV, VI: Dido and Aeneas. White Plains: Longman, 1988.

Hardie, Philip R., ed. Aeneid *Book IX*. By Vergil. Cambridge: Cambridge UP, 1995.

———. *The Epic Successors of Virgil: A Study of the Dynamics of a Tradition*. Cambridge: Cambridge UP, 1993.

———. "Fame and Defamation in the *Aeneid*: The Council of the Latins." Stahl, *Vergil's Aeneid* 243–70.

———. *Virgil*. New Surveys in the Classics 28. Oxford: Oxford UP, 1998.

———. "Virgil and Tragedy." Martindale, *Cambridge Companion* 312–26.

———. *Virgil's Aeneid: Cosmos and Imperium*. Oxford: Clarendon, 1986.

Harding, Davis P. *The Club of Hercules: Studies in the Classical Background of Paradise Lost*. Urbana: U of Illinois P, 1962.

Harris, William V. *Rome in Etruria and Umbria*. Oxford: Clarendon, 1971.

Harrison, S. J., ed. *Aeneid 10: With Introduction, Translation, and Commentary*. Oxford: Clarendon, 1991.

———, ed. *Oxford Readings in Vergil's Aeneid*. Oxford: Oxford UP, 1990.

Heinze, Richard. *Vergils epische Technik*. Leipzig, 1915.

———. *Virgil's Epic Technique*. Trans. Hazel Harvey, David Harvey, and Fred Robertson. Berkeley: U of California P, 1993.

Henry, Elisabeth. *The Vigour of Prophecy: A Study of Virgil's Aeneid*. Carbondale: Southern Illinois UP, 1989.

Hershkowitz, Debra. *The Madness of Epic: Reading Insanity from Homer to Statius*. Oxford: Clarendon, 1998.

Hexter, Ralph. "Imitating Troy: A Reading of *Aeneid* 3." Perkell, *Reading* 64–79.

———. "Sidonian Dido." *Innovations of Antiquity*. Ed. Hexter and D. Selden. New York: Routledge, 1992. 332–84.

Highet, Gilbert. *The Speeches in Vergil's Aeneid*. Princeton: Princeton UP, 1972.

Hinds, Stephen. *Allusion and Intertext: Dynamics of Appropriation in Roman Poetry*. Roman Literature and Its Contexts. Cambridge: Cambridge UP, 1997.

Hollander, Robert. *Il Virgilio dantesco: Tragedia nella Commedia*. Florence: Olschki, 1983.

Homer. *The Iliad*. Trans. Robert Fagels. New York: Viking, 1990.

———. *The Iliad*. Trans. A. T. Murray. 2 vols. Cambridge: Harvard UP, 1925.

———. *The Iliad of Homer*. Trans. Richmond Lattimore. Chicago: U of Chicago P, 1961.

———. *The Odyssey*. Trans. Allen Mandelbaum. Berkeley: U of California P, 1990. New York: Bantam, 1991.

———. *The Odyssey*. Trans. A. T. Murray. 2 vols. Cambridge: Harvard UP, 1938.

The Homeric Hymns. Ed. Susan C. Shelmerdine. Newburyport: Focus, 1995.

Horsfall, Nicholas. *A Companion to the Study of Virgil*. Mnemosyne Supp. 151. Leiden: Brill, 1995.

———. *Cornelius Nepos: A Selection, Including the Lives of Cicero and Atticus*. Oxford: Clarendon, 1989.

———. "Dido in the Light of History." Harrison, *Oxford Readings* 127–44.

———. *Virgilio: L'epopea in alambicco*. Naples: Liguori, 1991.

Hudson-Williams, A. "*Lacrimae Illae Inanes*." McAuslan and Walcot 149–56.

Hunt, J. William. *Forms of Glory: Structure and Sense in Virgil's* Aeneid. Carbondale: Southern Illinois UP, 1973.

———. "Labyrinthine Ways." In Bloom, *Virgil* 119–35.

Jaeger, Mary K. "Reconstructing Rome: The Campus Martius and Horace, Ode 1.8." *Arethusa* 28.2–3 (1995): 177–91.

Jenkyns, Richard. *Classical Epic: Homer and Virgil*. London: Bristol Classical, 1991.

———. *Virgil's Experience: Nature and History: Times, Names, Places*. Oxford: Oxford UP, 1998.

Johnson, W. R. *Darkness Visible: A Study of Vergil's* Aeneid. Berkeley: U of California P, 1976.

———. "*Dis Aliter Visum*: Self-Telling and Theodicy in *Aeneid* 2." Perkell, *Reading* 50–63.

Johnston, Patricia A., trans. *The Aeneid*. By Vergil. Newburyport: Focus Classical Lib., forthcoming.

———. "Juno and the Sibyl of Cumae." *Vergilius* 44 (1998): 13–23.

———. "The Storm in *Aeneid* 7." *Vergilius* 27 (1981): 23–30.

Jones, H. L., trans. *The* Geography *of Strabo*. 8 vols. Loeb Classical Lib. Cambridge: Harvard UP, 1917.

Josipovici, Gabriel. *Vergil Dying*. Windsor, Eng.: Windsor Arts Centre, 1980.

Kates, Judith. *Tasso and Milton: The Problem of Christian Epic*. Lewisburg: Bucknell UP, 1983.

Keith, A. M. *Engendering Rome: Women in Latin Epic*. Roman Literature and Its Contexts. Cambridge: Cambridge UP, 2000.

Kienast, Dietmar. *Augustus: Prinzeps und Monarch*. Darmstadt: Wissenschaftliche, 1982.

Klingner, Friedrich, ed. *Bucolica, Georgica, Aeneis*. By Vergil. Zurich: Artemis, 1967.

Knauer, Georg N. *Die* Aeneis *und Homer: Studien zur poetischen Technik Vergils mit der Homerzitate in der* Aeneis. Göttingen: Vendenhoeck, 1964.

———. "Vergil's *Aeneid* and Homer." *Greek, Roman and Byzantine Studies* 5 (1964): 61–84. Rpt. in Harrison, *Oxford Readings* 390–412.

Knott, John R., Jr. *Milton's Pastoral Vision: An Approach to* Paradise Lost. Chicago: U of Chicago P, 1971.

Knox, Bernard M. W. "The Serpent and the Flame: The Imagery of the Second Book of the *Aeneid*." *American Journal of Philology* 71 (1950): 379–400. Rpt. in Commager 124–42.

Laird, Andrew. "Approaching Characterisation in Virgil." Martindale, *Cambridge Companion* 282–93.

Leach, Eleanor Winsor. "Venus, Thetis, and the Social Construction of Maternal Behavior." *Classical Journal* 92 (1997): 347–71.

———. "Viewing the *Spectacula* of *Aeneid* 6." Perkell, *Reading* 111–27.

Lee, M. Owen. *Fathers and Sons in Virgil's* Aeneid: Tum Genitor Natum. Albany: State U of New York P, 1979.

Lerner, Gerda. *The Creation of Patriarchy*. Oxford: Oxford UP, 1986.

Lewis, C. S. *A Preface to* Paradise Lost. Rev. ed. Oxford: Oxford UP, 1960.

Livy. *History of Rome* (Ab urbe condita). Loeb Classical Lib. Trans. F. G. Moore. Vol. 8 (books 28–30). Cambridge: Harvard UP, 1988.

Llewellyn, Nigel. "Virgil and the Visual Arts." Martindale,*Virgil* 117–40.

Lloyd, Robert B. "*Aeneid* 3 and the Aeneas Legend." *American Journal of Philology* 78 (1957): 382–400.

———. "*Aeneid* 3: A New Approach." *American Journal of Philology* 78 (1957): 133–51.

Lucan. *Marci Annaei Lucani Pharsalia sive de bello civili libri decem*. Ed. A. E. Housman. Oxford: Oxford UP, 1927.

Lukács, Georg. *Soul and Form*. Trans. Anna Bostock. Cambridge: MIT P, 1974.

Lyne, R. O. A. M. *Further Voices in Vergil's* Aeneid. Oxford: Oxford UP, 1987.

———. "Vergil and the Politics of War." *Classical Quarterly* 33 (1983): 188–203. Rpt. in Harrison, *Oxford Readings* 316–38.

———. *Words and the Poet: Characteristic Techniques of Style in Vergil's* Aeneid. Oxford: Clarendon, 1989.

Mack, Sara. "The Birth of War: A Reading of *Aeneid* 7." Perkell, *Reading* 128–47.

———. *Patterns of Time in Virgil*. Hamden: Archon, 1978.

Mackail, J. W. *The* Aeneid *of Virgil*. Oxford: Oxford UP, 1930.

Mackie, C. J. *The Characterisation of Aeneas*. Edinburgh: Scottish Academic, 1988.

Macksey, Richard, and Eugenio Donato, eds. *The Structuralist Controversy: The Language of Criticism and the Sciences of Man*. Baltimore: Johns Hopkins UP, 1972.

Macrobius. *Saturnalia*. Ed. J. Willis. Leipzig: Teubner, 1963.

Malcovati, Henrica, ed. *Imperatoris Caesaris Augusti operum fragmenta*. Turin: Paravia, 1948.

Mandelbaum, Allen, trans. *The* Aeneid *of Virgil*. New York: Bantam, 1961. Fwd. W. Briggs, Jr. Berkeley: U of California P, 1982.

Martindale, Charles, ed. *The Cambridge Companion to Virgil*. Cambridge: Cambridge UP, 1997.

———. "Descent into Hell: Reading Ambiguity; or, Virgil and the Critics." *Proceedings of the Virgil Society* 21 (1993): 111–50.

———. *John Milton and the Transformation of Ancient Epic*. London: Routledge, 1986.

———, ed. *Virgil and His Influence*. London: Bristol Classical, 1984.

McAuslan, Ian, and Peter Walcot, eds. *Virgil*. Greece and Rome Studies. Oxford: Oxford UP, 1990.

McKay, Alexander G. "Recent Work on Vergil: A Bibliographical Survey, 1964–1973." *Classical Weekly* 68 (1974) 1–92.

McLeish, Kenneth. "Dido, Aeneas, and the Concept of *Pietas*." McAuslan and Walcot 134–41.

Merchant, Carolyn. *The Death of Nature: Women, Ecology, and the Scientific Revolution*. San Francisco: Harper, 1980.

Miles, Gary B. "The *Aeneid* as Foundation Story." Perkell, *Reading* 231–50.

Miller, John F. "The Shield of Argive Abas at *Aeneid* 3.286." *Classical Quarterly* 43 (1993): 445–50.

Miller, Paul Allen. "Sive deae seu sint dirae obscenaeque volucres." *Arethusa* (1989): 47–79.

Milton, John. *Complete Poems and Major Prose*. Ed. Merritt Y. Hughes. New York: Macmillan, 1957.

Mitchell, R. N. "The Violence of Virginity in the *Aeneid*." *Arethusa* 24 (1991): 219–38.

Moles, J. L. "Aristotle and Dido's *Hamartia*." McAuslan and Walcot 142–48.

Mulvey, Laura. *Visual and Other Pleasures*. Bloomington: Indiana UP, 1989.

Murrin, Michael. *The Allegorical Epic: Essays in Its Rise and Decline*. Chicago: U of Chicago P, 1980.

Mynors, R. A. B., ed. *P. Vergili Maronis opera*. Oxford: Clarendon, 1969. Rpt. 1972.

Nagy, Gregory. *The Best of the Achaeans: Concepts of the Hero in Archaic Greek Poetry*. Baltimore: Johns Hopkins UP, 1979.

Nethercut, W. R. "American Scholarship on Vergil." Bernard 303–30.

Nisbet, R. G. M. "Aeneas Imperator: Roman Generalship in an Epic Context." *Proceedings of the Virgil Society* 18 (1978–80): 50–61. Rpt. in Harrison, *Oxford Readings* 378–89.

Nugent, S. Georgia. "Vergil's 'Voice of the Women' in *Aeneid* V." *Arethusa* 25 (1992): 255–92.

———. "The Women of the *Aeneid*: Vanishing Bodies, Lingering Voices." Perkell, *Reading* 251–70.

O'Hara, James J. *Death and the Optimistic Prophecy in Vergil's Aeneid*. Princeton: Princeton UP, 1990.

———. "Dido as 'Interpreting Character' in *Aeneid* 4.56–66." *Arethusa* 26 (1993): 99–114.

———. *True Names: Vergil and the Alexandrian Tradition of Etymological Wordplay*. Ann Arbor: U of Michigan P, 1996.

Oliensis, Ellen. "Sons and Lovers: Sexuality and Gender in Virgil's Poetry." Martindale, *Cambridge Companion* 294–311.

Otis, Brooks. "The Odyssean *Aeneid* and the Iliadic *Aeneid*." Commager 89–106.

———. *Virgil: A Study in Civilized Poetry*. Oxford: Clarendon, 1964. Fwd. W. Briggs, Jr. Ann Arbor: U of Michigan P, 1995.

The Oxford Classical Dictionary. Ed. Simon Hornblower and Antony Spawforth. Oxford: Oxford UP, 1996.

The Oxford Companion to Classical Literature. Ed. M. C. Howatson. Oxford: Oxford UP, 1989.

Page, T. E. *The Aeneid of Virgil*. 2 vols. London, 1894–1900.

Parke, H. W. *Sibyls and Sibylline Prophecy in Classical Antiquity*. Ed. B. C. McGing. London: Routledge, 1988.

Parry, Adam. "The Two Voices of Virgil's *Aeneid*." *Arion* 2 (1963): 66–80. Rpt. in Commager 107–23.

Patterson, Frank A., gen. ed. *The Works of John Milton*. 18 vols. New York: Columbia UP, 1931–38.

Pavlock, Barbara. "Epic Tragedy in Vergil's Nisus and Euryalus Episode." *Transactions of the American Philological Association* 115 (1985): 207–24.

Pelling, Christopher. "The Triumviral Period." Bowman 1–69.

Perkell, Christine. "On Creusa, Dido, and the Quality of Victory in Virgil's *Aeneid.*" *Women's Studies* 8 (1981): 201–23. Rpt. in Foley 355–77.

———. "The Lament of Juturna: Pathos and Interpretation in the *Aeneid.*" *Transactions of the American Philological Association* 127 (1997): 257–86.

———, ed. *Reading Vergil's* Aeneid. Norman: U of Oklahoma P, 1999.

Petrarch, Francesco. *Africa. Francesco Petrarcha: Rime, trionfi e poesie latine.* Ed. Guido Martellotti. Milan: Ricciardi, 1951. 626–703.

Petrovych, Ivan. *Eneida.* Ed. O. F. Stavytski. Kiev: Radians'ka shkola, 1989.

Petter, Gerald. "Desecration and Expiation as a Theme in the *Aeneid.*" *Vergilius* 40 (1994): 76–84.

Pharr, Clyde. *Vergil's* Aeneid. Lexington: Heath, 1964. Rev. ed. Wauconda: Bolchazy, 2000.

Phillips, John. *Maronides; or, Virgil Travesty.* London: Brooks, 1673.

Pliny. *Natural History.* Vol. 9 (books 33–35). Trans. H. Rackham. Loeb Classical Lib. Cambridge: Harvard UP, 1968.

Porter, William M. *Reading the Classics and* Paradise Lost. Lincoln: U of Nebraska P, 1993.

Pöschl, Viktor. *The Art of Vergil: Image and Symbol in the* Aeneid. Trans. Gerda Seligson. Ann Arbor: U of Michigan P, 1962.

———. *Die Dichtkunst Vergils: Bild und Symbol in der* Aeneis. 3rd ed. Berlin: 1977.

Propertius. *Elegies.* Ed. and trans. G. P. Goold. Cambridge: Loeb Classical Lib., 1990.

Putnam, Michael C. J. "*Aeneid* VII and the *Aeneid.*" Putnam, *Essays* 100–20.

———. "*Aeneid* 12: Unity in Closure." Perkell, *Reading* 210–30.

———. "Anger, Blindness, and Insight in Virgil's *Aeneid.*" Putnam, *Vergil's* Aeneid 172–200.

———, ed. *Essays on Latin Lyric, Elegy, and Epic.* Princeton: Princeton UP, 1982.

———. *The Poetry of the* Aeneid: Four Studies in Imaginative Unity and Design. Cambridge: Harvard UP, 1965. Ithaca: Cornell UP, 1988.

———. "Possessiveness, Sexuality, and Heroism in the *Aeneid.*" Putnam, *Vergil's* Aeneid 27–49.

———. "The Third Book of the *Aeneid*: From Homer to Rome." *Ramus* 9 (1980): 1–21. Rpt. in Putnam, *Essays* 267–87.

———. "Turnus, Homer, and Heroism." *Literary Imagination* 1 (1999): 61–78.

———. *Vergil's* Aeneid: Interpretation and Influence. Chapel Hill: U of North Carolina P, 1995.

———. *Virgil's Epic Designs: Ekphrasis in the* Aeneid. New Haven: Yale UP, 1998.

Quinn, Kenneth. *Virgil's* Aeneid: A Critical Description. London: Routledge, 1968.

Quint, David. *Epic and Empire: Politics and Generic Form from Virgil to Milton.* Princeton: Princeton UP, 1993.

Raaflaub, Kurt A., and Mark Toher, eds. *Between Republic and Empire: Interpretations of Augustus and His Principate.* Berkeley: U of California P, 1990.

Ramsey, P. A., ed. *Rome in the Renaissance: The City and the Myth.* Binghamton: Medieval and Renaissance Texts and Studies, 1982.

Renehan, Robert. "Hera as Earth-Goddess: A New Piece of Evidence." *Rheinisches Museum für Philologie* 117 (1974): 193–201.

Richardson, Lawrence, Jr. *A New Topographical Dictionary of Ancient Rome.* Baltimore: Johns Hopkins UP, 1992.

Rimmon-Kenan, Shlomith. *Narrative Fiction: Contemporary Poetics.* London: Methuen, 1983.

Roman d'Enéas. Ed. J.-J. Salverda de Grave. 2 vols. Les classiques français du moyen age. Paris: Champion, 1929.

Ronsard, Pierre de. *La Franciade. Les œuvres completes de Pierre de Ronsard.* Ed. Paul Laumonier. Vol. 3. Paris: Lemerre, 1914–19. 1–176. Trans. in *Poems of Pierre de Ronsard.* Ed. and trans. Nicholas Kilmer. Berkeley: U of California P, 1979.

Rosenberg, Donald M. *Oaten Reeds and Trumpets: Pastoral and Epic in Virgil, Spenser, and Milton.* Lewisburg: Bucknell UP, 1981.

Rossi, Andreola. "Reversal of Fortune and Change in Genre in *Aeneid* 10." *Vergilius* 43 (1997): 31–44.

Rudat, Wolfgang E. H. "Milton's Dido and Aeneas: The Fall in *Paradise Lost* and the Vergilian Tradition." *Classical and Medieval Literature* 2 (1981): 33–46.

———. "Milton's Satan and Virgil's Juno: The 'Perverseness' of Disobedience in *Paradise Lost*." *Renaissance and Reformation* 15 (1979): 77–82.

Sainte-Maure, Benoît de. *Roman de Troie. The Story of Troilus.* Trans. R. K. Gordon. New York: Dutton, 1964. 1–24.

Salmon, Edward T. "The Evolution of Augustus' Principate." *Historia* 5 (1956): 456–78.

Schaar, Claes. *The Full Voic'd Quire Below: Vertical Context Systems in* Paradise Lost. Lund, Swed.: Gleerup, 1982.

Schelling, Friedrich W. J. *The Philosophy of Art.* Ed. and trans. Douglas W. Stott. Minneapolis: U of Minnesota P, 1989.

Scott, Kenneth. "The Political Propaganda of 44–30 B.C." *Memoirs of the American Academy in Rome* 11 (1933): 7–49.

Scullard, H. H. *From the Gracchi to Nero.* London: Routledge, 1959.

Seneca. *De clementia.* Ed. Carl Mosius. Leipzig: Teubner, 1914.

———. *Select Letters.* Ed. Walter C. Summers. London: Macmillan, 1962.

Servius. *Scholia Veronensia. Serviani in Aeneiadem commentarii.* Ed. G. Thilo and H. Hagen. Vol. 3, bk. 2. Leipzig: Teubner, 1902. 391–450.

———. *Serviani in Aeniadem commentarii, editio Harvardiana.* Amer. Philological Assn. Spec. Pubs. 1. Lancaster: Amer. Philological Assn., 1965.

Sims, James H. "A Greater than Rome: The Inversion of Virgilian Symbol from Camoes to Milton." Ramsey 333–44.

Slavitt, David R. *Virgil.* Hermes. New Haven: Yale UP, 1991.

Solmsen, Friedrich. "The World of the Dead in Book 6 of the *Aeneid*." *Classical Philology* 67 (1972): 31–41. Rpt. in Harrison, *Oxford Readings* 208–23.

Spence, Sarah. "The Polyvalence of Pallas in the *Aeneid*." *Arethusa* 32 (1999): 149–63.

———. *Rhetorics of Reason and Desire: Vergil, Augustine, and the Troubadours*. Ithaca: Cornell UP, 1988.

———. *"Varium et Mutabile*: Voices of Authority in *Aeneid* 4." Perkell, *Reading* 80–95.

Spenser, Edmund. *The Faerie Queen*. Ed. Thomas P. Roche, Jr. New Haven: Yale UP, 1981.

Stahl, Hans-Peter. "Aeneas—An 'Unheroic' Hero?" *Arethusa* 14 (1981): 157–77.

———. "The Death of Turnus: Augustan Vergil and the Political Rival." Raaflaub and Toher 174–211.

———, ed. *Vergil's* Aeneid: *Augustan Epic and Political Context*. London: Duckworth, 1998.

Steadman, John M. *Milton and the Renaissance Hero*. Oxford: Clarendon, 1967.

Steiner, George. *The Death of Tragedy*. New Haven: Yale UP, 1980.

Stewart, Douglas J. "Aeneas the Politician." Bloom, *Virgil* 103–18.

Storm, William. *After Dionysus: A Theory of the Tragic*. Ithaca: Cornell UP, 1998.

Suetonius. *De grammaticis*. Ed. Giorgio Brugnoli. Leipzig: Teubner, 1972.

———. *De vita caesarum*. Ed. and trans. John Carew Rolfel. Cambridge: Loeb Classical Lib., 1970.

Suerbaum, Werner. *Hundert Jahre Vergil-Forschung: Eine systematische Arbeitsbibliographie mit besonderer Berücksichtigung der* Aeneis. Aufstieg und Niedergang der römischen Welt 2.31.1. Berlin: Temporini, 1980.

Sullivan, John Patrick. "Dido and the Representation of Women in Vergil's *Aeneid*." Wilhelm and Jones 64–73.

Suzuki, Mihoko. *Metamorphoses of Helen: Authority, Difference, and Epic*. Ithaca: Cornell UP, 1989.

Syme, Ronald. *The Roman Revolution*. Oxford: Clarendon, 1960.

Tarrant, Richard. *Commentary to* Aeneid *12*. Cambridge: Cambridge UP, forthcoming.

———. "Poetry and Power: Virgil's Poetry in Contemporary Context." Martindale, *Cambridge Companion* 169–87.

Tasso, Torquato. *La Gerusalemne liberata*. Ed. Pio Spagnotti. 4th ed. Milano: Hoepli, 1912. Trans. as *Gerusalemne Liberata*. Ed. and trans. Anthony M. Esolen. Baltimore: Johns Hopkins UP, 2000.

Tennyson, Alfred. "To Virgil: Written at the Request of the Mantuans for the Nineteenth Centenary of Virgil's Death." *Alfred Lord Tennyson's Poetry*. 14 Mar. 2002 <http://tennysonpoetry.home.att.net/virg.htm>.

Thomas, Richard F. "The Isolation of Turnus: *Aeneid* Book 12." Stahl, *Vergil's* Aeneid 271–302.

———. *Reading Virgil and His Texts: Studies in Intertextuality*. Ann Arbor: U of Michigan P, 1999.

———. *Virgil and the Augustan Reception*. Cambridge: Cambridge UP, 2001.

———. "Virgil's Ecphrastic Centerpieces." *Harvard Studies in Classical Philology* 87 (1983): 175–84.

Tibullus. *Albii Tibulli aliorumque elegiae*. *Latin Library*. The Classics Page at Ad Fontes Academy. 12 May 1998. 19 Dec. 2001 <http://patriot.net/~lillard/cp/tib.html>.

Toohey, Peter. *Reading Epic: An Introduction to the Ancient Narratives.* London: Routledge, 1992.

Van Nortwick, Thomas. *Somewhere I Have Never Travelled.* Oxford: Oxford UP, 1992.

Varro. *M. Terentius Varro, Antiquitates rerum divinarum.* 2 vols. Ed. B. I. Cardauns. Wiesbaden: Steiner, 1976.

Veldeke, Heinrich von. *Eneit.* Ms. folium 282. Staatsbibliotek, Berlin.

Velleius Paterculus. *Roman History.* Ed. and trans. Frederick Shipley. London: Loeb Classical Lib., 1924.

Verbart, Andre. *Fellowship in* Paradise Lost: *Vergil, Milton, Wordsworth.* Amsterdam: Rodopi, 1995.

———. "Milton on Vergil: Dido and Aeneas in *Paradise Lost.*" *English Studies* 78 (1997): 111–26.

Vernant, Jean-Pierre. "Greek Tragedy: Problems of Interpretation." Macksey and Donato 273–95.

Vida, Girolamo. *Christiad.* Ed. and trans. Gertrude C. Drake and Clarence A. Forbes. Carbondale: Southern Illinois UP, 1978.

———. *De Arte Poetica.* Ed. and trans. Ralph G. Williams. New York: Columbia UP, 1976.

Voltaire. *The Henriade.* Trans. Charles L. S. Jones. Mobile: Smith, 1834.

Waltharius and Ruodlieb. Ed. and trans. Dennis Kratz. New York: Garland, 1984.

Webber, Joan M. *Milton and His Epic Tradition.* Seattle: U of Washington P, 1979.

Weinstock, Stefan. *Divus Julius.* Oxford: Oxford UP, 1971.

West, David A., trans. *The Aeneid.* By Vergil. Penguin Classics. London: Penguin, 1990.

———. "The Bough and the Gate." Harrison, *Oxford Readings* 224–38.

———. "*Cernere erat*: The Shield of Aeneas." *Proceedings of the Virgil Society* 15 (1975–76): 1–7. Rpt. in Harrison, *Oxford Readings* 295–304.

———. "The End and the Meaning." Stahl, *Vergil's* Aeneid 303–18.

West, Grace S. "Chloreus and Camilla." *Vergilius* 31 (1985): 22–29.

Whitman, Cedric H. *Homer and the Heroic Tradition.* Cambridge: Harvard UP, 1958.

Wilhelm, Robert M., and Howard Jones, eds. *The Two Worlds of the Poet: New Perspectives on Vergil.* Detroit: Wayne State UP, 1992.

Wilkinson, L. P. "The Language of Virgil and Horace." Harrison, *Oxford Readings* 413–28.

Williams, Gordon. *Technique and Ideas in the* Aeneid. New Haven: Yale UP, 1983.

Williams, R. D. "The *Aeneid.*" *The Cambridge History of Classical Literature: The Age of Augustus.* Vol. 2, part 3. Ed. E. J. Kenney and W. V. Clausen. Cambridge: Cambridge UP, 1982. 37–73.

———. *The* Aeneid *of Virgil.* 2 vols. London: St. Martin's, 1972–73.

———. "Changing Attitudes to Virgil: A Study in the History of Taste from Dryden to Tennyson." Dudley 119–38.

———. "The Pictures on Dido's Temple (*Aeneid* 1.450–93)." *Classical Quarterly* 10 (1960): 145–51. Rpt. in Harrison, *Oxford Readings* 37–45.

———. "The Purpose of the *Aeneid.*" *Antichthon* 1 (1967): 29–41. Rpt. in Harrison, *Oxford Readings* 21–36.

———, ed. *P. Vergili Maronis Aeneidos liber quintus.* Oxford: Oxford UP, 1960.

——, ed. *P. Vergili Maronis Aeneidos liber tertius*. Oxford: Oxford UP, 1961.

——. "The Sixth Book of the *Aeneid*." *Greece and Rome* 11 (1964): 48–63. Rpt. in Harrison, *Oxford Readings* 191–207.

Williams, R. D., and C. J. Carter. "Critical Appreciations II: Virgil, *Aeneid* XII.843–86." McAuslan and Walcot 167–79.

Wilson-Okamura, David, ed. *Virgil.org*. Macalester Coll. 13 Dec. 2000. 20 Mar. 2001 <http://virgil.org>.

Wiltshire, Susan Ford. "The Man Who Was Not There: Aeneas and Absence in *Aeneid* 9." Perkell, *Reading* 162–77.

——. *Public and Private in Vergil's* Aeneid. Amherst: U of Massachusetts P, 1989.

Wlosok, Antonie. "Vergil in der neueren Forschung." *Gymnasium* 80 (1973): 129–51.

Wofford, Susanne L. *The Choice of Achilles: The Ideology of Figure in the Epic*. Stanford: Stanford UP, 1992.

Woodford, Susan. *The Trojan War in Ancient Art*. Ithaca: Cornell UP, 1993.

Wright, M. R. "*Ferox virtus*: Anger in Virgil's *Aeneid*." Braund and Gill 169–84.

Zanker, Paul. *The Power of Images in the Age of Augustus*. Trans. Alan Shapiro. Ann Arbor: U of Michigan P, 1988.

Zarker, John. "Vergil's Trojan and Italian *Matres*." *Vergilius* 24 (1978): 15–24.

Zetzel, James. "Rome and Its Traditions." Martindale, *Cambridge Companion* 188–203.

Ziolkowski, Theodore. *Vergil and the Moderns*. Princeton: Princeton UP, 1993.

Films and Recordings

Berlioz, H. *Les troyens*. Sir Colin Davis conducting. 4 CDs. Philips.

Chinatown. Dir. Roman Polanski. 1974.

Clash of the Titans. Dir. Desmond Davis. 1981.

Cleopatra. Dir. Joseph L. Mankiewicz. 1963.

Gladiator. Dir. Ridley Scott. 2000.

The Godfather. Dir. Francis Ford Coppola. 1972.

La guerra di Troia. Dir. Giorgio Ferroni. 1962.

Holst, G. *The Planets*. Chicago Symphony Orchestra, James Levine conducting. Deutsche Grammophon.

Jason and the Argonauts. Dir. Don Chaffey. 1963.

La leggenda di Enea. Dir. Albert Band and Giorgio Rivalta. 1962.

Pulp Fiction. Dir. Quentin Tarantino. 1994.

Purcell, H. *Dido and Aeneas*. Les Arts Florissants, William Christie conducting. Erato.

Respighi, O. Pines of Rome *and* Fountains of Rome. Chicago Symphony Orchestra, Fritz Reiner conducting. RCA.

——. *Three Botticelli Pictures*. Orpheus Chamber Orchestra. Deutsche Grammophon.

Spartacus. Dir. Stanley Kubrick. 1960.

Star Wars. Dir. George Lucas. 1977.

Ulysses. Dir. Mario Camerini. 1955.

INDEX

Cross, Beverly, 33
Crowe, Russell, 33

Dante Alighieri, 6, 12, 18, 38, 39, 190,
    191–95
Davis, Desmond, 33
DiCesare, Mario A., 196
Dio Cassius, 116, 117, 121
Donatus, Tiberius Claudius, 11
Douglas, Gavin, 5
Douglas, Kirk, 33
Dryden, John, 177
Duckworth, George E., 21, 23
Dunaway, Faye, 32

Eden, P. T., 135
Edwards, Catherine, 131, 134, 135
Eliot, T. S., 25
Engar, Ann, 45
Ennius, 13, 39
Euripides, 21, 182, 183, 184, 189, 206

Fagles, Robert, 62
Fairclough, H. Rushton, 3
Fantham, Elaine, 30
Farrell, Joseph, 16, 17, 23, 29, 31
Farron, Stephen, 28, 119
Favro, Diane, 133
Feeney, Denis, 17, 20, 23, 30, 51, 62, 199
Ferroni, Giorgio, 33
Fichter, Andrew, 196
Fish, Stanley, 196
Fisher, Carrie, 33
Fitzgerald, Robert, 5, 7–10, 48, 51–52, 54,
    62, 69, 72, 77, 79, 132, 133, 134, 135, 136,
    160–61, 162, 168, 169, 171, 172, 173, 174,
    177, 196, 197
Ford, Harrison, 33
Fordyce, C. J., 3, 161
Fowler, Don P., 11, 17, 30, 31, 62, 63, 82
Frankel, Edward, 20
Freccero, John, 191
Fredricksmeyer, E., 77, 78
Fulvia, 116

Gaard, Greta, 148–49, 154
Galinsky, Karl, 14, 17, 20, 21, 28, 31, 32, 69,
    70, 78, 131, 134, 156
Gama, Vasco da, 40
Garrison, James D., 196
Genette, Gerard, 177
Gill, Christopher, 30
Gillespie, Stuart, 12, 24
Glare, P. G. W., 165
Godfrey of Boulogne, 40
Gottlieb, G., 30
Gracchus, Gaius Sempronius, 159, 160, 163,
    165, 166

Gracchus, Tiberius Sempronius, 159, 160,
    163–64, 166
Gransden, K. W., 3, 16, 17, 18, 28, 78, 100,
    102, 196
Greene, Thomas M., 196
Greenough, J. B., 146
Gregory, E. R., 196
Gregory I, 194
Griffin, Jasper, 12, 15, 23
Griffith, Mark, 19
Grimal, Pierre, 18, 140
Grimm, Richard, 20
Guarducci, Margherita, 126–27
Guiness, Alec, 33
Gurval, Robert, 14, 20

Habinek, Thomas, 20
Haecker, Theodor, 25, 40
Hall, Jane Harriman, 4
Hallett, Judith P., 44
Hamill, Mark, 33
Hamlin, Harry, 33
Hannibal, 159, 165
Hardie, Philip R., 3, 15, 23, 28, 29, 31, 46,
    182, 187, 189
Harding, Davis P., 196
Harris, Richard, 33
Harris, William, 116
Harrison, S. J., 3, 11–12, 17, 23, 69, 119
Hegel, Georg, 189
Heinze, Richard, 16, 20, 24, 25, 28, 30, 46,
    60, 61, 70, 81, 119, 182
Henry IV, 40
Henry, Elisabeth, 17, 131
Hershkowitz, Debra, 30
Hesiod, 51
Hexter, Ralph, 23, 30
Highet, Gilbert, 62, 180
Hinds, Stephen, 47, 140
Hollander, Robert, 190
Holst, Gustav, 32
Homer, 6, 13, 14, 15, 16, 19, 20, 21, 22, 24,
    28, 29, 39, 43, 46, 47, 54, 62, 66, 69,
    82–83, 84, 85, 87, 89, 94, 99, 102, 104,
    113, 120, 123, 133, 148, 172, 173, 174,
    190
Horace, 54, 133
Horsfall, Nicholas, 15, 17, 18, 20, 28, 159,
    160
Howard, Henry, 177
Hudson-Williams, A., 18
Humphries, Rolfe, 177
Hunt, J. William, 18, 76

Jacobi, Derek, 33
Jacoff, Rachel, 45
Jaeger, Mary, 44, 133
James, Sharon L., 44

Modern Language Association of America
Approaches to Teaching World Literature
Joseph Gibaldi, series editor

Achebe's Things Fall Apart. Ed. Bernth Lindfors. 1991.
Arthurian Tradition. Ed. Maureen Fries and Jeanie Watson. 1992.
Atwood's The Handmaid's Tale *and Other Works*. Ed. Sharon R. Wilson,
    Thomas B. Friedman, and Shannon Hengen. 1996.
Austen's Pride and Prejudice. Ed. Marcia McClintock Folsom. 1993.
Balzac's Old Goriot. Ed. Michal Peled Ginsburg. 2000.
Baudelaire's Flowers of Evil. Ed. Laurence M. Porter. 2000.
Beckett's Waiting for Godot. Ed. June Schlueter and Enoch Brater. 1991.
Beowulf. Ed. Jess B. Bessinger, Jr., and Robert F. Yeager. 1984.
Blake's Songs of Innocence and of Experience. Ed. Robert F. Gleckner and
    Mark L. Greenberg. 1989.
Boccaccio's Decameron. Ed. James H. McGregor. 2000.
British Women Poets of the Romantic Period. Ed. Stephen C. Behrendt and
    Harriet Kramer Linkin. 1997.
Brontë's Jane Eyre. Ed. Diane Long Hoeveler and Beth Lau. 1993.
Byron's Poetry. Ed. Frederick W. Shilstone. 1991.
Camus's The Plague. Ed. Steven G. Kellman. 1985.
Cather's My Ántonia. Ed. Susan J. Rosowski. 1989.
Cervantes' Don Quixote. Ed. Richard Bjornson. 1984.
Chaucer's Canterbury Tales. Ed. Joseph Gibaldi. 1980.
Chopin's The Awakening. Ed. Bernard Koloski. 1988.
Coleridge's Poetry and Prose. Ed. Richard E. Matlak. 1991.
Dante's Divine Comedy. Ed. Carole Slade. 1982.
Dickens' David Copperfield. Ed. Richard J. Dunn. 1984.
Dickinson's Poetry. Ed. Robin Riley Fast and Christine Mack Gordon. 1989.
Narrative of the Life of Frederick Douglass. Ed. James C. Hall. 1999.
Eliot's Middlemarch. Ed. Kathleen Blake. 1990.
Eliot's Poetry and Plays. Ed. Jewel Spears Brooker. 1988.
Shorter Elizabethan Poetry. Ed. Patrick Cheney and Anne Lake Prescott. 2000.
Ellison's Invisible Man. Ed. Susan Resneck Parr and Pancho Savery. 1989.
Dramas of Euripides. Ed. Robin Mitchell-Boyask. 2002.
Faulkner's The Sound and the Fury. Ed. Stephen Hahn and Arthur F. Kinney. 1996.
Flaubert's Madame Bovary. Ed. Laurence M. Porter and Eugene F. Gray. 1995.
García Márquez's One Hundred Years of Solitude. Ed. María Elena de Valdés and
    Mario J. Valdés. 1990.
Goethe's Faust. Ed. Douglas J. McMillan. 1987.
Hebrew Bible as Literature in Translation. Ed. Barry N. Olshen and
    Yael S. Feldman. 1989.
Homer's Iliad *and* Odyssey. Ed. Kostas Myrsiades. 1987.
Ibsen's A Doll House. Ed. Yvonne Shafer. 1985.
Works of Samuel Johnson. Ed. David R. Anderson and Gwin J. Kolb. 1993.

Joyce's Ulysses. Ed. Kathleen McCormick and Erwin R. Steinberg. 1993.
Kafka's Short Fiction. Ed. Richard T. Gray. 1995.
Keats's Poetry. Ed. Walter H. Evert and Jack W. Rhodes. 1991.
Kingston's The Woman Warrior. Ed. Shirley Geok-lin Lim. 1991.
Lafayette's The Princess of Clèves. Ed. Faith E. Beasley and Katharine Ann
    Jensen. 1998.
Works of D. H. Lawrence. Ed. M. Elizabeth Sargent and Garry Watson. 2001.
Lessing's The Golden Notebook. Ed. Carey Kaplan and Ellen Cronan Rose. 1989.
Mann's Death in Venice *and Other Short Fiction*. Ed. Jeffrey B. Berlin. 1992.
Medieval English Drama. Ed. Richard K. Emmerson. 1990.
Melville's Moby-Dick. Ed. Martin Bickman. 1985.
Metaphysical Poets. Ed. Sidney Gottlieb. 1990.
Miller's Death of a Salesman. Ed. Matthew C. Roudané. 1995.
Milton's Paradise Lost. Ed. Galbraith M. Crump. 1986.
Molière's Tartuffe *and Other Plays*. Ed. James F. Gaines and
    Michael S. Koppisch. 1995.
Momaday's The Way to Rainy Mountain. Ed. Kenneth M. Roemer. 1988.
Montaigne's Essays. Ed. Patrick Henry. 1994.
Novels of Toni Morrison. Ed. Nellie Y. McKay and Kathryn Earle. 1997.
Murasaki Shikibu's The Tale of Genji. Ed. Edward Kamens. 1993.
Pope's Poetry. Ed. Wallace Jackson and R. Paul Yoder. 1993.
Shakespeare's Hamlet. Ed. Bernice W. Kliman. 2001.
Shakespeare's King Lear. Ed. Robert H. Ray. 1986.
Shakespeare's Romeo and Juliet. Ed. Maurice Hunt. 2000.
Shakespeare's The Tempest *and Other Late Romances*. Ed. Maurice Hunt. 1992.
Shelley's Frankenstein. Ed. Stephen C. Behrendt. 1990.
Shelley's Poetry. Ed. Spencer Hall. 1990.
Sir Gawain and the Green Knight. Ed. Miriam Youngerman Miller and
    Jane Chance. 1986.
Spenser's Faerie Queene. Ed. David Lee Miller and Alexander Dunlop. 1994.
Stendhal's The Red and the Black. Ed. Dean de la Motte and Stirling Haig. 1999.
Sterne's Tristram Shandy. Ed. Melvyn New. 1989.
Stowe's Uncle Tom's Cabin. Ed. Elizabeth Ammons and Susan Belasco. 2000.
Swift's Gulliver's Travels. Ed. Edward J. Rielly. 1988.
Thoreau's Walden *and Other Works*. Ed. Richard J. Schneider. 1996.
Vergil's Aeneid. Ed. William S. Anderson and Lorina N. Quartarone. 2002.
Voltaire's Candide. Ed. Renée Waldinger. 1987.
Whitman's Leaves of Grass. Ed. Donald D. Kummings. 1990.
Woolf's To the Lighthouse. Ed. Beth Rigel Daugherty and Mary Beth Pringle. 2001.
Wordsworth's Poetry. Ed. Spencer Hall, with Jonathan Ramsey. 1986.
Wright's Native Son. Ed. James A. Miller. 1997.